COMING OF AGE IN MEDIEVAL EGYPT

Coming of Age in Medieval Egypt

FEMALE ADOLESCENCE, JEWISH LAW, AND ORDINARY CULTURE

Eve Krakowski

PRINCETON UNIVERSITY PRESS
PRINCETON & OXFORD

Published by Princeton University Press, 41 William Street,
Princeton, New Jersey 08540

In the United Kingdom: Princeton University Press, 6 Oxford Street,
Woodstock, Oxfordshire OX20 1TR

press.princeton.edu

Jacket art: Detail from "Abū Zayd and his son," Maqāmāt al-Ḥarīrī no. 49,
Bibliothèque nationale de France MS Arabe 6094, fol. 180r (1222, likely Egypt
or Syria).

Library of Congress Cataloging-in-Publication Data

Names: Krakowski, Eve, 1978– author.
Title: Coming of age in medieval Egypt : female adolescence, Jewish law,
and ordinary culture / Eve Krakowski.
Description: Princeton, New Jersey : Princeton University Press, [2017] |
Includes bibliographical references and index.
Identifiers: LCCN 2017020240 | ISBN 9780691174983 (hardcover : alk. paper)
Subjects: LCSH: Jewish women—Egypt—Social conditions—History—To 1500.
| Jewish women—Religious life—Egypt—History—To 1500. | Cairo Genizah.
Classification: LCC DS135.E4 K63 2017 | DDC 305.48/89240620902—dc23
LC record available at https://lccn.loc.gov/2017020240

British Library Cataloging-in-Publication Data is available

This book has been composed in Miller

Printed on acid-free paper. ∞

Printed in the United States of America

10 9 8 7 6 5 4 3 2 1

CONTENTS

LIST OF ILLUSTRATIONS

ACKNOWLEDGMENTS

THIS BOOK WAS WRITTEN with support from the Jacob and Hilda Blaustein Postdoctoral Fellowship in Judaic Studies at Yale University and the Stanley A. and Barbara B. Rabin Postdoctoral Fellowship in Judaic Studies at Columbia University. The dissertation from which it emerged was written with support from the Whiting Dissertation Fellowship at the University of Chicago.

I am grateful to the following people who read and commented on parts of the manuscript: Elisheva Baumgarten, Abraham J. Berkovitz, Robert Brody, Mark Cohen, Michael Cook, Arnold Franklin, Jonathan Gribetz, Brendan Goldman, Jennifer Grayson, Moshe Krakowski, Tamer el-Leithy, Ivan Marcus, Yifat Monnickendam, Ishay Rosen-Zvi, Seth Schwartz, Mathieu Tillier, Moulie Vidas, and Lev Weitz. Their questions and suggestions saved me from many embarrassing errors and pushed me to improve the book in countless ways. (The errors that no doubt remain are, of course, my responsibility alone.) Craig Perry and Oded Zinger read early drafts of almost every chapter—as did Marina Rustow, who also saved the day with her suggestions for several nearly finished ones. This book would have looked very different without them. Jessica Goldberg read the entire manuscript twice, once for a graduate seminar and once as a reader for Princeton University Press, and offered detailed advice that transformed the final version. I am also grateful to the other anonymous reader for the press for his or her valuable suggestions.

Norman Golb taught me to read the sources on which this book is based and insisted that I read them carefully. I would not have entered this field without his meticulous and patient instruction. I thank him and the other wonderful teachers at the University of Chicago who showed me how to be a scholar, especially Fred Donner and Jim Robinson. Marina Rustow never taught at the University of Chicago, but my thanks to her belong here too: since she agreed to act as reader on my dissertation seven years ago, she has taught me not only how to think about history, but also how to approach a conference interview, how to put together a grant application, the difference between "in press" and "forthcoming," and—by example—how it is possible to be an inexhaustibly enthusiastic, gracious, and generous teacher, mentor, and colleague. I am more grateful to her than I can say.

Parts of this book were written during the two years I spent as a postdoctoral fellow in the Program in Judaic Studies at Yale University. Ivan Marcus was a kind and supportive mentor to me during these two years, and I thank him, along with Steven Fraade, Christine Hayes, Hindy Najman, Eliyahu Stern, and Yishai Kiel, for making my time at Yale truly delightful. I can't imagine a better place to have begun life postdissertation. Chapters 2 and 7 fell into place during a year-long postdoctoral fellowship at the Institute for Israel and Jewish Studies at Columbia University. I am grateful to Jeremy Dauber, Elisheva Carlebach, and Seth Schwartz for graciously welcoming me to the institute and for many enriching conversations from which I learned a lot. The book came into final form during my first year at Princeton. Thanks to the many wonderful current and former colleagues who have made my start there a very happy one: Leora Batnitzky, Michael Cook, Yaacob Dweck, Jonathan Gribetz, Lara Harb, Bernard Haykel, Şükrü Hanioğlu, Martha Himmelfarb, George Kiraz, Satyel Larson, Lital Levy, AnneMarie Luijendijk, Naphtali Meshel, Hossein Modarressi, Michael Reynolds, Marina Rustow, Cyrus Schayegh, Sabine Schmidtke, Dan Sheffield, Moulie Vidas, and Qasim Zaman.

I chose to work on Geniza documents in graduate school because they were the most compelling sources I had ever read. It has been an unexpected bonus to discover that Geniza studies is an exceptionally friendly and collaborative field. It has been a pleasure over the last few years to work with and to get to know Phillip Ackerman-Lieberman, Mark Cohen, Arnold Franklin, Miriam Frenkel, Mordechai Akiva Friedman, Jessica Goldberg, Brendan Goldman, Jennifer Grayson, Geoffrey Khan, Tamer el-Leithy, Roxani Margariti, Renee Levine Melammed, Judith Olszowy-Schlanger, Ben Outhwaite, Craig Perry, Moshe Yagur, and Oded Zinger. I am especially grateful to Amir Ashur for sharing his dissertation with me early on; I could not have written my own dissertation or this book without it. For enjoyable and illuminating conversations about other matters late ancient, medieval, and modern, I thank Elisheva Baumgarten, Jonathan Decter, Yehuda Galinsky, Sarit Kattan-Gribetz, Sarah Pearce, Micha Perry, Meira Polliack, Paola Tartakoff, Rebecca Winer, and Rebecca Wollenberg.

I presented parts of this book at workshops and seminars at the Tauber Institute for the Study of European Jewry at Brandeis University, the Institute for Israel and Jewish Studies at Columbia University, the History Department at Johns Hopkins University, the Kevorkian Center for Near Eastern Studies at New York University, the Program in Judaic Studies at Princeton University, the Department of Jewish Studies at Rutgers University, and the Late Antiquity, Medieval, and Renaissance graduate seminar at the University of California, Los Angeles; and at conferences at the Institute for Advanced Studies in Princeton, the Institute for the Study of the Ancient World in New York, the University of Pennsylvania Law School, and the University of California, Los Angeles. Thanks to the organizers and participants for giving me the opportunity to talk about my work, and for their many thought-provoking comments that helped me to improve it.

A conference I helped organize at Yale in 2013 changed how I understand Geniza documents and their study. I am deeply grateful to the Program in Judaic Studies for sponsoring this conference, to Ivan Marcus for suggesting and encouraging it, to Marina Rustow for helping me to plan it, and especially to Roger Bagnall, Robert Brody, Andreas Kaplony, and Adam Kosto for being willing to spend three days advising Geniza scholars about our field and its prospects; their participation and insights proved invaluable. Some of the book's central arguments crystallized for me while I was teaching a seminar at Yale on marriage and kinship in medieval Egypt. I owe a lot to the students in that seminar, Yemile Bucay, Sarah Ifft, Jangai Jap, and Laura Speyer, whose astute and penetrating questions led me to consider aspects of my sources I had never thought about.

I am extremely grateful to Renee Reed for her cheerful assistance throughout my time at Yale, and to Sheridan Gayer at Columbia for facilitating my year there. Thanks to Karen Chirik and the other dedicated staff in the Department of Near Eastern Studies, to Baru Saul in the Program in Judaic Studies, and to Gayatri Oruganti in the Princeton Geniza Lab, who with their steadfast administrative support have helped me transition to life at Princeton.

It has been an extraordinary pleasure to work with Fred Appel of Princeton University Press. I am grateful to him and to Thalia Leaf for helping me get the manuscript to final submission, to Nathan Carr for his careful oversight of the book's production, to Lynn Worth for her judicious and discerning copyediting, and to Craig Noll for his thoughtful preparation of the indexes. Thanks to Matthew Harrison for preparing the amazing illustrations included in Chapter 8; to Peter Shalen for graciously working out the math in Chapter 1 for me and patiently explaining to me how it works; to George Kiraz for proofreading my Arabic transliterations; to Limor Yungman for proofreading my Hebrew ones; to Jay Winston for heroically taking on the mind-numbingly boring task of putting all my shelf marks and citations in order; and to Abigail Balbale for graciously consulting with me about the cover illustration.

Having written a book about women's dependence on their relatives, I am especially glad to end by thanking my own family, Peter, Catherine, and David Shalen; Rebecca, Israel, Tiki and Shana Krakowski; Marcia Shalen and my dearly missed grandfather Bob Shalen; Gitta and Roby Tabory; and Mindy Mermelstein. Their love and support looks very different from the family bonds described in this book, but I depend on it nearly as much. I am also deeply indebted to Lana Stryker, Barbara Alexander, and Szilvia Blasko, devoted caregivers who washed dishes, folded laundry, and spent time with my children while I was writing footnotes. My deepest thanks go to my husband, Moshe, and our children, Fruma Avigayil, Miriam, Shalva, Milka, Nomi, and Zev, and to God, for giving me this life with them.

TECHNICAL NOTES

THIS BOOK IS BASED on documents preserved in the Cairo Geniza, which are written in three languages—Hebrew, Aramaic, and Judeo-Arabic (Arabic in Hebrew script)—as well as on late ancient and medieval literary texts in these languages. Hebrew and Aramaic transcriptions follow the conventions of the *AJS Review*, except that צ is rendered as ṣ, ק as q, and final ה without a *mappiq* is usually not indicated (except in the case of a few words that are so commonly rendered with final "h" in English that they look strange without it, e.g., "*Torah*"). Initial and final *alef*s are not indicated. Arabic transcriptions follow the conventions of the *International Journal of Middle Eastern Studies*, except that the article "al" is not elided; initial *hamza* is also not indicated.

Most men mentioned in the Geniza had both Hebrew and Arabic names, which appear interchangeably and sometimes side by side in documents. Women almost always had Arabic names only. Names are rendered directly as they appear in documents, including nonstandard spellings, except that the word "son of" in men's patronymics is rendered as "b." whether it appears as *ben*, *bar*, or *ibn*; likewise, "daughter of" in women's patronymics is rendered as bt. whether it appears as *bat*, *berat*, *ibnat*, or *bint*. The only exceptions are scholars and jurists widely known by a name beginning in "ibn," e.g., Yosef ibn Migas. (Similarly, I identify the famous scholar Maimonides and his son Avraham Maimonides by these names rather than their lesser-known Arabic ones.) Names of dynasties, common place-names, and currencies appear in their standard English forms (e.g., Cairo, Fatimid, dinar); less common place-names are transliterated (except for Fustat, which is not generally common but appears often in this book). Arabic plurals take many forms; to avoid confusion for readers not fluent in Arabic, I have generally rendered plurals of words invoked within my English text with the Arabic singular followed by an English "s" (e.g., "*dār*s").

All translations in the book are my own, but in many cases I have benefited from previous scholars' editions and translations of Geniza documents. Publication data for all documents cited appears in the document index (where documents have been edited multiple times, only the latest publication is cited). Hebrew- and Arabic-language publications, both published medieval texts and works of modern scholarship, are cited by the English title appearing on the publication's title page when possible; otherwise they are transliterated. Biblical and classical rabbinic texts are cited according to the conventions of the *Jewish Quarterly Review*, except that tractates of the Palestinian Talmud are given as "pTractate" rather than "yTractate."

Square brackets [] in transcriptions indicate lacunae and questionable passages within a document. Slashes // // indicate words added by the scribe above or below the line. Parentheses () indicate words added to a translation for greater clarity, or to complete a partial literary citation. Ellipses without brackets . . . indicate my omission of words or phrases within a text or document. Words crossed out in transcriptions render words crossed out in the original document.

Finally, a few notes on dates and currencies: Geniza documents most often use the Seleucid calendar and secondarily give *anno mundi* dates. Both are rendered in their Gregorian equivalents. Dates of Gaonic responsa follow the chronology of Babylonian *ge'onim* provided by Brody, *The Geonim of Babylonia*. The most common currencies mentioned in Geniza documents are gold dinars and silver dirhams. Around 36–40 dirhams equaled a dinar: see Goitein, *Med. Soc.*, 1, Appendix D. The value of the dinar seems to have remained relatively stable throughout the centuries that this book covers. S. D. Goitein roughly estimated that two dinars equaled the monthly income of a lower middle class family, an estimate that Geniza and economic historians still accept; see ibid., 1:363.

ABBREVIATIONS

ADD.	Additional
AIU	Alliance Israélite Universelle (Paris)
ALAD	Khan, *Arabic Legal and Administrative Documents*
ARAB.	Arabic
ARAM.	Aramaic
AS	Additional Series
BL	British Library (London)
BODL.	Bodleian Library (Oxford)
CUL	Cambridge University Library (Cambridge)
DK	David Kaufmann Collection (Budapest)
EBD	Ashur, "Engagement and Betrothal Documents"
EI^2	*Encyclopaedia of Islam*, 2nd edition
ENA	Elkan Nathan Adler Collection (New York)
FGP	The Friedberg Geniza Project
HALPER	Center for Advanced Judaic Studies (Philadelphia)
HEB.	Hebrew
HUC	Hebrew Union College
JMP	Friedman, *Jewish Marriage in Palestine*
JNUL	Jewish National and University Library (Jerusalem)
JTS	Jewish Theological Seminary of America
KMD	Olszowy-Schlanger, *Karaite Marriage Documents*
LEWIS-GIBSON	Lewis-Gibson Genizah Collection (Cambridge)
MED. SOC.	Goitein, *A Mediterranean Society*
MISC.	Miscellaneous
MOSSERI	Jacques Mosseri Collection (Cambridge)
MT	Maimonides, *Mishne Torah*
NS	New Series

OHG	Lewin, *Oṣar ha-Ge'onim*
OR.	Oriental
PER	Papyrussammlung Erzherzog Rainer (Vienna)
PGP	The Princeton Geniza Project
PHIL.	University of Pennsylvania Museum
RNL	National Library of Russia (St. Petersburg)
TG	*Teshuvot ha-Ge'onim*
T-S	Taylor-Schechter Collection (Cambridge)
WEST. COLL.	Westminster College (Cambridge)

COMING OF AGE IN MEDIEVAL EGYPT

Introduction

SOMETIME IN THE EARLY twelfth century, a woman wrote to the Head of the Jews (*ra'īs al-yahūd*) in Fustat asking him to send her money for two orphan sisters whose care she was reluctantly supervising.[1] The girls were ten and thirteen years old and had no relatives to take care of them, and nothing to live on. They had been allotted two dinars from communal charity funds,[2] but for some reason (the letter is torn here, and parts are missing) the money had not actually been sent; without it, they had "only enough for a crust of bread." A childless widow who lived nearby had volunteered to teach them embroidery, and the letter's narrator was willing to check in on them once in a while. But she refused to take them into her household, even though the girls themselves wanted her to: "They constantly tell me, 'We want to come to you so that you can take care of us.'" She asked the *ra'īs* instead to provide the two dinars that the girls had been promised, along with extra funds to rent them a living space and to hire a religious teacher who could "teach them prayer, so they will not grow up like animals, not knowing *shema' yisra'el*" (the most basic of Jewish prayers).

This account of a mundane crisis, recorded not for posterity but to secure immediate help, captures incidentally mundane details attested in few other sources from twelfth-century Egypt: that preteen and teenage girls could live alone for some amount of time; that they were expected to receive a basic religious and vocational education that included learning prayer and embroidery, but could also get this far without having learned either; that when their relatives died, local women might step in to direct their care, but might also, without shame, refuse to house them. The specifics of the case might be unique, but the letter belongs to a vast textual corpus rich in other details of this kind: the Cairo Geniza documents, around 30,000 everyday papers—letters, legal records, administrative documents, and personal accounts—composed mainly

1. T-S 12.493.

2. About a month's income for a "lower middle class" household, according to the field's working estimate. See "Technical Notes" and n. 67 below.

by Jews in Fatimid and Ayyubid Egypt and Syria (969–1250) and preserved in a synagogue in Fustat (old Cairo).[3]

Geniza documents offer a different view of history from the chronicles, biographical texts, and religious treatises that tell us much of what we know about the medieval Middle East. Such works rarely discuss the ordinary people who populate these papers—especially ordinary women like these two sisters and their unwilling caretaker, who were neither married nor related to great men and whose world was far removed from centers of political power. These women, moreover, were Jews living in an Islamic society—otherwise visible only in Jewish legal works that are historically opaque.

This book considers how such ordinary Jewish women fit into the social order of the tenth- to thirteenth-century Islamic eastern Mediterranean, both as women and as Jews, and how two institutions central to that social order—kinship and law—shaped their lives. It does so by reconstructing a short stretch of women's early lives: the months or years between puberty and the start of first marriage, a period that I label *adolescence*, although no such term appears in my sources.

Why focus on adolescence? The months or years leading to a girl's first marriage set the stage for everything that happened to her afterward, in ways that make it a microcosm of the lives of "Geniza women."[4] The book makes two arguments focused on this brief interval, first about the structure and shape of the families with whom women lived, and second, about how and why Jewish courts came to govern many of the milestones they passed as they metamorphosed from children to adults. The documents those courts left behind are among the best sources we have not just for Jewish family life, but for why Jews in the medieval Middle East consistently turned to Jewish courts to structure it—and for what happened when they did so.

3. The documents were preserved alongside many literary fragments in a disposal chamber for written texts, commonly termed a *geniza*. The entire Geniza corpus contains around 330,000 pieces. Thirty thousand documents is an estimate, as they have not yet been catalogued in full. (The question is also complicated by the fact that many individual papers contain literary material on one side and documents on the other; see Rustow, "Petition to a Woman," Shweka, Rustow, and Olszowy-Schlanger, "The She'iltot, Recycling Manuscripts, and Efrayim b. Shemarya.") On *geniza*s among both Jews and Muslims, see Cohen, "Geniza for Islamicists," Cohen and Stillman, "Cairo Geniza," and cf. Ben-Shammai, "Is the 'Cairo Genizah' a Proper Name?" On the Geniza corpus and its transfer to libraries and private collections in the United States and Europe, see Reif, *Jewish Archive*, and Hoffman and Cole, *Sacred Trash*. A general introduction to the field of documentary Geniza research is forthcoming in Goldberg and Krakowski, "Documentary Geniza Research in the 21st Century" (a special issue of the journal *Jewish History*).

4. "Geniza women": For convenience, I use "Geniza" adjectivally throughout the book, as shorthand for "the people who produced and are described in Fatimid- and Ayyubid-era Geniza documents." I do not mean to imply by this that "Geniza people" comprised a single or coherent historical population, since as I note below, they didn't.

My first argument concerns women's kinship. Families in the premodern Islamic world are often assumed to have operated as cohesive patriarchal clans whose members lived together in extended households, preferred to marry each other, and were socially bound by their position in the family group. I suggest that the families documented in the Geniza operated differently from this. They are better understood as fluid social networks frequently disrupted and reconfigured by travel, divorce, remarriage, and death.

Both within households and as broader lineage groups, Geniza families were ordered not by their collective or unchanging structure, but by the dyadic personal loyalties that individual relatives bore each other. Consider, by way of analogy, the letter with which I opened. When these two sisters' relatives died, its author did not seek to replace their functions by assimilating both girls into an established household or even a coherent social group. Instead she asked different adults separately to provide specific aspects of their care. This disjointed simulacrum of a family was unusual in one respect: most unmarried girls mentioned in my sources—even fully orphaned girls like these—did live in households with older adults, a norm reflected in the sisters' plea that the letter's narrator take them in. But her refusal, based on her assumption that she could raise them without doing so, reflects an atomized conception of the support she should extend them that was also typical among blood relatives.

The personal commitments among kin that obligated such support—or occasionally, similar commitments shouldered by quasi or replacement kin like this woman—resembled those created through other forms of social association characteristic of this time and place, such as patronage and business relationships. Kinship and replacement kinship were unique, however, as almost the only such bonds available to women. The book follows women from childhood to early adulthood partly as a way to examine how a young woman's relationships with her birth relatives, or their replacements, shaped her social and economic position before and after marriage—determining the property to which she had access, the terms of her marriage contract and her capacity to enforce them, her power to divorce or gain leverage over an abusive or runaway husband, and even the domestic space that she controlled within her marital household.

How unique is this evidence to Jews? A major problem in Geniza research lies in defining the collection's limits as evidence for the broader history of the medieval Middle East. At stake in this problem are both the Geniza's uses as a source base and the social meanings of religious identity within the world that it reflects. Our letter illustrates one way in which Jewish belonging mattered in this world, through the support that Jewish communal and court officials sometimes offered to poor Jews, and especially to Jewish women, when their kin networks failed them. But more basic features of Jewish difference remain less clear. How similar were Geniza Jews' everyday lives to those of Muslims or Christians? How, and how far, did religious practice and belonging shape the ideas and institutions recognized by both Muslims and non-Muslims in medieval Islamic societies?

The book's second central argument addresses these questions with respect to Jewish law—a defining aspect of Jewish identity visible throughout the Geniza corpus, especially for women. Much of what we know about Geniza women comes from legal documents produced in rabbinic courts that oversaw their marriages, divorces, and property transfers. These courts recognized a distinctive rabbinic model of female maturity that casts girls in a series of discrete legal roles as they pass through puberty and into marriage: before puberty, as their fathers' chattel, without independent property or personal rights; after puberty, as autonomous legal agents; after marriage, as subjects mainly controlled by their husbands but who nonetheless retained some rights of their own. I read Geniza legal documents alongside both prescriptive rabbinic texts and Geniza documents of other kinds to examine how this rabbinic model fit Geniza Jews' social ideas about women's adolescence; that is, to compare how Geniza Jews approached adolescent girls as legal persons and as human beings.

My findings suggest that Geniza Jews' legal practices did not set Geniza women fundamentally apart from the Muslim and Christian women around them. I propose that this is because Jewish law was self-consciously distinctive, but worked similarly, as a category of difference, to other religious legal systems (Islamic, Christian, and Zoroastrian) in the medieval Middle East. Under the political conditions fostered by both the Fatimid and Ayyubid states, Islamicate ideas about religious law encouraged many Jews to cultivate a conservative stance toward technical rabbinic norms, including norms that theoretically dictated central aspects of women's lives. But this technical legal conservatism did not directly shape Jews' ordinary world: Geniza Jews routinely used rabbinic courts that carefully maintained rabbinic maturity laws even while understanding and structuring the early female life course according to social mores closer to those likely recognized by their Muslim (and Christian) contemporaries. This approach reveals the complicated fault lines between rabbinic legal practice and its practitioners' wider social universe, demonstrating that Jewish law did not straightforwardly determine Jewish women's social possibilities—and that read carefully, Geniza documents offer evidence for Middle Eastern social history in the broadest sense.

Kinship, Gender, and the Social Order

The fullest account written to date of non-elite women's lives in a medieval Islamic society is based on Geniza documents: S. D. Goitein's treatment of the subject in his monumental *A Mediterranean Society*.[5] Alongside panoramic

5. Published in six volumes between 1967 and 1993. Most of the material on women appears in Vol. 3 ("The Family," 1978) and Vol. 5 ("The Individual," 1988).

discussion of Geniza Jews' economic and political history and material culture, Goitein devoted the third of his five volumes to gender, marriage, and the family, a section of the work notable for its nuanced and empathetic portrait of women's private and public lives and the range of social and economic options that they faced. Some of the women he described were wealthy and relatively independent, deciding for themselves where they lived and with whom, managing and devolving their own property, and directing the education and marriages of their children, grandchildren, and sometimes former slaves. Others owned significant assets but exercised less agency over them, or over themselves; many more were much poorer, lacking not only enough property to require management in the first place, but also the food, clothing, and shelter that they needed to survive from day to day. Some had been widowed or divorced and had to provide for their young children as well as for themselves, while some were still married but to husbands who had abandoned them, or who beat them, or who stole from them.

Goitein's work on the Geniza is rightly viewed as one of the great historiographical achievements of the twentieth century. No scholar can approach this corpus without treading the ground that Goitein prepared through an astonishingly wide-ranging and creative synthesis of thousands upon thousands of fragmentary bits of evidence, themselves extracted painstakingly from thousands of documents and document fragments. But Goitein's treatment of any given topic was also messy, preliminary, and incomplete. This messiness was inevitable given the scale of his ambitions and the complexities of his source base; for precisely the same reasons, it has also been overlooked in the work's reception. Only in the past decade—as a critical mass of document editions and digitization projects has gradually accumulated—have a growing number of scholars begun to emerge from Goitein's long shadow, using Geniza evidence to write fresh histories that systematically expand as well as qualify his findings while considering foundational topics that he left unaddressed.[6]

6. Histories: see below, n. 53. Document editions: this study is a case in point. I could not have written it without Amir Ashur's study of Geniza betrothal and engagement documents (idem, "EBD"). I thank him for sharing it with me at an early stage of my research. Other major collections of editions published concurrent to *Med. Soc.* and since include Ackerman-Lieberman, "Partnership Culture"; Bareket, *Jews of Egypt* and *Jewish Leadership*; Ben-Sasson, *Sicily*; Frenkel, "*Yehudei Ḥalab*" and *The Compassionate and Benevolent*; Friedman, *JMP* and *Polygyny*; Friedman/Goitein, *India Book*; Gil, *Pious Foundations*, *Yehuda ha-Levi*, *Palestine*, and *Ishmael*; Goitein, *Palestinian Jewry*; Motzkin, "Judge Elijah"; Olszowy-Schlanger, *KMD*; Stillman, "East-West Relations"; Weiss, "Hillel" and "Halfon." Digitization projects: two have revolutionized the field. The Friedberg Geniza Project (http://www.jewishmanuscripts.org) offers a union catalogue of nearly the entire Geniza corpus (literary and documentary) together with high-resolution document images, bibliography, and cataloging data. The Princeton Geniza Project (https://etc.princeton.edu/genizaproject) offers a growing database of searchable document transcriptions and metadata. Plans are in

This book seeks to do the same for the women whom Goitein examined. In focusing on women's adolescence, I aim neither to recover teenage girls' own voices, nor to trace their daily routines in full. For all their intimate detail, Geniza documents do not easily lend themselves to either effort. Adolescent girls rarely speak for themselves through the Geniza corpus, while the men who wrote most of these texts rarely found reason to describe how their unmarried daughters spent their time, much less the concerns and interests that occupied their thoughts (or were supposed to).[7] But if the Geniza fails to disclose much that we wish to know about young women's lives, it tells us a great deal about the frameworks in which these lives unfolded. Unmarried and newly married women appear in hundreds of Geniza letters and legal documents: as beneficiaries of wills and gifts; recipients of private and public charity; workers, domestic companions, and domestic servants; and above all, as potential and actual brides, in many texts that describe transactions and negotiations surrounding their entry into marriage.

This is the data on which this book is based. To elucidate the roles that young women could inhabit and why, it draws on personal and administrative letters, court records, legal documents, and responsa preserved in the Geniza, alongside other responsa, legal codes, and commentaries that help explain them. I use this material to consider both the legal and social institutions shaping marriage, divorce, households, inheritance, education, labor, sexuality, and sociability among Geniza Jews and the factors that allowed a given woman to navigate these institutions, chief among them the assets and human relationships that she was able to accumulate by the time she married. Taken together, these conditions dictated not only her material well-being but also the choices that she could make: the "horizon of expectations" that she and others held about where she could go, how she could behave, and whom she could ask for help when she faced problems.[8]

---

progress for further digital projects that will make the corpus more accessible to nonspecialists while allowing specialists to better analyze and map it.

7. The Geniza preserved several hundred letters written or narrated by women at later stages of life, but I have identified only one document narrated by an unmarried girl, and it may have been composed for her by the scribe who wrote it: ENA 2348.1, an orphan's petition. Most women's letters, too, were written for them by male relatives or scribes, although some women (likely a small minority) were literate in Hebrew and perhaps Arabic and may also have known how to write. See Goitein, *Med. Soc.*, 2:183–185, on female literacy, and on women's letters see Kraemer, "Women Speak for Themselves" (Renee Levine-Melammed is preparing Kraemer's corpus for publication; see eadem, "Epistolary Exchanges"), and Wagner, "The Language of Women."

8. This term is borrowed from literary reception theory, where it describes the assumptions that readers in a given historical setting bring to a work. It was coined by Hans Robert Jauss, "Literary History as a Challenge to Literary Theory."

Among the variables deciding these horizons, two held pride of place: her natal kin, and the Jewish legal forums in which she was most likely to marry, divorce, and receive and transmit personal property. The book thus focuses especially on kinship and religious legal practice and suggests new ways of thinking about each.

Here I will briefly review and set in historiographical context my approaches to these two central subjects, which are discussed in greater detail in Chapters 1 and 2 and then developed throughout the rest of the book. To begin with kinship: Family history in the medieval Middle East has remained mostly uncharted territory since Goitein, both within Geniza studies and beyond it.[9] Beyond the Geniza, this gap partly reflects an evidence problem. Few systematic or archival records survive from the Islamic world before the Ottomans, precluding the methodical demographic analysis from which many histories of the family proceed. This impasse may begin to give way as the significant numbers of Arabic documents preserved in other ways become increasingly accessible.[10] In the meantime, however, only one work has exploited evidence of other kinds—mainly passages in chronicles, biographical dictionaries, and responsa—to examine closely nonroyal Muslim families in any region of the Middle East before the eighteenth century: Yossef Rapoport's pathbreaking 2005 study of divorce in Mamluk Egypt (1250–1517, later than the core Geniza corpus).[11] Studies of ruling dynasties and life at court are more common but tell us little about life beyond it.[12]

For their part, the European historians who first developed family history as a field have tended to focus on overarching historical questions

9. For a survey of work on women and the family in Geniza studies, see Krakowski, "The Geniza and Family History." As I note there, the PhD dissertation from which this book grew, "Female Adolescence in the Cairo Geniza Documents," was completed shortly before two other Geniza-based dissertations on aspects of gender, marriage, and the family: Craig Perry's study of domestic slavery in Fustat, "The Daily Life of Slaves," and Oded Zinger's study of marriage disputes in Geniza courts, "Women, Gender, and Law" (both completed in 2014). Together these three studies represent the first major return to the social history of Geniza women and families since Goitein.

10. On this problem, see el-Leithy, "Living Documents." Several major efforts to render medieval Arabic documents more visible and accessible are currently underway, including the Arabic Papyrology Database (http://www.apd.gwi.uni-muenchen.de:8080/apd/project.jsp), and Islamic Law Materialized, a project focusing on legal documents from thirteenth- to fifteenth-century Andalusia, Egypt, and Palestine (http://cald.irht.cnrs.fr/php/ilm.php).

11. Rapoport, *Marriage, Money and Divorce.*

12. On this point, see Bray, "The Family in the Medieval Islamic World." Studies of medieval Muslim women's lives have also focused mainly on elite and royal women. See, e.g., el-Cheikh, "The Harem," eadem, "Revisiting the Abbasid Harems," Cortese and Calderini, *Women and the Fatimids*, Humphreys, "Women as Architectural Patrons." Scholarship on women in Mamluk Egypt is more diverse; see Rapoport, "Women and Gender in Mamluk Society."

unconnected to regions south or east of the Mediterranean after the rise of Islam. Such questions include when and where the medieval European family first emerged as a commensurable social unit, or whether populations in different parts of Europe historically married and formed households according to distinctly different patterns.[13]

Islamicate families appear in this literature only fleetingly, as an imagined counterpoint to European ones. For example, a major debate in family history over the past half-century centers on evidence that late medieval and early modern northwestern Europeans maintained unusually weak ties with their extended kin. This debate began with John Hajnal and Peter Laslett, who cumulatively proposed that northwestern Europeans from at least the sixteenth century followed a distinctive "European marriage pattern" in which both men and women married relatively late, most couples established nuclear households at marriage, and many adults never married at all—a model that some economists credit for strengthening European labor markets and thus encouraging northern Europe's astonishing economic growth during this period and after.[14]

In contrast, Laslett classed southern European marriages in the same period as "Mediterranean": women married early, men relatively later; many couples joined complex households at marriage in which they lived with extended relatives, often across multiple generations; permanently single adults were rare; and the many widows created by this age imbalance at marriage usually remained single after their husbands died.

Hajnal and Laslett limited their typology to Europe and focused strictly on marriage and household formation, that is, on kinship ties expressed through coresidence in domestic units. But later scholars have assumed that Laslett's more enmeshed "Mediterranean" families mirror general kinship structures typical of the Islamic Mediterranean and broader Middle East.[15] This assumption echoes a long tradition of anthropological writing about Middle Eastern

13. For the first question see Herlihy, *Medieval Households*. For the second, see the following note.

14. Hajnal, "Two Kinds of Preindustrial Household Formation System," Laslett, "Family and Household as Work Group and Kin Group." The broader distinction between "weak" central and northern European kinship systems vs. "strong" Mediterranean ones comes from Reher, "Persistent Contrasts." On the debate surrounding Laslett's types, see below, n. 19. Economists: this thesis is reviewed (and judged unconvincing) in Dennison and Ogilvie, "Does the European Marriage Pattern Explain Economic Growth?"

15. See, for example, Reher, "Persistent Contrasts," 213, citing Goody, *Development of the Family and Marriage*, 6–33, on the differences between "Oriental" and "Occidental" family systems. Goody's treatment is based on Guichard, *Al-Ándalus* (although Goody is more tentative about these differences than Guichard, and in fact went on in *The Oriental, the Ancient, and the Primitive* to question the basic distinction between "eastern" and "western" family systems). For a critique of Guichard's portrayal of early Andalusian families, see Coope, "Marriage, Kinship, and Islamic Law."

cousin marriage (rooted in nineteenth- and twentieth-century accounts by European travelers and ethnographers, many of them reporting from rural areas), which typologizes historical Islamic and Middle Eastern families as extended patrilineal clans who jealously guarded their female members' sexual honor, lived in multigenerational patrilocal households, and favored patrilineal cousin marriage as a means of consolidating property and maintaining corporate solidarity within the family—a composite portrait that has also at times been invoked to explain Islamic patriarchy writ large.[16]

From a very different angle, papyrologists have extended Laslett's "Mediterranean" model to the eastern Mediterranean long before Islam, based on census returns that suggest marriages and households in first- to third-century Roman Egypt shared many of its core features (early female and later male marriage, near-universal marriage among both men and women, and a high proportion of complex households relative to nuclear ones).[17]

Within European historiography, Hajnal's "European marriage pattern" still holds empirical force (although historians have challenged the broader ideas about the weak European kinship that it inspired, arguing persuasively that beyond the household, extended kinship affiliations in Europe grew stronger, not weaker, in the early modern period).[18] In contrast, Laslett's "Mediterranean" model has long since dissolved, except as a useful heuristic model. Work on premodern populations throughout Spain, Portugal, and Italy has demonstrated that many marriages and households within all three regions, and across them, met the model's criteria only partly or not at all.[19]

16. Cousin marriage: see, e.g., Raphael Patai, "Cousin-Right in Middle Eastern Marriage." Holy, *Kinship, Honour, and Solidarity*, reviews much of this literature. Islamic patriarchy: e.g., Kandiyoti, "Bargaining with Patriarchy," Tillion, *The Republic of Cousins*. The idea that women's early marriage is typically "Mediterranean" also echoes (and was initially informed by) an anthropological tradition that views "honor and shame" cultures—in which women's virginity and chastity reflect honor and shame upon their male relatives, so that unmarried girls past puberty pose a social threat resolved through early marriage—as characteristic around the Mediterranean. See, e.g., Peristiany, ed., *Honour and Shame*, esp. the opening essay by Pitt-Rivers, "Honour and Social Status"; Gilmore, ed., *Honor and Shame and the Unity of the Mediterranean*, esp. the essay by Giovannini, "Female Chastity Codes"; and for a recent reckoning with this literature, Horden and Purcell, *The Corrupting Sea*, 485–523.

17. Bagnall and Frier, *The Demography of Roman Egypt*, 171–173; Huebner, *The Family in Roman Egypt*, 48–50, eadem, "Egypt as Part of the Mediterranean?" Martha Roth finds Laslett's typology useful for the ancient Near East: eadem, "Age at Marriage and the Household."

18. Sabean and Teuscher, "Kinship in Europe."

19. See the cogent review and summary of this literature in Viazzo, "What's So Special about the Mediterranean?" and for a more recent review of the long-term debates inspired by Laslett's types, see Sovič, Thane, and Viazzo, "History of European Families." Laslett's description of "eastern" European marriage and family patterns has also been qualified

An important outcome of this scholarship has been to underscore that urban and rural households differed at least as much as those in different broad geographic zones, and in particular, to demonstrate that large multigeneration residential compounds seldom flourished in either northern *or* southern European cities, except occasionally among the very wealthy.[20]

What this shift may mean for the Islamic Mediterranean has been sparsely addressed. Yet demographic studies of modern Islamic societies published over the last four decades—which happen to focus mainly on Mediterranean regions such as Egypt, Syria, and Turkey—contradict the "Mediterranean" model just as clearly. They suggest that households in the later Ottoman empire varied as much as those in preindustrial southern Europe, and that urban and rural households in some regions diverged along similar lines: many more people in nineteenth-century Cairo and Istanbul, for example, lived in small nuclear households than in multigenerational patriarchal compounds, which likewise could be found only occasionally among wealthy elites.[21] (Marriage timing, the other major crux of Laslett's model, has not been studied in the same detail.)

Both Ottoman social historians and anthropologists (the latter focused mainly but not exclusively on twentieth-century populations in formerly Ottoman regions) have also questioned classical anthropology's blanket depiction

---

by later research: Szołtysek, "Three Kinds of Preindustrial Household Formation System," idem, "Spatial Construction of European Family and Household Systems."

20. Lynch, *Individuals, Families, and Communities in Europe*, 9, 61–67. In medieval Genoa and Florence, for example, politically powerful extended patrician families clustered together in neighborhoods that they dominated socially and spatially, through privately owned defensive towers. But even these corporate family complexes comprised mainly small nuclear households—the most common type among elites and non-elites alike in cities across medieval and early modern Europe. Genoa and Florence: see Hughes, "Urban Growth and Family Structure," Goldthwaite, "Florentine Palace," idem, *Building of Renaissance Florence*, 104–106. Cf. for Renaissance Venice Brown, *Private Lives*, 195–197.

21. Istanbul: Duben and Behar, *Istanbul Households*, Duben, "Household Formation," idem, "Understanding Muslim Households and Families." Cairo: Fargues, "Family and Household." On rural Turkey in the same period, see Duben, "Turkish Families and Households," idem, "Understanding Muslim Households," McCarthy, "Age, Family and Migration"; on rural Egypt see Cuno, "Joint Family Households." Okawara, "Size and Structure," finds extended households to have been more common in late Ottoman Damascus. See further Olmsted, "A Case Study of the Arab World." Work on the earlier Ottoman empire is sparser but has yielded equally complex findings; Meriwether, *The Kin Who Count*, describes households among elites in eighteenth- and early ninteenth-century Aleppo as extremely variable, while Gerber, "Anthropology and Family History," finds nuclear households to have predominated in seventeenth-century Bursa. These studies mainly focus on ordinary households rather than the large complex ones maintained by Mamluk and then Ottoman military elites, inhabited by both kin and nonkin clients and slaves, which followed a different set of patterns. These have been best studied for the early Ottoman period; see especially Hathaway, *The Politics of Households*, and cf. Piterberg, "Mamluk and Ottoman Political Households," Sievert, "Family, Friend, or Foe," and Richards, "Mamluk Amirs."

of Islamicate and Middle Eastern families as cohesive patrilinies, on grounds that matter especially for women's history. These critiques highlight a range of Middle Eastern kinship systems past and present that contain demonstrably bilateral rather than purely patrilineal elements, meaning that these systems emphasized female kinship ties as well as male ones: daughters as well as sons received personal property from their parents or other birth relatives, remained socially connected to them after marriage, and relied on them socially and economically when they divorced.[22] A few ethnographies of urban and rural populations in twentieth-century North Africa go further and find these populations to have lacked commensurate extended kinship groups entirely.[23]

Do these findings reflect purely modern developments? As the richest available work on any premodern Middle Eastern kinship system, Goitein's "Volume 3" has been often cited in ways that suggest the answer may be yes—that at least in medieval Egypt, ordinary families behaved as archetypes of "classic (Middle Eastern) patriarchy," living as unified patrilineal clans within extended patrilocal households in which multiple generations of descendants, many of them married to their own paternal cousins, lived under the control of an aging patriarch and drew security from their family solidarity.[24]

22. Ottoman historians: e.g., Tucker, "Marriage and Family in Nablus," eadem, "Ties that Bound"; many of the essays collected in Zilfi, *Women in the Ottoman Empire*; and on divorce in particular, the sources cited by Rapoport, *Money, Marriage, and Divorce*, 3. Anthropologists: e.g., Peters, "Affinity in a Maronite Village," Maher, *Women and Property in Morocco*, and Friedl, "Women's Spheres of Action in Rural Iran." Cf. Pierre Bourdieu's distinction between official (patrilineal) kinship and practical (often also matrilineal) kinship in *Outline of a Theory of Practice*, 30–71, and Jack Goody's broad-ranging objections to depictions of "eastern" kinship systems as cohesive or patrilineal in *The Ancient, the Oriental, and the Primitive*.

23. Larson, "Tunisian Kin Ties Reconsidered," Geertz, "The Meaning of Family Ties," Rosen, "Social Identity and Points of Attachment," idem, "Muslim-Jewish Relations," idem, *Bargaining for Reality*, 63–94 (and cf. again Peters, "Affinity in a Maronite Village," for a similar argument for Lebanon). Rosen's and (Hilda) Geertz's accounts of social life in Sefrou, Morocco, as centered around dyadic ties rather than corporate groups reflect the subjectivist approach of Clifford Geertz—whose seminar at the Institute for Advanced Study was also attended by Goitein and Roy Mottahedeh, and whose impact can be discerned especially in Mottahedeh's work, from which I draw inspiration in this book, as discussed below; see further n. 29.

24. Sacchi and Viazzo, "Family and Household," 241, applying the model proposed by Kandiyoti, "Bargaining with Patriarchy," to Goitein's descriptions. For similar accounts of Goitein's Vol. 3, see, e.g., the reviews by M.A. Friedman (*Journal of the American Oriental Society*, 100, 1980, 128–131), Alfred Morabia (*Journal of the Economic and Social History of the Orient*, 25, 1982, 210–217), and Norman Stillman (*AJS Review*, 12, 1987, 157–163), and the sections on the family chosen for inclusion in *A Mediterranean Society: An Abridgment in One Volume*, rev. and ed. Jacob Lassner, Berkeley, 1999. As a measure of Goitein's casual reception along these lines in a broad range of scholarly contexts, see, e.g., Grossman, *Pious*, 46–47; Wansbrough, *Lingua Franca*, 26.

This reading is understandable, because it echoes Goitein's own reading of his findings. He begins the book by noting that although Geniza families appear too varied and complex to fit a single "defined sociological category," they nonetheless display typically "Mediterranean" features: "The bonds of blood were stronger than the ties of marriage. A man's family, foremost in his mind, was not the small one founded by himself but the larger one into which he was born. His family was, as is said in so many documents, 'the house of his father.'"[25]

Yet the heart of Goitein's Volume 3—the detailed document descriptions that make up most of the book, whose complexity he also acknowledges in this passage—offers a different picture from the one most readers have gathered from summary statements like this one.[26] Evidence hiding in plain sight throughout Goitein's work, and throughout the Geniza corpus itself, suggests that families in medieval Egypt were easily as diverse and complicated as Ottoman or European ones, if not more so. So does the only other work to have closely examined medieval families in this or any other region of the Middle East, Yossef Rapoport's study of Mamluk divorce.[27] Rapoport focuses on the economic matrix of divorce rather than the kinship systems permitting it or that it produced, and the Mamluk populations that he examines differed from Geniza Jews in some important ways. But his account nonetheless parallels the Geniza evidence in this respect. Far from coalescing as uniformly robust extended clans, the families and households that both these books describe appear extraordinarily varied and prone to constant change—routinely disrupted and reassembled through divorce, death, remarriage, and long physical separations between relatives of all kinds.

This book takes this counterevidence seriously. It describes a medieval society that was indeed patriarchal, kinship-oriented, and concerned with women's honor. But in all these features—its models of gender and kinship, as well as its ideas about female honor—I suggest that Geniza society looked little like a classic patriarchy. To understand how Geniza families affected women in particular, my starting point is not only the family as a domestic unit, but also wider kin networks encompassing relatives within households and others who did not live together—relationships that are often more visible in Geniza

25. *Med. Soc.*, 3:1.

26. This is true even on a terminological level. To my knowledge, Geniza documents never use the phrase "the house of the father" to denote a man's patrilineal clan, but rather the relatives who shelter a *woman* before her marriage and give her a dowry. On other terms for the extended family in some Geniza documents, see Chapter 1, n. 69. For more on this tension in Goitein's treatment on the family, see Krakowski, "The Geniza and Family History." On similar inconsistencies in Goitein's economic history, see Goldberg, "On Reading Goitein's *A Mediterranean Society*."

27. Rapoport, *Marriage, Money and Divorce.*

documents than domestic ones and that seem to have mattered equally to women's long-term fortunes. At both levels—both within households and within household members' wider kin networks—I find Geniza families to have been, above all, changeable and fluid, not only by demographic necessity, but beyond what even significant rates of mortality would have required.

This book's first chapter confirms quantitatively (to the limited degree that it is possible to do so) that divorce was common. Household arrangements varied widely even among living relatives. Children who grew up within a single unchanging family circle throughout their childhoods were likely exceptions rather than the rule. It argues, moreover, that Geniza Jews' *ideals* of kinship centered neither on patrilinies nor on solidarity groups of any kind, but rather on dyadic relationships between individual relatives—relationships that were heavily gendered not by genealogy (that is, not because they flowed through men rather than women) but in the obligations that they entailed and the options that they offered to male and to female relatives.

What kind of family system was this? Some of the evidence that I describe in the following chapters may fit parts of Laslett's "Mediterranean marriage pattern." Women do seem likely to have married earlier than men and rarely to have stayed single, and many Geniza Jews were likely to live in complex households, albeit small ones—although each of these conclusions is supported by such limited data that none of them is certain. On the other hand, my evidence more firmly contradicts one important aspect of Laslett's model: Geniza widows and divorced women alike often remarried rather than remaining single. My evidence also contradicts a central aspect of Mediterranean marriage as it has often been construed for the Middle East: I find close-kin endogamy to have been much rarer than assumed.

In other respects, Geniza families resemble what historians of early medieval French and German aristocracies have termed *cousinages* or *Sippen*—extended kinship groups bound together mainly through horizontal ties among living kin, whose households and inheritance patterns varied widely and whose shape was determined not "by specific genealogical constellations, but by individual members' positions outside their kin group"—except that representations of the family in Geniza texts seem to reflect a weaker sense of corporate identity.[28]

The closest parallel to Geniza families that I have found, however, appears in studies nearer home: historical works on other forms of social associations in the medieval Islamic world, especially the Islamic states that coalesced

28. Sabean and Tuscher, "Kinship in Europe," 4. This model was first proposed by Schmid, "Zur Problematik," "Structure of the Nobility," and adapted to France by Duby in *The Chivalrous Society* and numerous other works; for a review of this model and the argument that it lasted in France into the eleventh and twelfth centuries, see Livingstone, *Out of Love for my Kin*.

between Kirmān and Qayrawān after the Abbasid empire broke apart. In the 1970s and 1980s, Roy Mottahedeh, Goitein, and Abraham Udovitch argued that social relations under the Buyids and Fatimids (in tenth- and eleventh-century Iraq and Iran and in tenth- to twelfth-century North Africa, Egypt, and Syria) were ordered by informal but normative commitments between men.[29] These were dyadic ties formed through patronage and commercial cooperation among merchants and their agents, philanthropists and their beneficiaries, rulers and their retainers, rulers and their subjects, and any man who performed a service for another in almost any context. As the ideal Islamic *umma* assumed in the Qur'ān confronted the increasingly fractured and diverse Islamic polities that developed across the Middle East in the centuries after the Arab conquests, the Qur'ānic vision of a social order based on religious solidarity gave way to more flexible models grounded in ties of individual reciprocity.[30] These ties were not always permanent, but the expectations that men attached to them held enduring force and meaning. Foregrounding dyadic associations as a "basic unit" of social and political life allowed Mottahedeh especially to explain how early medieval Islamic *institutions* remained resilient without producing stable *organizations*—identifiable social groups lasting across generations.[31] While more recent work has tempered this approach through greater emphasis on the institutional power exercised by medieval Islamic states and their bureaucracies,[32] personal reciprocity remains essential to any account of the social and political fabric of post-Abbasid societies, among Jews and Christians as well as Muslims.

This model of social loyalties also clarifies much that seems otherwise baffling about Geniza kinship, as kinship bound together relatives living

29. Goitein, "Formal Friendship"; Mottahedeh, *Loyalty and Leadership*; Udovitch, "Formalism and Informalism," "Merchants and Amirs." All three scholars had been attending Clifford Geertz's seminar at the Institute for Advanced Studies in Princeton around this period.

30. Rustow, "Patronage in the Context of Solidarity," uses the terms "solidarity" and "reciprocity" to describe this shift, inspired partly by Schwartz, *Were the Jews a Mediterranean Society?* Cf. Mottahedeh, *Loyalty and Leadership*, 7–39, who makes a similar point in different words.

31. "Basic unit": Mottahedeh, *Loyalty and Leadership*, 4, citing Lapidus, "Muslim Cities and Islamic Societies," 49. On the distinction between institutions and organizations in medieval Islamic history, see Hofer, "Sufism, State, and Society."

32. Scholars have also noted that Mottahedeh overemphasizes the differences between medieval European and Middle Eastern political and economic organization. See Chris Wickham's review of *Loyalty and Leadership* (*International Journal of Middle Eastern Studies*, 13, 1981, 380–383; thanks to Marina Rustow for bringing this review to my attention), and more recently Goldberg, *Trade and Institutions*, 15, 120–179; Krakowski and Rustow, "Formula as Content." Recent studies have also complicated Goitein's and Udovitch's accounts of economic informalism. See Goldberg, ibid., Margariti, *Aden and the Indian Ocean*, and Ackerman-Lieberman, *The Business of Identity*.

dispersed in varying configurations throughout complex urban environments across distances great and small. Rather than stable corporate units, I suggest that the families reflected in the Geniza look something like the shifting patronage networks that Mottahedeh, Goitein, and Udovitch describe. Like patronage networks, families were anchored not by members' shared commitments to the abstract group, but by their local commitments to one another—commitments that like loyalties among nonkin were widely recognized and bore widely acknowledged meanings, but that could also be renounced.

This is no more than a metaphor and has its limits. But it is a metaphor I believe Geniza people would have recognized. They themselves applied common idioms to patronage and kinship, so that loyalties among nonkin may be understood as mimicking an ideal originally ascribed to ties of blood—although by the Geniza period, the analogy seems more often to have worked the other way; appeals to kinship gestured toward the core ideal of benefaction. It is moreover an especially useful analogy for my purposes, because kinship was not just one form of social loyalty among others but the one that mattered most to women.

The informal affiliations that scholars have studied so far were exclusively male, and so illuminate a social landscape without women. Attention to kinship helps fill this absence, because significant evidence suggests not only that Geniza women were bound to their kin in ways that partly resembled male clientele and patronage, but that these were nearly the only such bonds they maintained. With few exceptions—themselves mostly forms of replacement kinship, such as slavery and informal adoption of the kind described in the letter with which I opened[33]—women seem not to have created recognized social relationships with nonrelatives, or at least none that are visible in our sources—except, of course, with their husbands, who did not count as kin in the same way. Women who found themselves without relatives willing or able to support them could turn to Jewish communal or Islamic state officials for help, but with these women stripped of the protections that relatives could put in place, officials seem to have responded tepidly to these appeals. Kinship thus mattered to both men and women, but far more to women than to men. By the same token, kin obligations held special force when claimed by women (even if many women's relatives failed to live up to them). Women's honor, not sexual but social and reflected in their economic security and status within

33. On slaves as replacement kin for elite women in particular, see Perry, "The Daily Life of Slaves," 66–105. Free women seem to have formed kin-like connections with adults who took care of them after they had been orphaned, as in the letter described at n. 1 above. I discuss this evidence in Chapter 4, but the long-term relationships created by these arrangements deserve further study. See also ENA NS 17.31, an unusual legal document in which a father "sells" his infant daughter, whose mother had died in childbirth, to a married woman and gives up all claims over her upbringing and future property.

the households that they joined at marriage, seems to have weighed especially heavily on their own kin.

By following young women as they moved from childhood dependence on their relatives to the more complex social world that they lived in as adults, this book is partly an attempt to understand the gendered social order that this model of kinship created: how men and women alike understood the loyalties that they owed their daughters, sisters, and mothers; how these loyalties interacted with those that men maintained among themselves, including within legal and political institutions; how they shaped marriage for both men and women; why men honored these loyalties, or failed to; and what happened to women in both cases.

Religious Identity, Law, and Ordinary Culture

It is an irony of history that the largest documentary cache to survive the medieval Islamic world was preserved not by Muslims but by Jews—albeit Jews who lived side by side with Muslims and Christians in some of the most important Islamic cities of the day.

The people who wrote the Geniza documents—that is, the scribes and letter-writers who literally put pen to paper to produce them—were mainly sub-elite (or "middling"-class) Jewish men from cities and villages throughout the eastern Mediterranean, especially Egypt and Syria (including Palestine, a district of Syria in this period): most prominently Fustat itself, but also Cairo, Alexandria, smaller Egyptian towns such as Bilbays and Malīj, Jerusalem, Tyre, Damascus, Tripoli in modern-day Lebanon (sometimes termed in Geniza letters Tripoli al-Shām, a convention I have adopted here for clarity), Qayrawān, al-Mahdiyya, and the other Tripoli, in modern-day Libya.[34] The documents themselves describe and sometimes speak for a wider range of Jewish men and women from the same places: not only merchants, physicians, and scribes, but also craftsmen, tradesmen, and the very poor, together with their wives and daughters. Some were converts to Judaism, usually freed slaves who were formerly owned by Jews. But most had been born Jewish and likely descended from the late ancient Jewish populations of the Middle East, in both the east Roman and Sasanian empires.[35]

34. On the documents' geographic scope, see Goitein, *Med. Soc.*, 1:42–70, and the correction in Goldberg, "Geographies," 24–25, idem, *Trade and Institutions*, 306–309. See also Golb, "Topography." A complete map of the Geniza documents by provenance, date, and genre remains a major desideratum.

35. We know very little about Jews in Egypt between the second century and the early tenth, when the earliest Geniza documents appear. The evidence from Roman Palestine is much richer, while Sasanian Iraq and Iran fall somewhere in between, since the Babylonian Talmud contains an immense amount of data difficult to use as historical evidence.

We know little about these populations' movements in the intervening centuries, but some Geniza Jews' more recent ancestors seem to have moved west from Iran and Iraq in the late ninth and tenth centuries, as the Abbasid heartlands suffered a series of political and economic calamities.[36] By the eleventh century, when the Geniza record first reaches a critical mass, the Abbasid caliphate had collapsed in all but name, and Egypt had emerged as the political and economic center of the Islamic world. Fustat was its commercial heart—the focus of the buoyant economy of the Islamic eastern Mediterranean, and the portal through which trade across the Indian Ocean flowed into the Mediterranean, and through which immigrants and travelers passed to and from regions throughout the Middle East, North Africa, Byzantium, and even Europe.

Geniza documents reflect at every turn both their setting in the Fatimid (and then Ayyubid) Mediterranean and their writers' difference as Jews. Our letter about the orphan sisters, for example, is narrated in so-called middle Arabic, the common language of twelfth-century Fustat, and addresses its recipient using Fatimid petitionary formulae: "The (female) slave (*al-ʿabda*) . . . will act only on our lord's decision (*ra'y sayyidinā*)."[37] But it is *written* in Judeo-Arabic—Arabic in Hebrew script—and peppered with Hebrew phrases and honorifics, including a prestige title tied to the Palestinian gaonic academy, one of the major Jewish scholastic institutions in the eleventh-century Middle East (*ḥaver ha-yeshiva*, used to identify the volunteer widow's late father-in-law). It is addressed to the Head of the Jews, the leader of Jewish communal institutions in the Fatimid empire.[38] And part of its purpose is to secure a tutor who will teach the girls Jewish prayer.

What difference did this religious difference make? This is both a methodological question and a historical one. At stake methodologically are the

---

Egypt: Bagnall, *Egypt in Late Antiquity*, 275–278, Ilan, "Jewish Community in Egypt." Roman Palestine is covered by an enormous literature, much of it reviewed (and qualified) in Schwartz, *Imperialism and Jewish Society*. The most serious attempt to write a history of the Jews in Sasanian Iraq remains Neusner, *A History of the Jews in Babylonia*; on some of the reasons for this, see Schwartz, "Political Geography," 89–93. Evidence for Jews or Jewish life between the Arab conquests and the Abbasid period is extremely sparse. For a partial review, see Wasserstrom, *Between Muslim and Jew*, 17–46. Jews do appear in some eighth-century Egyptian papyri; see for now Hanafi, "Two Unpublished Paper Documents."

36. Ashtor, "Un mouvement migratoire," Goitein, "Rise of the Middle-Eastern Bourgeoisie," idem, *Med. Soc.*, 1:30–31, Gil, *Jews in Islamic Countries*, 676–679. The scale of this migration has recently been questioned: Ackerman-Lieberman, "Revisiting Jewish Occupational Choice," Goldberg, "The 'Maghribi Traders.'"

37. On these formulae in Fatimid petitions, see Khan, *ALAD*, 303–317, and on their use in Geniza letters, Cohen, "Four Judaeo-Arabic Petitions," idem, *Voice of the Poor*, 16–17.

38. I discuss the Palestinian and Iraqi gaonic academies and the Heads of the Jews in Chapter 2.

uses to which Geniza documents can be put. Do they illustrate Fatimid and Ayyubid social history writ large, or must we accept one Islamic historian's judgment that they "remain of marginal value" except for a narrowly particular history of the Jews?[39] At stake historically are the differences Geniza Jews' Judaism made for them and for the people around them—that is, how religion worked as a social category in the Fatimid and Ayyubid empires.

One way in which Geniza documents can help us to understand the nature of Jewish difference is by suggesting how Jews functioned as a social group. Decades of scholarship have made their group outlines relatively clear. On the one hand, the Jews we glimpse through the Geniza formed distinct social communities, defined both externally by their status as "protected" (*dhimmī*) non-Muslims who paid special taxes to the state, and internally by nearly exclusive bonds of kinship and by characteristic communal institutions—synagogues, courts, and systems of public welfare, all directed by overlapping networks of communal leaders.[40] This framework bound medieval Islamicate Jews together in ways that Jews arguably had not been in late antiquity. Yet Jewish communities were also politically and socially porous. Jews of all social strata participated in Fatimid and Ayyubid politics and institutional life, maintaining personal patronage ties with state officials, using Islamic *qāḍī* courts, and petitioning the state directly through its own *maẓālim* tribunals. They also formed patronage and business ties with Muslims and Christians beyond the purview of the state, lived in buildings with them, sometimes had children with them, and sometimes crossed communal lines entirely through conversion.[41] Viewed from this angle, Judaism appears as a primary but not totalizing social identity, grounded in an unusual form of group coherence that cut across some of the networks of reciprocal ties on which Fatimid and Ayyubid society ran.

39. Sourdel, *Medieval Islam*, 54, cited by Goldberg, *Trade and Institutions*, 26.

40. On these institutions, particularly in Fustat, see Goitein, *Med. Soc.*, 2:1–170, Gil, *Documents of the Pious Foundations*, Cohen, *Poverty and Charity*.

41. Jewish communal history is one of the best-developed areas of Geniza research. See the evaluations in Rustow, "The Genizah and Jewish Communal History," and Frenkel, Yagur, and Franklin, "Jewish Communal History." On Jews' use of *maẓālim* tribunals, see Rustow, "The Legal Status of *Ḏimmī-s*." Evidence for Jews' social contacts with Muslims and Christians is discussed throughout Goitein, *Med. Soc*, and more recently by Goldberg, *Trade and Institutions*, 140–141, 178, Margariti, "*Aṣḥābunā l-tujjār*" (on business connections among Jews and non-Jews involved in the eleventh-century Mediterranean and twelfth-century Indian Ocean trades), and Perry, "Daily Life of Slaves" (on slavery, conversion, and sexuality). Moshe Yagur (Hebrew University) is working on a dissertation that examines Geniza accounts of conversion in other contexts. See, e.g., CUL Or. 1080 J 21, a Geniza letter that mentions a marriage between a Jewish man and a Muslim woman. See also Chapters 1 and 5 on contacts between Jews and non-Jews within *dārs*.

In this book I am more interested in a further aspect of religion's social meaning that has been less studied—not only how Judaism defined Jews socially, but also how this group identity affected the ordinary shape and texture of their lives. By "ordinary" I mean to emphasize those parts of life that were not obvious religious flashpoints: the ideas, dispositions, and material practices that Geniza Jews took for granted when they were *not* praying, giving charity, or appearing before a rabbinic judge. Geniza Jews' Jewishness may have dictated the taxes that the state required them to pay, the range of courts that they chose to use, the holidays that they observed, a great many of their social bonds, and the texts that some of them read and wrote. But how far apart did it otherwise set them from their Muslim and Christian neighbors? Did they view the world in fundamentally different terms? Did they consume different goods, hold different notions of propriety or beauty, or think differently about filial bonds, childhood friendships, or death? Most importantly for my purposes, did they live in differently shaped households, hold different views of marriage and kinship, or cast women in a different range of social roles?

These questions are unlikely to share a single answer. Some may not be answerable at all, given the unique quality of the evidence the Geniza preserves. Still, most scholars have assumed that Geniza documents can indeed be used for Islamic (or more aptly here, Islamicate)[42] social history, because as a group, Jews were too loosely differentiated to have maintained radically different social or cultural norms from those of the Muslims and Christians around them. Goitein begins *A Mediterranean Society* on this reasoning, noting that Geniza Jews "mingled freely with their neighbors, and therefore cannot have been very much different from them."[43] This expectation informs all later attempts to explain Geniza documents in light of Islamic or Christian evidence. And it seems validated whenever these comparisons have proven useful. But without systematic comparative studies against which to weigh their findings, few Geniza scholars have directly developed this assumption, or sought to pin down its limits.[44]

I argue here that an unexpected evidence base can place this assumption on a firmer footing: texts describing Jewish law and legal practice. Rather

42. Marshall Hodgson coined this term precisely to flatten distinctions among members of different religious groups in medieval Islamic societies and to highlight their shared culture: *The Venture of Islam*, 1:58–60.

43. Goitein, *Med. Soc.*, 1:70–71.

44. The one major exception has occurred in economic history, where a lively debate has developed over how eleventh-century Geniza merchants' Jewish identity affected their commercial practices. See Goldberg, "Geographies," 32–40, and the literature reviewed there, and Ackerman-Lieberman, *Business of Identity*. Cohen, *Poverty and Charity*, 243–252, also addresses the interplay between Islamicate and rabbinic models in Geniza Jews' treatment of the poor.

than illustrating Jewish particularity alone, legal evidence used throughout this book supports the field's working assumption that Geniza Jews were not "much different" from the non-Jews around them. The Jewish girls whom I examine here likely resembled their Muslim (and probably Christian) neighbors in many basic respects. But this evidence also demonstrates that we cannot ignore Geniza documents' Jewish features to assume so. Instead, it is precisely by attending closely to what *is* distinctively Jewish about these documents that we can begin to see what may *not* be—and thus begin to use them, tentatively and carefully, as evidence for Middle Eastern and Islamic as well as Jewish social history.

How so? The book's approach to Jewish law and Jewish difference in a nutshell is as follows. Jewish law stands out as a central aspect of Jewish identity in the medieval Islamic world, both within the Geniza and elsewhere—especially throughout the library of prescriptive legal writings produced by medieval rabbinic jurists. By the tenth century, when our documents begin, scholars working in the gaonic *yeshivot* (scholastic academies in Iraq whose heads represented themselves as heirs to the rabbis who appear in the Babylonian Talmud) had stabilized an enormous range of rabbinic legal teachings from Roman and Sasanian late antiquity into a unified discursive system equipped with its own textual canon, technical vocabulary, and hierarchy of established norms. Jurists in Iraq, Egypt, the Maghrib, and Andalusia maintained and developed this system during the following centuries via increasing numbers of responsa and legal digests, codes, and commentaries written in Aramaic, Hebrew, and Judeo-Arabic. Without the Geniza, these legal texts would contain most of what we know about Jews' lives in the medieval Middle East. With it, we can, of course, see far beyond these legal texts. But more than this, we can also glimpse beneath them, to the human settings in which medieval rabbinic law was produced and received. The Geniza corpus contains thousands of legal documents issued by and for rabbinic courts (*batei din*) throughout Fatimid and Ayyubid Egypt and Syria. These documents not only illuminate how rabbinic law worked in practice within rabbinic courtrooms. Read alongside other kinds of Geniza documents, they also suggest the roles that rabbinic legal practice played *outside* the courtroom: why and how Jews used rabbinic courts, what they accomplished in doing so, how the laws upheld there shaped their ordinary culture, and how they did not.

This is the approach I take here. Female adolescence is a good subject through which to examine these questions, because of the clear-cut and unusual way in which rabbinic law defines women's coming-of-age. Throughout the book, I compare rabbinic maturity laws both to Geniza legal documents about unmarried and newly married girls, and to Geniza evidence of other kinds concerning such girls' adolescence.

I use three main bodies of prescriptive rabbinic texts to do so. First is the classical rabbinic literature from late antiquity: the Mishna and Tosefta,

Babylonian and Palestinian Talmuds, and occasionally legal *midrashim*.[45] Although I sometimes note discontinuities and tensions within these sources, my main interest lies not in their meaning within late ancient Judaism but in their medieval legacy—how medieval jurists read, codified, and struggled with the traditions that these sources preserve.

The second group includes gaonic texts composed in Abbasid and Buyid Iraq, the earliest postclassical rabbinic (or Rabbanite)[46] legal writings that we possess. These can be further grouped into three categories: a) the early (likely late eighth- and ninth-century) legal codes *Halakhot Pesuqot* and *Halakhot Gedolot*; b) later legal monographs and biblical and Mishnaic commentaries written by Se'adya b. Yosef—*ga'on* of the *yeshiva* of Sura in Baghdad from 928 and 942 and a revolutionary intellectual figure who transformed the intellectual focus and output of the *ge'onim*—and his successors in the tenth and early eleventh centuries; and c) gaonic responsa—legal answers issued by the *yeshivot* to individual queries that they received from Jews in Andalusia, North Africa, Iraq, and elsewhere, which survive mainly in later literary collections.[47]

Third, I draw on postgaonic Rabbanite texts produced by jurists close to the orbit of Geniza Jews, who wrote in conversation with each other and with the *ge'onim*. Among these, I draw most often on three sets of works, because they contain the most material relevant to my subject: a) responsa issued by Yiṣḥaq al-Fāsī, as his name suggests, a native of the Maghrib, who headed a rabbinic academy in Lucena from the late 1070s or slightly after, until his death in 1103; b) the legal writings of Moshe or Mūsā b. Maymūn, better known as Maimonides—a student of al-Fāsī's student Yosef b. Me'ir ibn Migas, and the greatest rabbinic author of the Islamic Middle Ages, who spent his adult life in Fustat until his death in 1204 and served twice as *ra'īs al-yahūd* there—especially his responsa, Mishna commentary, and his monumental legal code the *Mishne Torah*; and c) responsa issued by Maimonides' son Avraham, who likewise served as *ra'īs* in Fustat from 1204 to 1237.[48]

45. For an introduction to these sources, see Strack and Stemberger, *Introduction to the Talmud and Midrash*.

46. The term "Rabbanite" denotes rabbinic Jews in the medieval Islamicate world, as a counterpart to Karaites, on whom see below. Here I use it interchangeably with "rabbinic" to describe medieval Jews, but use "rabbinic" only when describing late ancient Jews.

47. See Brody, *Geonim of Babylonia*, for an exceptionally clear introduction to these sources. See ibid., 216–230, on this dating for *Halakhot Pesuqot* and *Halakhot Gedolot*.

48. Al-Fāsī's responsa are preserved in several collections old and new (listed in the bibliography) but have not been studied systematically as a group. In contrast, enough has been written on Maimonides' legal writings to fill a mid-sized library; see by way of introduction Twersky, *Introduction to the Code*, Cohen's forthcoming *Maimonides and the Merchants*, and on his responsa, Goitein, "Maimonides as Chief Justice." Abraham Maimonides' responsa are known through the Geniza; see Friedman, "Responsa of R. Abraham Maimonides."

Finally, a note on my use of Karaite sources: Not all Geniza Jews recognized rabbinic law. Some were Karaites, who followed a different prescriptive legal system developed in ninth-century Iraq, Iran, and Palestine, and based, at least in theory, directly on the Hebrew Bible. Recent scholarship demonstrates that far from living as isolated sects, Karaites and Rabbanites worked together politically and sometimes intermarried, and that Karaites often used Rabbanite courts.[49] This book touches comparatively on Karaite law and uses documents about Karaites as evidence for Jewish social practice. But it focuses exclusively on rabbinic law when discussing *legal* practice, because surviving Rabbanite legal documents vastly outnumber Karaite ones.[50]

Comparison between these prescriptive texts and my Geniza evidence yields two consistent conclusions. On the one hand, the Rabbanite court officials and jurists described in the Geniza worked hard to reproduce a conservative version of rabbinic law, as codified and explained by the *ge'onim* and their successors. Officials took care to treat unmarried and newly married girls as rabbinic legal persons whenever they entered a rabbinic courtroom, fixing their formal economic and personal status in ways closely aligned with gaonic and later Rabbanite prescriptive norms. Yet on the other hand, these same Jews understood young women differently as *social* persons. Beyond the narrow sphere of rabbinic legal performance and juridical writing, Geniza Jews managed and understood young women's property, support, labor, sexuality, mobility, marriage choices, and household arrangements according to models different from those assumed by rabbinic maturity law—and closer to those captured by Islamic law, which allowed young women greater legal agency after marriage than they could achieve before it, regardless of their age.

Most research on the social dimensions of medieval Jewish law has examined traces of legal change—evidence that medieval jurists responded to contemporary realities by rejecting, adapting, or expanding older legal traditions.[51] I find similar evidence in some cases. But the most striking disjunction in my evidence is not between the laws that jurists had inherited and those that they changed to meet the needs of their day. Rather, these two contrasting findings—Geniza Jews maintained rabbinic maturity laws yet structured young women's lives differently from what rabbinic law envisions—highlight the distance between the entire sphere of rabbinic legal writing and practice

49. Rustow, *Heresy*.

50. Almost all the Karaite legal documents preserved in the Geniza are marriage and premarital contracts. See Olszowy-Schlanger, *KMD*, "Lettre de divorce," and "Karaite Legal Documents."

51. Outstanding examples include, from different angles, Soloveitchik, "Halakhah, Hermeneutics, and Martyrdom," idem, *Wine in Ashkenaz*, Fram, *Ideals Face Reality*, Baumgarten, *Practicing Piety*, and most directly relevant to this study, Cohen's forthcoming *Maimonides and the Merchants*.

on the one hand and Geniza Jews' accepted social norms on the other. This tension could lead Rabbanite court officials to enforce rabbinic laws unevenly (for example, they often ignored pleas made by socially unprotected women, regardless of their legal merits) but rarely to change or deny them directly.

One of the book's main conclusions is thus that medieval Jews who practiced rabbinic law conservatively did not always see the world in rabbinic terms. At least some and likely many of their ordinary cultural ideas were not religiously differentiated at all, but shared equally among Muslims, Jews, and Christians in medieval Islamicate societies. At least in this case, Islamic legal traditions of recent vintage were closer to these shared ideas than Jewish ones developed many centuries earlier.

This does not demonstrate, of course, that Jews lived exactly like the Muslims and Christians around them. The Jewish girls whom I examine in this book may well have differed from their Muslim and Christian contemporaries along other lines due to class or group mores that lie beyond our purview to discern, at least until a base of comparable evidence for the other two groups has been amassed and assessed. But it does suggest at least that the social differences created by Jewish law—the most obvious and central aspect of Jewish particularity visible in our sources—were slighter than we might expect.

Nor does it mean that rabbinic legal practice lacked all social meaning. Even the most practically trivial elements of the law can be said to have mattered at some level as long as Jewish litigants and court officials continued to reenact them, even if they rarely affected how things worked in ordinary time. Certain elements of Jewish law could matter a great deal more than this. One example that left its mark throughout the Geniza is the husband's unilateral right to rabbinic divorce, which bound many women to husbands who had abandoned them; in contrast, Islamic law permits judges to divorce women in their husbands' absence.[52] But overall, the evidence I examine here suggests that rabbinic legal practice packed more impact through its form than through its content. The Jews who ran and used Geniza courts cared more about reproducing a coherent system of legal behaviors that they and others understood as authentic Jewish law than about the specific ideas or social structures that this law embodied.

Why should this be the case? Here, too, I suggest that our best answers lie in considering Geniza legal practice against a history close to it in time and place—in this case, the history of early Islamicate legal cultures. The Iraqi *ge'onim* who developed the normative legal system that Geniza courts strove to maintain worked in Abbasid Baghdad during the eighth through early eleventh centuries. During this period not only Jewish but also Muslim, Christian,

52. On abandoned wives in the Geniza, see below, Chapter 1, n. 2; on Muslim women's recourse to judicial divorce in Mamluk Egypt, see Rapoport, *Money, Marriage, and Divorce*, 76–78.

and Zoroastrian religious elites began to produce new forms of legal writings, which share important features even if they are not precisely cognates. All of these literatures developed side by side within an open legal marketplace in which Abbasid state courts, Islamic *qāḍī* courts, and non-Muslim religious communal courts eventually came to operate side by side. All approach religious law as a *technical* system of normative rules, that is, one maintained by legal experts who have mastered a specific textual canon and a repertoire of methods for using it. All present these rules as binding on the entire religious group, elites and laypeople alike. And all therefore invest with political authority the legal specialists who maintain and administer these rules.

Most of these developments, which I survey in the book's second chapter, have been well studied in isolation, but they rarely have been viewed together. Yet once we do so, it is obvious that they form a common history. Each of these legal systems was unique, but all came to define the religious groups they belonged to in similar terms. Viewing early medieval Jewish law as part and parcel of this history helps explain why it looks the way it does—including the law practiced in Geniza courts, which operated in an environment deeply informed by Abbasid models. More broadly, it helps explain why many Geniza Jews took pains to negotiate their disputes and record their transactions in line with rabbinic norms, by suggesting how Islamicate assumptions about religious law may have conditioned Jewish communal elites and non-elites alike to take seriously the technical norms of rabbinic law. This stance politically strengthened Jewish court officials who lacked hard powers of rule, and it encouraged non-elite Jews to use Jewish courts and value the law that they dispensed even if many of its details no longer made much sense to them.

This history thus suggests that non-Islamic religious law played a mutually comprehensible role within early medieval Islamic social orders, one recognized in its basic outlines by Muslims and non-Muslims alike. By extension, it helps explain how rabbinic Judaism, a product of pre-Islamic late antiquity, survived and flourished in the vastly different environment of the medieval Islamic world during a period when around 90 percent of Jews worldwide lived under Islamic rule.

Most importantly for the concerns that animate this book, this history further suggests that the evidence I describe throughout the following pages may not have been unique to Jews, or at least not unique to them by virtue of their religious practices. Thus, this history helps explain the limits of rabbinic doctrines to control or explain Jewish women's lives. The Jewish courts in which women married, divorced, and acquired property practiced a technically conservative form of rabbinic law, but one sufficiently constrained and selective that its practical outcomes depended on factors that lay beyond the letter of prescriptive legal texts—especially on a woman's kin and the support that they offered her both in court and elsewhere. Jewish law and the communal institutions that administered it affected women in important ways, but proved ultimately less important to their fates than did the gendered networks of kinship and patronage in which men and women alike remained embedded, both within court and beyond it.

Geniza Documents and "Geniza Society"

A few words are in order about my documentary sources and how I use them throughout the book. The Geniza corpus is uniquely valuable not only for its size, but also for its density and for the diversity of the genres that it contains. Because the Geniza chamber was essentially a garbage disposal rather than an archive, it preserved all manner of ephemera usually lost to history. The documents span widely different genres and are unusually varied in form and content, so that they allow us to glimpse the Jews of Fatimid and Ayyubid Egypt and Syria within a broad geographic context as they moved and communicated with others from the Mediterranean to the Indian Ocean, and from multiple angles of vision, as they wrote to their relatives, to their business associates, to their own communal elites, to Islamic state officials, and as they recorded the responsibilities that they owed each other in their own religious courts.

Goitein mined all of these genres to build the great composite portrait presented in *A Mediterranean Society*. Some of the most fruitful and accomplished work in Geniza historiography published since then, however, has treated subsets of documents defined more tightly by region (e.g., Roxani Margariti's study of the port of Aden and Miriam Frenkel's of Jewish communal leaders in Alexandria), by period (e.g., Marina Rustow's study of Karaite-Rabbanite relations in the eleventh century), by genre (e.g., Mordechai Akiva Friedman's study of Palestinian-style Rabbanite marriage agreements and Judith Olszowy-Schlanger's study of Karaite ones, Geoffrey Khan's study of mainly Arabic-script Fatimid and Ayyubid state and legal documents, Mark Cohen's work on charity lists and appeals from Fustat, and Phillip Ackerman-Lieberman's study of rabbinic partnership contracts), or by genre *and* period (Jessica Goldberg's economic history based on early eleventh-century commercial letters).[53] These latter genre-based studies have expanded not only our historiographical knowledge but also our understanding of the documents

53. Margariti, *Aden*, Frenkel, *The Compassionate and Benevolent*, Rustow, *Heresy*, Friedman, *JMP*, Olszowy-Schlanger, *KMD*, Khan, *ALAD*, Cohen, *Poverty and Charity*, Ackerman-Lieberman, *The Business of Identity*, Goldberg, *Trade and Institutions*. Several Geniza studies have also focused on communal leaders in Fustat in the eleventh century: Cohen, *Jewish Self-Government*, Bareket, *The Jews of Egypt 1007–1055*, eadem, *The Jewish Leadership in Fustat*. Zinger, "Women, Gender and Law," and Perry, "The Daily Life of Slaves," both take a synthetic approach closer to the one employed here.

themselves, the scribal conventions they followed, and how people used them. Not all documentary genres within the corpus have been studied as carefully, but the powerful results of this work demonstrate that they should be—that any given type of Geniza document presents a composite of unique features and recurring scribal formulas, which scribes creatively deployed in ways that they and their audiences understood but that are easy for us to miss.[54]

This book returns to Goitein's approach of treating the Geniza corpus as a grand archive even though the Geniza chamber was not a literal one. Because the subjects that I examine here are neither addressed fully nor directly within any single subset of documents, I have chosen to take advantage of the Geniza's full promise by casting my net widely across time and space within the corpus and across documents of many different kinds (while, however, sticking to the "classical" Geniza period and regions, that is, mainly to the Fatimid and Ayyubid eastern Mediterranean, ca. 969–1250; some of my evidence ranges a bit earlier and later, from the earlier tenth century to the end of the thirteenth).[55] But I have also sought to benefit as much as possible from recent work on smaller subcorpora and its implications by paying close attention to formulas and conventions used within documents of different genres. Many of the arguments that I advance in the following pages developed from attempts to understand these formulas, by comparing them to each other and against Jewish and Islamic texts of other kinds. This approach often helps to clarify not only why the letters and legal documents cited here look as they do, but also what they were supposed to accomplish for the people who wrote and received them.

Geniza documents can be difficult to class by type, since some merge features from multiple genres. Nonetheless, most of the documents discussed in the following pages fall into four basic categories.[56]

First, I rely on legal documents produced by rabbinic courts, some issued to litigants, and others that court officials kept for their own records. Because of the book's partly legal focus, these documents' features, functions, and development are discussed at length in the following chapters, especially in Chapters 2 and 7. For reasons addressed in Chapter 2, Geniza legal documents are extremely variable and thus especially difficult to classify. But among them, those cited most frequently throughout the book revolve around marriage

54. See on this point Krakowski and Rustow, "Formula as Content."

55. Some of my material also ranges into regions beyond the edge of Fatimid control, particularly eleventh-century Zirid North Africa and Seljuq Syria.

56. This list is nearly exhaustive of the Geniza's major genres, but not entirely. I have made little to no use of certain document types that proved to contain no evidence relevant to my subject, e.g., Arabic-script Fatimid state documents preserved in surprisingly large numbers within the Geniza chamber, or Jewish administrative records listing communal funds and property, or commercial accounts and lists. State documents: see Khan, *ALAD*; Marina Rustow is currently working on a book about this material. Administrative records: see Gil, *Pious Foundations*. Accounts and lists: see Goldberg and Udovitch, "Lists."

and its attendant financial transactions: marriage contracts proper (that is, *ketubbot*), engagement and betrothal documents, dowry lists, and reconciliation agreements between husbands and wives. Besides marriage documents, some of my evidence also comes from wills and legal testimonies about young women's property.[57]

Second, a different group of legal sources cited throughout the book falls into a no-man's land between documents and prescriptive texts: legal queries sent to elicit responsa and almost always preserved alongside them. The book draws both on queries and responsa that survived individually within the Geniza, and on others contained within the literary responsa collections discussed above, as evidence both for the situations that the queries portray and for the juridical reasoning that the responsa reflect. Although they are not legal documents, responsa often describe cases that unfolded within the same courts that produced our documents, and so illuminate them from another angle.[58]

The third group comprises personal letters sent between relatives and business and social associates and by poor men to their charitable patrons (or hoped-for patrons). Because Geniza people rarely wrote to each other for the sheer pleasure of communicating their thoughts, but rather for immediate practical purposes, Geniza letters are most easily described by the reasons for which they were written. Those I discuss most often include brief charity petitions sent by poor Jewish men to wealthier ones, framed either as third-party recommendations or as direct appeals, usually written by professional scribes and following conventions borrowed from petitions to the Fatimid state;[59] commercial letters exchanged by merchants, mainly to give instructions, share market information, and share information about their own and other merchants' business activities, but also containing bits of communal, family, and personal news;[60] and personal letters of other kinds, most often between family members, both men and women, which vary more in their length and content.[61]

57. On these genres and the work done on them to date, see below, Chapters 1, 2, 7, and 8, and Krakowski, "The Geniza and Family History."

58. Many studies of medieval Jewish communities in Europe and the Middle East draw evidence from responsa, but they have rarely been studied as instruments in their own right. For an exciting step in this direction, see Zinger, "Towards a Social History of Responsa."

59. These are discussed in detail in Cohen, *Poverty and Charity*, and idem, *Voice of the Poor*. See also idem, "Four Judaeo-Arabic Petitions."

60. Most of the eleventh-century commercial letters were published by Gil, *Ishmael*; their forms and uses are closely analyzed in Goldberg, *Trade and Institutions*, "The Use and Abuse of Commercial Letters," "Friendship and Hierarchy," and "Mercantile Letters." Commercial letters from the twelfth century have not been as carefully studied as a corpus, but many have been published: Goitein/Friedman, *India Book*.

61. In contrast, private noncommercial letters have not been studied systematically as a group, although 100–150 such letters sent by or to women are now being prepared for publication; see above, n. 7.

Fourth and finally, I have relied on administrative letters and records written by or to Jewish communal officials, mainly in Fustat. Here I draw most often on four subtypes. First, there are communal appeals by poor men and women meant to be read aloud in synagogue, asking for financial help or—more often in the case of women—for help obtaining a divorce or other legal rights (these are more common in the early eleventh century than after).[62] Second, there are petitions to communal officials, including the Heads of the Jews (which largely replaced these communal appeals in the mid-eleventh century), sent by poor men and especially poor and socially struggling women. Again, these ask both for money and for social assistance of other kinds; like private petitions, they were written mainly by scribes and modeled on *maẓālim* petitions submitted by individuals to the Fatimid state.[63] Third, there are letters exchanged between officials or between officials and people working on their behalf, about legal cases, public charity, and communal crises and affairs.[64] And fourth, there are records of the Jewish communal charity funds of Fustat, especially lists of poor men and women who had received bread or clothing from the communal dole.[65]

Working with this range of sources has been illuminating but also daunting. The same breadth that makes the Geniza richer than most smaller or more orderly collections also creates major interpretive problems. Some of these come from the state of the texts themselves, which are often fragmentary and faded. Others have to do with first-order interpretation: Many cannot be dated with any precision. Some passages are not self-evident even at a semantic level. Others can readily be translated but remain inexplicable anyhow, since the people who wrote and originally read them took for granted an entire social universe closed to modern readers—a problem that even the closest attention to their conventions and idioms cannot always solve.

But even when Geniza documents can be confidently dated, deciphered, translated, and parsed, they pose other historical difficulties when used as a group. Not only do they describe people spread over three centuries and across more than 2,000 miles, but they describe them irregularly, in two ways. First, the corpus is spread unevenly across time and space. Eleventh-century

62. These appeals have not been systematically studied either, but see preliminarily Goitein, *Med. Soc.*, 2:169–170, and Ben Sasson, "Appeal to the Congregation."

63. See again Cohen, *Poverty and Charity*, and idem, *Voice of the Poor*. On these petitions' parallels with Fatimid state petitions, see Rustow, "Diplomatics of Leadership," Goitein, *Med. Soc.*, 2:34–35, Cohen, *Jewish Self-Government*, 245.

64. On some of these letters' material features and their parallels with Fatimid state documents, see Rustow, "The Diplomatics of Leadership." Examples appear in many published Geniza collections focused on Jewish communal leadership, e.g., Friedman, *Polygyny*, and Bareket, *The Jews of Egypt*, but they have not otherwise been assessed as a genre.

65. These, too, are discussed most thoroughly in Cohen, *Poverty and Charity*, and idem, *Voice of the Poor*.

Geniza documents come mainly from Egypt and Syria and occasionally the Maghrib and Fatimid Sicily. But the political map of the Middle East shifted in the mid-eleventh century. In the west, Bedouins invaded across Ifrīqiyya and the Maghrib; in the east, Seljuq Turks toppled Islamic states and populations from Central Asia to Syria. These upheavals collapsed communications among Middle Eastern Jews, isolating Fatimid Jewry more than it had been before. The corpus reflects these changes; many more documents from the twelfth and thirteenth centuries are from Egypt alone.[66]

Second, Geniza documents are also spread unevenly across social and economic strata. In one respect the Geniza is consistent: almost all the people who appear in it lived in cities or sizable towns rather than the countryside. But here the consistency ends. The corpus covers nearly the full range of urban classes that can be imagined—from elite courtiers attached to the Fatimid and Ayyubid states to merchants great and petty, to craftsmen, tradesmen, and masses of the indigent poor—but does so erratically.[67] This lumpy distribution is most obvious in the case of personal letters. Perhaps the section of the Geniza to have attracted the most attention from scholars in other fields is a group of some 750 commercial letters sent by an interconnected group of eleventh-century Mediterranean merchants. Nearly all were exchanged among a group of around fifty men, half of them members of just six extended family networks.[68] In contrast, few letters written by merchants connected to Iraq or Andalusia survive (possibly because these merchants would have been attached to the "Babylonian," that is, Iraqi-rite, synagogue of Fustat rather than

66. A relatively smaller but still significant number of twelfth- and thirteenth-century documents come from Syria. See Goitein, *Palestinian Jewry*, 229–343, Prawer, *Latin Kingdom*, and Goldman, "Jews in the Latin Levant."

67. It is easier to identify Geniza people by occupation than to untangle the class and status categories that they implicitly or explicitly recognized. The most comprehensive attempt to do so remains Goitein, *Med. Soc.*, 1:75–126, who suggests five economic strata (the uppermost elite, including courtiers and major communal officials; a broad "middle class" of merchants, professionals, and artisans, further divided into upper and lower sections; an urban lower class; and a rural peasant class). See also ibid., 2:61–65, 3:418–420, 5:526. Cf. Gil, *Ishmael*, 597–606. (For a comparative account of occupations by sector derived from medieval Islamic literature, see Shatzmiller, *Labour*, 369–398.) But these were not rigid categories, and in any case class seems not to have been merely a function of prosperity (as is clear from Cohen's eloquent description of the "respectable" shame-faced poor, *Poverty and Charity*), but something closer to what Roger Bagnall describes for fourth-century Egypt: "a combination of group identity and a relational sense, combining in a consciousness of one's standing in the world" (*Egypt in Late Antiquity*, 226).

68. Most are edited in Gil, *Ishmael*, and idem, *Palestine*. The six families are those of Nahray b. Nissim, the Tāhirtī, Tustarī, and ibn ʿAwkal families, and the relatively less densely represented Khalīla and Qābisī families. See Gil, *Jews in Islamic Countries*, 663–722, and the literature cited there; I identified these six families as figuring in about half of all Geniza commercial letters based on Gil's edited corpora.

the "Palestinian" one that housed the Geniza chamber)—much less by the textile workers who processed the flax that any of these merchants dealt in.[69] No other related group of letters is this large, but several other subcorpora from the twelfth and thirteenth centuries likewise cluster around particular individuals and families whose bundled papers seem to have been deposited wholesale in the Geniza chamber.[70] It can be difficult to judge whether differences in these letters' tone and in the behaviors that they capture reflect broad social and cultural changes over these centuries, or narrower differences between the particular circles of (literate and well-connected) men whom they happen to describe.

Legal and administrative documents and petitions reveal a wider swath of men and women, rich and poor, who used rabbinic courts and sought help from communal officials and private patrons. These texts often tell us more about these people's private lives than do commercial letters. But they are limited in a different sense, because the people whom they describe rarely appear in the corpus more than once. This means that aside from clues internal to a given document—the places and the sums of money it names, the story it tells, and the honorifics it employs—the people who appear in it can rarely be placed within a known social setting. These sources are rich in breadth but poor in depth, revealing a complex social landscape whose internal geography we cannot map precisely.

In sum, "Geniza Jews" were not a single population so much as several overlapping segments of several overlapping ones, united mainly by the findspot of the documents that describe them—that is, by the fact that they or their descendants happened to discard their papers in the disposal room of the Palestinian-rite synagogue of Fustat. How then can this collection be used as a unified historical source, and why attempt to do so?

Approaching the Geniza as a corpus yields rewards different from those achieved by chopping its contents into discrete subcorpora. Addressing the frustrations created by fourth-century Egyptian papyri, Roger Bagnall notes that in the case of fragmentary and isolated texts, "a thousand points of light do not of themselves add up to illumination."[71] But in Geniza research as in papyrology, some of these points do create wider trails of light once they are brought together, revealing patterns that otherwise we might not see.

69. As suggested by Goitein, *Med. Soc.*, 20–22, although see the questions raised by Goldberg, "Methodology."

70. These include a different group of merchants active across both the Mediterranean and the Indian Ocean in the twelfth century, and in the early thirteenth century, the children and associates of the Rabbanite judge Eliyyahu b. Zekharya. See Goitein/Friedman, *India Traders* and the Hebrew *India Book* volumes, and Motzkin, "Judge Elijah."

71. *Egypt in Late Antiquity*, 10.

For all its chaos and complexity, the corpus itself suggests that the populations who produced it were socially and culturally coherent in important ways. "Geniza Jews" may have been widely and unevenly dispersed, but they shared a common set of Jewish and Islamic institutions, spoke a common language, and lived in a coterminous region across which many individuals regularly traveled. It is therefore no surprise that in many cases they also shared a common set of social codes, expectations, and dispositions rooted in this common landscape—what Bourdieu termed a shared *habitus*.[72] To reconstruct this shared world and the people in it without losing sight of their diversity, I have tried wherever possible to identify regional and social variations in my evidence and to trace changes in institutions, practices, and ideas over time. In many cases I must admit that my evidence has resisted these efforts, allowing me to discern fine-grained differences between individual cases (or groups of cases) but not to explain them systematically. In all cases, moreover, diachronic developments within communal institutions have proven easier to detect than changes in ideas and practices surrounding young women, marriage, or kinship; and the lives of wealthy and well-connected girls easier to see from multiple angles than those of poorer ones—whom we hear about mainly through their suffering. Most centrally, however, I have sought throughout the book to handle these problems by avoiding broader claims for my data than it can reasonably support. In the end I am hopeful that it can support quite a bit. Some of the analysis that follows rests on thin or negative evidence, as I note in presenting it. But the basic cruxes of my argument—Geniza Jews' ideas of kinship, and the conservatism of their forms of rabbinic legal practice—appear consistently enough in a broad enough range of sources that I trust that they are meaningful.

The book is divided into three main parts. Part I introduces the two institutions that I argue made the greatest difference to Geniza women's lives: the family and the rabbinic legal system. Chapter 1 addresses Geniza kinship and family structures, while Chapter 2 examines Geniza courts and the Islamicate legal environment in which they functioned.

The rest of the book develops the arguments introduced in these two opening chapters through a close study of women's coming-of-age. Part II examines how Geniza Jews understood and managed adolescence as a stage of women's lives. Chapter 3 defines "adolescence" itself as a legal and social category, focusing on women's age at first marriage and the sexual ethics surrounding marriage timing. Chapter 4 discusses adolescent girls' economic position and activities: their access to personal property, vocational training and labor, and sources of economic support, and addresses how Geniza Jews' dowry regime

72. Bourdieu, *Logic*, 53, *Outline*, 72; for the phrase "shared *habitus*," see e.g., Bourdieu, *Homo Academicus*, 3.

affected young women's financial lives both before they married and after. Chapter 5 examines the social control of adolescent girls, especially their virginity and physical mobility.

Part III focuses on women's transition to early adulthood through first marriage, its roots in and impact on their kin and social networks, and how it did and did not change their practical legal position. Chapter 6 focuses on endogamous and exogamous marriage choices in law and practice and the ideas about kinship that they reflect. Chapter 7 examines young women's marriage agreements as legal instruments—the rights that they afforded different women, and the kin support on which these rights depended—through a corpus of over 100 Geniza marriage documents from the twelfth and early thirteenth centuries that contain personal stipulations about both spouses' behavior within marriage. Chapter 8 follows young wives into the marital household, focusing on the expanded social universe that they inhabited as wives connected to their husbands' relatives as well as their own kin. The Conclusion briefly sums up the book's main findings and notes some of their implications for the history of the family and of Jewish law in the medieval Middle East.

PART I

Women in a Patronage Culture

CHAPTER ONE

The Family

SOMETIME BETWEEN 1046 and 1090, a woman named Hayfā' bt. Sulaymān submitted a petition to an unnamed Jewish official in Fustat.[1] She had arrived in the city alone and friendless, "a feeble stranger" with a two-year-old son in tow, desperately seeking the runaway husband who had deserted her in Jaffa. Rejected by her own relatives ("God knows what I suffered from them and their words"), and finding no help from a brother-in-law in the north Egyptian town of Malīj, she told the official that he was her last hope: "I have no one to whom I can turn with my complaint, except God and your honor." She asked him to write on her behalf to a Jewish court in Palestine, where she believed her husband had now returned, to pressure him to either return to her or divorce her—an outcome that would at least permit her to remarry.

This story was not unusual. Geniza documents mention abandoned wives so often that the topic easily deserves a book of its own.[2] Constant mobility meant that many men spent more time apart from their wives than with them. Men traveled for many reasons: business, religious pilgrimage, simple wanderlust, or to evade the poll tax, poverty, debt, and the financial burden of family itself. "I was bankrupted in Alexandria (by debts owed to) Muslims," a man writes from Fustat in an early twelfth-century charity petition; "My children and old mother were starving. I could not bear to sit and watch them in that state, so I fled."[3] For the women that they left behind, the hierarchy of options

1. T-S 13 J 8.19. The dating is uncertain. It comes from T-S 13 J 21.2, another letter that Hayfā' seems to have sent shortly after this one, addressed to Nahray b. Nissim, whose extant corpus stretches between these dates. See Goitein, *Med. Soc.*, 3:197, on the two letters, and Goldberg, "Geographies," xvii–xviii, on dating Nahray's correspondence.

2. As Goitein notes, *Med. Soc.*, 3:189. A full study of this subject has not yet been written; for a valuable start, see Zinger, "Long-Distance Marriages" (Friedman, "Crisis in Marriage," qualifies parts of Zinger's analysis).

3. T-S 13 J 18.14.

available to Hayfā' was typical too. Divorce was common, but a Jewish woman could not divorce her husband in his absence.[4] In the meantime, a woman left without adequate means of support could seek help in two arenas: first and ideally, among her birth (and sometimes marital) relatives, or if this failed, from the government, writ small or large—either the class of administrative and legal authorities who ran Jewish courts and synagogues in the Fatimid and Ayyubid empires, or the Fatimid and then Ayyubid states themselves.

The rest of this book attempts partly to trace how Geniza women developed resources, or failed to, as they entered adulthood: to identify the factors in women's early lives that landed some in hopeless situations like the one Hayfā' faced, and that provided others with a range of social, legal, and economic options that she lacked. This chapter and the next introduce the two institutions most visible in her letter, whose particular structure and character are central to much of what will follow: the family and the Jewish community—most importantly, since so many of the documents that I use are legal papers produced by the Rabbanite court of Fustat, the rabbinic legal system.

Patriliny and Its Limits

First, the family. Family ties loom large throughout the Geniza corpus. Geniza letters consistently assume that parents, children, and siblings will remain emotionally attached to one another and materially and socially support each other, and each other's children, throughout their lives. "I have no one but God and you," a widow old enough to have a daughter on the verge of marriage writes to her brother from Tripoli in the 1060s,

> May the Creator not deny me the sight of you! All this year, O my brother, I looked for a letter to come from you . . . when they told me you were ill, I went out of my mind. I swore not to eat in the daytime nor to change my clothes, nor to enter the bathhouse—neither I nor my daughter—until I received a letter from you.[5]

This intense affective ideal, which far outweighed the love that husbands and wives were expected to feel for each other, may be the most striking aspect of the family relationships described in the Geniza. Passages like this led Goitein to describe Geniza families as cohesive extended patrilineal clans—"the house of the father" bound firmly together by "the bonds of blood."[6]

4. This set them apart from Muslim women; see Introduction, at n. 52.

5. T-S 10 J 14.20. The letter is addressed to Yeshu'a b. Isma'īl al-Makhmūrī, a merchant associated with Nahray b. Nissim in the mid-eleventh-century.

6. *Med. Soc.*, 3:1; cf. ibid., 1:73. See my discussion of these passages and their reception in the Introduction.

But stories about women like Hayfā' complicate any attempt to draw a unified picture from these statements of affection. When men died or abandoned their wives and children, what "house of the father" did they leave behind? How constant were the "bonds of blood," and did they matter to all relatives in the same ways, or in equal measure? Much of our evidence suggests that for many people, the answers to these questions were messy and far from obvious. Closer attention to gender complicates matters too. Because women as well as men maintained significant relationships with their own birth relatives, the patrilineal family must have been porous even as an abstract idea: although the formal genealogies preserved in the Geniza exclude women, maternal kinship ties mattered a great deal in social practice.[7]

This chapter seeks to make sense of this counterevidence, by examining how kinship did and did not work to bind Geniza people together, focusing first on demography and then on ideology. The first part of the chapter examines Geniza families on the ground and concludes from the most systematic data available that both households and immediate family groups were more variable and fluid than has been supposed. The second part zooms out to examine Geniza Jews' ideas about kinship more broadly, among extended as well as immediate relatives. It presents a different way of understanding Geniza families—as fluid networks bound together by relationships among individual relatives rather than as predictably structured solidarity groups. I will argue both that Geniza Jews considered family ties centrally important, and that they were not attached to any particular form of household or family structure as ideal. It was the *kinship bonds* between individual relatives that mattered, not the shape of the broader *family group* that these bonds produced—a distinction that affected women in particular in crucial ways.

THE REAL SHAPE OF GENIZA FAMILIES

Much of the available Geniza evidence for family demography is anecdotal and impressionistic. But the corpus provides one means to consider family structures somewhat more systematically, through the many marriage agreements that it contains. The Jewish legal record preserved in the Geniza includes some 1,500 to 2,500 texts that document the formation of marriages—both

7. On Geniza genealogies, see below, n. 74. Cf. Goody's argument that pure patrilinies are impossible within most Eurasian societies, *The Ancient, the Oriental and the Primitive*. Indeed, as Goitein notes (*Med. Soc.*, 3:5), some Geniza letters explicitly reflect a shadow concern with matriliny, as when the early thirteenth-century schoolteacher and scribe Shelomo b. Eliyyahu writes to his brother from Fustat: "Hibat Allāh b. al-ʿAmmānī . . . betrothed my paternal aunt's daughter . . . Inform him . . . that she is not honored by him; but he by her and by the rest of her pure and noble house, *from her maternal ancestors*" (CUL Add. 3343).

formal marriage contracts (*ketubbot*) and a range of auxiliary legal deeds and declarations ratifying engagements, betrothals, dower payments, dowry transfers, and individual social and financial agreements between couples and their relatives.[8] Many documents of both types contain three formulae that reveal specific aspects of the couple's family circumstances at the moment they were composed: whether the bride's and groom's fathers were living or deceased; whether the bride was a first-time bride, a widow, or a divorced woman; and whether she had agreed or refused to live with particular relatives immediately after marriage. These clauses illuminate three basic aspects of family and household structure: paternal mortality during a daughter's childhood and adolescence, remarriage, and household formation at marriage.

Among the entire corpus of currently available Geniza marriage documents, I have identified 381 documents[9] that contain at least one of these three formulae.[10] Except for residence stipulations, present in a small subset of these documents,[11] these formulae appear in a given fragment largely by chance; honorifics indicating whether an individual is living or deceased seem to appear idiosyncratically in legal documents in general, whereas clauses identifying the bride as a virgin or nonvirgin, included in all Rabbanite and Karaite *ketubbot*, appear in extant *ketubbot* fragments as an accident of preservation. These documents' distribution therefore likely parallels that of the overall corpus of Geniza marriage documents. They describe marriages between couples whose dowries and promised dowers place them within a broad range of socioeconomic classes. Most can be readily identified as formally Rabbanite, but a

8. 1,500–2,500: This is a loose estimate, extrapolated from the total number of marriage documents that I have been able to identify. See below, n. 10, and see Chapter 7 on these agreements more generally.

9. This is the total number of relevant documentary *texts*, rather than of *manuscripts*. Some manuscripts, usually fragments of records maintained by the Rabbanite court, include multiple texts pertaining to different marriages.

10. Only a fraction of Geniza marriage documents have been published to date, mainly in three collections: Ashur, "EBD" (Rabbanite engagement, betrothal, and other premarital contracts); Friedman, *JMP* (Rabbanite Palestinian-formula *ketubbot* and betrothal contracts), and Olszowy-Schlanger, *KMD* (Karaite *ketubbot* and betrothal documents). Nearly all of the "Babylonian" (Iraqi-formula) Rabbanite *ketubbot* preserved in the Geniza remain unpublished. (On these editorial choices, see Krakowski, "The Geniza and Family History.") I identified these 381 marriage texts from a much larger group of about 1,500 texts, themselves located through the Friedberg Geniza Project catalogue, references in prior scholarship, and several unpublished lists prepared by S. D. Goitein and Mordechai Akiva Friedman and stored in the Geniza laboratory at Princeton University. I am also extremely grateful to Oded Zinger for sharing his personal research database with me, which included several dozen marriage documents not identified elsewhere. The remaining texts that I examined either do not include the relevant formulae, or were composed later than 1250.

11. These formulae appear in 25 of 381 documents (6.5 percent).

small percentage are either Karaite legal documents, or they ratify "mixed" marriages involving a Karaite spouse.[12] Finally, while all exhibit paleographic and formulary features typical of the "classical" Geniza period and a bit earlier—roughly between 950 and 1250—most are only partly preserved; only a slight majority can thus be securely dated.[13] About half of these come from eleventh- and twelfth-century Fustat, with much smaller concentrations from tenth- and eleventh-century Syria, tenth- to thirteenth-century rural Egypt, and eleventh- to thirteenth-century Cairo and Alexandria. (See Figure 1.1 and Table 1.1.)

What can systematic review of these formulae tell us? Like most subcorpora preserved in the Geniza, the documents in which they appear are an inherently uneven evidence base. Unlike census results gathered and preserved in order to keep tabs on the demographic makeup of a given population, Geniza marriage documents were composed for unrelated reasons and preserved as a group by chance, facts that limit their usefulness in several ways. First, they do not yield anything like a global picture of family and household demographics. They provide no usable data at all for many questions fundamental to the study of marriage and family systems, including the prevalence of polygamy; proportions of men and women remaining unmarried; fertility rates; infant mortality; either men's or women's precise ages at marriage, first reproduction, and death; and—because the select data points that they do preserve are frozen at the moment of each couple's marriage—shifts in household composition over time, either significantly before or after a particular marriage was contracted. For this reason, I use the terms *family* and *household* here in the broadest possible sense, to denote a) a group of living relatives who viewed their genealogical ties as creating some form of social connection among them; and b) a group of socially connected individuals (mostly relatives, but also nonrelatives such as slaves and household dependents) living together at a given point in time in a shared space, or several contiguous ones, within a building.

Second, the documents' haphazard material preservation makes it impossible to detect precisely how the particular measures that they do preserve may have varied over time or between regions and social classes. As a group, Geniza marriage documents cover a relatively broad chronological and geographic

12. Twenty-nine of these 381 texts (7.6 percent) feature a Karaite bride and/or groom.

13. 226 texts are explicitly dated or securely datable to a specific period (this is 59 percent of the total). I classed documents as datable when they either included a *rashut* formula naming the current *ra'īs al-yahūd* (on whom see Chapter 2), or mentioned people known from other Geniza documents. I did not rely on names appearing in only one or two other documents unless they were particularly distinctive. I also chose not to classify undated documents solely on paleographic grounds. Some Geniza scholars routinely date documents by identifying individual scribes' handwriting, but these identifications are ad hoc and often contested; see Goldberg, "Methodology," eadem, "Geographies," xvii–xviii.

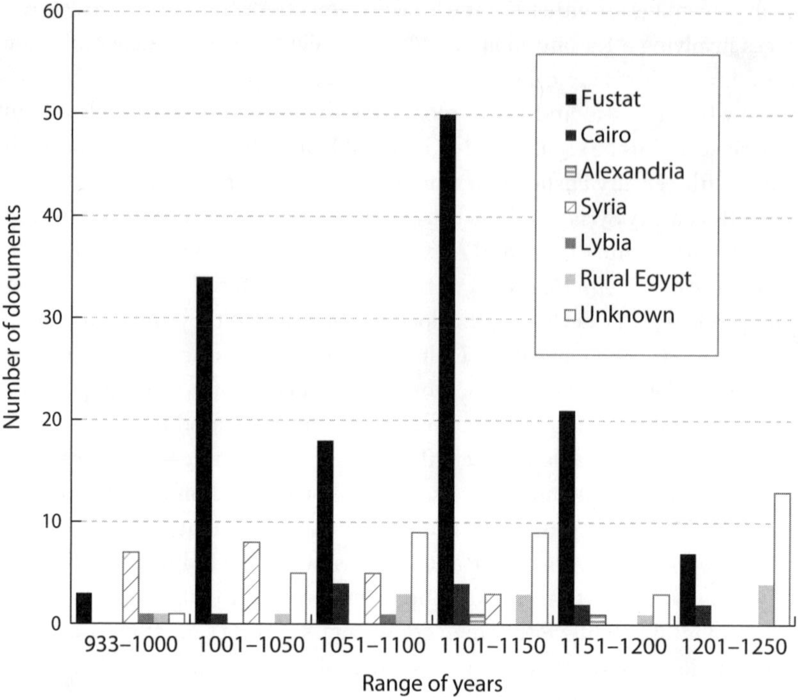

FIGURE 1.1. Datable marriage documents with demographic data, 933–1250

range. But only a fraction are preserved in full; this is largely a corpus of fragments, many undatable and of uncertain provenance. The demographically significant formulae that they contain often appear in bits and pieces, on small scraps of paper that contain little else. Instances of each can be tracked in isolation, but they cannot easily by correlated with each other, nor fully separated into discrete subgroups representative of specific micro-populations.

Geniza marriage documents thus cannot be used like census records (or like the parish registers that historians of early modern Europe have mined for demographic data). What they do offer is something far more basic, but still significant: dispersed and fragmentary as they are, this corpus of documents is the closest we can come to a representative record of the Jewish populations of Fatimid and Ayyubid Egypt and Syria. Evidence internal to the corpus itself suggests that Jews of all types were more likely to turn to Jewish courts to document their marriages than any other type of transaction, personal or economic.[14] This widespread use of Jewish marriage documents means that they likely constitute the single most widely diffused and characteristic body

14. See Chapter 7.

Table 1.1. Datable marriage documents with demographic data, 933–1250

	Lybia	Syria-Pal.	Fustat	Cairo	Alexandria	Rural Egypt	Unknown	**Total (by date)**
933–1000	1	7	3			1	1	**13**
1000–1050		8	34	1		1	5	**49**
1050–1100	1	5	18	4		3	9	**40**
1100–1150		3	50	4	1	3	9	**70**
1150–1200			21	2	1	1	3	**28**
1200–1250			7	2		4	13	**26**
Total (by region)	**2**	**23**	**133**	**13**	**2**	**13**	**40**	**226**

of papers available in the Geniza. They preserve data about couples from a broad range of economic strata, as suggested by the wildly ranging values of the financial arrangements that they ratify. And while the corpus as a whole tilts toward the urban Rabbanite population of eleventh- and twelfth-century Egypt, particularly Fustat, it also preserves trace evidence of marriages in rural tenth-century Egypt; among eleventh- and twelfth-century Egyptian Karaite Jews; and among both Rabbanite and Karaite Jews in parts of the tenth- and eleventh-century Levant, most notably Jerusalem and coastal Syria.

Grouping these documents by period and region provides a crude test of their overall coherence, while considering them together permits the use of undatable documents, yielding a larger sample than would otherwise be accessible. In what follows, I use these contracts as a basic measure of variety, which capture certain fundamental features defining and limiting family networks and households within the broadly defined population that they document. (In Chapter 6, I will use a similar, overlapping corpus of marriage document formulae to examine the closely related question of endogamy.)

MAPPING THE EVIDENCE: THREE DATA POINTS

Mortality

Whatever forms of marriage, family, and household a society may aspire to, death complicates them in practice. Precise mortality rates in the medieval Middle East remain generally unknown.[15] But documents containing the first of our three formulae demonstrate that for the populations documented in the Geniza, they were high enough to constrain families and households

15. For some initial work on life expectancy, see Nawas, "Profile," 455, and the studies cited there, all based on biographical dictionaries of Islamic scholars (*ʿulamāʾ*), following Bulliet's approach, "Quantitative Approach," *Conversion*. On mortality in Mamluk Egypt during the Black Death, see Dols, *Black Death*, 172–200, "General Mortality"; Borsch, *Black Death*, 24–25.

significantly. Scribes writing in Judeo-Arabic often marked individuals' names with one of two possible Hebrew honorifics identifying them as living or dead: *s"t*, for *sofo tov* ("may his end be good") in the former case, and *n"'e*, for *nuḥo 'eden* ("may he rest in Eden") in the latter. These markers appear in Geniza material of all kinds, both legal and nonlegal, including many marriage documents. One group of texts in which they appear is especially important: legal documents composed for a woman entering first marriage. As far as we can tell, most women married by their early twenties; many married earlier, in their early or mid-teens.[16] A central argument of the following chapters will be that first marriage acted as a major watershed in women's early lives, ushering them into economic and social adulthood. When a first-time bride's marriage documents add one of these markers to her father's name, given alongside her own as her patronymic, they reveal whether he was still living by the time she had reached this crucial turning point.

Seventy-eight of these 381 documents identify a first-time bride's father as either living or dead.[17] As a whole, they include a remarkably high proportion of women orphaned from their fathers before first marriage: 31, a full 40 percent, mark the bride's father as dead. While this sample is relatively small, it is internally consistent across time and place. Because it contains relatively many complete or largely preserved documents—as each must be well-preserved enough to include both the bride's patronymic and a clause identifying her as previously unmarried—an unusual majority (72 percent) can be securely dated. Among these datable documents, subgroups from each century between the tenth and the twelfth yield very roughly similar ratios: in documents from the tenth century, 40 percent of brides' fathers are marked as deceased, as are 33 percent from the eleventh century and 52 percent from the twelfth. The ratio from the thirteenth century (to 1250 only) is relatively lower: 25 percent. (See Figure 1.2.)

By the time they formally or informally contracted a first marriage, close to half the women who appear in this corpus thus no longer had a living father. This finding does not effectively capture much about male mortality itself, since many men married and produced sets of children several times across their lifetimes. But it provides a striking measure of mortality's effects on family coherence, demonstrating how often men (and by extension, other relatives too) died before their children—both daughters and sons, who generally reached full social maturity later than their sisters[18]—had become socially adult.

16. The evidence for this question is admittedly limited; see Chapter 3.

17. Almost all of these explicitly append *s"t* or *n"'e* to the bride's patronymic. In a few cases, I identified the bride's father as living because he is cited as appearing in court (e.g., T-S NS 224.58).

18. Judging from sporadic references to men's ages when they married or entered business apprenticeships, e.g., T-S Misc. 25.133 (an undated letter that mentions a

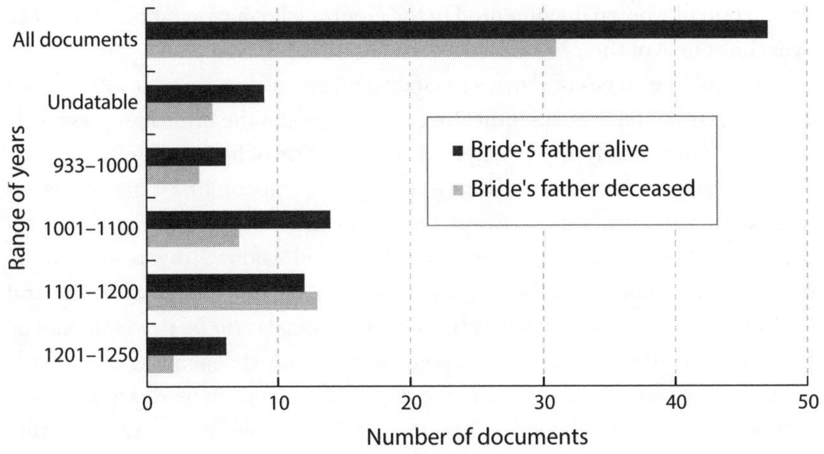

FIGURE 1.2. Women whose fathers died before they married, 933–1250

Remarriage

Not only death disrupted households and family networks; both were also subject to social upheavals, most visibly through disrupted marriages. Geniza letters and legal documents alike routinely describe men socially or physically estranged from their wives, spouses renegotiating their marital obligations, and above all, divorce. Bills of divorce themselves are one of the most common genres of Geniza documents.[19]

These texts create a strong impression that marriage among Geniza Jews was a volatile and often temporary arrangement. But this impression is difficult to quantify. Few of the Geniza documents that mention divorce and marital strife map neatly onto those recording the formation of marriages; we have no way to know how many marriages actually ended in divorce or separation, nor to calculate precisely how either outcome affected family groups more broadly. However, the second of our formulae offers a point of entry to both questions, by suggesting the frequency of *remarriage*—specifically, the

sixteen-year-old bridegroom); T-S 20.127 (a merchant letter, mid-eleventh century, that describes the writer's start in trade at age sixteen); T-S 10 K 7.1 (*Megillat Evyatar*, a literary polemic attacking the *ra'īs al-yahūd* David b. Dani'el, which identifies him as about twenty years old when he married in 1082); T-S 24.78 (a lengthy letter from Alexandria, 1131, in which a father complains at great length about his son, who is still unmarried at age twenty-two; this is not the source of the complaints). Compare to the data for women's ages at first marriage discussed in Chapter 3. See also Frenkel, "Adolescence."

19. This evidence parallels narrative and literary evidence for other medieval Middle Eastern populations. Rapoport, *Money, Marriage and Divorce*, provides a detailed assessment of its economic bases in Mamluk Egypt.

proportion of women documented in the Geniza who married more than once over the course of their lifetimes.

Two different types of clauses in Geniza marriage documents capture rates of remarriage. First, clauses indicating whether or not the bride had previously been married typically appear after the first mention of her name, often in auxiliary marriage documents and almost always in *ketubbot*: first-time brides are labeled "virgin" (Heb. *betula*, Aram. *betulta*, or Arab. *bikr*), while brides entering a second or later marriage are varyingly termed "widow," "divorced woman," or very occasionally, "nonvirgin" (Aram. *be'ulta*). Second, both Rabbanite and Karaite *ketubbot* routinely specify the formal minimal *ketubba* payment paid by the groom in order to ratify the marriage, which differed depending on whether the bride had been married before; the standard amounts in medieval Egyptian *ketubbot* were twenty-five dirhams (usually designated by the Aramaic *zuz*) for first-time brides and twelve and a half for widows and divorced women.[20]

Fragments of one or both of these clauses appear in 297 of the marriage documents included in my corpus.[21] Taken together, they suggest a high rate of remarriage among Jewish women in Fatimid and Ayyubid Egypt—so much so, that more than half the women in this population who married once may have gone on to marry again. The precise number is uncertain, but can be roughly estimated, as follows: among these 297 documents overall, 63 percent (186 of 297) were composed for women entering a first marriage, while 37 percent (111 of 297) feature brides who had been married before. However, because the pool of first-time brides documented in this corpus includes those women who would go on to remarry, this percentage of remarriage *documents* may correspond to a higher percentage of *women* remarrying within the population that it represents—likely anywhere from 37 percent up to 59 percent.[22]

20. For the legal background, see Friedman, "Minimum Mohar," and idem, *JMP*, 1:244–257.

21. Goitein summarizes results from a similar survey of 243 Geniza marriage documents, *Med. Soc.*, 3:274. His findings differ from those I present below in reflecting an even higher proportion of remarriage documents. I cannot explain this discrepancy, as Goitein does not list the documents he used in this survey, and I have been unable to locate any record of them among Goitein's papers preserved in the Geniza Laboratory at Princeton University. However, the appendices of marriage documents presented at the end of Vol. 3 of *Med. Soc.* provide some possible clues: Goitein there describes a number of reconciliation documents between couples who had not formally divorced as "remarriages," and includes references to documents composed after 1250, which I have not considered.

22. This problem is further complicated by the possibility that some women were remarrying for a second or third time. The possible percentages given here presume that the proportion of women going from a second to a third marriage was at least no greater than the proportion of women going from a first to a second one. Peter Shalen graciously worked out these percentages for me and explains them thus: "If x is the percentage of married women who marry a second time, and if we assume that the percentage of women who marry a (k + 1)-th time among women who have married k times is also no greater

(The uncertainty derives from the possibility that the pool of remarried brides may also overlap to some unknown extent, since some women who married twice may have gone on to marry a third or even fourth time, a distinction that our documentary formulae do not reveal.)

As with the evidence for paternal mortality, this overall proportion holds roughly consistent within this corpus across time and space, with one exception. Of thirteen documents that can be securely dated to the tenth century (about half from Syria and half from rural Egypt and Fustat), all thirteen were composed for first-time brides. This handful of documents is too small to prove much of anything, but it is conceivable that remarriage was less common among Levantine and Egyptian Jews in the tenth century than it became later. In contrast, datable eleventh- through thirteenth-century documents include remarkably high percentages of remarriages: previously married brides appear in 41 percent of datable documents from the eleventh century, 44 percent from the twelfth, and 44 percent from the thirteenth. Allowing for overlaps within the pools of first-time and later brides documented in these subgroups, these proportions suggest rates of female remarriage anywhere between 41 percent and 69 percent for the eleventh century, and between 44 percent and 78.5 percent for the twelfth and thirteenth. (See Figure 1.3 and Figure 1.4.)

Somewhere between a large minority and a comfortable majority of Jewish women in Fatimid and Ayyubid Egypt (and, less certainly, Syria) thus passed through more than one marriage over the course of their lives. Can this finding tell us anything more about how these women's first marriages ended—specifically, about how many of these remarriages followed divorces rather than a husband's death?

The documents themselves provide some indication, although a limited one. Among the 186 documents in this corpus that feature remarrying brides, 47 explicitly identify the bride as either a widow or a divorced woman. Within this subgroup, divorced women outnumber widows by a factor of nearly three to one: 33 brides are termed divorced women, whereas only twelve are identified as widows (the other two women are described as both widows *and* divorcées, likely meaning that these were their third marriages). Remarkably, these identifications also indicate that divorce itself could be just as temporary as marriage: a full 17 of the 33 divorced women had divorced the same man whom they were remarrying.

To be sure, this subsample is small and thinly spread. Still, it suggests that a significant number of women remarrying had previously divorced a husband. And of course, these numbers do not capture all divorced women or

---

than x, then the total number T of marriages is constrained by the inequalities $n(1+x) \leq T \leq n(1+x+x2+\cdots) = n/(1-x)$, where n is the number of women who marry at least once. The percentage of marriages that are remarriages is $y = (T-n)/n$. We therefore have $x/(1+x) \leq y \leq x$, so that $y \leq x \leq y/(1-y)$." (Personal communication, Nov. 6, 2016.)

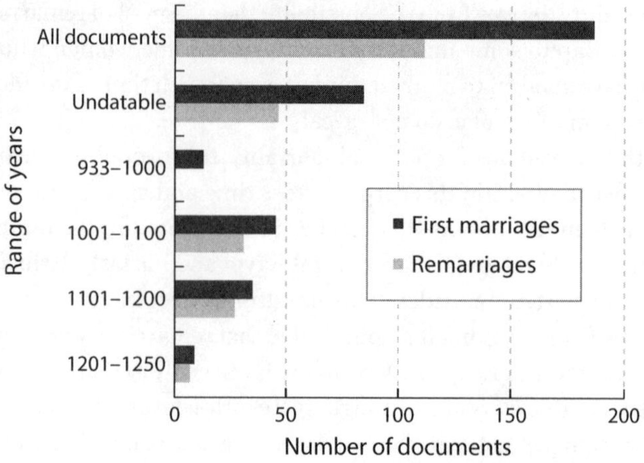

FIGURE 1.3. First marriages vs. remarriages in Geniza marriage documents, 933–1250

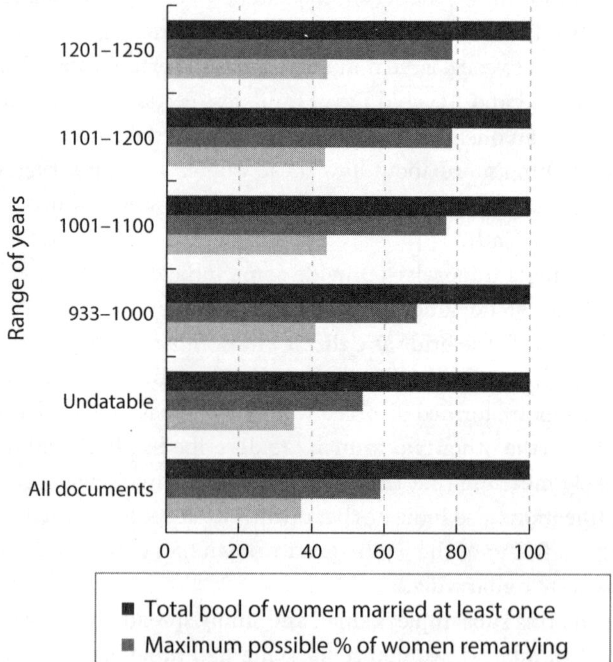

FIGURE 1.4. Predicted percentages of women remarrying, 933–1250

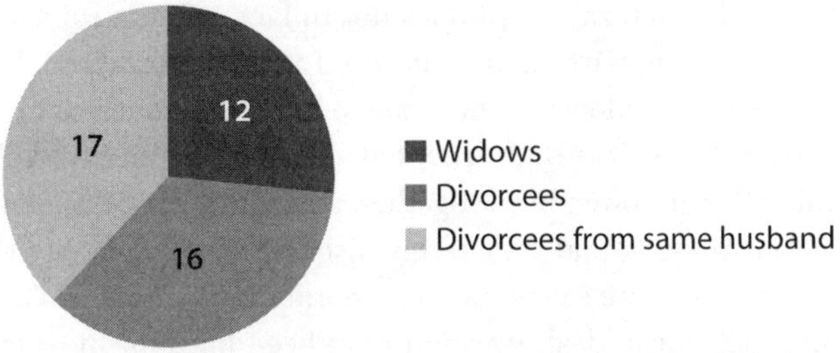

FIGURE 1.5. Divorced women and widows in remarriage documents, 933–1250

estranged wives among Geniza Jews. Some women divorced a first husband without going on to remarry; others separated from their husbands without a formal divorce. This robust rate of female remarriage thus offers just one limited data point among the many possible marital rearrangements suggested by more anecdotal Geniza sources—one that supports the impressionistic sense created by these sources, that Geniza marriages were unstable agreements that could be renegotiated, dissolved, and then refashioned (even between the same man and woman) as often as they were maintained.

This finding also suggests the instability of other family ties clustered around marriage. Rifts in a marriage could radiate outwards to change relationships between both spouses and other relatives socially connected by their union—especially their children, as in the case of Hayfā' bt. Sulaymān's husband, who abandoned her together with their young son. Frequent divorce and spousal estrangement thus made immediate and perhaps extended kin relationships less predictable and uniform than they would have been due to mortality alone.

Households

The rates of paternal mortality and women's remarriage discussed so far help suggest the field of possibilities within which Geniza families took shape. Our final formula sheds light on one aspect of families' actual composition in practice: their organization as domestic groups within a shared household. Geniza households have been widely described as extended and patrilocal, with multiple generations of patrilineal relatives living together in a single household. This view stems from Goitein's conclusion, repeated several times throughout *A Mediterranean Society*, that new brides typically moved in with their husbands' relatives, who felt an "urge, and almost moral obligation" to live near each other (either in one dwelling or in adjacent ones), so that "housing was organized so as to secure the coherence of the extended family."[23]

23. *Med. Soc.*, 3:36; 3:69, 3:150–151, 4:82, 4:85–86.

In my view, the Geniza record does not in fact reflect a robust ideological preference for any particular household form. Geniza people's "moral obligation(s)" about residence seem to me to have been idiosyncratic and uncertain: as we will see, it is both true that relatives—especially siblings and parents and children—often lived together, and that they did so in many different ways, for reasons that they rarely discussed in writing but that often appear to have been more economic than moral.[24] But even had Geniza Jews held a strong patrilocal ideal, it would have been hard for most families to realize it equivalently in practice, given the messy realities of urban housing in Fatimid and Ayyubid cities, particularly in Fustat (as Goitein also acknowledges in some of these passages, a caveat that has, however, received less enduring attention).[25]

During the tenth and eleventh centuries, overlapping with the earliest layer of Geniza documents, Fustat's population expanded dramatically, transforming the city from a widely spaced network of aristocratic estates into a bustling mercantile center.[26] Physically, Fustat expanded internally rather than externally: new roads were gradually built between existing ones, creating a dense patchwork landscape bound externally by the Nile to the west and Cairo to the east, and internally by the irregular layout of its earliest pathways (*akhṭāṭ*).[27] Non-elite domestic housing developed haphazardly in this complex space. Eleventh- and twelfth-century Geniza property deeds describe private dwellings of all shapes and sizes standing alongside shops, markets, houses of worship, workshops, mills, and ruins.[28] An early gift document composed in Fustat in 959 already foreshadows this pattern: Menaḥem *levi* b. Tamim testifies that among other properties, he has given his son El'azar two residences in *Qaṣr Edom* (the "Roman" quarter, where a Byzantine fortress had stood before Fustat's founding), which border, to the east, a residential property owned by a Jewish man; to the north, flour mills in the "marketplace of the Greeks"; to

24. I have encountered few documents that praise cohabitation with relatives as a general social ideal. Those few describe motives that seem as much material as moral, e.g., T-S 12.780, a late eleventh-century letter: "I decided to live in my mother's presence (that is, in her dwelling), that I might earn a livelihood and benefit from it completely (that is, avoid paying rent), and gain from the *merit* of this."

25. *Med. Soc.*, 3:36–37, ibid., 4:82. In both places, Goitein describes the housing system documented in the Geniza as shaped by the opposing forces of "family cohesion and mobility." On Goitein's inconsistent descriptions of Geniza households as both extremely varied and normally patrilocal, see Krakowski, "The Geniza and Family History."

26. Fustat was reputedly established as a garrison town in 642, shortly after the Arab conquest of Egypt. The earliest literary descriptions of its topography date to the ninth century. Garcin, "Habitat Médiéval," 152–162, idem, "Toponymie et Topographie," describes Fustat's development under the Fatimids mainly from literary sources. See also Denoix, "Notes."

27. See especially Garcin, "Toponymie," 131–132.

28. Goitein, *Med. Soc.*, 4:12–24.

the west, another Jewish residential property, and to the south, the "alley of the poor."[29]

Most of what we know about life inside these scattered dwellings comes from Goitein's own painstaking reconstruction of the Geniza evidence. His findings suggest that living spaces in Fustat varied widely. Geniza documents typically denote residential properties by the Arabic *dār* or its Hebrew equivalent, *ḥaṣer*, terms applied equally to a single-story house or a multistory building containing an internal courtyard, and to a group of multistory buildings surrounding a common courtyard. Individual *dār*s could be three stories or even taller. The first floor (*qāʿa*) was often uninhabited, containing the open courtyard, a communal sitting room (*majlis*) open to all residents, and areas used as commercial space or for storage. Residents generally lived on the upper floors, which were divided into multiple distinct apartments (*ṭabaqa*s) and living areas (*manzil*s or *maskan*s), each possessing a variety of small chambers grouped around one or more central room or rooms. (The two illustrations in Chapter 8 depict what some of these buildings may have looked like.)[30] While some *dār*s were owned by a single proprietor, many were shared among several co-owners, who might live in or rent out their portions. These partial owners were by no means always genealogically related; nonkin, including Jews, Muslims, and Christians, routinely co-owned and lived side by side within a single property.[31] Finally, both ownership and occupancy seem to have shifted frequently. The enormous number of property transactions, rental agreements, and relocations mentioned in Geniza

29. Bodl. MS Heb. b. 12.6 + Bodl. MS Heb. b. 12.29. "Marketplace of the Greeks": *shuq ha-yevanim*, to my knowledge a location not mentioned in any other Geniza document. Jacoby, "Byzantine Trade with Egypt" 58, suggests it may have been a *funduq* (here, a commercial inn).

30. Goitein, *Med. Soc.*, 4:47–81, idem, "Mansion in Fustat." Geniza documents provide a wealth of detail about domestic architecture in Fatimid and Ayyubid Fustat not available in any other sources, and much more might be done with the evidence they provide. On the history of excavations at Fustat (themselves incomplete and difficult to interpret) and their relationship to the Geniza evidence via Goitein, see Harrison, "Fusṭāṭ Reconsidered."

31. Each formally owned a portion of the property calculated from an abstract total of twenty-four shares, a convention derived from Islamic inheritance law; see Goitein, *Med. Soc.*, 4:82–83; Petry, "Fractionalized Estates," 107. These formal shares did not always correspond to the actual division of living space within a *dār*. See, for example, T-S 12.544 (1147, Fustat; a wife indemnifies her husband against possible claims by a Muslim neighbor that the couple was occupying more than the one-sixth of the property she officially owned); Maimonides, *Responsa*, no. 94: "The heirs of a *dār*, who were paternal cousins, lived there together . . . completely intermingled . . . without (regard) to who lived (where), and without each designating a dwelling of his own."

documents—not only between regions, but also between *dār*s in the same city or town—suggests a high rate of residential turnover.[32]

In short, much of the urban population described in the Geniza lived not in large, homogeneous residential compounds, but in disparate, changeable, and often fragmented living spaces. Scattered references in Geniza documents and responsa suggest that under these conditions, relatives and individuals grouped, and often then regrouped, themselves within households in a wide variety of ways. We read about a married woman whose father had gifted her the *dār* in which she lived, on the condition that he, her mother, and her brother might continue to live in one of its apartments (other portions were rented out to lodgers);[33] four paternal cousins growing up together in a small *dār* that they had jointly inherited, who could not agree on a plan for divvying up its two apartments once two of them married;[34] two sisters who owned a *dār* together, sold off two-thirds of it, and lived together on the remaining upper floor with their husbands and children; and, in the same text, a widow whose husband had purchased separate lodgings for each of his married sons, but who gathered them back after his death, together with their spouses and children—fifteen people in all—to live in the portion of a *dār* where they had grown up, so that they could save money by renting off their own properties.[35]

These isolated descriptions imply that Geniza households could be heterogeneous and changeable. But they are hard to interpret in and of themselves. This is not only because, like so much of the documentary Geniza, they are stratified across time and place. Equally importantly, casual references to individuals living in a given household often leave their precise relationships and respective stages of life unclear (as when a wife writes her husband, away on travel: "I grasp your hands, as does my mother, my maternal aunt, the wife of my paternal uncle, and [. . .] who is in the *dār*").[36] Because even households in robustly predictable complex residence systems necessarily change over time—expanding as children marry and bring in spouses and children of their own, and contracting as older members die—descriptions that leave this context unclear do little to clarify overall household composition.

Fortunately, the last of our three marriage document formulae provides a means to approach this problem somewhat more systematically, if not to

32. Some documents also describe individuals' relocation between portions of a single *dār*. See *Med. Soc.*, 4:84.

33. T-S 13 J 3.3.

34. Maimonides, *Responsa* no. 94.

35. Maimonides, *Responsa* no. 13. The two sisters complained that she had turned the *dār* into a public inn (*funduq*), overfilling the latrines and using up the building's water supply, and demanded that the extra tenants leave.

36. DK 238.3, addressed to ʿAllān b. Ḥassūn, a twelfth century India trader (on ʿAllān, see Goitein, "Portrait," idem, *Med. Soc.*, 5:221–222).

resolve it definitively. The most coherent body of evidence for household composition in the documentary Geniza appears in a small group of marriage documents that record residence agreements between spouses. These agreements appear both in documents composed before marriage, and occasionally in reconciliation documents composed to resolve disputes between married couples, usually during the early stages of a marriage.[37] Many specify the terms under which both spouses (but more often the wife) will live together with various extended relatives, either her husband's or her own.

I have identified 29 marriage documents that contain this type of coresidence agreement, including 23 premarital documents and six reconciliation documents.[38] Ten can be securely dated, most to twelfth-century Fustat, when Rabbanite marriage documents began to include personal stipulations dictating husbands' and wives' behavior within marriage.[39] While marriage document stipulations fossilized by the thirteenth century into generic fixed formulae that provide little detail (in the case of residence clauses, most often stating simply, "her lodging is up to her"), 25 of these 29 earlier documents describe the particular relatives with whom the wife or couple will reside, e.g., "She will live with this groom's mother as long as there is peace between them"; "He will live with her and her parents in the *dār*."[40] Two others specify that the wife will not live with *any* relatives: "He will lodge her in a separate place set aside for her, and will not compel her [to live with anyone else], neither a nonrelative of his or a relative."[41]

These agreements thus reveal the particular kin with whom spouses lived in early marriage. (They do not usually describe the nonkin, slaves and orphan dependents, who may have lived with them as well.)[42] Because they describe only the start of a couple's married life, these documents do not illustrate the entire cycle through which Geniza households may have passed over the course of one or more generations. But precisely for this reason (and unlike

37. This is sometimes explicitly stated, as in T-S 16.35, drafted several months after the couple's marriage. Other reconciliation documents are less clear, and may have been composed later; but even they almost always mention one or both spouses' parents and very rarely involve couples who themselves already have children, giving the impression that the marriages they describe were relatively recent ones.

38. Ashur, "*Haggana*," reviews these and related clauses in Geniza marriage documents.

39. See Chapter 7. A few are earlier: Bodl. MS Heb. a. 3.32, a *ketubba* from 1064, Ramle, and T-S 13 J 6.33 (late eleventh century), a list of contract stipulations for a Karaite-Rabbanite marriage.

40. T-S Misc. 8.97, T-S NS J 378. Generic thirteenth-century clauses: see Chapter 7, n. 13.

41. T-S AS 151.244. The other agreement that contains this kind of clause is T-S 8 J 5.3 + T-S NS 259.37. Two others state only that the bride will live with her husband's relatives or dependents, without specifying who they are (T-S 6 J 2.2, T-S NS 224.104).

42. Except in the case of two documents in which the husband promises to provide his wife with a slave woman: T-S 8 J 4.18c, and ENA 3755.6.

the inchoate evidence provided by references elsewhere in the Geniza record), they serve as a meaningful comparative measure of household *formation* at marriage. At the same time, they also pose more daunting interpretive problems than either of the two marriage document formulae examined thus far.

Let us begin where these agreements are most useful. Following a classification system first developed by Peter Laslett and E. A. Hammel in 1974, family historians often define household forms partly by the people with whom married couples live: in *simple* or *nuclear* households, one couple lives alone with their minor children, whereas in *complex* households couples and their children live with other relatives.[43] Complex households can be further divided into *extended* households, in which one couple and their children live with individual extended relatives, e.g., either spouse's mother or siblings, and *multiple* households, in which more than one couple and their children live together (usually a married couple and their parents, and/or one or more sets of married siblings).[44] Complex households of both types may also be described by the genealogical relationships between their members: in *patrilocal* households, couples live with one or more of the husband's relatives, and in *matrilocal*, with the wife's.[45]

Geniza residence agreements tell us the most about complex households formed when a couple married. Most of these complex households—those described in 17 of the 25 documents (68 percent) that discuss a new wife living with relatives after her marriage—are not multiple but extended: the bride agrees to share a household with her husband's or her own single mother, sometimes together with the mother's unmarried children, or (much less often) with her husband's single father or unmarried siblings.[46] Fourteen of these extended households are patrilocal—the wife agrees to live with her husband's mother *or* father and/or siblings—and three are matrilocal: she agrees to live with her own mother. In contrast, only eight agreements (24 percent) describe multiple family households shared by a wife or couple and their married parents; these are divided evenly between patrilocal and matrilocal households, shared either with the husband's or the wife's parents. (See Figure 1.6.)

Only a quarter of the new couples described in this corpus thus joined a household headed by an older married couple, and those that did so were just as likely to move in with the wife's parents as with the husband's. But most

43. Laslett and Hammel, "Comparing Household Structure."

44. Multiple households can be further classed as *stem family* households, in which only one married child lives with a set of parents at marriage, or *joint family* households, in which several married children and their spouses do so.

45. In this schema, nuclear households are termed *neolocal*. See further Kertzer, "Household History."

46. One of the documents labeled "patrilocal, extended family: father only" in Fig. 1.6 mentions a stepmother married to the groom's father (T-S 8 J 4.18c).

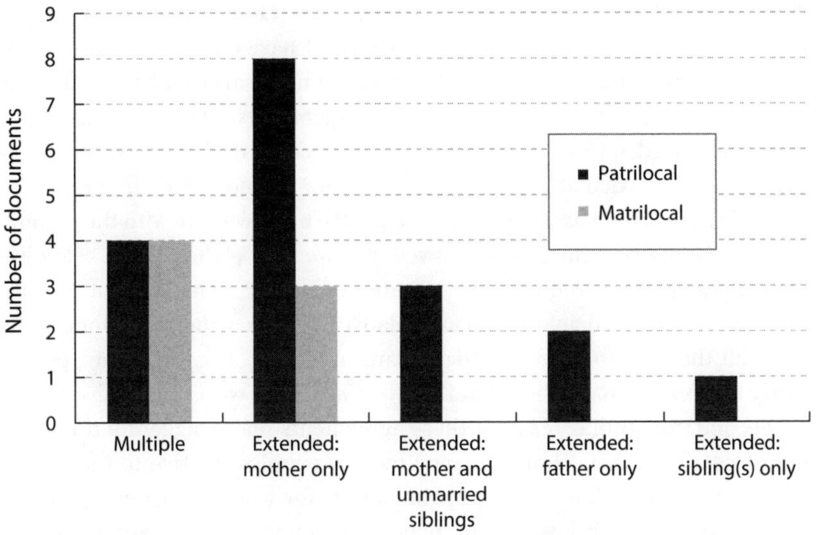

FIGURE 1.6. Complex households in Geniza marriage agreements

newlyweds (three-quarters of our sample) did neither. Rather, new couples who formed complex households with their relatives mostly moved in with one or more single relatives—most often, the husband's mother, sometimes together with her still unmarried children.[47]

This finding is persuasive despite this sample's small size, because it follows logically from everything else we know about Geniza families. Given how many men died before their daughters reached social adulthood, and how many marriages ended in divorce or social estrangement even before this point, it is obvious that most couples cannot have lived—or lived together—long enough to form a household with any of their married children. Honorifics attached to *grooms'* fathers' names in Geniza marriage documents (omitted above because they do not distinguish men's first marriages from later ones, and are thus useless as a measure of paternal morality) make this even clearer: a full 71 percent of the documents I have identified that provide this information indicate that the groom no longer had a living father at the time of marriage.[48]

In other respects, however, these residence agreements are less useful. First, there is no way to know how common the complex households that they

47. It is also possible that some of these older women were not yet widows but lived with a married child, apart from their husbands; see below, n. 54.

48. I have identified 123 marriage documents in which the groom's patronymic is accompanied by either *s"t* or *n"e*; 87 of these have *n"e*, indicating that the groom's father was dead by the time the marriage document was composed.

describe may have been relative to nuclear ones. Only two of our 27 agreements promise that a wife will live alone, and I have found only three other Geniza passages that do so.[49] But this does not necessarily mean that nuclear households were this rare: marriage agreements described living arrangements that needed to be negotiated in court because they were viewed as socially fraught, particularly for women (since they are more often framed as the wife's obligation than as the husband's, e.g., "the bride will live with the groom's mother //and his brother// in one dwelling (*maskan*)"; "she will not cease living with her mother, and will not separate from her.").[50] This was not the case for couples who lived apart from any relatives, who may therefore not usually have felt the need to formalize these plans in writing. Even in letters, people rarely had reason to mention that they were *not* living with any relatives.

Second, for similar reasons, these agreements may exaggerate the number of patrilocal households formed by new couples relative to matrilocal ones, which were viewed as less problematic for women (or perhaps more accurately, for the relatives who usually negotiated these agreements on women's behalf).[51] Scattered references to living arrangements in other types of Geniza documents support these suspicions; they describe a much higher proportion of matrilocal households and neolocal households than do our clauses.[52]

49. See above, n. 41. It is also possible that these two documents describe seminuclear arrangements in which the wife lived within a *dār* with her in-laws but didn't share living space with them; see Chapter 8. Three other passages: T-S 10 J 12.14, Maimonides *Responsa* no. 23, ibid., no. 239.

50. T-S 8 J 5.22, engagement contract, Fustat, 1162; T-S 13 J 6.33, text of premarital stipulations, late eleventh century. Only one residence clause in my corpus explicitly mentions the husband's residence: Bodl. MS Heb. a. 3.32, a Palestinian-formula *ketubba*, possibly from 1064, Ramle, which specifies that the wife's mother "will live with *them* (that is, the husband and wife) in the apartment (*dira*)." The most obvious reason for this convention is that husbands were socially (although not legally) considered responsible for their wives' lodging. See Chapter 7.

51. See Chapter 7.

52. I have identified 24 responsa, letters, and other legal documents that mention the relatives with whom a wife or couple shared a *dār*. Six describe a wife or couple living with the husband's relatives, versus twelve with the wife's; five describe neolocal households; and one a couple who lived with both the husband's and wife's relatives. On the other hand, these references resemble our residence agreements in describing mostly extended rather than multiple joint households across generations; but they include some multiple joint households shared by married siblings and cousins (absent from our marriage agreements). With the husband's relatives: T-S 10 J 9.13, ENA NS 2.11, T-S 13 J 9.4, T-S 13 J 8.23 (and others about the same couple; see part 2 of Chapter 8), Maimonides, *Responsa*, nos. 34 and 94. With the wife's relatives: DK 238.3, ULC Or. 1080 J 173, ENA 3792.4, T-S 13 J 23.5, T-S 13 J 3.3, Maimonides, *Responsa*, nos. 9, 13 (story 1 in the query), 30, 96, 229, 362, and 418. Couples living alone: T-S 10 J 12.14, T-S 16.288, Maimonides, *Responsa*, nos. 13 (this text offers evidence for both neolocal and patrilocal arrangements, since it describes a widow's

Finally, our agreements fail to resolve a basic question that the standard terminology that I have used so far (nuclear, extended, patrilocal, matrilocal, etc.) elides, but that is actually not clear: did married couples routinely live together? No matter what form of coresidence they ratify, almost all the residence agreements in our corpus are formulated as conditions placed on the *wife's* residence alone. Other legal documents sometimes also distinguish wives' lodging from their husbands' in this way. For example, a *ketubba* composed in Tyre in the early eleventh century stipulates that the bride will live there for the first year of her marriage, whereupon her husband must move her to Acre, into a property included in her dowry—but which her father retains the right to inhabit as well, "whether he is alone or with his wife and children, and whether for a visit or as his permanent dwelling."[53] This convention raises the possibility that married couples may have sometimes maintained separate residences as a matter of course, and not only when husbands travelled abroad. But once again, there is no clear way to know: some documents clearly do describe husbands and wives sharing domestic space, while others are ambiguous.[54] And this question is further complicated by polygamous marriages, in which husbands may have lived at different times with different wives in separate households. Some marriages described in the Geniza were polygamous, but it is impossible to determine how common they may have been.[55]

married sons who lived on their own but then moved in with her; see above, n. 35), 23, and 239. Relatives of both the husband and the wife: T-S 12.780. This breakdown differs slightly from the one given in Krakowski, "Female Adolescence," 275–277, because I subsequently reevaluted some of the cases summarized there and identified several new ones.

53. T-S 13 J 6.14.

54. Couples living together: for example, in T-S AS 151.24, an undated marital reconciliation agreement, the husband pledges to move with his wife to a new residence "among Jewish neighbors"; T-S 8 J 34.8, an undated betrothal contract, contains a stipulation to take effect if the couple leaves a certain residence (the document is too fragmentary to be understood further); Bodl. MS Heb. a. 3.42, a Karaite-Rabbanite *ketubba*, Fustat, 1117, notes that the wife will not charge her husband rent for the apartment (*dira*) "in which they currently live." Ambiguous: for example, in T-S 13 J 22.2, a will from the mid-eleventh century, Fustat, a woman leaves the *dār* "in which she lived" to two slave girls and to the communal charity fund (*qodesh*), and a different property to her husband. As in T-S 13 J 6.14, cited above (at the previous note), documents that clearly describe wives living apart from their husbands mainly involve older couples with married children, e.g., T-S 13 J 23.5, an undated letter sent by a woman in Raqqa, to her son: "Your father is in one city, your brother in another, and you in another; and you have all left me with your sister, and this was as you wished"; Maimonides, *Responsa* no. 30, which describes a newlywed wife whose mother came to live with her in Alexandria, while her father remained in Qūṣ.

55. For evidence of co-wives living in separate dwellings (possibly separate living chambers within a single *dār*) see, for example, T-S 13 J 3.1, T-S 8.116, and more generally Friedman, *Polygyny*, Chapter 6. Medieval Islamic legal literature normatively assumes that marriages will be polygamous and that husbands will rotate between wives living in different residences; see Ali, *Marriage and Slavery* 100, and below, Chapter 8. No study

These agreements therefore do not transparently capture the entire range of households formed by Geniza Jews at marriage. Still, as a limited marker of household diversity, they are suggestive. Read with an eye to both what they record and what they likely omit (most nuclear and some extended matrilocal households), this small group of agreements suggests that Jews in Fustat—and, as far as we can tell, in other Fatimid and Ayyubid cities too—never developed a uniform household system. Rather, families and individuals grouped themselves in households in a variety of ways. Some unknown number of couples and single people may at times have lived alone or with only their minor children. Many others formed households with both birth and marital relatives, for a range of social and economic reasons that can often be reasonably surmised. Our evidence most clearly suggests that widowed and divorced women often ended life sharing space with one of their married sons or daughters (or their daughters-in-law), probably because they had nowhere else to go. These women's unmarried children, too, might live for a while under a brother, sister, or sister-in-law's roof. Married cousins and siblings might live in adjacent households, or even within a single apartment, which they had jointly inherited from a common parent or grandparent. Similarly, married women might live with or next to one or both of their parents, in property that these parents had given to them as a dowry but still needed to live in themselves.[56]

Rethinking Kinship

Although our evidence for household formation is incomplete, it underscores how important kinship bonds were among Geniza Jews: blood relatives did often live together, even if we cannot tell exactly how often. But the variety of different ways in which they did so, together with the other limited demographic data at our disposal, suggest that these bonds could produce many different kinds of family groupings that were neither stable nor predictable. When we take into account the changes created by mortality, divorce, spousal estrangement, and male mobility (unquantifiable but omnipresent in the Geniza record), it seems nearly certain, for example, that most children did

---

has yet assessed the actual frequency of polygamy in any medieval Islamic society, although preliminary evidence suggests that in Mamluk Egypt, at least, it was rare; see Rapoport, *Money, Marriage, and Divorce* 111. On the difficulty of quantifying rates of polygamy from Geniza evidence, see Friedman, *Polygyny*, 1–6.

56. For references to married women living in their own dotal property, see, e.g., T-S 13 J 6.14, T-S 12.624 (*ketubba*, c. 1090, Alexandria), T-S 13 J 2.3, T-S 8 J 34.8, Bodl. MS Heb. a. 3.42, Bodl. MS Heb. e. 98.56, Mosseri IV 19.1, ENA 2727.14b, sect. 2, T-S 12.544 (Fustat, 1147), T-S K 6.118b, T-S 13 J 22.2, Maimonides, *Responsa*, no. 59, Yiṣḥaq al-Fāsī, *Responsa*, ed. Leiter, no. 172. See further Krakowski, "Adolescence," 201, at n. 29.

not grow up within a single unchanging household inhabited by a fixed group of relatives throughout their childhoods, or interacting with a similarly fixed set of kin beyond the household.

How far does this evidence set Geniza Jews apart from any other premodern population? Even where patriarchal clans have prevailed as a social ideal, mortality necessarily made family forms more varied on the ground. Too many people in the premodern world died young for most families to have lived together across multiple intact generations, no matter how normative this arrangement may have been in theory. Many scholars have argued that this does not matter, or at any rate that it matters only partly; the ideal itself exerts powerful social force even when it is infrequently realized. This point is worth emphasizing wherever it applies, and might perhaps be extended even to the other markers of domestic variety that I have just reviewed. But I suggest that it is a moot point in this case, because the Geniza documents offer almost no evidence that their writers held such an ideal in the first place. In the rest of this chapter I will argue instead that they recognized a different type of kinship ideal entirely.

Beyond the accidents of demography, how then did Geniza Jews *understand* genealogical relationships, how they worked and how they ought to?

Geniza documents rarely invoke either the family or kinship as abstract categories.[57] One of the few documents I have found that does so is a faded and cryptic letter sent to a woman in Egypt by a female relative who had fled Palestine for Tripoli al-Shām after the Seljuq invasion of Jerusalem in 1073.[58] Her husband and son had disappeared, leaving her and her other children "dying of hunger" and envying the prisoners of war, who at least "have someone to feed them and give them to drink." She mentions a web of relatives with whom she has been in contact. Their relationships to her, and to each other, are impossible to reconstruct in full, but they include a cousin or uncle who had supported her when she arrived in Tripoli al-Shām, and another relative, the brother of "that man" (perhaps meaning her husband) who had likewise helped him when they first arrived, but stopped when "he (i.e. the husband) sued them over an inheritance; they severed ties, and not one of them will talk to me." She asks the recipient to ask a communal leader—perhaps Yehuda b. Se'adya, the first Egyptian Head of the Jews—to send her money to redeem some boxes of books she had pawned, but notes that he may refuse to help her because he, too, is angry with her husband. Emphasizing her social isolation, she begs the recipient to recognize their relationship and to help her:

57. On the difficulties surrounding Geniza terminology for the extended family, see below, n. 69.

58. Lewis-Gibson Misc., 35.

> Have mercy on me, you and your sister and your mother, as much as you're able . . . don't neglect me. Maintain (our) kinship and (our) blood (*al-ahliyya wa-al-dam*) and stay bound to me through correspondence (*mukātaba*). When I was in Jerusalem, your correspondence and favor[59] came to me abundantly, as between sisters; now you have severed me.

This appeal is striking partly for what it does *not* say. Even as one of the few Geniza documents we possess that directly appeals to kinship in the abstract, it makes no mention of these women's shared *family* as a solidarity group. The predictable domestic structures missing from our demographic data are also missing here. At no point does the author try to claim her relative's help by gesturing to the broader family to which they both belong: neither by mentioning a household where they had once lived together, nor the hope of one day doing so, nor by invoking the extended family itself, either as a conceptual ideal (e.g., "remember we are both daughters of the so-and-so clan") or as embodied in other relatives they share (e.g., "remember our grandmother and help me for her sake").

In short, this letter reflects a model of family relations in which kinship matters a great deal, but "the house of the father" as a social unit figures not at all. The ideals it emphasizes inhered not in the *family group* (*al-ahl*) its author shared with her relatives, but rather in the personal *kinship bonds* between them (*al-ahliyya wa-al-dam*). Kinship itself appears from this passage as a social association that was supposed to command inherent loyalty—specifically, regular correspondence and financial help—but that did not always actually do so. Rather, kinship bonds needed tending to bear social meaning, which meant that they could also be dissolved: the author begs the recipient to maintain their kinship ties rather than sever them as her other relatives have done.

This atomized model of kinship bears little resemblance to the clan-based solidarities that scholars have tended to ascribe to the premodern Islamic world in general, and to the Geniza populations in particular. But it should be immediately familiar to anyone who has read a charity petition, letter of recommendation, or commercial letter preserved in the Geniza. Our letter represents kinship as a type of *personal loyalty* similar to others well-known throughout the Geniza corpus and beyond it: the reciprocal patronage and commercial relationships that helped order social, political, and economic activity among Muslims and non-Muslims alike within a range of post-Abbasid Islamic states.

59. *Ḥaḍḍ*, for *ḥaẓẓ*; see Diem and Radenberg, *Dictionary*, 44. It is not clear whether this means financial support or more intangible social benefaction.

Among several important studies that have examined these reciprocal relationships and the roles that they played in Buyid, Fatimid, and Ayyubid society, the most useful starting point is Roy Mottahedeh's classic account of political culture at the tenth- and eleventh-century Buyid court, *Loyalty and Leadership in an Early Islamic Society*. Mottahedeh explained Buyid politics as organized primarily by local commitments between individuals that were durable in *form*—they followed coherent and recognized codes of conduct—but not in the specific personal *formations* that they created; they produced no equally durable associations "within groups that [were] not composites of ties between individuals."[60] "Acquired loyalties" formed by choice through specific social acts thus outweighed "loyalties of category," created de facto among all members of a given class or group by virtue of their common membership.[61] Among these acts, Mottahedeh highlighted especially forms of political benefaction, or *niʿma*, which created ongoing mutual expectations between benefactor and client that lasted as long as both maintained them.

Mottahedeh describes a world far removed from the middling- to lower-class Egyptian and Syrian Jews who produced most of the Geniza documents. But Marina Rustow has demonstrated that Geniza Jews shared a common vocabulary of reciprocal benefaction with the Buyid narrative texts that he examined. Geniza documents use terms like *niʿma, khidma* (service), and *riʿāya* (protection) to describe an enormous variety of binding social relationships—political ties, business associations, charitable patronage, and apprenticeship (and as I will argue in Chapter 6, affiliation through marriage)—in similar ways to Buyid texts. These terms reflect a "common code" of social affiliation recognized by men at all levels of the social ladder.[62] Without invoking Mottahedeh's work, other scholars, including Goitein, Abraham Udovitch, and Jessica Goldberg, have argued that Geniza merchants likewise depended professionally on dyadic relationships maintained between individuals, rather than on fixed mercantile groups or guilds.[63]

How can this literature help us understand Geniza kinship? To begin with, it underscores how foreign the self-contained "house of the father" that has been viewed as normative across the premodern Middle East might have been to Geniza people. Solidarity-based extended patriarchal clans have often been central to rural social orders (especially nomadic ones, including those reflected in the foundation texts of both Judaism and Islam: ancient Israel

60. Mottahedeh, *Loyalty*, 6.

61. Ibid., 72–78.

62. Rustow, "Benefaction," "Formal and Informal Patronage," *Heresy*, 89–91 and passim.

63. Goldberg, *Trade and Institutions*, 123–150, "Backbiting," expanding on previous work by Goitein (*Med. Soc.*, 1:164–169) and Udovitch ("Formalism and Informalism"). For evidence that shifting personal ties played a central role in the practical functioning of Jewish communal institutions, see Chapter 2.

and seventh-century Arabia), but not to the very differently organized urban milieux in which Geniza Jews lived, from which hermetically closed groups of any kind were mostly absent.[64] By the same token, this literature clarifies much about how kinship did work in this social universe. The forms of reciprocal social associations on which Geniza society ran may once have been modeled on loyalties among kin. This is at any rate how classical Muslim jurists understood the early Islamic institution of clientage, *walā'*.[65] But by the Geniza period, I suggest that the reverse had become true: our letter thus understands kinship itself as a social bond that works in similar ways to other dyadic social ties.[66]

I do not mean to suggest that kinship was literally identical to either patronage or commercial partnership. Indeed, patronage and commercial association were not identical to each other either; commercial letters, for example, emphasize business associates' equality to each other, whereas petitions cast patronage as hierarchical.[67] But Mottahedeh's model of "acquired loyalties" offers a useful way to think about how relatives in the Geniza talk to and about each other, in the many letters and other documents within the corpus that resemble this one, but that unlike it, do not address kinship directly as a concept.

Three of these similarities are especially worth noting, along with the ways in which kinship differed from other social loyalties with respect to each. First, as I have already noted, just as Geniza Jews describe patronage and commercial ties as a function of individual relationships between men, they also consistently describe kinship as a function of individual relationships between relatives, rather than of larger family groups. This is true not only of the few letters that explicitly invoke kinship as an abstract ideal, but also of several more standard features of Geniza discourse. Geniza letters often identify people by their ties to a specific relative (e.g., "Send my regards to Abī Zikrī Yehuda b. Menashe, and to the judge Abī 'Alī, *his brother*"), but seldom by naming them as members of a particular family group.[68] Likewise, relatives

64. On the limited evidence for large complex households in medieval cities east and west, see the Introduction.

65. Crone, *Roman, Provincial and Islamic Law*, 40.

66. Mottahedeh himself does not address kinship at length, but labels it an unstable category of social organization compared to acquired loyalties between nonkin. Contrary to what I argue here for Geniza Jews, he suggests that among Buyid elites, the two were also fundamentally different; *Loyalty*, 5.

67. Goldberg, "Friendship and Hierarchy."

68. T-S 10 J 14.26, a letter written by Nahray b. Nissim in the 1060s; I have elided the honorifics appended to both men's names. Geniza mercantile letters do, however, refer to male relatives who operate as close business associates as "the sons of so-and-so," e.g., "The *ḥaver* R. Ḥayyim conducted business in an ugly manner with his in-laws, the sons of (*benei al-*) Baradānī" (T-S 10 J 5.10 + T-S 10 J 11.13).

rarely emphasize their ties by referring to their shared family, but instead by naming their particular genealogical relationship: "my brother," "my mother," "my paternal uncle," and so on.[69] More distant relatives who wished to emphasize their social closeness did so by using these expressions too, assimilating their relatively weaker kinship bonds to these more centrally important ones. "I am your brother or your son," writes Shelomo b. Eliyyahu, a schoolteacher and scribe in early thirteenth-century Fustat, to his cousin (and father-in-law) Abū al-Faraj, to remind him of their blood relationship.[70] (This is what our letter's author is doing when she describes her female relative's previous correspondence with her as being like that "between sisters.") These expressions suggest that like both patronage and commercial cooperation, kinship ordered society not by carving it into tightly defined groups, but by offering individuals a characteristic form of social relationship that they could marshal to form personal networks of social affiliation for themselves.

Here one important distinction must be made. Whereas benefaction and commercial relationships did not outlive the parties involved, kinship was different in one respect: Geniza documents do display strong concern for patriliny across generations. Memorial lists and geneaologies, polemics, personal letters, and even legal documents preserved in the Geniza discuss and invoke paternal lineage in ways that reveal a profound preoccupation with vertical kinship.[71] Exalted ancestry was understood to legitimate claims to power—as when, during a major battle for control of the Palestinian gaonic *yeshiva* in the early 1050s, both factions supported their respective leaders by pointing to their noble lineage; Yosef *ha-kohen* b. Shelomo, the previous *ga'on*'s son, as a member of the priestly caste on the one hand, and his rival Dani'el b. ʿAzarya as a descendant of King David on the other.[72] Descent from respected forefathers could also validate far more humble claims, as when a late eleventh-century charity petition urges the recipient to assist its bearer because he descends

69. Geniza documents do use terms for the extended family, but they are not often invoked ideologically. Goitein (*Med. Soc.*, 3:425, n. 2), singles out *bayt* and *dār* (in this sense, both meaning something like "house") as the most common of these terms. In my experience, however, it is often unclear whether these words denote an entire extended family group or the members of a physical household, or in the case of *bayt*, a wife (as Goitein notes here, the latter problem applies also to uses of the term *ahl*). The two other terms that Goitein mentions—the strange construct form *baytat* (attached to a name, or sometimes appearing decoupled from one, as *bayta*) and the term *ʿitra*—are uncommon in my experience, and appear infrequently in the PGP database; from the citations that I have found, both appear most unequivocally in the sense of "family" in genealogical and memorial lists, on which see below, n. 74. Cf. Introduction, n. 26.

70. T-S 12.69. This phenomenon is even more extensive in papyri from Greco-Roman Egypt; see Dickey, "Literal and Extended Use of Kinship Terms."

71. See Franklin, *This Noble House*, Goitein, *Med. Soc.*, 3:2–6.

72. Franklin, *This Noble House*, 115–118, and cf. Rustow, *Heresy*, 323–330.

"from the sons of (worthy) fathers and substantial householders."[73] The medieval Middle Eastern Jews who produced this material manifestly understood *nasab*, patrilineal descent, as an essential component of personal worth. But precisely because *nasab* was tied to *personal* worth, it was rarely used to highlight bonds between two or more living relatives; instead, lineage claims too created (imagined) individual networks, in this case vertical ones spread out across time, rather than horizontally distributed groups of living kin.[74]

The second similarity between kinship and other social loyalties lies in the commitments that relatives owed each other. Like ties produced by benefaction, kinship imposed mutual obligations between relatives, central among them those that our letter-writer demanded from her relative: social affiliation and financial and social support. Here, too, kinship differed in some respects from other social bonds, especially among close kin. It created some obvious and widely felt social and economic obligations among relatives that other forms of social loyalty did not: parents usually devolved property on their children and sometimes more extended relatives, and kin lived together rather than with their business associates or political clients (the few nonkin who lived in households, slaves and domestic dependents, were themselves viewed as quasi or replacement kin for this reason).[75] But the ways in which obligations among kin were *understood* nonetheless resembled those produced by acquired loyalties, so much so that Geniza documents discuss them in similar ways. For example, the ongoing correspondence (*mukātaba*) that our author seeks with her relative was an expected feature of patronage and commercial relationships too, one that helped maintain both parties' commitment to each other, and signaled this commitment to others, since the delivery of letters and their reading were public acts.[76]

But this model of social commitment also allowed individuals to decline these obligations, a point that brings me to the third similarity between kinship and acquired social loyalties: both could be denied and terminated. Once again these parallels are not exact, precisely because acquired loyalties had to be created, whereas kinship was inborn. Official kinship—the recognized fact

73. T-S 18 J 4.4. This is a common trope in charity petitions; see Cohen, *Poverty*, 67–70.

74. Goitein's treatment of Geniza memorial lists (idem, *Med. Soc.*, 3:2–6) suggests that this is the case, but also states that these lists sometimes name horizontally linked relatives as well. I thank Arnold Franklin, an expert in this material, for confirming that while Geniza memorial lists and genealogies "do incorporate members of multiple branches of a family, that fact isn't really emphasized visually or textually. They appear just as lists of names . . . all of which are understood to be the descendants of a common ancestor. So . . . the horizontal connections between family members . . . (don't) seem to have been the primary concern of the records themselves." (Personal communication, Sept. 30, 2016).

75. See Introduction, n. 33.

76. See Franklin, "More Than Words on a Page," esp. 289–293, and see the discussion of Shelomo b. Eliyyahu and his father-in-law in Chapter 8.

of being genealogically related to another person—therefore existed whether one acknowledged it or not, and Geniza documents sometimes imply that failing to acknowledge it could stain one's social honor.[77] But people often did so anyway. If official kinship was immutable, Geniza documents make clear that *practical* kinship—Pierre Bourdieu's term for living associations between relatives, as opposed to those recognized only on paper—could decay in much the same ways as any other form of social affiliation.[78] One could sever correspondence with a relative, and all that it implied, just as effectively as with a client or a business partner (*inqiṭāʿ*, the term our letter uses for severing a written correspondence, is often used this way in commercial and political contexts too).

Indeed, Geniza Jews tend to mobilize kinship ideals precisely at points when they are being shirked or ignored. Some of the strongest expressions of family affection found in the Geniza were composed to preserve fraternal bonds in danger of unraveling. In 1058, Labrāṭ b. Moshe b. Sughmār, a merchant in al-Mahdiyya, Ifrīqiyya, wrote to his brother Yehuda in Fustat: "You are not only a brother to me, but a younger brother and an oldest son. . . . You are dearer to me than the world, and all that is in it."[79] While this passage can easily be read as a straightforward declaration of brotherly love, Labrāṭ was not simply being demonstrative, but working to repair a potential falling-out with Yehuda over a business disagreement. He had rebuked Yehuda for losing some of his merchandise in a shipwreck, and Yehuda had responded indignantly; Labrāṭ now hastened to declare that he had only been upset at Yehuda for failing to tell him about what had happened, as "you would have done . . . to any other man whose merchandise you held," but that he was prepared to postpone (although not forgive) the debt. In this context, this letter's affirmation of fraternal intimacy served the same function as one couched in terms of benefaction (*niʿma*) to a business associate. Nor were Labrāṭ's assurances unnecessary. He elsewhere makes clear that he maintains quite different relationships with other relatives equally close to him by blood, including another brother from whom he is estranged, about whom he notes: "I mostly deal with him by keeping away from him completely, and considering him non-existent."[80]

Labrāṭ and Yehuda were merchants, and it may be natural that they approached their fraternal relationship partly as a merchant association. But not only merchants behaved this way. Many, if not all, of even the closest kin relationships described in the Geniza appear just as socially contingent; and not only in adulthood, but from the very outset. This was to some extent a natural

77. As in the letters I discuss in the section on dotal charity in Chapter 4.

78. Bourdieu, *Outline of a Theory of Practice*, 33–38, *Logic of Practice*, 166–187.

79. T-S 16.179.

80. Bodl. MS Heb. b. 13.49, composed the previous year.

outcome of the variability of families themselves. Frequent divorce and high mobility meant that like the young son of Hayfā' bt. Sulaymān, whose story opened this chapter, children whose parents divorced or physically separated might grow up never meeting their fathers—or, more rarely, mothers—at all.[81] When parents remarried, siblings and half-siblings might live apart and affiliate with entirely different relatives from each other. But many Geniza letters suggest something more than this: parents, children, and siblings could retain radically different personal loyalties even within a single immediate family.

For example, writing from Damascus just before the First Crusade, a destitute man who had abandoned his wife and young children in Tyre almost a year earlier insists that he can neither return there nor bring the family to Damascus.[82] Yet he also expresses passionate concern for his eldest son Murajjā, whom he accuses his wife and her father of mistreating and neglecting: "The child is neglected, lonely, starving and naked; he has no one to take mercy on him nor to guide him. You (the boy's grandfather) direct your anger against him and shut him out!" He ends the letter by demanding that his wife send Murajjā to live with him in Damascus, on pain of abandoning her and their other children: "Otherwise I shall leave for the furthest of places, and the children will die." This father's unequal investment in his different children, and Murajjā's own precarious position between his warring father, mother, and grandfather, suggest the profound variability of practical kinship ties among people of all ages and all social levels documented in the Geniza. Even the most intimate family relationships could potentially be activated or deactivated at will, according to individual choice and circumstance.

Women and Kinship

In sum, viewing kinship in light of Mottahedeh's work on *ni'ma* suggests that Geniza families were uneven in part because practical kinship itself functioned as one variety of the personal ties that ordered much social life in the medieval Middle East, which tended to be durable in form but flexible in execution, and were embodied mainly in the immediate loyalties that individuals bore each other. It follows that when we step *outside* the family, we may expect to find

81. Geniza letters and legal documents describe fathers treating children from past marriages in a wide range of ways. Like Hayfā' bt. Sulaymān's husband, many men who neglected or divorced their wives also severed ties with their children; for numerous examples, see Cohen, *Poverty*, Chapter 6. But others did not; many Geniza documents describe divorced husbands pledging financial support for minor sons and daughters, as well as estranged spouses battling for social control of their children. For the former, see, e.g., Bodl. MS Heb. d. 66.7; for the latter, see the letter discussed immediately below. This subject merits far more dedicated attention than it has yet received.

82. Phil. E 16516.

kinship working to situate people within society at large in much the same ways as personal ties created by other means.

And when it comes to men, this expectation is often fulfilled. Abundant Geniza material, much of it created in order to document, regulate, and perpetuate social ties among men, demonstrates that men could form socially beneficial relationships in many ways: through professional association; shared study; common travel; political, professional, social, or material patronage; *and* ties of blood. Male kinship ties—both those formed at birth and those forged through marriage, which I will discuss at greater length in Chapter 6—paralleled and often converged with many of these other forms of social affiliation.[83] Among the subcorpus of Geniza merchant letters composed in the eleventh century, for example, brothers and cousins who worked as business partners stand out as enjoying clear advantages.[84] Likewise, men of all social classes appear in Geniza letters appealing to their own relatives for material and professional aid, as well as for more intangible benefits, such as socially useful introductions to others. But if men often depended significantly on the social ties they shared with relatives, they rarely did so exclusively. And many did not do so at all; the Geniza describes men who worked in different sectors from their fathers or brothers, lived far away from them, and maintained personal networks mainly or exclusively with nonkin. In the physically and sometimes economically mobile urban society documented by the Geniza corpus, the family into which a man was born did not rigidly fix his eventual place in life, although it did much to determine what place he could expect to achieve.[85] Male kinship served instead as one centrally important form of social constraint and social capital among many, alongside a range of other, similarly shaped personal ties.

But things were different for women. In contrast to men, the Geniza provides scant evidence that women could routinely socially affiliate with nonkin (except through forms of replacement kinship, usually created by coresidence

83. I argue in Chapter 6 that men also formed recognized social alliances by marrying each other's female relatives, a tendency that both further underscores the parallels between kinship and other types of social affiliation and provides further context for the instability of marriage itself.

84. Most notably the Tāhirtīs of Qayrawān, immigrants from Ifrīqiyya who maintained merchant partnerships with each other for three generations. On the Tāhirtīs, see Gil, *Jews in Islamic Countries*, 693–704; on family merchant partnerships more generally, see Goitein, *Med. Soc.*, 1:180–183. Here as elsewhere, our evidence for informal social organization is strongest for the eleventh-century merchants, who left so many personal letters in the Geniza. Professional cooperation is more difficult to see among male relatives whose occupations did not require them to correspond regularly with each other. Still, it is obvious from naming patterns that doctors and specialized craftsmen often ran in families as well; see Goitein, *Med. Soc.*, 1:79–80, 3:40–42.

85. Socio-economic class and class mobility remain major underexplored questions in Geniza social history. Much more work needs to be done on both topics; for now, the most comprehensive treatment remains Goitein's, discussed above, Introduction, n. 67.

in a household during childhood, or with slaves at any point during a woman's lifetime).[86] This does not mean that women had no contact with people outside their families and households; letters addressed to nonrelatives frequently contain messages for the recipient's wife, mother, sister, or daughters, for example.[87] But whatever personal contacts may have prompted these greetings, they seem rarely to have created the sort of meaningful social identification that fostered durable associations among men. Thus, while women often appear in legal documents buying, selling, or renting property to nonkin, they seldom if ever appear *represented* in court by nonkin.[88] Similarly, women's private charity petitions almost always address their birth or marital relatives, again in stark contrast to those composed by or for men, which routinely seek *ni'ma* from nonrelatives.[89] This is equally true of ties between women themselves. Women may well have had female friends outside their families—with whom they worked or among whom they lived in *dār*s and neighborhoods—but these friendships are nearly invisible in the Geniza corpus.

The thesis that emerges piecemeal from these clues, and that will be tested and elaborated throughout the rest of this book, is that women's relationships with their own relatives were central to their lifelong social and economic welfare. It is no accident that the majority of complex households described in our marriage document corpus involve a single older mother living with her married son or daughter. Almost all Geniza material pertaining to women suggests that kinship ties held critical significance for adult daughters, both within marriage and after. Like the widow whose frantic letter to her brother is cited near the beginning of this chapter, most women who outlived a marriage, or who were unhappy within one, found themselves with "no one left but God and you"—a standard appeal formula in women's petitions, both those sent to their own relatives and to communal officials like the one whom Hayfā' addressed (on whom more in the next chapter). "I have no one left but God and you" is one of several such formulas that present a female petitioner's weakness and need in terms of her isolation, that is, her detachment from a network of supportive relatives. Such women are routinely labeled "cut off," "lonely," and "alien" (that is, without birth or marital relatives in the city or region in which they find themselves).[90]

86. See Introduction, n. 33.

87. Particularly in the eleventh and early twelfth centuries, these greetings are sometimes oblique, extended to "your house," or to "the one who is with you," both euphemisms for "your wife." See Goitein, *Med. Soc.*, 3:160–162.

88. Women do occasionally (if rarely) appear in legal documents asking nonkin men to act as witnesses on their behalf, most famously in T-S 10 J 7.10, a remarkable deed of testimony involving Wuḥsha (Karīma bt. 'Ammār); see below, Chapter 5, n. 8.

89. Cohen, *Poverty*, 192–193.

90. "Cut-off": *munqaṭi'a*: cf. above, immediately after n. 78, and see also above, n. 1. This term is ubiquitous within the Geniza, and also common in Fatimid state petitions; I

It thus mattered greatly to women, almost certainly far more than it did to men, that even immediate kin could not always be relied on for help; many "cut off" and "lonely" women had living relatives, who could not or chose not to support them. The following chapter will examine the option of last resort available to women whose family members failed them: the Jewish community and its legal institutions.

---

thank Marina Rustow for sharing with me a section of her forthcoming book on Fatimid petitions that addresses this material. See also Cohen, *Poverty and Charity*, 194. I am currently planning a systematic study of this and related formulae in private letters and women's petitions from the Geniza.

CHAPTER TWO

The Courts and the Law

WITHOUT RELATIVES WHO WERE willing or able to support her, where could a woman like Hayfāʾ bt. Sulaymān turn? Because women did not maintain social bonds with nonrelatives, she could not seek help in the way most obviously open to a man, by appealing to a stranger for charity. She could, however, appeal to several overlapping legal and political institutions: to a Jewish or an Islamic court, or to the Islamic state or Jewish communal officials.

For women, arguably the most socially important of these forums was the Jewish court (*bet din*). The *bet din* is the Jewish communal institution best documented within the Geniza corpus, and one that was central to women's lives. So long as she remained Jewish, it was primarily in Jewish court that a woman could hope to escape a ruinous marriage or achieve any other basic social and economic goal: receive an inheritance, contract or renegotiate a marriage, or pass on her property after she died. Yet women also faced considerable challenges in court, which they could overcome only by seeking help through other means. The letter cited at the start of Chapter 1, in which Hayfāʾ asked a Jewish communal leader in Fustat to write to the *bet din* of Acre on her behalf, illustrates the most common of these options: petitioning an official outside the court for support in a lawsuit.[1] If this failed, women could also circumvent the Jewish leadership entirely, or try to force its hands, by turning to an Islamic *qāḍī* or to state officials, a point that women do not shy away from emphasizing in petitions. "I appeal to my lord . . . and to the community," says a typical (undated) letter narrated by a woman seeking divorce, "to grant

1. T-S 13 J 8.19; see Chapter 1, n. 1 (I locate the court that Hayfāʾ mentions in Acre based on T-S 13 J 21.2). Petitions to Jewish communal officials from isolated women like Hayfāʾ are common. They suggest that although women could not seek private patrons among nonkin, they could appeal to communal officials in their public roles, a norm that must have strengthened officials' own political capital. See Cohen, *Poverty and Charity*, 147, Zinger, "Women, Gender and Law," 46–58.

me justice from (my husband). Otherwise I will be forced to go to *the nations of the world*"—meaning, to an Islamic court—"that they may save me."[2]

If examining Geniza families and households reveals the extent to which women depended on individual kin relationships, examining Geniza courts allows us to locate them within a broader social setting ordered by both individual and group affiliations. Geniza legal documents reveal the social opportunities and constraints that women encountered not only among their blood and marital relatives, but also as members of the Jewish community and subjects of the Fatimid and Ayyubid states.

They also offer unusually close evidence for the social effects of a different kind of institution: medieval rabbinic law itself. Beginning in the Abbasid period, rabbinic and other religious elites began producing libraries of prescriptive texts detailing the ritual and personal laws that they expected their followers to obey, including many that theoretically dictated central aspects of women's lives. Geniza legal documents suggest how these texts dictated legal practice on the ground, within rabbinic courts whose coercive powers were limited but that were nonetheless widely used by Jews despite their access to other legal venues.

This chapter provides an introduction to these courts focused on the broader Islamicate legal culture in which they operated, a context that helps explain how they administered rabbinic law. In the first section of the chapter, I explain why Fatimid and Ayyubid rulers permitted their Jewish subjects to operate their own courts, and discuss the puzzle presented by these courts' success despite their lack of effective enforcement mechanisms. The second and third sections provide one answer to this puzzle, by arguing that rabbinic court officials gained social legitimacy in part by engaging in legal practices, and issuing legal products, understood to bear a particular type of technical religious legal authority widely accepted throughout the medieval Islamic Middle East. The chapter's second section traces how this model of authority developed among both Muslim and *dhimmī* religious elites in Abbasid Iraq. In the third and final section, I examine its impact on Jewish legal practice in Fatimid and Ayyubid Egypt through a close reading of Geniza legal documents—one of the main source types used throughout the rest of the book, and the one most central to its arguments about the law—as social and political instruments.

Legal documents were ubiquitous in medieval Islamic societies. Although Muslim jurists theoretically viewed written records as suspect, the very reason for this mistrust—documents' capacity to acquire a life of their own, independent of the people who appear in them—rendered them indispensable in

2. T-S 18 J 3.2. See Zinger, "Women, Gender and Law," 116–124, on this theme in women's petitions. See ibid., esp. Chapters 3 and 4, on socially unprotected women's tenuous position in the courtroom.

legal practice. This was especially true in Jewish courts, whose officials used documents—specifically, technically valid private deeds—to assert legal authority. Documentary production was not the only reason for rabbinic courts' success. But it is one worth taking seriously among others, and one particularly important for my purposes, because it helps explain not only what drew Jewish litigants to rabbinic courts, but also the type of legal system that they encountered there. The political conditions under which these courts operated encouraged officials and litigants alike to reproduce closely the technical forms of rabbinic law; yet they also limited its social impact, ensuring that women's legal outcomes often depended on factors other than the letter of prescriptive law.

Rabbinic Courts and the Islamic State

Jews in major cities and some smaller towns throughout Fatimid and Ayyubid Egypt and Syria maintained local communal courts that oversaw, ratified, and recorded transactions, agreements, and arguments among Jews (they did not handle cases between Jews and Muslims or Christians): sales, gifts, loans, commercial contracts and disputes, and those related to marriage, divorce, and inheritance. These courts have a long prehistory, but it is difficult to trace. Classical rabbinic and early medieval (gaonic) texts composed in the Sasanian empire, in Roman Palestine, and in Abbasid Iraq often mention rabbinic judges; but they offer few reliable details about the political contexts in which these judges functioned, and it is not clear whether documents produced in their orbit survive.[3] In contrast, the Geniza corpus contains thousands of rabbinic legal documents produced in Fatimid and Ayyubid Egypt and Syria, especially Fustat. (Dozens of Karaite legal documents were also preserved in the Geniza, but we know much less about the courts that produced them.)[4]

The earliest Geniza legal documents predate the Fatimid conquest. They attest to a mature tradition of Hebrew and Aramaic legal diplomatics known to scribes throughout tenth-century Egypt and Syria—in Damascus, Jerusalem, and Fustat, and in towns such as Qugandima and Tinnīs in the Nile

3. On rabbinic courts in late antiquity, see below, n. 66. Second-century Greek, Aramaic, and Hebrew legal documents featuring Jews survived in the Judean desert, but it is not clear whether they are distinctively rabbinic; see Cotton, "Change and Continuity in Late Legal Papyri" and the scholarship cited there. A marriage contract from fifth-century Antinoopolis presents an important exception: Sirat at al., *La 'Ketouba' de Cologne*. On rabbinic courts in Abbasid and Buyid Iraq, see Brody, *Geonim of Babylonia*, 57–58, and Simonsohn, *A Common Justice*, 135–142.

4. Most of these are marriage documents; see Olszowy-Schlanger, *KMD*. On the problem of Karaite courts, see eadem, "Karaite Legal Documents," "Lettre de Divorce Caraïte." The question is complicated by the fact that at least some Karaite documents were composed by Rabbanite scribes: Rustow, *Heresy*, 266–288.

FIGURE 2.1. T-S. Ar. 18 1.136. Entries in a court notebook from the rabbinic court of Fustat, 1159. On the left-hand page a woman's dowry items and their values are listed, together with the conditions attached to her marriage (see also Chapter 7). Reproduced by kind permission of the Syndics of Cambridge University Library.

Delta—but are so few in number that it is impossible to recover much about the institutional contexts in which they were composed.[5] This changes dramatically from the start of the early eleventh century, when far more documents begin to appear; their language gradually changes to Judeo-Arabic; and they reveal an increasingly coherent and formalized court system centered in Fustat, which remains abundantly documented through the beginning of the Mamluk period.

This corpus provides a form of granular evidence for ordinary legal practice unlike any available from elsewhere in the pre-Ottoman Middle East, which has yet to be systematically exploited. Although Geniza legal documents have been subject to detailed study for more than eighty years, they have never been closely examined as a record of legal practice: that is, as

5. Published dated tenth-century Geniza documents include: from Egypt, T-S 12.154 (Qugandima, 945), Bodl. MS Heb. b. 12.6 and Bodl. MS Heb. b. 12.29 (Fustat, 959), T-S 12.462 (Fustat, after 966), T-S 12.499 (Fustat, 969), and from Syria, T-S AS 146.66 (Damascus, 933), T-S 16.181 (same, multiple documents), and Bodl. MS Heb. d. 65.30 (Damascus, 956).

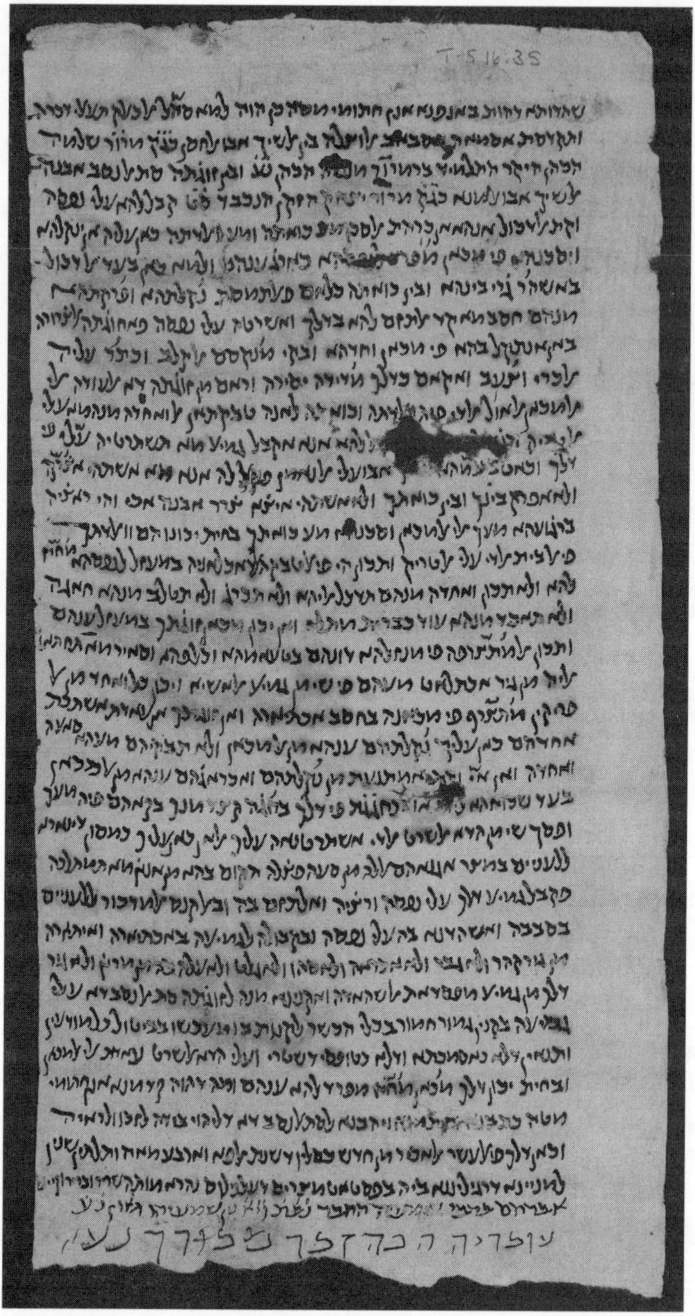

FIGURE 2.2. T-S 16.35. A legal document issued to a woman by the rabbinic court of Fustat, ca. 1118. The document records her husband's promise to move her into a separate room away from her mother and sisters-in-law and not to let them disturb her there. (See further Chapter 8.) Reproduced by kind permission of the Syndics of Cambridge University Library.

the residue of a complex legal system whose institutional habits they reveal.[6] Such an assessment will be possible only after close diachronic study of the entire Geniza legal record—a major desideratum in Geniza studies, but one that lies beyond the scope of this chapter. In what follows, however, I preliminarily assess Geniza legal documents to pursue the more modest goal of explaining rabbinic legal authority in medieval Egypt from an angle that prior scholarship has not addressed in detail, namely the social ideas about religious law that helped shape these documents' production and that contributed to their utility.

JEWISH SELF-GOVERNMENT AND ITS LIMITS

A scholarly paradigm dominant among Jewish historians for much of the twentieth century viewed medieval Jews as essentially detached from the political fabric of the states in which they lived. This approach emphasized Jews' organization within what Salo Baron termed "almost extraterritorial" autonomous communities (in Yitzhak Baer's words, "immanent creations in our people's history," and in Goitein's, "a state not only within the state, but beyond the state")—self-enclosed, transregional hierarchies that interacted with non-Jewish governments only peripherally, through the Jewish political elites to whom kings and caliphs alike delegated the task of communal self-rule.[7] Implicit in this model was the assumption that these elites exerted direct, uncomplicated authority over the Jewish populations whom the state had entrusted to their control.

For the Jews documented in the Geniza, it has become increasingly clear that this picture is an illusion, and one incompatible with the structure of both Fatimid and Ayyubid rule. It is true that Geniza Jews, both Rabbanite and Karaite, formed coherent social communities bound together by near-exclusive ties of kinship and ordered by an array of distinctive communal institutions, chief among them synagogues, courts, and systems of public welfare. But membership in these communities was neither formal nor tightly policed, and their boundaries were permeable, breached often through social contacts with Muslims and Christians and occasionally through conversion.[8] Recent scholarship has emphasized that this porousness extended also to Jewish communities' political organization, which was "jagged" and complex, mirroring

6. Goitein is the only scholar to have provided a general account of legal practice in the Geniza corpus, *Med. Soc.*, 2:311–344. This survey is a remarkable achievement, but only scratches the surface of the available evidence, as noted by Zinger, "Women, Gender and Law," 24–39.

7. Baron, *Jewish Community* 1:vii; Baer, "Origins of the Organization of the Jewish Community," 3, Goitein, *Med. Soc.*, 2:1.

8. See Introduction, at n. 41.

their members' mixed social commitments.[9] Far from supporting a hegemonic communal hierarchy, both empires' political cultures ensured that the channels of power accessible to individual Jews neither ran in a single top-down stream within the Jewish community, nor were confined to it.

Both the Fatimids and Ayyubids ruled their empires according to a model of government established by the Abbasids, which permitted religious courts run by and for non-Muslims to operate alongside Muslim judges (*qāḍīs*) and in the shadow of the state's own system of legal tribunals, through which any subject, whether Muslim or non-Muslim, could present appeals (*maẓālim*, literally "[complaints against] abuses") directly to the government.[10] The Abbasids began directly appointing *qāḍīs* in the 770s, under the caliph al-Manṣūr; a century later, the nominally Abbasid governor ibn Ṭūlūn began holding *maẓālim* sessions directly with his subjects. The Fatimids absorbed and expanded both institutions, allowing *qāḍīs* of diverse legal affiliation to operate under the authority of a formally Ismāʿīlī chief judge (*qāḍī al-quḍāt*) while also responding to complaints and requests filed through *maẓālim* petitions at court.[11] Ṣalāḥ al-Dīn, the founder of the Ayyubid dynasty, cultivated a program of Sunnī reform in Egypt powered by the establishment of new religious institutions and the consolidation of existing ones, including a more robustly centralized judiciary under exclusive Shāfiʿī control.[12] But neither he nor his descendants collapsed the difference between *qāḍī* and *maẓālim* courts, nor did they bar *qāḍīs* of other legal schools from holding local judicial positions. Under the Ayyubids as under their predecessors, the result remained an atomized political system in which rulers, bureaucrats, and judges maintained authority through a mixture of bureaucratic structures

9. See Rustow, "The Genizah and Jewish Communal History" (the term "jagged" appears there), and Cohen, "Jewish Communal Organization."

10. That is, the Abbasid empire was legally pluralist, in ways similar to its Roman and Sasanian predecessors. For Rome, see Ando, "Legal Pluralism in Practice," and see further below, n. 66.

11. Before al-Manṣūr's reign, local *qāḍīs* throughout the empire had been appointed by provincial governors. The Fatimids replaced the Mālikī *qāḍī* of Fustat and installed the Ismāʿīlī ʿAlī b. al-Nuʿmān as *qāḍī al-quḍāt*, a position occupied by Ismāʿīlī judges at least until the reign of Badr al-Jamālī (1074–94), when the history of the office becomes obscure. In 1131, the *wazīr* al-Afḍal appointed four chief judges from different *madhhabs*, presaging the multiple-*qāḍī* system established by the Mamluks. See Tillier, "Les 'premiers' cadis de Fusṭāṭ," idem, "The *Qāḍīs* of Fusṭāṭ-Misr," idem, "Du pagarque au cadi," Walker, "The Relationship Between Chief *Qāḍī* and Chief *Dāʿī*," Lev, *State and Society*, 133–140, Allouche, "Establishment of Four Chief Judgeships." On the development of the *maẓālim* system in Egypt, see Tillier, "*Qāḍīs* and the Political Use of the *Maẓālim* Jurisdiction"; Marina Rustow's forthcoming book on *maẓālim* petitions will address continuities under the Fatimids.

12. Shāfiʿī *qāḍīs*: Lev, *Saladin in Egypt*, Jackson, *Islamic Law and the State*, 53–54. On *maz ʿālim* under the Ayyubids: Nielsen, *Secular Justice*.

and personal patronage networks, allowing for multiple points of contact between Muslim officials and elite and non-elite Jews alike.[13]

Against this backdrop, Jewish communal history during the core Geniza centuries can be roughly divided into two distinct periods. From the Fatimid conquest of Egypt until the last third of the eleventh century, Jewish political organization was particularly diffuse and multifocal. For much of this period, the Palestinian *ge'onim* (heads of the Rabbanite academy in Jerusalem, who claimed institutional descent from the Sanhedrin)[14] asserted authority over Rabbanite Jews under Fatimid control, in part by requesting investiture documents from successive Fatimid caliphs. But the actual power that they exerted over individuals and institutions alike was limited and contingent. It was limited even in conception, because major Fatimid cities housed up to three sets of Jewish courts, synagogues, and overlapping administrative bureaucracies, respectively affiliated with the Palestinian *ge'onim*; their Iraqi counterparts, the *ge'onim* of Baghdad (who represented themselves as heirs to the rabbinic leadership of the Sasanian empire); and the Karaite academy in Jerusalem.[15] But the reality was even messier than this tripartite schema suggests, since local leaders affiliated with each center often maintained social and financial ties with both of the others, as well as with courtiers associated directly with the Fatimid court.[16] And it is not clear, for example, how directly the Palestinian *ge'onim* controlled even the rabbinic law court affiliated with the Palestinian-rite synagogue of Fustat, let alone those operating in smaller towns throughout Egypt.[17]

13. See Humphreys, *From Saladin to the Mongols*, 22–23, on the importance of patronage networks in Ayyubid politics.

14. The academy (*yeshiva*) is attested in Jerusalem as early as 935 and remained there until shortly after the Seljuq conquest of Jerusalem in 1073, when it relocated to Tyre and then to Damascus, where it eventually fades from view. Maṣliaḥ b. Shelomo, the son of its last known head, adopted the title *ga'on* when he became *ra'īs* in Fustat in 1127, and later *ru'asā'* continued to use it into the Mamluk period (on the office of *ra'īs*, see immediately below). See Wechsler, "New Data from Saadia," Gil, *Palestine* (English ed.), 490–776, Goitein *Palestinian Jewry*, 52–114, Cohen, "Administrative Relations," idem, *Jewish Self-Government*, 79–101; on Maṣliaḥ's lineage, see Goitein, "Prayers from the Geniza for Fatimid Caliphs," 50–51, and for a list of all known Palestinian *ge'onim*, Rustow, *Heresy*, 363.

15. Rustow, *Heresy*, 3–35, including a detailed review of earlier studies.

16. Rustow, *Heresy*, 67–108, eadem, "The Genizah and Jewish Communal History," Ben-Sasson, "Varieties of Inter-communal Relations," Bareket, *Fustat on the Nile*.

17. A petition submitted on behalf of the *ga'on* Shelomo b. Yehuda (r. 1025–51) asks the Fatimid caliph al-Mustanṣir (r. 1036–94) to recognize his authority over Rabbanite judges throughout the empire: T-S 24.43. This reveals that Shelomo claimed control of the courts, but another surviving petition submitted around the same time suggests that his control may have been limited in practice; it asks al-Mustanṣir to recognize the local authority of a judge in Alexandria whom Shelomo had already appointed. (T-S NS 320.45.) See further Goitein, "New Sources on the Palestinian Gaonate," idem, "Local Jewish Community," Rustow, *Heresy*, 87–99, and on Efrayim, Bareket, *Fustat on the Nile*, 129–159.

Jewish communal authority became more centralized between the 1060s and 1090s, as a single communal leader operating in Fustat and Cairo, the Head of the Jews (*ra'īs al-yahūd*) gradually acquired control over Jewish institutions throughout the Fatimid empire. The office of *ra'īs* lasted throughout the Ayyubid period and beyond, overseeing an increasingly institutionalized court system whose judges were directly appointed from the capital. Yet painstaking documentary work has revealed that the office of *ra'īs* was not, as scholars once thought, created from above by the Fatimid state, but was the product of efforts by a shifting network of local Jewish elites to consolidate their own administrative authority.[18] This distinction matters because it shaped the character of the office. Even into the Ayyubid period, when the office of *ra'īs* became a hereditary post held by Maimonides' descendants, there is ample evidence that his practical authority and that of his entourage continued to depend as much on the patronage ties they maintained with their subjects as on the approval of the state.[19]

In their dealings with each other as well as with non-Jews, Jewish leaders and Jewish non-elites thus took active part in the political culture of the empires in which they lived. This realization has helped make sense of much evidence overlooked by older models, and has unlocked an entire vocabulary of social and political relationships previously hidden from view within the Geniza corpus.[20] At the same time, it complicates aspects of Jewish communal life that once seemed straightforward. Eliding the state's complex relationship to its Jewish subjects had allowed scholars to view rabbinic authority as monolithic and uncomplicated, a natural outcome of medieval Jews' own uniform piety. If this idea now appears untenable, it becomes necessary to explain how power was actually distributed within Jewish communal institutions. In the case of rabbinic courts, the problem is particularly acute: at first glance, it is not at all clear what hold rabbinic judges and court scribes possessed over the litigants who appeared before them.

18. Cohen, *Jewish Self-Government*. (See further Rustow, *Heresy*, 99–107.) Cohen's study ends with Maṣliaḥ b. Shelomo's tenure in 1126, and the later *ru'asā'* have not been studied as thoroughly. See preliminarily Goitein, "The Title and Office of the Nagid," idem, "Twilight of the House of Maimonides," Ben-Sasson, "Maimonides in Egypt," Friedman, *India Book*, 4:227–252, idem, "*Teshuvat R. Yeḥi'el bar Elyaqim*," and the following note.

19. This is illustrated by the best-studied political episode involving a *ra'īs* after Maṣliaḥ: a communal dispute between factions supporting and opposing liturgical innovations imposed by Avraham Maimonides (r. 1204–37). Goitein, *Med. Soc.*, 5:474–496, idem, "Documents on Abraham Maimonides," Rustow, "Limits of Communal Autonomy," 140–146, Russ-Fishbane, "Between Politics and Piety," Friedman, "Abraham Maimonides on Leadership."

20. Rustow, "Benefaction," and see further Goldberg, "Friendship and Hierarchy."

WHY DID LITIGANTS USE *DHIMMĪ* COURTS?

Legal Practice in the Bet Din

Because so little systematic work has been conducted on Geniza courts, there is a great deal that we do not yet understand about how they operated. Most of the legal documents preserved in the Geniza were produced by the *bet din* of the Palestinian-rite Rabbanite synagogue of Fustat in which the Geniza chamber itself was housed, and which eventually became the central law court of the *ru'asā'* (Heads) under Mevorakh and after. But the relationships between this court and others—including both a court that seems to have been housed in the Iraqi-rite synagogue of Fustat at least through the eleventh century,[21] and local rabbinic courts elsewhere throughout Egypt and Syria—remain to be traced in detail, as do its composition, personnel, and most importantly, the nature of its legal practices. Rabbinic courts were staffed by a minimum of three judges, who under the *ru'asā'* were headed by a career chief judge and assisted by career court scribes.[22] But it is not yet clear how these figures interacted to produce the legal documents from which we know them, much less how these interactions evolved over time. As we will see, almost all Geniza legal documents are framed as private deeds of testimony—records of transactions, agreements, and declarations that disclose little about the courtroom protocols and interactions that led to their production. Some scholars have assumed that many of the legal events described in these testimonies actually resulted from judges' hierarchical rulings, while others have viewed them as outcomes of some form of mediation.[23]

But even with these gaps in our knowledge, two features of the Geniza legal record raise obvious questions about the nature of these courts' political power. First, the Jews who appear in it freely used Islamic *qāḍī* and state *maẓālim* courts in addition to Jewish ones.[24] Rabbanite jurists viewed this as a problem to the extent that it directly challenged their own authority. Court officials and prescriptive legal authors alike harshly condemned Jews who unilaterally sued a Jewish opponent in Islamic court in order to secure a better outcome than they could expect before the *bet din*, especially

21. T-S 13 J 1.10 is a rare surviving document produced by this court.

22. See above, n. 6.

23. For the former view, see Goitein, *Med. Soc.*, 2:334–345, Ackerman-Lieberman, "Commercial Forms and Legal Norms." For a nuanced discussion of Goitein's argument highlighting the many ambiguities that it leaves unresolved, see Zinger, "Women, Gender and Law," 31–38.

24. *Qāḍī* courts: Marglin, "Jews in *Sharī'a* Courts," summarizing previous treatments; *Maẓālim* courts: Rustow, "The Legal Status of *Ḍimmī-s*."

if they did so after the case had already been heard there.[25] But this does not amount to a claim to legal exclusivity. On the contrary, most rabbinic legal authors assumed that their adherents would procure Islamic legal documents as proof of certain kinds of transactions, and found legal grounds for permitting them to do so. They also permitted litigants to pursue another Jew in Islamic court, even without his consent, if he had already been summoned before a Jewish court and had refused to obey its directives.[26] (In other words, it was fine to invoke Islamic power against another Jew, as long as one did so to support rather than undermine Jewish communal leaders' decisions.) Geniza documents routinely reveal Jews appealing to Islamic courts for both reasons, often with explicit permission from the *bet din*; they also reveal that leaders themselves routinely turned to *maẓālim* tribunals to gain leverage in their own political conflicts.[27] Some documents also suggest that court personnel could be relatively sanguine about Jews who bilaterally agreed to bring cases before a *qāḍī* without involving the Jewish court at all, although these actions are naturally less visible in the primarily rabbinic legal corpus preserved in the Geniza.[28] However Jewish courts exerted

25. That is, to override the *bet din*'s decision, or to pursue rights recognized in Islamic but not rabbinic law. This disapproval was gendered; cases of the latter type mentioned in both prescriptive texts and Geniza documents often involve women's inheritance and divorce rights. See Zinger, "Women, Gender and Law," 46–72.

26. Rabbinic jurists are often described as monolithically opposed to Jews using non-Jewish courts in all circumstances, but their opposition was in fact more qualified than this. On the nuances of classical and medieval rabbinic approaches to this question, see Simonsohn, *A Common Justice*, 57–60, 184–195. Maimonides, writing almost two centuries after the latest texts that Simonsohn discusses, condemns use of Islamic courts more severely than his predecessors: "Anyone who pursues judgment in non-Jewish courts . . . is wicked, and it is as if he disgraced and insulted and raised his hand against the Torah" (*MT*, *Sanhedrin*, 26:7, based on bGit. 88b but using far harsher language). But even he permits litigants to sue an opponent who refuses to cooperate with the *bet din* in Islamic court, as long as the *bet din* agrees (ibid., and see also *MT*, *Malve ve-Love*, 27:1, Maimonides, *Responsa* no. 193). See further Cohen, *Maimonides and the Merchants*, and the next note.

27. Permission from the *bet din*: *Med. Soc.*, 2:401–402. For example, T-S 13 J 1.6, Fustat, 1024, a document appointing an agent to locate a woman's husband and sue him for divorce in a court of his choosing, "either Jewish or non-Jewish." Petitions from communal leaders: see most recently Rustow, "The Legal Status of *Ḏimmī-s*," 316–319.

28. See, for example, Mosseri VII 27, an administrative letter from the first half of the eleventh century that describes a woman excommunicated by the local court of Ṣahrajt, Egypt, for having sued her husband for divorce before a *qāḍī*. On the verso, however, a witness testifies that the couple had mutually agreed to appear before the *qāḍī*—a version of events that court officials in Fustat seem to have viewed as exculpatory. This may have changed under Maimonides' influence during the Ayyubid period; see idem, *Responsa* nos. 27, 408, and on Maimonides' possible long-term effects, see Cohen, "Correspondence and Social Control."

authority, it was not by claiming sole jurisdiction over Jewish litigants, even the most loyal ones.

The *bet din* was not unique in this respect, since Muslim litigants also had access to more than one legal venue at a time.[29] But a second feature of its authority was particular to Jewish (and presumably other *dhimmī*) courts alone: for most of the period documented in the Geniza, its officials lacked direct means of coercion.[30] A few Geniza documents from the early eleventh century mention rabbinic judges sentencing Jews to flogging for specifically religious offenses (e.g., keeping a shop open on the Sabbath), although none make clear whether the floggings were to be administered by agents of the Jewish community or of the state, or indeed whether they actually occurred at all.[31] After this, references to corporal punishments imposed directly by court officials disappear from the Geniza record; the *bet din* seems to have been able to punish Jewish litigants physically only by turning them over to the state for judgment.[32] Short of this, rabbinic courts had three means of suasion at their disposal: they could require litigants to swear oaths of varying religious weight, fine them for legal infractions or for breach of contract, or excommunicate them, a form of social ban that theoretically prevented them from interacting with other Jews.

These are not necessarily trivial sanctions. But surviving documents suggest that in practice, all three were limited coercive tools. Fear of lying under oath might encourage a litigant's cooperation when he was in the courtroom, but could not ensure that he would show up there in the first place nor obey officials' orders after he left.[33] The fines stipulated in Geniza documents can be remarkably large, but this mattered little if there was no way to force

29. Including not only *qāḍī* vs. *maẓālim* courts, but also *qāḍī*s from different *madhhabs*. See Rapoport, "Legal Diversity" (on the Mamluk period, but with some implications for earlier centuries).

30. *Qāḍī*s did not maintain their own police force either, and were subordinate both to the *qāḍī al-quḍāt* and to state officials. They nonetheless possessed far greater executive power than did the *bet din*, not only because some controlled armed guards, but also because *qāḍī*s maintained closer ties with state officials and often worked with them to administer punishments and confiscate goods. Goitein, *Med. Soc.*, 2:364–373, Goldberg, *Trade and Institutions*, 162–163. See also Tillier, "Judicial Authority and Qāḍīs' Autonomy," on ideas about *qāḍī*s' judicial autonomy in the Abbasid period, and Lange, *Justice, Punishment and the Medieval Muslim Imagination*, 44–48, for comparative discussion of *qāḍī*s' penal authority under the Seljuqs.

31. T-S 8 J 7.18 (written by Efrayim b. Shemarya, about a Sabbath-violating shopkeeper), T-S 18 J 1.6 (1028, Cairo, about a ritual slaughterer accused of malpractice), T-S 13 J 33.4 (about a cantor accused of slandering a communal official).

32. Goitein, *Med. Soc.*, 2:371, Rustow, *Heresy*, 73.

33. Both Jewish and Islamic legal tradition take oaths very seriously, a value reflected in medieval Islamicate political culture: Mottahedeh, *Loyalty and Leadership*, 42–50. On courtroom oaths in Islamic law, see Bechor, *God in the Courtroom*, 16–142; on gaonic use

litigants to pay them; in fact, all available evidence indicates that they were routinely renegotiated and rarely, if ever, paid in full.[34] Excommunication, the most severe punishment that the court could apply, bore theoretically drastic personal and economic consequences. But it was nearly impossible to implement perfectly—Geniza evidence for people isolated by the ban is remarkably thin on the ground—a shortcoming that meant it was best imposed infrequently, lest its overuse damage court officials' own credibility.[35]

Jewish courts thus lacked effective means to enforce judgments or the terms of contracts that they had issued, or even to compel litigants to appear before them in the first place. Yet the same record that reveals this also demonstrates that they remained robust and well-patronized institutions throughout the Fatimid and Ayyubid periods. Even without any tangible mechanisms forcing them to do so, many Jews went to considerable expense to negotiate interpersonal conflicts and document their transactions in rabbinic court. Why did they do so? What did Jews hope to achieve by turning to the *bet din* that they could not have achieved equally well by turning to a *qāḍī*, filing a *maẓālim* petition, or engaging in purely social negotiations outside the courtroom?

The Nature of Rabbinic Power

Scholars' answers to this question have mostly focused on the advantages that rabbinic courts presented as convenient, low-risk forums for dispute resolution. The most complete and cogent account appears in Jessica Goldberg's *Trade and Institutions in the Medieval Mediterranean*, which traces the legal choices described in Geniza commercial letters from the eleventh century.[36] On the one hand, these letters reveal the hidden social costs of legal action before the *bet din*, describing lawsuits there as time-consuming public spectacles that hurt the professional reputations of all involved. On the other hand, turning to a *qāḍī* was riskier; Jewish merchants were less socially powerful or legally competent in Islamic courts than in Jewish ones, faced greater procedural charges there, and exposed themselves to potential imprisonment, torture, and loss of goods. Geniza merchants responded to these possibilities in multiple ways: by protecting their transactions through written contracts and acts of witnessing that could potentially be deployed in either legal arena, while attempting to resolve disputes extrajudicially when this was possible, and bringing suit primarily in Jewish court when it was not. These choices

of oaths as a coercive mechanism, see Libson, *Jewish and Islamic Law*, 113–15; on attitudes toward oaths reflected in the Geniza, see Goitein, *Med. Soc.*, 2:156, 340–41.

34. Goitein, *Med. Soc.*, 2:330–31, Rustow, *Heresy*, 251–52, Zinger, "Women, Gender and Law," 251–57.

35. See Rustow, *Heresy*, 204–206, and the literature cited there.

36. Ibid., 150–164.

suggest that Jewish courts were effective precisely because they operated alongside more powerful Islamic legal venues to which litigants could also turn. The threat that one's legal opponent could potentially escalate his case to a *qāḍī* court or state tribunal placed greater pressure on both parties to cooperate with each other before things went that far, and thus helped ensure merchants' commitment to the Jewish legal arena.

This model convincingly explains how rabbinic courts could be effective despite their executive limitations, within the space carved out for them by other Fatimid and Ayyubid institutions. As Elka Klein first argued about thirteenth-century Barcelona (in direct response to Baron and Baer), medieval Jewish institutions were not always engaged in a zero-sum competition for authority with the non-Jews who ruled above them.[37] They could instead gain strength from policies that furthered kings' and caliphs' own interests. But if the Geniza legal record supports Goldberg's account of complementary Jewish and Islamic legal powers, it also allows us to extend this model further. Documents produced by and for rabbinic courts themselves suggest that they attracted litigants not only by providing comfort and security to well-connected Jewish sub-elites in the shadow of the state's hard power. Beyond this, rabbinic judges and scribes also wielded their own more active forms of soft power over Jews of the lower as well as middling classes.

One such form of power, which I will not explore in detail although it merits close attention in its own right, lay in the *bet din*'s control of resources. Bureaucratic correspondence, legal documents, and administrative records all reveal that from at least the early eleventh century on, rabbinic judges and other court personnel routinely administered Jews' estates, choosing between competing heirs' claims and allotting—or denying—support and property to widows and orphans. They also controlled charitable bequests, often left as perpetual endowments (Heb. *heqdesh*, Arab. *waqf*) for the community's poor and for the upkeep of synagogues and scholars.[38] Another less tangible, yet equally important, source of rabbinic court officials' power is more germane to the concerns of this book: their claim to specialized legal knowledge of a kind that carried cultural weight throughout Fatimid and Ayyubid Egypt and beyond—among not only Jews and other *dhimmīs*, but also the Muslims who ruled over them.

The Islamic societies that developed from the remains of the classical Abbasid empire (750–945) shared certain common social and political assumptions. These included the idea of an Islamic social order that comprised different religious groups, both Islamic and *dhimmī*, each possessing characteristic

37. Klein, *Jews, Christian Society and Royal Power*, 142–161; on this point among Fatimid and Ayyubid Jews, see the studies by Rustow cited above, ns. 16 and 19.

38. Gil, *Pious Foundations*, 21–22. On charitable endowments more generally, see ibid., 1–118, Goitein, *Med. Soc.*, 2:112–137, Cohen, *Poverty and Charity*, 200–211.

bodies of religious law (*sharīʿa*): detailed corpora of normative rules dictating their members' ritual and social behavior, articulated in written prescriptive texts, and (in some cases) administered in communal religious courts. This model resonates with Muslim political theorists' general agreement that laws must proceed from some form of prophetic revelation to be legitimate,[39] although Muslims were naturally more concerned with explaining and justifying their own *sharīʿa* than that of others. The role of non-Islamic law in the Islamic public sphere never became an explicit focus of medieval Islamic thought. But medieval *dhimmī*s' own writings reveal that many Muslim rulers implicitly valued *dhimmī* loyalty to *dhimmī* legal tradition. Jewish and Christian texts written under the Buyids, Fatimids, Ayyubids, and Mamluks alike suggest that accusing another Jew or Christian of deviating from authentic Jewish or Christian law could be a successful strategy for gaining Muslim rulers' sympathies.[40]

This stance shaped Jewish and Christian leaders' own self-presentation, both when communicating with state officials and with the populations whom they hoped to lead. The idea that medieval Jews naturally used Jewish courts out of naïve piety has been justly criticized. But this does not mean that the specifically rabbinic legal character of the Geniza courts' practice did not matter. In a milieu where almost everyone (or at any rate, almost all elites) took the idea of religious law seriously, rabbinic courts' claims to rabbinic legal expertise were crucial to their social legitimacy.

Some Geniza evidence indicates that Fatimid and Ayyubid bureaucrats occasionally lent their own weight to the *bet din*'s authority. Several documents describe *qāḍī*s and state officials who went so far as to directly sponsor rabbinic legal practice, redirecting Jewish litigants who had appeared before them to a Jewish court for judgment or further legal action. For example, a document issued by the rabbinic court of Alexandria in 1152 describes a mutual declaration made by two men annulling the terms of a settlement they had previously reached there, so that they might settle the case anew through a quittance drawn up in Muslim court and written according to an Islamic formulary.[41] The declaration was formalized and recorded before a represen-

39. On medieval Islamic theories about natural and divine law, see Crone, *God's Rule*, 3–16, 259–285.

40. In state petitions, Jewish communal leaders sometimes accuse each other of religious innovation (*bidʿa*), an argument that applies Islamic ideas about authentic *sharīʿa* to non-Muslim law—and that thus suggests state officials understood *dhimmī* legal legitimacy in these terms. This rhetoric becomes more pronounced in the Ayyubid and especially Mamluk periods, but is visible earlier; for examples, see Cohen, "Jews in the Mamluk Environment" (esp. 439–340), Rustow "The Legal Status of *Ḍimmī-s*," 316–319, idem, "Limits of Communal Autonomy," el-Leithy, "Coptic Culture and Conversion," 435–439.

41. Bodl. MS Heb. d. 68.99. One of the litigants, Shemu'el b. Yehuda, appears as both litigant and trustee in many Egyptian rabbinic court papers from the 1130s through the

tative of the local *qāḍī* who had accompanied the men to court, apparently because he did not want to give them the quittance without ensuring that they had properly voided their earlier rabbinic-formula agreement. These cases are not numerous enough to clearly attest to a Fatimid or Ayyubid version of what Klein termed Jewish "autonomy by design," that is, some form of systematic government policy requiring Jews to involve Jewish courts in their affairs. [42] But they do suggest that the dual legal arena in which most Jews participated was implicitly sanctioned by the state.

But more often, the Geniza legal corpus indicates that Islamicate ideas about religious law bolstered Jewish courts indirectly by providing jurists, judges, scribes, and litigants with a shared conceptual framework for understanding rabbinic legal practice and a common idiom for expressing its importance and authority. These ideas and idioms pervade medieval Rabbanite legal literature and legal documents alike—including some features that have come to be seen as intrinsic to rabbinic legal discourse even though they emerged fully only during the Abbasid period. To understand how the Jews documented in the Geniza understood, developed, and deployed these ideas, we must begin by stepping back in time and over a thousand miles east, to Abbasid Iraq, where these ideas developed and where Jewish legal texts first began to be published and circulated in written form.

Prescriptive Law and Religious Identity

By the time the Fatimids conquered Egypt in 969, the forms of legal practice and discourse that would hold sway throughout their rule and after had already taken shape. Medieval Islamicate legal culture emerged from late ancient precedents, but developed its characteristic features under the Abbasids in eighth- and ninth-century Iraq and Iran. This legal culture was the product of enormous historical changes that altered the social meaning of religious affiliation among populations throughout the Middle East, and thus changed how elites and non-elites alike understood their own religious identities and their allegiances to the religious leaders who claimed authority over them.

RABBINIC LAW AND GAONIC LEGAL WRITING

For Rabbanite Jews, of course, the idea of religious law long preceded the Abbasids. The vast core of what medieval Jews recognized as rabbinic law developed before the Islamic conquests, in Roman Palestine and Sasanian Iraq. It is known through an interrelated corpus of works widely assumed to have

1160s: Goitein, *Med. Soc.*, 3:9, 296–297. For other examples, see Maimonides, *Responsa* no. 191, and below, Chapter 6; see also Goitein, *Med. Soc.*, 2:405–406.

42. Klein, *Jews, Christian Society and Royal Power*.

been composed between the first and sixth or seventh centuries, although some were first published in writing only in the eighth century. The longest and ultimately most influential of these is the Babylonian Talmud, a massive, multilayered compilation of legal, narrative, exegetical, and homiletical discussions among rabbinic elites in the Roman and Sasanian empires, which Jews in pre- and early Islamic Iraq apparently preserved through oral recitation. The Talmud provides little concrete information about how it came to exist in the form in which it has come down to us, and scholars disagree about many of the most basic aspects of its textual history, including when it was redacted, under what conditions, and why.[43] What is clear, however, is that for its late ancient creators—the anonymous scholars who compiled the text and who narrate its final discursive layer—*talmud*, the study of legal and narrative traditions, was a creative scholastic activity aimed at generating legal norms through dialectical analysis of traditions, not merely an unfiltered transmission of such traditions.[44]

At some point, this activity stopped and was replaced by a different form of legal learning, one that seems to have evolved most significantly under the Abbasids in the eighth and ninth centuries. By the time the Abbasid empire dissolved in the tenth century, rabbinic authors across the Middle East had come to view the Talmudic text as the canonical basis of a fixed system of normative law. Rather than engage in open-ended analysis of traditions, as does the Talmud itself, jurists now used them to derive unambiguous legal meaning. This transformation was largely accomplished by scholars affiliated with the gaonic *yeshivot* of Iraq, located originally in Sura and Pumbedita on the Euphrates, and from around 890 in Baghdad, the Abbasid capital.[45] We know only slightly more about these *yeshivot* than we do about rabbinic institutions in late antiquity. The only detailed accounts of their history and operation appear in two texts from the later tenth century—a historical responsum by the *ga'on* Sherira b. Ḥananya, and a brief work by the otherwise unknown Natan

43. Most scholars date the Talmud's latest layer to the sixth or seventh centuries, but arguments have been raised for as early as the fifth century and as late as the eighth (or even after). For summaries of the central debates in this field, see on the Talmud's dating, Kalmin "Formation and Character" (to which should now be added Halivni, *Formation of the Babylonian Talmud*); on its institutional setting, Becker, "Comparative Study of 'Scholasticism,'" 95–97; and on its authors' intellectual motives, Vidas, *Tradition and the Formation of the Talmud*, 3–9.

44. See especially Vidas, ibid., 115–149, who argues that this scholastic innovation was central to the Talmudic authors' own self-conception, in opposition to contemporary rabbinic "transmitters" who simply preserved traditions—an ideology that contrasts sharply with the gaonic conservatism described below.

45. 890: This date is attested for the *yeshiva* of Pumbedita; the Suran academy may have moved later, but was located in Baghdad by 928. Brody, *Geonim of Babylonia*, 36, Gil, *Jews in Islamic Countries*, 340, 342–343.

ha-Bavli—both written to persuade Jews in Ifrīqiyya of gaonic authority at a time when it was already failing.[46] But if the *ge'onim* left few reliable historical traces, they did produce a body of works that attest to one of the most important intellectual developments in the history of Judaism: the canonization of the Talmud.

Sometime in the eighth century, gaonic scholars began transcribing and disseminating the first known written copies of Talmudic passages, rendering them portable texts that could be studied far beyond the walls of the *yeshivot* themselves.[47] They did so while forwarding claims for the Talmud's authority that its own authors had never fully expressed. The *ge'onim* treated the Talmud as a form of scripture in the broadest sense: as a closed literary corpus whose contents bore inherent religious authority because they appeared within it and that overrode the authority of competing traditions that did not.[48] (They did not, however, make claims for its exclusivity, but accepted both extra-Talmudic oral traditions and those preserved within other rabbinic works, including the Palestinian Talmud, as valid supplementary sources of normative law.)[49] This stance appears as early as the turn of the eighth century in a famous polemical letter composed by Pirqoy b. Baboy, who identifies himself as the student of a student of Yehuday (*ga'on* of the Suran *yeshiva* around 760). Addressed to rabbinic Jews in Ifrīqiyya and Andalusia, it outlines an aggressive pro-Iraqi ideology based directly on the Talmudic expertise of Iraqi gaonic scholars, who "establish (every) matter on its foundations, and (every) law in its true form, bringing proof from Scripture, and from Mishna, and from Talmud."[50] In contrast, Pirqoy dismisses Palestinian gaonic legal expertise because it derives not from in-depth textual study but from reference to lived religious custom

46. Sherira's responsum: Lewin, *Iggeret*. See further Brody, "Epistle." Natan's account: Neubauer, *Mediaeval Jewish Chronicles*, 2:78–88, Friedlander, "Arabic Original." See further Ben-Sasson, "Structure, Goals, and Content," Brody, *Geonim of Babylonia*, 26–30.

47. Danzig, "From Oral Talmud to Written Talmud." These copies were produced for export only; within the *yeshivot* themselves, the Talmud continued to be transmitted as a formally oral text. (That is, students may have kept private written copies [*hypomnemata*] of Talmudic passages, but did not circulate them as publicly published texts [*syngrammata*]. On this distinction in early Islamic literature, cf. Schoeler, "Writing and Publishing.") Brody, "*Sifrut ha-Ge'onim ve-ha-Teqst ha-Talmudi*," idem, *Geonim of Babylonia*, 156–160, Elman, "Orality and the Redaction of the Babylonian Talmud," Fishman, *Becoming the People of the Talmud*, 20–65.

48. On this stance, see Brody, *Geonim of Babylonia*, 161–66. However, the *ge'onim* did not sacralize each word of the Talmudic text, but rather its "dialogical skeleton." (The phrase is Brody's, ibid., 160.) Again compare Schoeler, "Writing and Publishing," for Islamic parallels.

49. Brody, *Geonim of Babylonia*, 121–122, 171–184, Libson, *Jewish and Islamic Law*, 16–67.

50. Lewin, "*Mi-Seridei ha-Geniza*," 395, 397. On Pirqoy, see Spiegel, "Pirkoi Ben Baboi Controversy," Brody, *Geonim of Babylonia*, 113–117.

(*minhag*) in Palestine, which he argued had become corrupted under Roman rule.

Equally importantly, gaonic scholars produced the first post-Talmudic rabbinic legal texts, which extract binding norms from the Talmud's dialectical and narrative flow. The earliest of these—including the earliest extant gaonic responsa and *Halakhot Pesuqot*, a practical legal digest of the Talmud—seem to have been composed in the later eighth century, shortly before Pirqoy's letter. The *ge'onim* continued to write in these genres throughout the ninth and early tenth centuries. Then between 928 and 942, the Suran *ga'on* Se'adya b. Yosef al-Fayyūmī, a native of Egypt and arguably the most influential rabbinic author of the early Middle Ages, single-handedly transformed the scope and variety of gaonic composition. Se'adya was the first rabbinic author to write works under his own name and the first to write works in Judeo-Arabic. Among many other innovations, he composed the first comprehensive collection of legal document formularies, the first monographs on discrete legal topics, and the first commentary (formulated as a glossary) on a classical rabbinic work, the Mishna. Se'adya's successors in the later tenth and early eleventh centuries adopted these innovations and extended them to include systematic exegesis of the Talmud itself.[51]

The achievement of the *ge'onim*, both before and after Se'adya, was thus to translate late ancient rabbinic legal culture into a replicable tradition of written prescriptive law that drew on the Babylonian Talmud as its core canon. This tradition's most striking characteristic is its profound conservatism, both with respect to the Talmud itself and to a large body of oral legal and interpretive customs surrounding it that were maintained within the *yeshivot*. The *ge'onim* presented themselves as the only legitimate custodians of these traditions, but admitted to creating almost no new legislation themselves; the innovations that they did introduce were almost entirely procedural rather than substantive and tended to be camouflaged through assimilation to existing Talmudic categories, expressions, and proof-texts.[52]

This stance served to promote the *ge'onim*'s own religious authority above that of their rivals in Palestine and that of local rabbinic elites in North Africa and Andalusia. But it had effects that extended far beyond this immediate

51. On gaonic literature before and after Se'adya, see Brody, *Geonim of Babylonia*, idem, *Sa'adyah Gaon*. See also Drory's groundbreaking *Models and Contacts*, 126–146, which demonstrates that Se'adya's literary innovations proceeded from earlier Karaite ones. My periodization of rabbinic legal writing in this section departs from that of Drory, who emphasized the disjunction between Se'adya and previous *ge'onim*. This is not to minimize Se'adya's impact, about which Drory is certainly correct, but rather to point to the equally important conceptual and literary developments that preceded him in the eighth and ninth centuries, and from which his ideas about textuality and legal authority emerged.

52. See especially Brody, "Were the Geonim Legislators?" idem, *Geonim of Babylonia*, 171–184.

aim, and that eventually outlived the *ge'onim* themselves. The Iraqi *yeshivot* declined politically throughout the later tenth century, and their literary output ceased in the early eleventh century.[53] By this time, however, their conceptions of law and traditions of legal discourse had spread westward, traveling with Abbasid Jews who had migrated to the Fatimid realm; with Syrian and Egyptian Jews who had traveled to Iraq to study in the *yeshivot* and then returned home; and above all, with the responsa and other texts that the *ge'onim* disseminated throughout the Islamic world.[54] Long after the *yeshivot* collapsed, the scholastic culture that they had developed continued to flourish among rabbinic elites in the Fatimid empire, in Andalusia, and (in a different form) even in Christian Europe, where in-depth study of Talmudic texts seems to have been adopted as an important religious activity sometime in the tenth century.[55] The Geniza reveals the extent to which this culture was absorbed even by Jews politically enmeshed with the Palestinian *ge'onim*, and even by those *ge'onim* themselves: by the tenth century and possibly earlier, Iraqi legal texts had come to be studied in the Palestinian *yeshiva*, and Iraqi legal formulae dominated the documents produced by the Palestinian Rabbanite court of Fustat.[56]

LEGAL WRITING AS AN ABBASID PHENOMENON

Why did the gaonic project succeed so spectacularly? The answer probably does not lie, as scholars once believed, in any support that they may have received from the Abbasid government. There is no evidence that the Abbasid caliphs maintained contact with the *ge'onim* during their heyday, or even knew that they existed.[57] But in another sense, the gaonic approach to rabbinic law

53. Although a gaonic *yeshiva* reappears in Baghdad in the twelfth century; see Gil, *Jews in Islamic Countries*, 448–467.

54. On Jewish migration from Iraq, see above, Introduction, n. 36. A vast literature addresses the transregional ties maintained by the *ge'onim* with Jews further west. See especially Ben-Sasson, *Qayrawan*, idem, "Varieties of Inter-Communal Relations in the Geonic period," Gil, "The Babylonian Yeshivot and the Maghrib in the Early Middle Ages," idem, *Jews in Islamic Countries*, 150–206, and Brody, *Geonim of Babylonia*, 126–132.

55. For a persuasive account of the Iraqi origins of European rabbinic scholastic culture, see Soloveitchik, "Third Yeshivah of Bavel," *Essays*, Vol. 2. (However, I am not convinced by Soloveitchik's suggestion that this culture developed from a nongaonic "third *yeshiva*" in Iraq.)

56. Palestinian *yeshiva*: Brody, *Geonim of Babylonia*, 117. Iraqi legal formulae: Friedman, *JMP*, 21–31, esp. 26, n. 58, and see below, "Documents and Legal Practice." At the same time, Iraqi gaonic law eventually absorbed a number of "Palestinian" elements, so that, as Robert Brody notes, "The tradition which came to dominate medieval Judaism . . . was actually an amalgam of [these] two strands of tradition" (*Geonim of Babylonia*, 122).

57. Brody, *Geonim of Babylonia*, 337–340, Gil, *Jews in Islamic Countries*, 121–124, Cohen, "Administrative Relations," Rustow, *Heresy*, 67, and the literature cited ibid., 7–8.

may be seen as a distinctly Abbasid phenomenon—one that developed alongside similar legal cultures throughout the Abbasid empire in the eighth to tenth centuries, which then collectively endured within the coherent Islamicate cultural landscape that survived its fragmentation.

The *ge'onim* were not the only religious elites in the early Abbasid empire to begin producing a written literature outlining a body of prescriptive legal norms with which laypeople and elites alike were expected to comply. The first systematic written account of Islamic law, Mālik b. Anas' *al-Muwaṭṭa'*, was composed in the 760s, within at most a few decades of the earliest gaonic legal texts. *Al-Muwaṭṭa'* was reportedly commissioned by the caliph al-Manṣūr, possibly in opposition to the legal scholarship based on individual reasoning (*ra'y*) in fashion among jurists in mid-eighth-century Iraq. Rather than derive legal norms through rationalist dialectic, it extracts them from the lived practices (*'amal*) of the Islamic community of Medina. By the 830s, however, a new form of Islamic legal writing had begun to develop. It rejected both pure rationalism and Mālik's emphasis on communal practice and instead located normative legal authority within a body of canonized sacred texts, the *Qur'ān* and *ḥadīth*. This shift was systematized most effectively by a single scholar, Muḥammad b. Idrīs al-Shāfi'ī, a native of Palestine (or, by other accounts, Yemen) who had studied with Mālik in Medina before spending considerable time in Iraq and then Egypt. Shāfi'ī's writings, compiled as *Kitāb al-Umm* after he died in 820, circulated among scholars in ninth-century Iraq, Egypt, and Mecca, several of whom wrote secondary works adopting and extending his rulings and interpretive methods. This "community of interpretation"[58] developed alongside others clustered around Mālik's teachings and those of the scholars Abū Ḥanīfa al-Nu'mān b. Thābit and Aḥmad b. Ḥanbal. By the early tenth century they had coalesced into the enduring legal schools (*madhhab*s) of Sunnī Islam, each with its own distinct methodologies, doctrinal traditions, and cumulative literature—but all of which, like Shāfi'ī and unlike his predecessors, related to the *Qur'ān* and *ḥadīth* as canonical sources of normative law.[59]

(Evidence for Abbasid investiture of *ge'onim* does survive from the early thirteenth century; see Grayson, "Jews in the Political Life of Late-Abbasid Baghdad.") More plausibly, state officials may have recognized the exilarch (*resh galuta*), a hereditary Jewish official. See Gil, *Jews in Islamic Countries*, 88–91, Brody, *Geonim*, 68–69 (but note the objections raised in Rustow, *Heresy*, 68–69), and on the exilarch in the Sasanian period, Herman, *A Prince Without a Kingdom*.

58. This term comes from El Shamsy, *Canonization and Islamic Law*, 167 and following.

59. This account is particularly indebted to El Shamsy's recent *Canonization and Islamic Law*. See also Abd-Allah, *Mālik and Medina*, and Brown, *The Canonization of al-Bukhārī and Muslim*. For a survey of scholarship on the formation of the *madhhab*s more generally, see Melchert, *The Formation of the Sunni Schools of Law*, xiv–xxviii.

Christians and Zoroastrians also adopted new forms of religious legal writing at this time. Bishops in the Melkite, West Syrian, and East Syrian churches all produced legal corpora under the early Abbasids. These collectively included Arabic translations of late ancient canons, new synodal legislation, and individually authored compilations written in a question-and-answer format that suggests they began as collections of individual responsa issued to local ecclesiastical judges. The earliest and best developed of these literatures is that of the East Syrian church, which developed in Baghdad during the same decades that Shāfiʿī was composing the contents of *al-Umm*, thanks largely to the efforts of the Patriarch Timothy I (r. 780–823). Timothy produced his own book of rulings and commissioned a Syriac translation of a similar work written in Pahlavi by the late eighth-century Iranian bishop Išōʿbōkt. Together with the book of rulings of Timothy's successor Išōʿ bar Nūn, these works helped to form the basis of all later East Syrian law, upon which bishops in later centuries drew to create systematic legal codes. Timothy and Išōʿ bar Nūn were not the first East Syrian bishops to write legal texts, but they addressed a broader range of lay practices than had earlier ecclesiastical authors. By recasting numerous contemporary social norms (including many descended from Sasanian practices) as legitimately Christian, they created an enduring framework of prescriptive *legal* norms dictating ordinary Christians' behavior, particularly in matters of marriage and inheritance.[60] Less is known about medieval Zoroastrianism, but those of its elites who survived after the Islamic conquests also began producing novel legal works in the early ninth century, including *Rivāyat*s, collections of legal queries and answers likely compiled from individual responsa. The earliest of these consists mostly of rulings issued by Ādurfarrbay ī Farroxzādān, high priest of the province of Fārs under the caliph al-Maʾmūn (r. 815–833).[61]

To be clear, none of these legal literatures are directly cognate to each other. While the legal concepts that they outline overlap in many places, the earliest Abbasid-era Islamic, Christian, Zoroastrian, and Jewish legal texts are written in different languages (respectively, Arabic, Syriac, Pahlavi, and Hebrew-Aramaic) and lack the close structural similarities shared by other literary genres that emerged in Arabic among Muslims and then Jews and

60. See Weitz, "Syriac Christians in the Medieval Islamic World," "Shaping East Syrian Law," and *A God-Fearing House*. By Christianizing lay customs, including ones of Sasanian origin, Timothy and other Abbasid-era Syriac jurists were continuing a trend begun by their seventh-century predecessors (but that does not appear to predate the Arab conquests): Payne, "Christianity and Iranian Society," 203–204.

61. See Macuch, "Pahlavi Literature," 130–151; on Zoroastrians in Iran after the Muslim conquests, see Choksy, *Conflict and Cooperation*. Michael Stausberg has argued that the idea of a (written) Zoroastrian sacred canon also originates with this literature: "Invention of a Canon."

Christians in later centuries, such as scriptural exegesis (*tafsīr*) or systematic theology (*kalām*). Each legal literature developed on a different scale: Sunnī Muslim writings vastly outnumber those of the *ge'onim*, which in turn dwarf the east Syrian legal corpus. They also developed at a different pace. For example, Islamic authors were already writing topic-driven, named-author legal monographs in the late eighth century, whereas the *ge'onim* began doing so only in the mid-tenth century.

But Jewish and other religious legal literatures produced during the Abbasid period nonetheless share fundamental similarities. It is no surprise that in the tenth and eleventh centuries, when Rabbanite Jews and East Syrian Christians respectively adopted Arabic as a language of legal discourse, they immediately began to apply Islamic legal terminology (e.g., *sharīʿa*, *fiqh*, *madhhab*, *muftī*, and so on) to their own legal systems and practices.[62] This vocabulary was easily assimilated, because even before this linguistic shift, Muslim and non-Muslim jurists alike had come to share common ideas about the nature of religious legal knowledge, the aims of religious legal writing, and the role of prescriptive law in defining religious groups.

By the time the Buyids toppled the Abbasids in all but name, elite Jews, Muslims, Christians, and Zoroastrians alike had come to view the law as an expert discipline, one derived from *technical* traditions of legal knowledge—traditions whose mastery required assimilating detailed repertoires of established formulas (terms, phrases, proof-texts, narrative units, and patterns of discourse, encoded, for Muslims and Jews in particular, within a multilayered textual canon), along with implicit and explicit rules for how and how not to deploy them.[63] Among all four groups, this form of expertise generated political power for their specialists; Muslim jurists sometimes served as *qāḍīs* and enjoyed varying degrees of socially recognized "epistemic authority" even when they did not,[64] while Jewish, Christian, and Zoroastrian ones often

62. Beginning respectively with Seʿadya b. Yosef in the tenth century and the Iraqi Christian author Abū al-Faraj ʿAbd Allāh ibn al-Ṭayyib in the eleventh. On the latter, for now see Weitz, "Syriac Christians in the Medieval Islamic World," 437; Mathieu Tillier is currently working on this question. On Islamic terms in Seʿadya's biblical commentary more generally, see Friedenreich, "Islamic Sources," 361–368.

63. This formulation borrows from Talal Asad's famous definition of Islam as a set of discursive traditions that "seek to instruct practitioners regarding the correct form and purpose of a given practice," embodied in "authoritative formulas" that carry regulatory power (idem, "On the Idea of an Anthropology of Islam"). But the *legal* traditions I am concerned with here are more formally and precisely defined than the broad range of intellectual and embodied practices Asad addresses, a distinction that the term *technical* is intended to capture.

64. For this phrase, see Hallaq, *Authority, Continuity and Change*. On the complex relationship between the *ʿulamāʾ* and the Abbasid state, see especially Zaman, *Religion and Politics*.

acted as hierocratic communal leaders whose claims to leadership depended partly on their legal knowledge. Muslim and *dhimmī* jurists alike therefore wrote for political as well as purely scholastic aims, using the common medium of responsa, among other genres, to disseminate practical legal norms to the audiences they addressed—in all four cases, transregional confessional communities comprising laypeople as well as elites, whose identity as groups they sought to define partly by these norms. Finally, by the late ninth century, at least, Muslims and non-Muslims alike recognized as natural that broad religious communities might comprise various subgroups (*madhhab*s) who subscribed to somewhat different normative frameworks. For Muslims, these included not only Sunnī movements but also Shīʿī ones that coalesced during the eighth and ninth centuries and began to produce legal works in the tenth; for Jews, they included both Rabbanites and Karaites.[65]

Like the texts themselves, this understanding of prescriptive law and its role in the social order had roots in late antiquity, but crystallized fully only during the Abbasid period, in the context of large-scale social changes that transformed religious cultures across the Middle East.[66] Two of these

65. Shīʿism under the Abbasids: see especially Hodgson, "How Did the Early Shiʿa Become Sectarian?" Crone, *God's Rule*, 70–124, 197–218, Dakake, *Charismatic Community*. Tenth-century Shīʿī legal writing: Newman, *The Formative Period of Twelver Shiʿism* (on Imāmī *ḥadīth* collections), and Cilardo, *The Early History of Ismaili Jurisprudence*. For a description of Karaism and Rabbanism as *madhhab*s, see Rustow, *Heresy*.

66. Until recently, scholars had assumed that the ideas about religious legal identity I have just described were already broadly accepted among Jewish and eastern Christian communities in the pre-Islamic Middle East. But recent studies of Christian communities in the Sasanian empire and Jewish ones in Roman Palestine have qualified this paradigm from multiple angles. On eastern Christians, see Payne, "Christianity and Iranian Society," Tannous, "Syria between Byzantium and Islam," and Papaconstantinou, "Between *Umma* and *Dhimma*"; on Roman Jews, Lapin, *Rabbis as Romans* (especially 98–125), and (focusing not on law but on rabbinic culture more broadly) Schwartz, *Imperialism and Jewish Society* (cf. also idem, "Rabbinization in the Sixth Century," "The Political Geography of Rabbinic Texts"). In what form, then, can these ideas—or the judicial institutions that they reflect—be identified before the Arab conquests? First, the institutional precedents: both the pluralistic Abbasid legal system and the *dhimmī* religious communal authorities who operated within it developed from late Roman and Sasanian models. Roman and Sasanian imperial and provincial state courts alike coexisted with other legal venues, including ecclesiastical courts in the Roman empire, and in both regions, lower-order officials and local elites who provided judicial services with varying degrees of state recognition. In this context, the Palestinian and Babylonian Talmuds describe rabbinic judges in Roman Palestine and in Sasanian Iraq as mediating marriage and property disputes among Jews—as bishops in the Sasanian empire may have done among Christians, although even this much is uncertain. At least in Palestine, rabbinic judges are portrayed as catering mostly to limited circles of local followers, not as forming a coherent legal network (see especially Lapin, ibid.; the question has not yet been systematically examined in the Sasanian context, but on the messiness and complexity of the evidence see Herman, *Prince Without a Kingdom*, 194–209). Second, the ideological precedents: prescriptive law is of course

changes are particularly worth noting. First, during the eighth to tenth centuries a large (if still uncertain) proportion of the inhabitants of the Middle East came to consider themselves Muslims, a transformation that intensified the social meaning of religious identity for Muslims and non-Muslims alike. Mass conversions created a Muslim community held together by Islam itself rather than by Arab ethnicity. One important consequence for those who did *not* convert was that they, too, were increasingly identified by religion, that is, as members of some other non-Muslim religious community (primarily Jewish, Christian, or Zoroastrian). The pagan populations of late antiquity all but disappeared over the course of the first Islamic centuries. By the reign of al-Mutawakkil (r. 847–861), the Abbasids had come to define the remaining non-Muslims over whom they ruled as "protected peoples" (*ahl al-dhimma*), each equipped with its own leaders and communal institutions, but subject to special taxes and social disabilities—a social model that Muslim jurists eventually retrojected to the early Islamic caliph ʿUmar b. al-Khaṭṭāb, but that in fact developed fully only in the late eighth and early ninth centuries.[67]

Second, literary production in Arabic increased dramatically during the same period, the result of the spread of spoken Arabic and of an affordable writing medium, paper; the growth of a professional class of bureaucratic scribes; and imperial and private patronage of written scholarship. Muslim, Christian, and Jewish scholars translated a vast library of Greek philosophical and scientific texts into Arabic, while Muslims began composing not only legal literature but also original Arabic works of philology, theology, historiography, exegesis, and poetry, among others. This literary revolution had profound epistemological consequences: groups whose textual traditions had been formally oral now began to view the written word as a legitimate vehicle for the transmission of knowledge.[68]

---

central to rabbinic self-definitions from the Mishna on. Beginning in the sixth century, Syriac Christian authors such as the Patriarch Mar Aba (r. 540–552) also began to define Christian identity partly in terms of obedience to legal norms, using rhetoric that foreshadows later Islamicate models. But none of these rabbinic or ecclesiastical claims seem to have been either as widely diffused among late ancient Jewish and Christian communities, or as broadly recognized as characteristic of them by others, as they would become in the medieval Islamic world. This is particularly clear in the case of Christian communities; see especially Payne, ibid. On late Roman legal pluralism, see further Humfress, *Orthodoxy and the Courts*, 29–61, Kelly, *Petitions, Litigation, and Social Control*, and Simonsohn, *A Common Justice*, 25–62; and on Sasanian judicial institutions, ibid., Macuch, "A Zoroastrian Legal Term in the Dēnkard," and Shaki, "Dādwar."

67. On this legal category and its evolution under the Abbasids, see Levy-Rubin, *Non-Muslims in the Early Islamic Empire*, esp. 58–87.

68. See especially Schoeler, *Genesis of Literature in Islam*, idem, "Writing and Publishing," Toorawa, *Ibn Abī Ṭāhir Ṭayfūr*, 7–34, Rustow, *Heresy*, 37–41, and on the Greco-Arabic translation movement, Gutas, *Greek Thought, Arabic Culture*.

It is against the backdrop of these two major developments—increasing confessionalization in the context of Islamization on the one hand and widespread textualization and the birth of Arabic writerly culture[69] on the other, unfolding within the open legal arena fostered by the Abbasids—that the *ge'onim* of Iraq, like other religious elites in the same time and place, began disseminating copies of a sacred canon (the Talmud) as well as extracanonical legal texts dictating norms to the broad religious community over whom they claimed leadership. Because little evidence for Jewish life in Abbasid Iraq has survived beyond the gaonic corpus, it is unclear what impact these writings had outside of the limited circles of loyalists who had studied in and maintained active ties with the *yeshivot*.[70] We know much more about the ideological battles that the *ge'onim* waged against each other and other Jewish religious elites than we do about how their legal teachings were received among other classes of Jews. This is particularly true in the eighth and ninth centuries, when distinctions between even elite rabbinic and nonrabbinic Jewish groups still may have been relatively porous, and the reach of their institutional centers remains uncertain.

By the early Fatimid period, however, matters come into clearer focus. The earliest legal documents preserved in the Geniza were written around the same time as Se'adya's groundbreaking legal works. By this point, and certainly by the early eleventh century, when the Geniza legal corpus picks up in earnest, religion had become a more universally primary element of social identity for members of all Middle Eastern confessional groups—elites and non-elites alike—than it had ever been before the rise of Islam.[71] By this time, these groups had also commonly come to understand religion as necessarily involving prescriptive law. Among rabbinic Jews (those loyal to the Iraqi and Palestinian *yeshivot* alike), this law was essentially that developed by the Iraqi *ge'onim*; in Egypt and Syria as elsewhere in the medieval Islamic world, to belong to the Rabbanite *madhhab* meant (at least in commonly accepted theory) to obey the normative legal frameworks described in gaonic and postgaonic literature.

Documents and Legal Power

It is in this context that the politically fluid but socially coherent local Jewish communities of the Fatimid and Ayyubid periods developed, and that rabbinic courts operated within them as politically and socially important institutions.

69. The term is Toorawa's, ibid.

70. This is true of Jews both within Iraq and elsewhere, since our evidence for the *ge'onim* comes almost entirely from their correspondence with loyalists in other regions, especially Ifrīqiyya. See above, n. 54.

71. On this point, see the references cited above, n. 66, especially Papaconstantinou, "Between *Umma* and *Dhimma*."

It must be emphasized that not all *dhimmī* groups under the Fatimids seem to have constructed similar legal identities. Conspicuously, there is no evidence that Coptic Christians maintained courts similar to the Jewish ones revealed by the Geniza.[72] Nonetheless, in the case of Jews, the history of prescriptive legal writing under the Abbasids and afterward explains many of the social ideas about religious law that may have helped legitimize *dhimmī* courts for their Jewish users and for Muslim officials alike.

This history does not, however, tell us much about how Geniza courts enacted or profited from these ideas in practice. How far did the thousands of prescriptive norms detailed in medieval Rabbanite texts shape what actually went on inside rabbinic courtrooms? And how, in turn, did court officials draw power from the Islamicate model of legal authority that these texts assume?

The best place to begin looking for answers to these questions is in the vast corpus of legal documents preserved in the Geniza—not only because of the often fascinating stories that they tell (and for which historians have most often examined them), but also because of their drier, and thus more easily overlooked, formulaic features. In the last part of this chapter, I will argue that disentangling three of these features in particular—the *documentary genres* in which these documents are written, the *substantive content* of the transactions that they ratify, and the *legal languages* that they employ—reveals them as hybrid artifacts, which draw on a complex dual register of rabbinic and Islamic documentary conventions that mirrors the dual legal arena in which they were produced. This interplay of registers offers some of the clearest evidence we possess both for the far-reaching social impact of prescriptive rabbinic law in Fatimid and Ayyubid Egypt, and for its social limits.

72. Few Coptic legal documents survive after the ninth century, and none after the eleventh. Moreover, some ninth- and tenth-century legal documents involving Copts are in Arabic and feature Islamic legal conventions. See Richter, "Coptic Papyri and Juristic Papyrology," 418–419, Abbott, "Arabic Marriage Contracts Among Copts," and Gaubert and Mouton, *Hommes et villages du Fayyoum*. (For similar documents among Melkite Christians, see Richards, "Some Muslim and Christian Documents from Sinai," Pahlitzsch, "Ein arabischer Kaufvertrag.") I thank Sebastian Richter and Johannes Pahlitzsch for these references. Beyond this, we know little about how Coptic communities organized themselves internally under the Fatimids. Still, it is noteworthy that Coptic elites began to produce legal writings in the mid-eleventh century, after the Fatimids had transformed Egypt into an Islamic imperial center—around the same time that Jewish courts in Egypt became more formalized and centralized. See Rowberry and Khalil, "A Brief History of Coptic Personal Status Law," 104–116, and on the lack of evidence for Coptic courts, see Mikhail, *From Byzantine to Islamic Egypt*, 149–159.

RABBINIC LAW ON THE PAGE AND ON THE GROUND

My main purpose in this section is to demonstrate that Geniza courts drew much of their prestige and power from the same approach to religious law that animated Rabbanite legal writing. Although this may seem self-evident, it is worth demonstrating directly, because Geniza legal documents bear a complicated relationship to prescriptive Rabbanite texts that has yet to be explained fully.

On the face of it, there are good reasons to suppose that rabbinic legal texts directly affected what occurred in rabbinic courts. That is certainly the impression created by Rabbanite legal authors, who often address their teachings to court scribes and judges—both overtly in specialized genres such as gaonic formulary books and responsa, and implicitly in legal compositions such as Maimonides' *Mishne Torah*, which includes sections on oaths, testimony, and other aspects of court procedure.[73] While it need not follow that courtroom staff always adhered to these instructions, the Geniza does reveal that Rabbanite court officials in Fatimid and Ayyubid Fustat were avid consumers of gaonic and postgaonic rabbinic legal literature. This is evident not only from the vast numbers of postclassical rabbinic legal texts preserved within the Geniza chamber—from which, in many cases, we know of their existence in the first place—but also from book lists and personal copies of legal texts belonging to leaders of the "Palestinian" Rabbanite court of Fustat from as early as the turn of the eleventh century.[74]

Surviving evidence thus suggests that theoretical jurists and acting judges considered themselves to be engaged in a common enterprise. But because Geniza legal documents differ from Rabbanite legal texts in their tone, structure, and terminology, the precise nature of their interaction has proven remarkably difficult to untangle. Goitein, for example, seemed to suggest that what happened in rabbinic courtrooms may have only vaguely paralleled theoretical rabbinic law.[75]

73. But not on the production of legal documents, a topic that Maimonides treats only briefly and in passing.

74. Book lists: Allony, *Jewish Library*, docs. 1–3. Personal copies: Shweka, Rustow, and Olszowy-Schlanger, "The She'iltot, recycling manuscripts and Efrayim b. Shemarya," on Iraqi gaonic legal passages copied by Efrayim b. Shemarya, head of the Palestinian-rite synagogue of Fustat c. 1007–1055.

75. See especially *Med. Soc.*, 2:327: "Reviewing the vast legal material embedded in the Geniza records one gets the impression that it was not so much the contents of the law applied as the authority administering it which gave the parties the feeling that they were judged according to 'the Law of the Torah.'" This conclusion somewhat resembles what I suggest below: that Geniza documents' authority derived from their form rather than their content. But Goitein's treatment suggests that Geniza documents' Jewish authority was embodied mainly in generic legitimizing statements (e.g., that a document conforms to "the law of Moses and Israel") rather than in their overall formulation or content, and

This perception echoes similar claims about Islamic legal practice that extend back to Weber's notion of an arbitrary and pragmatic "*Kadi-justiz*" decoupled from prescriptive Islamic law, or indeed from any predictable system of normative rules.[76] More recent scholarship has challenged this consensus for Islamic courts as well as Jewish ones, arguing that practice and doctrine in both contexts bore clear dialectical relationships to each other.[77] I share in this emerging view, which is firmly supported by the evidence examined throughout this book. But work on this subject to date has not clearly explained *how* this relationship worked within the Geniza courts. We remain uncertain how even case-specific responsa solicited from jurists by judges and litigants were actually used once issued, much less how the detailed rules outlined in medieval rabbinic monographs, codes, and commentaries relate to the complex and fragmentary patchwork of legal behaviors visible in the Geniza legal record.

To illustrate how Geniza documents' forms and formulae can help clarify this problem, the final section of this chapter turns from the global to the particular, focusing closely on a single exemplar, a draft of a testimony about a young woman's dowry, composed in Fustat in 1124.

Anatomy of a Legal Document

Our sample document is a record of testimony written in the distinctive handwriting of Ḥalfon b. Menashe, the most prolific court scribe known from the Geniza (his dated documents span nearly four decades, from 1100 to 1138).[78] It tells a clear and straightforward story: when Sitt al-Ahl bt. Yosef Abū Yaʿqūb al-Lebdī married Abū al-Surūr Peraḥya b. Binyamin, her dowry was publicly appraised (a practice mentioned in many documents from the eleventh and twelfth centuries). Anxious to ensure his wife's claim to this property, Abū al-Surūr asked her brother Zayn to promise him before two unnamed witnesses that all of the items on display, together with a *dār* also included in her dowry, belonged to her absolutely, and that neither he nor his absent brother Abū

leaves unclear their meticulous technical rabbinic validity, on which I focus below. Cf. Zinger, "Women, Gender and Law," 26.

76. Weber, *Economy and Society*, 2:976–980. For a theoretical critique of this idea, see Crone, "Weber, Islamic Law, and the Rise of Capitalism." Among historians of Islamic law, Weber's "*kadi-justiz*" has been adopted perhaps most influentially (although without direct reference to Weber) by Schacht, *Origins of Muhammadan Jurisprudence.*

77. Islamic courts: see especially Hallaq, "Model Shurūṭ Works," idem, "From Fatwās to Furūʿ," idem, "*Qāḍīs* Communicating," Powers, *Law, Society, and Culture*, and Masud, Peters, and Powers, *Dispensing Justice in Islam.* Jewish courts: see especially Ackerman-Lieberman, *The Business of Identity*, idem, "Commercial Forms and Legal Norms," and cf. the studies cited by Zinger, "Women, Gender, and Law," 26, n. 13.

78. The document was preserved in six separate fragments—T-S NS 211.8, T-S NS J 460, T-S NS J 112, T-S NS 323.11, T-S 8.138, and T-S AS 152.19—joined by Goitein and M. A. Friedman; see eidem, *India Book*, 1:34b.

al-Barakāt would try to take any of it back after the wedding. Zayn agreed, declared that he had given her the items unconditionally, and eight months later—well into the couple's marriage and long after Sitt al-Ahl's dowry had been listed in her *ketubba*—Abū al-Surūr asked the two witnesses to sign this document testifying to what they had heard.

Like most Geniza legal documents produced during the eleventh through thirteenth centuries, this document is written in a mixture of Judeo-Arabic, Aramaic, and Hebrew,[79] which I have rendered with different emphases (Arabic, Hebrew, *Aramaic*) in the following complete translation.

> *Testimony that was before us, we, the witnesses whose signatures are below. Thus it was*: When the Creator—may His memory be exalted and His names be sanctified—facilitated a union between Abū al-Surūr o(ur) t(eacher) and m(aster) Peraḥya ha-levi, (his) C(reator) g(uard him), the son of o(ur) t(eacher) and m(aster) Binṣyamin ha-levi, the honored elder; and Sitt al-Ahl, who is divorced from a betrothal, the daughter of o(ur) t(eacher) and m(aster) Yosef the elder, called Abū Ya'qūb al-Lebdī, (may he) r(est) in E(den), we came on the day of the dowry evaluation (taqwīm al-qumāsh), on which she entered (marriage) to him—which was the middle tenth of the month of Sivan of the year 1435 of documents (= 1124).[80] Her younger brother Zayn was present.
>
> When the entire dowry was finished being appraised and had been figured to the last dirham,[81] as is customarily done, and we had begun to leave, *this* Abū al-Surūr caught up to us and asked us to wait a moment. We stopped in the front hallway of the dār where the dowry was—namely, the large dār in Qaṣr al-Sham'[82] in Fustat belonging to Abū Ya'qūb al-Lebdī, may God be pleased with him, which was previously known as b. al-Zaffān. Then *this* Abū al-Surūr immediately came out to us, and his (brother)-in-law Zayn b. al-Lebdī, the brother of *this* Sitt al-Ahl, was with him.

79. Tenth-century Geniza legal documents are written in Hebrew or in Hebrew and Aramaic (see above, n. 5, and below, n. 84). Judeo-Arabic documents begin to appear in the early eleventh century and overtake the corpus by the mid-eleventh, although some Hebrew documents reappear in the early thirteenth century. (For some possible explanations of this latter shift, see Goitien, *Med. Soc.*, 1:15, Lieberman, "Legal Pluralism.")

80. 1435: as here, most Geniza documents are internally dated by the Seleucid calendar (which they often term the "era of documents").

81. Or, "had been figured as a single sum," as per Friedman's translation. See idem, *India Book*, 1:252, n. 27.

82. The "fortress of wax." *Qaṣr al-Sham'* was the site of the original garrison town of Fustat, where many Jews and Christians lived in later centuries. Both the "Palestinian" and "Babylonian" Rabbanite synagogues of Fustat were located there. Raymond, *Cairo*, 12–13, Gil, *Pious Foundations*, 93–96.

He said to him in our presence, "I'm afraid of what may happen.[83] I want you to testify to me before these people that you have already given all of the dowry, //together with the dār that is in the Silver Lane (Darb al-Fiḍḍī) in Qaṣr al-Sham'// to this sister of yours, as a gift. Stand guarantee for your brother about this, to reassure me, so that I may enter (marriage) with proof. And if (you) had intended to take back any of it, take it away from me now."

He said to him, "If we had intended (to do this) with any of it, we would not have brought it." And he had us witness for him that he had given all of the dowry that had been brought (there) for *this* sister of his, which had now been appraised, as noted (above)—//together with the aforementioned *dār*—as an immediate gift// in her marriage contract, for her and no one else, ~~and that he had~~ and that he gave her all of this immediately, as a complete, open, and public gift, given by a healthy person and not as a gift granted from a deathbed, *a public* gift, *a complete, decisive, final, valid and enduring* gift, a gift *that may not* be revoked. And that he had already pledged to stand guarantee for his brother, Abū al-Barakāt, (his) C(reator) g(uard him), in all of this—for him and for his heirs after him, with the most trustworthy and thorough guarantees, and as an enactment of the sages.

We performed qinyan with him for all of this—of his free will and not through coercion—for his sister, *this* Sitt al-Ahl the wife of *this* Abū al-Surūr; through a complete, stringent act of acquisition (qinyan), (performed) with an implement that is suitable for performing qinyan, (effective) immediately, nullifying all *secret depositions and conditions*, neither through compulsion nor coercion nor force nor inattention nor error, nor is he rendered defective by illness nor any of the other things that may invalidate testimony.

We went on our way. The ketubba was written after this, detailing the entire aforementioned dowry to which the gift pertained //and the aforementioned dār//. *This* Abū al-Surūr betrothed her on Tuesday, the aforementioned 26th of Sivan, and *this* Sitt al-Ahl took possession of // the entire dār// and the entire aforementioned dowry, and acquired ~~it~~ //all of this//, and acquired it.

This Abū al-Surūr asked us to certify this, and we acceded to his request and wrote this document for him, with what we verify of this testimony in the month whose date was aforementioned, and we gave it to him to be in his possession as a right and proof, and we delayed

83. Lit., "I am afraid of the consequences of time," a phrase sometimes used in Geniza documents that list the dowry independently of the *ketubba*. Ashur, "EBD," 88–89.

our signing until the month of Shevat of the year 1436 of documents in Fustat, Egypt. Valid, clear, and enduring.

GENRE. The events that this document describes are easy to follow, but its form and purpose in recording them are not. What was it supposed to accomplish, and how?

First, the question of genre. Part of the reason Geniza legal documents are difficult to parse is that they often look quite different from the fixed document types described in gaonic formulary books. Portions of three such collections survive, written by Se'adya b. Yosef in 926 and by Hayya b. Sherira and Shemu'el b. Ḥofni in the early eleventh century.[84] All provide dozens of templates for distinct document types, including loan deeds, quittances, sale contracts, partnership contracts, marriage contracts, dowry allocation deeds, and others. But with only a few exceptions (primarily divorce deeds, manumission deeds, bills of sale, *ketubbot*, and wills), most rabbinic legal documents preserved in the Geniza bear little systematic resemblance either to these gaonic models, or to each other. This document is a case in point: it might conceivably be described as either a gift deed or a dowry allocation deed, but does not entirely match Se'adya's or Hayya's models of either type. Nor does it precisely resemble other Geniza documents that might also reasonably be described in these terms, even those written by the same scribe.[85]

84. On Se'adya's formulary book, see Brody, *Geonim*, 257–259. Brody and Menahem Ben-Sasson are preparing an edition of this work based on Geniza fragments (*Sefer ha-Shetarot le-Rasa"g*, an expansion of eidem, "Fragments from Saadya's 'Sefer ha-Edut ve-ha-Shetarot'"). I thank them for graciously sharing it with me. For Hayya's book, see Assaf, "*Sefer ha-Shetarot le-Rav Hayya*." Shemu'el b. Ḥofni's formulary book has not yet been edited; Zvi Stampfer is currently working on fragments of this text preserved in the Geniza. Se'adya's and Hayya's books differ considerably, at least judging by the fragments that have survived; Hayya's is a collection of complete model texts in Hebrew and Aramaic, Se'adya's a Judeo-Arabic monograph that provides instructions for drafting documents of different types. See also Aptowitzer, "Formularies of Decrees and Documents," an apparently earlier collection of purely Aramaic gaonic formularies.

85. Se'adya's and Hayya's collections each include formularies for a gift deed and a dowry allocation deed (Ben-Sasson and Brody, *Sefer ha-Shetarot le-Rasa"g*, nos. 11, 39; Assaf, "*Sefer ha-Shetarot le-Rav Hayya*" nos. 8, 25). Our document omits features included in all four model texts (e.g., both Se'adya's and Hayya's gift formularies include clauses about the gift's public setting, which are absent here; both also describe dowry allocation deeds as enumerating the dowry items), but includes others that they omit or even deem unnecessary (e.g., the warranty clause; see below, n. 108 and after). For an example of another dotal gift deed composed by Ḥalfon b. Menashe that looks quite different from this one, see T-S 12.567. This internal variety renders it unlikely that scribes were working from a single set of fixed templates, as some scholars have assumed: Weiss, "Formularies (Shetarot) Reconstructed from the Cairo Genizah." On this point, see Ackerman-Lieberman, "Partnership Culture," 73.

Despite this textual variability, documents produced by the *bet din* of Fustat during its best-recorded period (the eleventh through early thirteenth centuries) share certain basic generic features. Like this one, they often include nonstandardized narrative accounts of litigants' interactions within and outside the courtroom, but assume a single basic legal form: instead of formal judgments issued by judges or other court officials, almost all are framed as probative[86] records of witness testimony, either to a legal act (e.g., a sale, gift, or betrothal) or to a verbal declaration (in this case, to Zayn's declaration that he has already gifted Sitt al-Ahl's dowry to her). As in this case, many of these testimonies are iterative; that is, they do not record entire cases from start to finish, but rather describe discrete legal events occurring in the course of longer transactions and arguments that left cumulative paper trails as they unfolded. (Sitt al-Ahl's dowry, for example, was described not only here but also in her *ketubba* and probably in other documents composed before and after she married.)[87] Finally, these iterative records seem often to have been produced in multiple variant versions, some issued to specific litigants—this one is clearly Abū al-Surūr's copy—and some archived by court officials.[88] But because very few legal documents made their way into the Geniza as easily recoverable archives, complete collections of these papers rarely survive. The documents that we have, as numerous as they are, are thus only a small remnant of all that the courts originally produced.[89]

Taken together, these features suggest that rabbinic documents in Fatimid and Ayyubid Egypt served more limited functions than in late antiquity, when classical rabbinic texts describe many written legal instruments that are dispositive as well as probative. Their function perhaps was more limited even than documents in Abbasid Iraq, where rabbinic courts may have issued formal records of judgment (although our evidence for this, and for Iraqi rabbinic courts

86. That is, they provide evidence of events that have independently occurred, in contrast to *dispositive* documents, which directly create a legal outcome. The only exceptions are divorce and manumission deeds, which hold a unique status in rabbinic law that ensured their strict standardization, attested already in the Mishna (mGit. 9:3–4; this status comes from Deut. 24:1–4 and is analogized to manumission, for example, in mGit. 1:4, tAZ 3:16). See also Holtz, "To Go and Marry Any Man."

87. These may have included an engagement or betrothal document, a separate dowry list, gift deeds for Sitt al-Ahl's real estate, and other testimonies composed during this dispute.

88. Cf. Ackerman-Lieberman, "Legal Writing in Medieval Cairo."

89. This description is messier than Goitein's, who identifies three main types of Geniza legal documents: "depositions" containing litigants' and witnesses' statements about a case, "acquittals" in which the parties release each other from future obligations, and "acknowledgements" of their remaining obligations (*Med. Soc.*, 2:334). This rubric comfortably fits some documents in the corpus, but not all (our document about Sitt al-Ahl's dowry, for example, is neither precisely a deposition nor an acknowledgement).

in general, is extremely limited).[90] In contrast, the Geniza legal record consists almost entirely of private deeds produced as evidence for individual litigants' benefit, and retained by both litigants and court personnel to use or consult in support of future claims. Our document, produced a full eight months after the events that it describes, indicates that acts of witnessing were not always ratified in documents, but only when documentation was required; Abū al-Surūr almost certainly commissioned this one as counterevidence to claims that his brothers-in-law had made, or that he feared they might make, to Sitt al-Ahl's property.[91]

This generic shift is not difficult to understand. It parallels documentary practice among contemporary Islamic courts and notaries. Surviving medieval Islamic documents and formularies from at least the tenth century and onward are also mostly probative records of formally oral acts, produced for individual litigants who preserved them in defense of future claims, often composed iteratively over the course of complex transactions, and that likewise display considerable fluidity across regions and period—although Geniza documents stand out even in this context for their extreme variability, and because of the complete absence of formal judgments from the corpus.[92]

Geniza documents' overall formulation is thus broadly Islamicate, a feature that suggests that legal processes in rabbinic courts may have resembled those in Islamic ones. But it need not imply that rabbinic courts administered Islamic rather than rabbinic law. On the contrary, when we turn away from questions of genre to those of legal content and language, it becomes clear that Geniza documents constantly appeal to rabbinic tradition—not despite their Islamicate legal character, but as part and parcel of it.

SUBSTANTIVE LAW. If almost all Geniza legal documents share a single basic form, their substantive content is more variable. The acts and agreements that they describe range widely, imposing differing obligations on the

90. On the dispositive character of legal documents cited in the Babylonian Talmud, see Gulak, *Legal Documents in the Talmud*, 40–45. Records of judgment in Abbasid Iraq: Se'adya's formulary collection includes a model deed of judgment (Heb. *pesaq din*, Arab. *kitāb faṣl al-qaḍā'*, Ben-Sasson and Brody, *Sefer ha-Shetarot le-Rasa"g* no. 29). A fragment of a gaonic legal monograph on court procedure preserved in the Geniza states that at the close of a case, the court's chief judge should record his and his colleagues' opinions in a document (*kitāb*). HUC 1185, fol. 3.

91. Acts of witnessing: Goldberg, *Trade and Institutions*, 157–158.

92. Some of these features first appear in Islamic formulary collections from eighth- and ninth-century Iraq and in Islamic documents from Abbasid Khurasan; they begin to appear in surviving documents from Egypt only in the tenth century. Wakin, *The Function of Documents*, Khan, "Pre-Islamic Background," idem, "Remarks on the Historical Background," idem, *ALAD*, 7–55. On similar features in later documentary corpora from Mamluk Egypt and Syria, see Müller, "Settling Litigation Without Judgment" and el-Leithy, "Living Documents."

individual spouses, business partners, and other litigants for whom they were produced. A betrothal document composed in Cairo in 1108 stipulates that a groom, Natan *ha-levi* b. Yiṣḥaq, may travel without his wife, Sitt al-Bayt bt. Natan, whenever he wishes; another composed in Fustat less than two decades later, in 1124, categorically forbids the groom, Avraham b. Yakhin, to travel and prevents him from compelling his wife, Dalāl bt. Yosef *ha-meshuḥrar*—a former slave's daughter—to do so.[93]

This flexibility, above all else, suggests that Geniza courts may have hewed only loosely to prescriptive rabbinic norms. But this impression fails to capture these documents' consistent deference to the technical substance of rabbinic law.

Geniza documents' substantive rabbinic character is easy to miss, because both classical and medieval rabbinic law permit broad freedom of contract among parties to any financial transaction (*davar shel mammon*, a category encompassing not only commercial law but also many aspects of family law).[94] The *bet din*'s pervasive use of private deeds as an administrative tool thus meant that litigants could arrange their affairs differently from rabbinic legal models without violating rabbinic law itself. A contract like Avraham b. Yakhin's forbidding a husband from travelling is thus valid in rabbinic contract law—even though absent such a contract, rabbinic marriage law does not limit husbands' freedom of movement in this way. The idiosyncratic agreements ratified in Geniza documents are overwhelmingly of this type. Among the thousands of documents that I have examined, I have yet to find one stipulating terms clearly forbidden by prescriptive Rabbanite (i.e., gaonic and postgaonic) legal discourse.[95]

In fact, despite the variability of their terms, Geniza documents are as legally conservative as the prescriptive texts on which they draw. They pervasively invoke and reproduce rabbinic legal definitions and ideas—many familiar from both gaonic and postgaonic prescriptive writings, and some known primarily through the Geniza corpus itself but that also appear in contemporary Rabbanite responsa.[96] They do so in large part through the legitimating

93. 1108: T-S 8 J 4.22v. 1124: T-S 8 J 5.3 + T-S NS 259.37.

94. The core rabbinic passage establishing this principle is bBB 126b; the principal exceptions to it are contracts whose terms directly contradict rabbinic prohibitions ("that make conditions on what is written in the Torah," mBB 8:5). See the detailed discussion in Elon, *Jewish Law*, 123–132.

95. A possible exception is BM Or. 10126.6 (cited by Ackerman-Lieberman, "Commercial Forms and Legal Norms," 1041), a document from Bilbays, 1239, that mentions a loan granted at fixed interest—an outright violation of rabbinic law. But on closer inspection, the document does not clearly state whether this transaction had been ratified before the *bet din*, or in an Islamic legal venue that it also mentions.

96. An example of the latter type is the divided (preliminary and deferred) groom's dower, discussed in Chapter 4.

formulae that validate their contents (discussed below), but also through the substance of the agreements that they ratify.

This substantive conformity takes two main forms. First, Geniza agreements almost always assume that the financial and marital transactions and institutions they describe will be governed by rabbinic legal norms unless otherwise stated. This is the case in Sitt al-Ahl's dowry document, which makes sense only given the assumption that as her husband, Abū al-Surūr expected to have tangible rights to the property listed in her *ketubba*—an assumption rooted in rabbinic law, which grants husbands profit from and control over their wives' dowry, rather than Islamic law, which does not.[97] Second, for all their latitude and variety, these contracts' contents often echo the terms of rabbinic legal literature. Some Geniza documents endorse conditions identical to rabbinic laws concerning marriage and commerce, providing litigants with written promises of rights that they theoretically held according to prescriptive law in any case.[98] Others modify these rules—within the limits permitted by rabbinic law—while nonetheless engaging them in conversation (e.g., clauses that exempt husbands from obligations that rabbinic marriage law imposes on them).[99] In either case, they reveal their writers' close affiliation with the substance of medieval rabbinic legal writing.

LEGAL LANGUAGE. If Geniza documents' overall form is Islamicate and their legal content primarily rabbinic, their most prominent technical feature combines aspects of both legal cultures: the authenticating formulae that signal their legal validity.

Specialized validation formulae authenticating a document and the events that it describes appear in most surviving Middle Eastern legal documents from the second millennium BCE onward.[100] In the Fatimid period, as long before it, these clauses allowed documents produced by one scribe to be accepted by other legal experts and were thus central to their long-term efficacy. In the case of the Geniza corpus, identifying this technical language can be

97. See Chapter 4, at n. 42.

98. Phillip Ackerman-Lieberman has closely examined this feature of the legal corpus in the context of documents about commercial partnership. See especially idem, "Commercial Forms and Legal Norms." For such stipulations in marriage documents, see below, Chapter 7.

99. E.g., premarital documents that stipulate that the husband will not have to give his wife clothing but that she will control her own labor, a tradeoff that directly echoes classical rabbinic texts that link these two marital obligations. See Chapter 7, ns. 39–40.

100. On ancient Aramaic documentary formulae before and contemporary to the earliest known rabbinic ones (which are preserved only in rabbinic literary citations), see Gross, *Continuity and Innovation in the Aramaic Legal Tradition*. On early Islamic documentary formulae, see the articles by Khan cited above, n. 92.

challenging, first because the specific clauses used in any given document vary unpredictably, and second, because most documents include clauses drawn from two distinct formulaic repertoires, rabbinic and Islamic.

The clauses included in our sample document about Sitt al-Ahl illustrate these repertoires and their uses. By far the most prominent and pervasive type of legal language in the Geniza corpus belongs to a recurring group of distinctively rabbinic clauses in Hebrew, Aramaic, or both. This document includes four of these: (1) a series of *gift validations* authenticating Zayn's gift to Sitt al-Ahl;[101] (2) a *qinyan*, or acquisition clause, formally ratifying his declaration;[102] (3) a *receipt clause* describing the document's transfer to Abū al-Surūr; and (4) a *document validation clause* affirming the document's legal legitimacy.[103] While such clauses are common to many Middle Eastern documentary traditions, their formulation here is recognizably gaonic. All four closely parallel passages in both Seʿadya's and Hayya's formulary collections; three appear in rudimentary form already in the Babylonian (or, in one case, Palestinian) Talmud.[104] It is not clear whether Seʿadya's more elaborate versions are his own inventions, developed from the brief Talmudic references at his disposal, or whether they reflect existing scribal traditions that he merely codified.[105] In either case, the fact that Ḥalfon and other Egyptian scribes con-

101. These appear in the fourth paragraph, beginning with "as an immediate gift// in her marriage contract."

102. This clause appears in the fifth paragraph ("We performed qinyan with him for all of this," etc.). *Qinyan* (acquisition) is a rabbinic legal construct that originally served to effect a sale: the buyer hands the seller an item that the seller grasps, thereby granting the buyer ownership of the property he is purchasing in exchange. See especially bBM 45b-47b. *Qinyan* clauses are used in medieval rabbinic documents to validate all legal acts and declarations. They are the most common type of validating clause in Geniza legal documents.

103. Both (3) and (4) appear in the document's final paragraph. Receipt clause: "We gave it to him be in his possession as a right and proof." Validation clause: "Valid, clear, and enduring."

104. Gift validations: The formula "an immediate gift" parallels formulae cited in mGit. 7:3, pGit. 7:3, bBB 135b, and bBM 19a, and appears with slight variations in Seʿadya's and Hayya's gift deed formularies. Both formularies also include the formula "*a public* gift, *a complete, decisive, final, valid and enduring* gift." (Ben-Sasson and Brody, *Sefer ha-Shetarot le-Rasa"g* no. 11, Assaf, "*Sefer ha-Shetarot le-Rav Hayya*" no. 8). *Qinyan* clause: the formula "an implement suitable for performing *qinyan*" is cited in bBM 47a and in both gaonic collections (Ben-Sasson and Brody, ibid., Introduction, part 7; Assaf, ibid., doc. 3 and throughout). (The accompanying formula "nullifying all *secret depositions and conditions*" is gaonic; see, e.g., Assaf, ibid., doc. 8.) Receipt and document validation clauses: both are ubiquitous in both gaonic collections; the latter is first cited in bBB 160b.

105. Some of the earliest Geniza legal documents, written within one to two decades of Seʿadya's formulary book, already employ versions of many of its characteristic formulae (although they are mainly in Hebrew, whereas Seʿadya's versions are mainly in Aramaic). See, for example, Assaf, "*Shetarot ʿAtiqim*" docs. 13–15. This suggests either that these formulae were already in use before Seʿadya codified them, or that they rapidly penetrated

tinued to deploy these formulae in Hebrew-Aramaic long after having adopted Judeo-Arabic as a primary documentary language suggests that they understood them to hold distinctive rabbinic legal authority.

Less prominently, Geniza court documents sometimes use Judeo-Arabic legal phrases that can also loosely be described as gaonic even though they do not appear directly in gaonic models. Our document includes one clause cluster of this type, intermingled with the *qinyan* clause: (5) a series of phrases affirming Zayn's *volition and capacity* to perform a *qinyan*—and, by extension, to grant Sitt al-Ahl the property that he has given her.[106] Neither Se'adya nor Hayya cite this clause, but it resembles the Hebrew-Aramaic volition clauses that they do employ more closely than it resembles contemporary Arabic Islamic ones, and was probably understood as a characteristically rabbinic formula.[107]

In contrast, Geniza scribes also draw on a different repertoire of Judeo-Arabic terms and phrases, one that is neither gaonic nor even Jewish, but rather echoes the technical language of Islamic law. Our document contains two such clauses: (6) a *warranty* pledge guaranteeing Zayn's gift to Sitt al-Ahl against potential claims made by their brother Abū al-Barakāt,[108] and (7) a *property transfer* clause describing Sitt al-Ahl's physical acquisition of her dowry.[109] Neither of these clauses is obviously rabbinic. Gaonic formularies include a standard Hebrew-Aramaic warranty clause, but it is more elaborate than this brief Judeo-Arabic passage and is moreover not applicable to gifts,[110] while property transfer clauses do not appear in gaonic models at all.

to Egypt after he developed them. But the whole question needs to be considered more systematically. For a review of some document formulae attested in early gaonic responsa, see Olszowy-Schlanger, "Formules Juridiques," 24–25.

106. These appear in the fifth paragraph, embedded within and following the *qinyan* clause.

107. Volition clauses appear in the Geniza corpus in two basic variants: a Hebrew-Aramaic version that closely echoes formulae cited by Se'adya and Hayya (Ben-Sasson and Brody, *Sefer ha-Shetarot le-Rasa"g*, Introduction part 7; Assaf, "*Sefer ha-Shetarot le-Rav Hayya*" 22; and cf. bBB 154a), and the Judeo-Arabic version that appears here—which more closely parallels this Hebrew-Aramaic version than it does contemporary Islamic volition clauses (see Khan, *ALAD*, 204). Some Geniza Judeo-Arabic volition clauses do begin with a short phrase that directly echoes Islamic ones, however: "with validity with respect to me, (my) acts being legal, acting voluntarily (*fī ṣiḥḥa minnī wa-jawāz 'amr ṭā'i'an*)" (e.g., T-S 13 J 2.15; cf. Khan, ibid.).

108. This clause appears at the end of the fourth paragraph: "He . . . pledged to stand guarantee (*bi-ḍamān (al-)darak*) for his brother . . . in all of this—for him and for his heirs after him," etc.

109. In the sixth paragraph: "(She) took possession of //the entire *dār*// and the entire aforementioned dowry," etc.

110. Ben-Sasson and Brody, *Sefer ha-Shetarot le-Rasa"g*, Introduction, part 7. Assaf, "*Sefer ha-Shetarot le-Rav Hayya*": for the warranty clause, see, e.g, doc. 1; for its exclusion

But neither is precisely Islamic either. Both employ terms standard in medieval Islamic warranty and property transfer formulae but are more cursory than real Islamic clauses of either type; and Muslim jurists, too, view warranty clauses as irrelevant to gifts.[111] In other words, these clauses marshal what is clearly Islamic legal language, but they do so imprecisely compared to Islamic legal documents.

The technical language in these documents thus falls into two distinct registers: a core of careful, detailed rabbinic formulae that appear mostly in Hebrew-Aramaic (clauses 1–4 in our sample document) but sometimes in Judeo-Arabic (clause 5), and a secondary layer of more cursory, informal Islamic legal terms and phrases in Judeo-Arabic (clauses 6–7). This contrast extends to the narrative portions of some documents, which use Islamic legal language in a similarly casual way. For example, our document's third paragraph cites Abū al-Surūr as asking Zayn to "stand guarantee (*taḍmanu* . . . *al-darak*)" for him so that he may enter marriage "with proof (*'alā bayān*)," both Islamic legal terms that bear no particular technical meaning here but that serve to frame the core rabbinic legal content that follows.[112]

Geniza scribes' uneven use of these two registers suggests that they relied on gaonic and quasi-gaonic formulae to legitimate their products, but that they did so while participating in a broader legal arena whose culture and vocabulary were thoroughly Islamicate. Geniza documents' Islamic terminology has been noted as possible evidence that they were intended to be usable in Islamic as well as Jewish courts (a version of what Muslim jurists term *iḥtiyāṭ*, "precaution," the practice of composing documents that can be used before *qāḍīs* of different legal schools).[113] Yet few Jewish court documents appear designed to hold up as Islamic legal instruments. Instead, they use Islamic terms in ways that reflect Jewish scribes' natural fluency in the language of Islamic court process, the common currency of the open legal marketplace in which Jews as well as Muslims participated. While the nature of this marketplace renders it likely that Jewish court documents may sometimes have ended up marshaled as evidence before Muslim judges (another question that deserves to be examined in greater detail), their intended legal authority seems to have been squarely rabbinic.

from gift deeds, see doc. 8. Both a version of this clause, and the idea that it does not apply to gift documents, appear already in the Talmud, bBM 15a.

111. On Islamic warranty clauses, see Wakin, *The Function of Documents*, 60–63, 90–91; Khan, *ALAD*, 26–28. On property transfer clauses, see Wakin, ibid., 53–56, Khan, ibid., 25.

112. On *ḍamān al-darak* for warranty, see Wakin, ibid. (Geoffrey Khan has argued that this Arabic term itself has Aramaic origins; see idem, "Pre-Islamic Background of Muslim Legal Formularies," 214–223.) On *bayyina*, see Brunschvig, "Bayyina," *EI²*; for *bayān* as a Judeo-Arabic equivalent, see Blau, *Dictionary*, s.v. *bayān*.

113. Ackerman-Lieberman, "Copy or Likeness," idem, "Legal Pluralism."

DOCUMENTARY PRODUCTION AND POLITICAL POWER

Using Sitt al-Ahl's dowry document as an exemplar, I have argued that Geniza legal documents combine rabbinic substantive elements and Islamicate procedural elements. To return to the questions with which the chapter opened: how can these mixed features help explain the nature of rabbinic courts' authority over Jewish litigants, and the ways in which this authority determined their experiences in court?

They do so, first, by supporting the broad thesis advanced in the chapter's first two sections: rabbinic court officials were able to mobilize power in part by asserting a type of religious legal authority that held broadly accepted social meaning across religious groups in the post-Abbasid Middle East. For the Jewish litigants who appeared before the *bet din*, legal action of any kind offered only one means of organizing social agreements. Yet both they and the Islamic state officials who ruled over them shared common expectations about the nature and authority of religious legal tradition. We have seen that these expectations sometimes led *qāḍīs* and state bureaucrats to recognize the *bet din*'s jurisdiction over Jewish litigants. But the prominence in the Geniza legal record of hybrid rabbinic-Islamicate documents—functionally similar to contemporary Islamic ones, but crafted with close attention to technical rabbinic norms—suggests that court officials more routinely claimed authority by demonstrating their rabbinic legal expertise in ways that made recognizable sense to all participants in the Fatimid and Ayyubid legal arenas; including by producing, distributing, retaining, and assessing written records that litigants, Jewish elites, and Islamic officials alike viewed as technically valid in rabbinic law. These documents' careful craftsmanship, combined with the sheer density and volume of output reflected by the surviving corpus, suggest that court officials relied partly on *documents themselves* to maintain rabbinic legal norms and in turn to support their own legal authority. Litigants must have valued the documents that the *bet din* produced, or it would not have produced so many of them. This demand not only allowed scribes and judges to demonstrate their legal expertise. It also offered a means by which they could directly regulate litigants' behavior, most concretely by refusing to produce a given document until the parties involved had met their legal conditions.[114] Documents, in short, were tools of power that reproduced and drew on prevailing ideas about religious law no less than were prescriptive texts—certainly not the only such tools to which rabbinic courts had access, but the most visible ones to have survived.

In this respect, the very fabric of the Geniza legal corpus helps explain how Islamicate ideas about religious law strengthened the *bet din* as an institution,

114. This is most clearly documented surrounding the courts' regulation of marriage. See Chapter 7, n. 35.

granting it a hold on litigants that it might not have otherwise possessed. Yet these same features also help explain the limits of this form of soft power—its limits as a means of rule, but also as a means of enacting the law itself.

For all their technical validity, most Geniza documents were composed to ratify agreements and transactions animated by social concerns different from those that animate prescriptive texts, as is evident from the wide diversity of their terms. Most of these documents are private, probative deeds rather than records of judgment, and the agreements and transactions that they ratify vary widely from case to case. This diversity reveals how flexible this form of technical legal practice could be, but also how incapable it therefore was of fully shaping litigants' broader lives. Respect for rabbinic law might inspire a couple on the verge of marriage to procure a valid betrothal document defining the conditions of their union, or prompt a dying man to commission a technically meticulous rabbinic will; but these choices alone did not decide what the couple would require of each other, or how the man would divide his property.

What, then, did determine these decisions? The rest of this book will use female adolescence as a case study for answering this question, focusing on the distance between the technical forms of rabbinic legal practice and its practitioners' ordinary cultural motives and assumptions. But one thing is clear at the outset: litigants' own social capital in the courtroom—most obviously, their personal relationships with court officials or their affiliates—must have played a major role in the outcomes they received there.

This was intrinsic both to the political contexts within which rabbinic courts operated and to the products they offered and from which they drew social force. Geniza courts' executive weakness fostered an uneven form of legal practice, one prioritizing rules that could be comfortably maintained without any assumption of coercive power. We will not fully understand how litigants and court personnel came to the terms recorded in Geniza documents without a great deal of further work on the courtroom processes from which they emerged. Even so, it is not difficult to understand how a courtroom culture that vested authority in the formal features of private agreements might in practice favor some (better socially positioned) litigants over others. Court officials concerned primarily that a couple's *ketubba* was formulated properly, for example, had little reason to care whether its terms were grossly more favorable to either party. What is more, it was easier for them to ensure the *ketubba*'s proper formulation than to force either party (but in practice, almost always the husband) to honor its terms if he did not wish to do so, no matter what the prescriptive texts said. Here human relationships cannot but have begun to matter: given communal leaders' own social and political dependence on the reciprocal ties that they maintained with other men—both those above and below them, Jews and Muslims alike—this was all the more true when the husband was well-connected and his wife was not (as I will demonstrate more concretely in Chapter 7). These conditions help explain why women like Hayfā' bt. Sulaymān, who lacked robust kinship ties, often fared poorly in court and were compelled to appeal to communal officials to intercede on their behalf.

In that case, how did a woman end up like Hayfā', or in a far better position? Having offered a general introduction to the family and the legal system—the two social institutions most central to the lives of all women who appear in the Geniza corpus—in the next three chapters I will consider how both institutions defined and positioned women on the verge of adulthood, in the period between puberty and first marriage.

PART II

Unmarried Daughters

CHAPTER THREE

A Ripened Fig

AGE AT FIRST MARRIAGE

GENIZA DOCUMENTS LACK A specific vocabulary for young women between childhood and adulthood. The most common word applied to the girls discussed in this book, *ṣabiyya* ("young woman"), was also used interchangeably for infants and toddlers and for married women with children of their own. Yet almost all women spent some stretch of time, either months or years, in which they were no longer treated quite as children nor yet as adults. This liminal period is easiest to define as starting at physical puberty and ending with first marriage. Both events were social milestones in a young woman's life that changed how others viewed her and what possibilities were open to her. Both were also legal turning points that changed her formal status in rabbinic law. I have therefore chosen to call this interval "adolescence," even though my sources themselves use no such term. Geniza Jews may not have had a word for adolescence, but they nonetheless recognized it a distinct stage of women's lives, during which their position both within rabbinic courts and in society at large was different than it had been before or would be after.

The next three chapters will examine how Geniza Jews understood and managed this adolescent period. This chapter begins by describing its basic boundaries—women's adolescence as defined by rabbinic law, and as it emerges from Geniza evidence for women's age at first marriage.

Female Adolescence in Rabbinic Law

THE *BOGERET*

Female adolescence is a complex but clear category in rabbinic law. Classical rabbinic texts divide the early female life course into three different stages:

childhood, pubescence, and full maturity. This schema first appears in the Mishna:

> The sages drew a metaphor for women: an unripe fig, a ripening fig, and a ripened fig. An unripe fig: while she remains a child. A ripening fig: these are the days of her youth (*ne'ureha*). For both of these—her father owns rights to any property she may acquire[1] and to her labor, and may annul her vows. A ripened fig—once she matures (*bagra*), her father retains no authority over her.[2]

This passage bases a young woman's personal status on her physical maturity. As a sexually undeveloped child and in early puberty—when she is an "unripe" or a "ripening fig"—her father controls her socially and economically. Once she matures fully, becoming a "ripened fig," he loses his authority over her.[3]

At first glance, this three-part schema seems needlessly complicated. If a girl's father holds the same power over her throughout both childhood and early puberty, why distinguish them as two separate stages? The answer seems to lie in this distinction's function as a gloss on biblical law. The Hebrew Bible describes the early female life course differently from this rabbinic passage. Numbers 30 states that a father may veto his daughter's vows, and thus effectively control her legal actions, as long as she remains "in (his) household, in her youth (*ne'ureha*)"; when she marries, this right passes directly to her husband.[4] According to Numbers, then, women remain legally subject to their fathers until first marriage, no matter how old they are—a model at odds with the Mishna's rule that a physically mature daughter gains independence from her father whether she is married or not. To resolve this problem, the Mishna here and elsewhere defines the biblical term *na'ara*, "maiden," not as a generic word for an unmarried woman, but as a technical term that describes girls who have begun but not yet finished puberty.[5] The Mishna can then reinterpret the Bible's statement that a father controls his daughter's vows during "her youth" (*ne'ureha*) as applying only to this brief period of early puberty. Later classical rabbinic and early

1. Lit., "that which she finds."

2. mNid. 5:7.

3. I should note that another Mishnaic passage would appear to suggest a different model, in which a daughter remains under her father's control until marriage: "She is always under her father's authority until she enters her husband's authority through marriage" (mKet. 4:5). But this dictum appears shortly after another passage (mKet. 4:1) that assumes the same tripartite model as our Mishna in Nid.; the Talmud (bKet. 46b) and later commentators thus assumed that its "she" refers to a daughter who is not yet mature (the point being that she enters her husband's authority only at marriage, rather than at betrothal).

4. Numbers 30:4–17.

5. For other early rabbinic references to this definition of *na'ara*, see, e.g., mKet. 3:8, mNed. 11:10, tKet. 1:5.

gaonic sources refine this definition even further, limiting women's "youth" or "maidenhood" (*na'arut*) to the first six months of chronological and physical puberty: a girl becomes a *na'ara* once she is at least twelve years old and has at least two pubic hairs, and becomes fully mature (*bogeret*) six months after that.[6] At that point, her father's authority over her dissolves and she becomes legally independent—at least until she marries and falls subject to her husband's control.

The purpose of this rabbinic passage, then, is to justify the third stage that it describes: a distinctive legal period of female *adolescence* between middle puberty and first marriage, in which the *bogeret* (mature unmarried daughter) is an autonomous legal actor free from both her father's and her future husband's authority. Other rabbinic texts provide further details. A father may sell his minor daughter into slavery or marry her off to whomever he pleases, "even to a disgusting man afflicted with boils." But as an adolescent she gains control over her person; she and she alone may marry herself. Whereas a father owns his minor daughter's labor and property, in adolescence she becomes economically independent from him.[7]

This rabbinic idea is extremely unusual. It departs not only from biblical precedent but from most other systems of ancient and late ancient Middle Eastern law. Throughout ancient Mesopotamia and Egypt as in the Hebrew Bible, daughters seem to have remained under a father's or appointed guardian's legal control until they married.[8] Papyri from Roman Egypt also recognize fathers' authority over their daughters at first marriage and

6. The threshold of twelve years comes from mNid. 5:6; two pubic hairs are invoked as a definitive sign of puberty in mNid. 5:9. The notion that *na'arut* lasts six months is cited, e.g., in bKet. 39a, bNid. 45a, bQid. 79a, pYev. 1:2. Classical rabbinic sources do not explicitly consolidate these different principles into a unified framework; however, the concept that *na'arut* begins once a girl grows two hairs after age twelve seems implicit, for example, in bNid. 45b-46a. In any case, this is the interpretation given by the earliest gaonic sources, e.g., *She'iltot* 133 (ed. Mirsky, 4:268), *Halakhot Gedolot* (*Hilkhot Mi'un*), and articulated in later gaonic responsa (e.g., Mueller, *TG Mizraḥ u-Ma'arav*, no. 97; Harkavy, *Zikhron Kamma Ge'onim*, no. 74). Some early medieval Rabbanite sources reflect slight variants of this schema; see Friedman, *JMP*, 1:217, n. 3. On the tension between individual physical development and chronological age as criteria for maturity in rabbinic sources, see Meacham/Frenkel, *Sefer ha-Bagrut*, 17–25.

7. "A disgusting man": bKet. 40b. The three rights that the mature daughter acquires in mNid. 5:7, to her own property, labor, and vows (see above, at n. 2), imply that she becomes an independent legal actor, an implication assumed throughout classical and medieval rabbinic literature.

8. See the summary of scholarship on paternal power in the ancient Near East in Marsman, *Women in Ugarit and Israel* 50–54, 255–260. Kawashima, "Could a Woman Say No?" argues that the very concept of an autonomous daughter is conceptually impossible in the Hebrew Bible, which does not recognize individuals' legal status beyond the patriarchal clan.

sometimes well beyond, as do the few legal texts that have survived from Sasanian Iran.[9]

Islamic maturity law falls somewhere between this pre-Islamic consensus and the rabbinic model, but on balance lies closer to the former. Although the classical texts of Sunnī Islamic law recognize girls' maturity—*bulūgh*, achieved at menarche or by age fifteen, according to most opinions—as a legally meaningful turning point, its implications are neither wide-ranging nor clear-cut.[10] On the one hand, most (if not all) medieval Muslim jurists allowed a mature girl to acquire and use her own assets, even if she had not yet married, as long as she could demonstrate that she had good sense (*rushd*)—the same criterion required of mature boys (although in practice, medieval *qāḍīs* in some times and places seem to have much more readily denied the *rushd* of girls and women than that of boys).[11] But in other respects, Islamic adolescence was sharply gendered, and here jurists recognized marriage rather than maturity as the major threshold in young women's lives. Unlike an adolescent son, a virgin (*bikr*) daughter remained in her father's physical custody (*ḥaḍāna*) until she married, no matter what her age.[12] Most importantly, she could not choose to marry herself, but had to be married off by her father or male guardian, even (according to most schools) against her will.[13] Only once she had married a first time and become formally nonvirgin (*thayyib*) could a woman live alone and marry herself.

Given how far she departs from deeply entrenched norms that had prevailed throughout the Middle East since antiquity, and that likewise continued to inform Islamic law throughout the Middle Ages and beyond, the rabbinic

9. For the Egyptian papyri, see Arjava, "Paternal Power," 155–159, eadem, *Women and the Law*, 32–34, and cf. Yiftach-Firanko, "Law in Graeco-Roman Egypt," 551–552. For Sasanian Iran, see Hjerrild, *Studies*, 19–76.

10. The Mālikīs viewed 18 years as the upper limit. See "Bāligh," *EI²*.

11. Property rights conditioned on maturity and *rushd*: based on the Qur'ān, 4:6. Medieval jurists widely agreed that before this point, minor children were under interdiction (*ḥajr*) and could not control their own property. Jurists disagreed about how and when interdiction should be lifted for different types of people, but most concurred that unmarried girls could potentially leave interdiction after they matured. This view was not universal, however: the Mālikīs argued that women remained under interdiction until marriage, or even for one or more years after. See, e.g., Shāfiʿī, *Kitāb al-umm*, *Al-taflīs*, Chapter 11, for the majority view, and ibn Rushd, *Bidāyat al-mujtahid*, *Kitāb al-ḥajr*, for a review of the various schools' approaches, with special focus on Mālikī jurists. On the interdiction of adults more generally, see Arabi, "The Interdiction of the Spenthrift." Medieval *qāḍīs*: Rapoport, *Money, Marriage and Divorce*, 23–24. For the effects of Mālikī law on women in the medieval Islamic west, see Shatzmiller, "Women and Property Rights in al-Andalus and the Maghrib."

12. De Bellefonds, "Ḥaḍāna," *EI²*.

13. See Ali, "Money, Sex, and Power," 86–108, eadem, "Marriage in Classical Islamic Jurisprudence," 17–18, and see further below, Chapter 6, ns. 83–84.

bogeret presents a puzzle.[14] It is not clear what social meaning this unusual legal idea held even among late ancient rabbinic Jews; in fact, rabbinic narrative passages consistently describe mature daughters as passively subject to their parents' marriage choices.[15] But however obscure her social history may be, the autonomous *bogeret* appears as a well-defined legal category throughout classical rabbinic literature, and was universally accepted as an uncontroversial aspect of normative law by medieval rabbinic jurists, gaonic and postgaonic alike.

FIRST MARRIAGE AND RABBINIC ADOLESCENCE

How long was rabbinic adolescence expected to last? Legally, it could easily not happen at all. The *bogeret*'s independence coexists with another rabbinic legal principle that can potentially render it irrelevant: a father's right to marry off his minor daughter whenever he wishes. (If her father dies, other relatives may also marry a minor girl in their care, although she retains the right to annul the marriage through a procedure termed *mi'un* until she reaches maturity.)[16] Women whose fathers or guardians choose to marry them off as minors never reach autonomous adolescence, but instead pass directly from childhood to marriage. At least some rabbinic authors viewed this as ideal: the early rabbinic sage 'Aqiva, for example, describes female adolescence as a moral hazard akin to prostitution: "*Do not profane your daughter to make her a whore* (Lev. 19:29): this refers to one who delays his mature daughter" (that is, from marrying).[17]

The legal category of the *bogeret* is thus contingent rather than necessary; it holds no implications for women's age at first marriage. This is partly because rabbinic law decouples puberty from women's sexuality. Physical puberty can alter a woman's legal status, but it does not affect her identity as a potential wife. A minor daughter can be entered into a physically consummated marriage at the astonishingly young age of three years, long before she reaches legal maturity.

The idea that "a girl of three years . . . is legally fit for intercourse" stands essentially unchallenged in late ancient rabbinic literature.[18] Zoroastrian texts

14. The most systematic attempt to explain the *bogeret* remains Bamberger, "Qetanah, Na'arah, Bogereth," who argues that she is an accidental byproduct of the rabbis' real aim: to limit the impact of biblical virginity and rape laws by redefining the term *na'ara* (used in many of the biblical verses outlining these laws) as narrowly as possible.

15. Schremer, *Male and Female*, 126–142.

16. See Schremer, *Male and Female*, 106–108; Dinari, "*Hishtalshelut*," 320–323. Islamic law recognizes a very similar idea; see below, n. 80.

17. BSan. 76a. On this theme in rabbinic literature, see Schremer, *Male and Female*, 109–111; cf. Katzoff, "Age at Marriage," 11–12.

18. bAZ 37a, alluding to a widely cited principle established in mNid. 5:4. See the detailed discussion in Schremer, *Male and Female*, 102–106, 113–125.

also identify three years as the minimal threshold for marriage, suggesting that this was not a distinctively rabbinic concept, but one common among Jews and non-Jews alike in Sasanian Iraq and Iran.[19] From our perspective, this is of course a profoundly disturbing, indeed horrifying, idea. Modern scholars confronted by this aspect of rabbinic law have therefore understandably tended to respond apologetically, by emphasizing occasional rabbinic passages that criticize child marriage. But in fact, these passages do not resolve the problem, because none oppose prepubescent marriage for the same reasons that most modern societies do. The text most frequently cited on this topic objects that girls married as minors may end up married to men whom they dislike: "Rav said, 'It is forbidden for a man to betroth his daughter until she matures and states, 'I want so-and-so.'"[20] Others condemn child marriage because it is nonprocreative: "Those who play with little girls delay the Messiah . . . because they marry minors who are not capable of childbearing, as R. Yosi said, 'The son of David (i.e., the Messiah) . . . will come only after all the souls in the storehouse are exhausted.'"[21]

A few rabbinic passages go further by implicitly acknowledging that child marriage may be unpleasant for the child herself. Citing a tradition that permits both a minor bride and her father to delay her wedding, the Babylonian Talmud, for example, notes that a father might want to do so on the reasoning that his daughter "does not know" what marriage entails, but once married may "rebel and leave, and come and fall back on me."[22]

19. See, e.g., *RAF*, ed. Skjærvø and Kiel, no. 12. I am very grateful to Yishai Kiel for bringing this parallel to my attention and for sharing this work in progress with me.

20. bQid. 41a/81b.

21. That is, after all the children destined to be born have been. bNid. 13b; the same passage appears in *Kalla Rabbati* 2:4, referring to "wasted seed" (i.e., masturbation) rather than prepubescent intercourse. See Satlow, *Tasting the Dish*, 246–260. Cf. also *Avot de-Rabbi Natan*, 56: "One who marries his daughter as a minor diminishes procreation, loses his money, and comes close to murder"; tYev. 8:4/bYev. 61a-b: "A man should not neglect procreation . . . and should not marry a barren woman, an old woman, an *aylonit*, a minor, or one unfit to give birth." (On the *aylonit*, a woman without secondary sex traits, see Lev, "*Aylonit*.") Rabbinic passages about young girls' *subjective* sexual development are even less consistent. Some imply that women develop active sexual desire around puberty, e.g., bQid. 81b: a girl in middle childhood can act as chaperone for an adult woman, because "she understands the taste of intercourse but will not hand herself over for intercourse." (Cf. bBer. 24a. For *ta'am bi'a* as "the taste of intercourse," see bSan. 19b.) Others describe girls as experiencing sexual desire much earlier. The Talmud illustrates the Mishna's ruling that "a girl of three years . . . may be betrothed through intercourse" through several startling anecdotes in which women describe enjoying sex as young children: bNid. 45a. It is difficult to know what to make of this extraordinarily unsettling passage, which has no parallels in any other rabbinic text (and which most medieval commentators left untouched). But it can be read most straightforwardly as a hermeneutic response to the Mishna that it elaborates.

22. bKet. 57b; for the legal background, see tKet. 5:1. And on the same page (bKet. 57b): "One should not arrange to marry a minor in order to marry her when she is a minor,

Even these passages, however, neither describe child marriage as uniquely morally repulsive, nor outlaw its practice because of the trauma experienced by minor brides. Moral opposition to pedophilia as modern societies understand it, as self-evident as it appears to us, is not clearly reflected in these late ancient sources.[23] Equally importantly, these passing objections never materialized into practical law, at least as it was codified by the medieval jurists who followed: the *ge'onim* and later Rabbanite authors universally understood the rabbis of late antiquity to have permitted physically consummated child marriage.[24]

Between Puberty and Marriage in Medieval Egypt

Did the women who appear in Geniza documents typically pass through a period of legal adolescence between puberty and marriage? Enough Geniza legal documents identify unmarried girls as mature to suggest that they did. Most women documented in the Geniza spent some time in which the *bet din* would have formally recognized them as a *bogeret* should the question have happened to arise—although the evidence makes it hard to gauge how long this interval typically lasted. (The short intermediate stage of "maidenhood," *na'arut*, on the other hand, is almost invisible in the Geniza, and it may be that in practice, courts rarely bothered with it.) The widespread existence of this adolescent period, moreover, seems to have been no coincidence, but due at least in part to a newfound disapproval of child marriage expressed by both Jews and Muslims in some parts of the medieval Middle East, whose traces are likewise recoverable in the Geniza corpus. This ideological shift not only made adolescence normative for most women documented in the Geniza, it also gave adolescence a different social meaning than it holds in rabbinic law. Rather than being defined by young women's legal agency, the period after puberty stands out in Geniza sources as the point at which young women became socially marriageable.

---

but one may make arrangements to marry a minor when she matures. Isn't this obvious? One might suppose that this might cause her (i.e., the minor whose wedding is being planned) to become immediately afraid and to fall ill." Cf. pKet. 5:3: "If she is a minor and wishes to mature (before marrying), we heed her."

23. For a similar conclusion about ancient Rome, see Hopkins, "The Age of Roman Girls at Marriage," 310, and cf. Caldwell, *Female Transition*, 266–306. To my knowledge, this question has not been closely examined for either Roman Palestine or the Sasanian empire. Indeed, literature on historical ideas about childhood sexuality is generally sparse, despite the central role that this question played in the development of family history as a field, through Philippe Ariès' seminal *Enfant et la vie familial sous l'Ancien Régime*. See Egan and Hawkes, "Imperiled and Perilous," 357, and the literature cited there.

24. See below, n. 61.

AGE AT FIRST MARRIAGE

Women's age at first marriage holds important demographic and economic consequences. Evidence that women in early modern northwestern Europe tended to marry relatively late, for example, underpins the distinctive "European marriage pattern" first described by John Hajnal, in which women often worked for years as domestic servants before marrying in their middle to later twenties, accumulating personal property that they then brought with them into marriage and pooled jointly with their husbands to establish nuclear households.[25] This marriage system produced households, household economies, and labor markets different from those common during the same period in southern Europe, where a woman typically married younger and seldom worked for long before doing so, instead marrying mainly with property that she had received as a dowry from relatives or through charity, and that was often held separately rather than communally within marriage.[26]

Although it is clear that the marriages documented in the Geniza were dowry-based, evidence for their timing is limited. (I will discuss evidence for women's labor before marriage and for dowry transfers further below, in Chapter 4.) Jews in the medieval Middle East, like the Muslims and Christians around them, married in several stages.[27] Two of these are required by rabbinic law: *qiddushin* (also called *erusin*) is a form of betrothal or inchoate marriage that legally binds a couple as man and wife, but they consummate the marriage and live together only after a formal marriage ceremony (*nisu'in*). Beginning in the twelfth century, some Rabbanite Jews in Egypt not only began formalizing betrothal (*qiddushin*) through written contracts, but also contracting nonbinding engagement or match agreements (*shiddukhin*) before betrothal.[28] Geniza marriage documents describe couples as typically becoming either engaged or betrothed well before they physically married, with the gap between initial contract and marriage lasting anywhere from a

25. Hajnal, "Two Kinds of Preindustrial Household Formation System." See Introduction, n. 14.

26. See the sources cited in the Introduction, n. 14, and in Chapter 4, ns. 7–8 and 129–132.

27. On nonbinding betrothal, contracted marriage, and consummation in Islamic law, see Delcambre, "Khiṭba" (*EI²*), Ali, *Marriage and Slavery*, 75–80. On inchoate vs. consummated marriage in Syriac law (with reference to Coptic practices in Egypt), see Weitz, "Syriac Christians," 113–132.

28. On *shiddukhin*, *qiddushin*, and *nisu'in* in classical rabbinic literature and in the Geniza period, see Friedman, *JMP*, 1:192–195; idem, "*Shiddukhin ve-Erusin*"; Ashur, "EBD," 54–71, "Shiddukhin." Karaite Jews in Fatimid and Ayyubid Egypt and Syria-Palestine also typically contracted *qiddushin* and *nisu'in* separately; see Olszowy-Schlanger, *KMD*, 123–127. Couples who became engaged through *shiddukhin* usually entered binding *qiddushin* only once they were ready to consummate the marriage; see Ashur, "EBD," 19–21.

few months to several years.[29] Despite the complexity of this legal process, and of the social arrangements surrounding it,[30] in this book I use "first marriage" to denote what happened after the wedding ceremony, since this is the point at which Geniza documents themselves begin to describe women as wives, with all of the social changes that I will argue this entailed.

Unfortunately, very few Geniza sources mention individual brides' ages either at the wedding or at any of these earlier stages. The handful of sources that do specify how old girls were when (or before) they married supply quite varied information. Some describe girls marrying before or just after having reached legal maturity. For example, a *shiddukhin* contract composed for a nine-year-old orphan girl named Sutayt in Bilbays in 1218 notes that the marriage would be consummated three years later, that is, after she turned twelve.[31] But others describe girls who remained unmarried significantly later than this. A query sent to the Egyptian Rabbanite jurist Yehuda b. Yosef in the late eleventh century asks whether a *shiddukhin* contract drafted by a man for his fifteen-year-old daughter should be viewed as holding legal weight.[32] A legal query sent to Avraham Maimonides in the early thirteenth century mentions two unmarried sisters whose father had been in India for fifteen years; both daughters, then, were at least this old and likely older, and neither had yet married.[33] A court record from Fustat, 1118, describes Sitt al-Ahl, the daughter of the India trader Yosef Lebdī, as having becoming betrothed sometime after reaching legal maturity; we learn from a different document that this betrothal eventually failed and that Sitt al-Ahl ended up marrying another man six and a half years later, when she was at least eighteen or nineteen years old or perhaps older.[34]

29. Ashur, "EBD," 94–97.

30. Marriage did not always entail a complete change in a new bride's circumstances. As I will argue in Chapter 5, some Geniza women may have had sexual contact with their future husbands before "consummation" at marriage; conversely, some women continued to live in the same households, with the same relatives, after marriage as they had before (see Chapters 1 and 8).

31. T-S 8 J 9.13; see below, n. 38.

32. T-S G 1.18.

33. ENA 4020.41. (Friedman, "Responsa of R. Abraham Maimonides," 48 n. 52, identifies T-S Misc. 27.3.2 as the second half of this document.)

34. First betrothal document, Nov. 1118: T-S NS 184.58 + 62 + 50 + 71 +70 + 74 + 72 + 98. Second betrothal document, June 1124, which terms Sitt al-Ahl "divorced from betrothal": T-S NS J 460 + NS J 112 + NS 211.8 + NS 323.11 + T-S 8.138 + T-S AS 152.19. Divorces from betrothal are mentioned regularly in documents and responsa and, as in this case, must have delayed these women's first marriages by months or years. See, for example, T-S 8 J 14.25v, a legal document about a girl who had been "betrothed several times," and T-S 13 J 16.5, an early thirteenth-century administrative letter about a girl in Bilbays, Egypt, who wished to contract a betrothal but could not prove to the local rabbinic court that she had properly dissolved a different betrothal eight months earlier. Other Geniza texts that

It is also unclear how many women documented in the Geniza never married at all. This is another important distinction between the European and "Mediterranean" models: late marriage in preindustrial northwestern Europe was accompanied by relatively large proportions of permanently single women, who seem to have been rarer in southern Europe. Geniza documents almost never mention older never-married women, but this does not mean that none existed; because so many legal documents and responsa were composed to document conflicts within marriage, it is possible that permanently unmarried women simply left a lighter footprint in the Geniza record.[35]

Minor and Mature Brides

The most that we can conclude from these sporadic Geniza references is that the women who eventually married typically did so within a range of ages, perhaps most often sometime between their early teens and early twenties. But if our evidence for this subject is poor, it does make one thing clear: few girls married earlier than this. At least among Jews in Fatimid and Ayyubid Egypt, true child marriage seems to have been rare. This question has been debated more than any other discussed in this book.

S. D. Goitein, Mordechai Akiva Friedman, Amir Ashur, and Avraham Grossman have all examined evidence for child marriage among Jews in medieval Egypt and in the medieval Middle East more broadly. Their conclusions differ dramatically. Goitein, Friedman, and Ashur, all Geniza specialists, have cumulatively identified fifteen references to minor brides in Egyptian documents and legal queries composed throughout the tenth to thirteenth centuries.[36] Balanced against the thousands of Geniza documents that mention marriages in general, all three scholars take this small group of texts as evidence that child marriage was unusual. Grossman, however, views this as

---

mention unmarried girls in their teens include T-S 8 J 27.14, a fragmentary legal query about a sixteen-year-old girl betrothed in her father's absence, and T-S 8 J 22.29, a virtually indecipherable query that mentions an unmarried girl of sixteen.

35. On the lack of clear Geniza evidence for never-married women, see Goitein, *Med. Soc.*, 3:62–65, and cf. Rapoport, *Marriage, Money and Divorce*, 38–39, 43. Goitein's discussion focuses partly on women appearing in a sample communal charity list, most of whom are described as wives, widows, or divorced women. None are explicitly described as never married, but 12 of the 42 are identified only by name, vocation, or another description, and may conceivably have never married. Such ambiguous references appear in other document genres, too. Cf. ibid., 173, where Goitein describes sisters mentioned in their brothers' marriage agreements (in clauses about whether the new bride would have to live with them) as "spinsters." This is possible, but it is equally possible that these dependent sisters were younger women who would eventually go on to marry, or that they were widows, divorced women, or even wives living apart from their husbands.

36. Goitein, *Med. Soc.*, 3:76–79; Friedman, "Marital Age" (cf. idem, "Ethics," 86–87); Ashur, "EBD," Chapter 6. These cases are listed and described in Krakowski, "Female Adolescence," Appendix A, and see below, n. 38.

an argument from silence, since other texts may simply fail to describe brides as minor even when this was the case. He concludes from a survey of medieval responsa that child marriage was extremely common, perhaps even normative, among Jews in the medieval Islamic world, including in Egypt. Grossman's argument has been widely influential and is often cited as the last word on the subject.[37]

There are two reasons, however, to conclude that Goitein and other Geniza specialists are correct: few women among the core Geniza populations married before legal maturity. First, the evidence for minor marriage is actually thinner than Grossman allows, or even than Goitein, Friedman, and Ashur have noted. This is because most of the texts that mention child marriage identified by all four scholars, Geniza documents and responsa alike, describe inchoate marriages (*qiddushin*) rather than consummated ones (*nisu'in*). Most of these inchoate marriages were consummated only later, usually once the bride reached legal maturity. In the case of the fifteen Geniza documents and legal queries assembled by Goitein, Friedman, and Ashur, only two clearly refer to minor brides married through *nisu'in*, both at age eleven. Another five describe brides engaged or betrothed before maturity but married only after maturity. The remaining eight documents are unclear. They either record minors' engagements or betrothals without noting when the match would be consummated, or mention minor girls who "married" using the ambiguous verb *zawwaja*, which can signify either betrothal or marriage.[38]

The same is true of the broader corpus of medieval Rabbanite responsa on which Grossman draws. Numerous gaonic responsa composed during the ninth to eleventh centuries, most answering questions of unknown provenance, discuss legal problems surrounding *qiddushin* conducted for minor girls. Many of these are obviously academic rather than prompted by actual legal cases. But more importantly, few clearly describe physically consummated marriages.[39] The few exceptions appear in legal queries and responsa sent to and from Ifrīqiyya and Andalusia, to which I will return below.

37. Grossman, "Child Marriage," idem, *Pious and Rebellious*, 33–43. Influential: see, e.g., Libson, "Betrothal of an Adult Woman," 185, Lamdan, "Child Marriage," 42, Frenkel, "Adolescence," 264, n. 5.

38. Two child marriages: T-S Ar. 47.244, Fustat, 1047; T-S 12.242, undated. Five deferred consummations: ENA NS 1.89a, Fustat, undated; Bodl. MS Heb. c. 13.20; Maimonides, *Responsa*, nos. 196/364; Mosseri IV 3, Alexandria, early thirteenth century; T-S 8 J 9.13, Bilbays, 1218. Eight ambiguous cases: T-S AS 146.66, Damascus, 933; T-S 13 J 8.31, Alexandria, 1042; T-S 12.397 + T-S AS 155.329 + T-S G 1.5a, Egypt, late eleventh century; ENA 1822A.23, Egypt, possibly c. 1082–94 (two cases mentioned); Maimonides, *Responsa*, nos. 34, 85; T-S 8.112, Bilbays, early thirteenth century.

39. Krakowski, "Female Adolescence," Appendix C. Two other gaonic responsa discuss girls betrothed or married at thirteen: Mueller, *TG Mizraḥ u-Ma'arav*, no. 197, and Assaf, *TG*, no. 8 (composed by Shemu'el b. Ḥofni, d. 1013).

Second, outside of this small group of cases, the Geniza corpus also contains a different form of positive evidence indicating that most brides were legally mature by the time they became betrothed. It is not just that only a few documents mention minor brides while most do not; as Grossman notes, this finding proves little on its own. More to the point, the vast majority of Geniza marriage documents contain some form of consent or agency clause either demonstrating that the bride has willingly consented to the marriage, or recording her appointment of an agent (*wakīl*) to betroth or marry her.[40] Such clauses indicate that these brides were legally mature, since minor girls lack legal agency and may be married by their fathers whether the girls grant consent or not.

Assent and agency clauses appear in Karaite and Rabbanite marriage documents of all kinds—*shiddukhin* contracts, *erusin* contracts, and *ketubbot*—but provide the strongest evidence for a bride's maturity when they appear in Rabbanite betrothal contracts (which, as noted above, rabbinic courts in Fustat began to produce separately mainly in the early twelfth century).[41] Assent clauses are standard in all Geniza *ketubbot* from across the Fatimid and Ayyubid periods (Palestinian- and Iraqi-formulary Rabbanite *ketubbot*, as well as Karaite *ketubbot*), but precisely because *ketubbot* were highly standardized documents, this may not mean much; scribes may simply have included the bride's assent as a matter of routine because they were accustomed to employing a formulary that contained it, even when it was not legally necessary. (However, if the scribes *were* accustomed to this formulary, this custom may itself suggest that most brides were expected to be legally mature.) Conversely, assent and agency clauses appear irregularly in engagement (*shiddukhin*) documents. But this, too, is not especially meaningful, because *shiddukhin* agreements were nonbinding and thus did not require the bride's legal consent even if she was mature.[42]

Betrothal documents, however, are more helpful. Unlike *ketubbot*, they do not follow a fixed formulary and are more likely to describe the actual legal

40. Goitein alludes to this point elsewhere (*Med. Soc.*, 3:102), but not in his discussion of child marriage. See also Friedman, "Marital Age," 163 n. 12.

41. Twelfth century: see Chapter 7. But they are foreshadowed by Palestinian-formulary *erusin* contracts from the tenth and eleventh centuries; see below, at ns. 44 and 45. Assent clauses typically appear in *ketubbot* but not betrothal contracts; agency clauses appear in both. For their legal background and formulation, see Friedman, *JMP*, 1:179–181, 216–232; Olszowy-Schlanger, *KMD*, 205–207, 212–217. (Friedman and Olszowy-Schlanger disagree about the origins of the agency clause; see Friedman, "Relationship.") A few contracts include an explicit maturity clause (e.g., "she is entirely mature, has reached puberty, and holds authority over herself," JNUL Heb. 4 577.4/98, Tyre, 1023).

42. Of twenty-two known *shiddukhin* contracts from the twelfth century and after, one identifies the bride as a minor, one identifies her as mature, and five contain agency clauses. See Ashur, "*Shiddukhin*," Krakowski, "Female Adolescence," 90.

roles assumed by participants in the betrothal ceremony; unlike *shiddukhin*, they ratified legally binding agreements to which mature brides did need to signal consent. The assent and agency clauses that they contain thus offer a reasonably reliable index of women's maturity status at marriage.

Both Karaite and Rabbanite betrothal documents preserved in the Geniza contain either assent clauses, agency clauses, or references to the bride's agent, but because Karaite maturity law is less clear than its Rabbanite counterpart, I will focus here on the evidence provided by Rabbanite documents. I have identified twenty-five Rabbanite betrothal documents that are sufficiently complete to reveal whether the bride was represented by an agent (*wakīl*).[43] Of these, three are early Palestinian-formulary betrothal contracts from a single court register, composed in Damascus in 933; none refer to an agent representing the bride.[44] The remaining twenty-two documents were composed in Egypt, primarily Fustat, all but one in the twelfth century.[45] Five of these describe the bride herself accepting the betrothal; another fifteen contain an agency clause or mention a bride's formal agent.[46] Only one clearly describes the bride's father as betrothing her without her explicit consent; another may do so, but it is too fragmentary for this to be certain.[47] In sum, of the documents composed in Egypt, twenty (91 percent) clearly involve brides who were legally mature at betrothal, while either one or two (4.5 percent or 9 percent) do not mention a formal agent and therefore may possibly, although not necessarily, have been composed for minor brides.

This group of documents is small, but it suggests more clearly than any other body of surviving evidence that most Egyptian betrothals documented in the Geniza were composed for legally mature brides. (Damascus is another story, to which I will return shortly.) This finding is limited to the twelfth century, but because this is due to a clear change in documentary production (this is when betrothals in Egypt began to be contracted separately in writing), there is no reason to assume that it reflects a shift in the practice of child marriage in this period—especially since the known cases of child marriage identified by Goitein, Friedman, and Ashur are no more heavily concentrated in the eleventh century than in the twelfth.

43. Krakowski, "Female Adolescence," Appendix B 2 (excluding nos. 18 and 21, which are too fragmentary to reveal whether they contained an agency clause, and no. 24, which is a different genre of document but which affirms the bride's maturity).

44. T-S 16.181a-c.

45. The one exception is T-S 18 J 1.3, a Palestinian-formulary Rabbanite *ketubbat erusin* from Fustat, 1007.

46. Bride herself accepts: Krakowski, "Female Adolescence," Appendix B 2, nos. 11, 13, 22, 23, and 27. Agency clause or agent mentioned: ibid., nos. 4–6, 8–10, 12, 14–16, 19–20, 25–26, 28.

47. Consent clearly lacking: T-S 8 J 5.21 (no. 17 ibid.). Ambiguous: T-S 6 J 12.1 (no. 7 ibid.).

Taken together, the available evidence thus supports these three scholars' conclusion that few Jewish girls in medieval Egypt were physically married as minors. It also suggests further that even inchoate (nonconsummated) marriage was relatively uncommon before legal maturity. Incidental comments in Geniza letters and other kinds of legal documents (from both the eleventh and twelfth centuries) further corroborate this conclusion, by casually associating female maturity with both betrothal and marriage: "When she matured, one of the woman's sons wished to betroth her"; "When one of the girls had matured, someone sought to betroth her"; and so on.[48]

Can this evidence tell us anything more about women's specific ages at marriage? It is unclear how closely rabbinic court officials considered girls' physiological development before deeming them mature. Some documents do describe court officials investigating girls to determine their legal status. For example, a fragmentary legal document datable to the tenth or early eleventh century (based on the coinage it mentions) testifies that a girl had been found "mature (*bāligh*,[49] the Arabic equivalent of *bogeret*) before two witnesses" before her betrothal.[50] But others imply that girls were often automatically assumed to be legally mature once they turned twelve (or perhaps twelve and a half), without close attention to whether they showed physical signs of puberty.[51]

It is possible, then, that some girls described as mature in these documents were as young as twelve. This is almost certainly true of the handful of brides betrothed as minors, and may be true of others. For these girls, adolescence as I define it in this book was extremely short and unimportant. But clearly this was not true for all women, and likely was not the case for most. Among the few sources discussed above that explicitly name a bride's or unmarried girl's age, it

48. ENA 2808.15a, undated; Maimonides, *Responsa* no. 58 (here *zawāj* might also mean "marriage," but the narrative makes clear that she was betrothed only after maturity). See also T-S 8.104, an undated will leaving the testator's three minor daughters one hundred dinars each to "use as a dowry after they mature," and T-S 12.461, an eleventh-century will leaving funds to two daughters to be spent on their dowries once they "reach full maturity." Cf. also Maimonides, *Responsa* no. 37 (repeated ibid., no. 90): "They arrived in Alexandria as unmarried virgins, and remained there until they matured and married."

49. Geniza documents routinely use this masculine form for girls.

50. T-S 10 J 28.1. See also ENA 1822A.23 (late eleventh century), which specifies that an orphan about to be betrothed has not yet grown "two" (referring to pubic hairs); and T-S Ar. 50.198, a fragmentary responsum about a thirteen-year-old betrothed girl that mentions her "signs of maturity" (*ḥujja bagrut*, l. 18; *simanei bagrut*, l. 19).

51. Two engagement and betrothal contracts drafted for minor brides state that they will marry at age twelve, without addressing their physical development: T-S 8.112, T-S 8 J 9.13. Prescriptive texts also sometimes casually describe maturity as a direct function of age, e.g., *TG Sha'arei Ṣedeq*, 4:3:6, a responsum of Se'adya b. Yosef's: "Her maturity occurs when she reaches twelve and a half years and one day." Most prescriptive texts, however, explicitly condition maturity on physical development.

is *only* those girls betrothed as minors who are described as being married right at legal maturity (or at age twelve); the other passing references that I identified involve young women who married at least a few years later than this.[52] A query submitted to Maimonides in the late twelfth century describes thirteen years as the *minimum* age at which girls could be expected to marry.[53] At least in Egypt, the majority of Rabbanite women probably spent at least a year or two, if not considerably more, with the legal status of *bogeret*.

How representative is this evidence of marriage patterns among Muslims and Christians in Egypt, or of Jews, Muslims, or Christians elsewhere in the medieval Islamic world? Very little comparative work has been done on women's age at marriage among other medieval Islamicate populations. The few sources that have been examined suggest that at least in medieval Egypt, Muslim girls may have also typically married at maturity or beyond. This evidence is too thinly spread to be at all conclusive. Still, it is consistent. Among a small group of published Islamic marriage contracts from ninth- to twelfth-century Egypt, most identify the bride as mentally or physically mature.[54] Yossef Rapoport has surveyed later references in *fatwā* literature and narrative texts from Mamluk Egypt that paint a similar picture.[55]

However, some rabbinic responsa suggest that matters may have been different elsewhere. The same query to Maimonides cited above (sent from an unknown location) that describes thirteen as the minimum age for marriage goes on to state that this is not true in all places; the custom of the Jews of Damascus "is to marry girls of eight or nine."[56] It is unclear whether this refers to betrothal or physical marriage. Although this passage was written two and a half centuries after the three early-tenth-century betrothal contracts from Damascus mentioned above,[57] it is remotely conceivable that they are connected; perhaps these documents do not mention the bride's agent because they were produced for minor brides. On the other hand, this fact may merely reflect changing scribal conventions. We possess very few other marriage agreements from the tenth century against which to compare these three documents.

Both gaonic and local responsa also describe child betrothal and child marriage as more common in Andalusia and the Maghrib (especially Ifrīqiyya) than they appear to have been in Egypt. A number of legal queries sent from western North Africa to Iraqi *ge'onim* describe girls betrothed as minors, or casually describe such betrothals as expected. For example, a query sent from tenth-century Qābis notes, "In our region, one who betroths

52. See above, at ns. 32–34.
53. Maimonides, *Responsa*, no. 427.
54. Grohmann, *Arabic Papyri*, Vol. 1, nos. 38, 40–42, 44; Khan, *ALAD*, nos. 32–33.
55. Rapoport, *Marriage, Money and Divorce*, 38–39.
56. Maimonides, *Responsa*, no. 427.
57. At n. 44.

a woman with a ring gives the ring to his agent, so that he may give it to her before witnesses—or to her father, if she is a minor."[58] Several tenth- and eleventh-century Andalusian responsa explicitly describe marriages consummated with extremely young minor brides: "Dina was orphaned from her father as a minor of about six years, and her mother misled her and married her to Re'uven—a forty-year-old. He secluded himself (that is, lived together) with her for around three years, and then died"; "You asked about that orphan whose relatives betrothed her to Shim'on, and he had sex with her when she was a minor"; "Re'uven betrothed Shim'on's daughter, who was a minor, and lived with her for a time."[59] The fourteenth- to fifteenth-century Maghribī jurist Shim'on b. Ṣemaḥ Duran describes child marriage as a longstanding social norm: "Indeed, we see that most people marry their daughters as minors . . . the practice in all later (i.e., medieval) generations . . . has been to marry daughters as minors." [60]

DEVELOPING DESIRE: AGE AND SEXUAL IDENTITY

The low proportion of child marriages documented in the Geniza is thus not self-explanatory. If Jewish girls in medieval Ifrīqiyya and Anadalusia, like Jewish girls in late antiquity, occasionally or perhaps often married before puberty, why did girls in Egypt typically not do so? The answer seems to lie in a sexual ethics averse to prepubescent marriage common among both Jews and Muslims in at least some regions of the medieval Islamic Middle East.

58. Harkavy, *Zikhron Kamma Ge'onim*, no. 65. See also the very similar comment in *TG Sha'arei Ṣedeq*, 3:3:12 (from tenth-century Qayrawān) and cf. Mueller, *TG Mizraḥ u-Ma'arav*, no. 12; T-S Misc. 28.186; Ginzberg, *Ginzei Schechter* II, no. 65. These queries all address inchoate rather than consummated marriages, and some texts from Ifrīqiyya explicitly describe minor betrothals consummated only at puberty or after: Assaf, *TG*, no. 8; Mosseri IIIa 11 (a family letter from al-Mahdiyya, eleventh century). Cf. the story from *al-Faraj Ba'd al-Shidda* cited at the beginning of Chapter 5. Marital age among Muslims in this region has not yet been studied, but note preliminarily an Islamic *fatwā* from twelfth-century Ifrīqiyya about a physically immature ten- or thirteen-year-old girl whose father married her but did not let her live with her husband right away. On the other hand, another *fatwā* from thirteenth-century Fez describes a mentally immature bride who has been physically married for nearly two years. Idris, "Le Mariage," I:59, no. 71; III:124, fourth case.

59. Mueller, *TG Mizraḥ u-Ma'arav*, nos. 186, 184; ibn Migas, *Responsa*, no. 173. See also Mueller, *TG Mizraḥ u-Ma'arav*, no. 187: "Shim'on died . . . leaving two daughters, the elder around six years old and the younger around four. . . . (Their mother) betrothed them . . . and they are still betrothed and have not yet consummated."

60. Duran, *Sefer Tashbeṣ*, 4:1:19. Shim'on's older contemporary Yiṣḥaq b. Sheshet Parfat states in a responsum that "people are usually careful not to marry their daughters as minors" (citing Rav's dictum, see above, n. 20), but then admits that such marriages are actually common: "nowadays (people) are accustomed to behaving leniently in this matter" (*She'elot u-Teshuvot*, no. 127).

This was a shift in social norms rather than in legal ones. Medieval Muslim and Jewish jurists alike agreed that child marriage was legally permitted (this is equally true of Karaites as well as Rabbanites, and for that matter also of Syriac Christians).[61] Yet it is a shift nonetheless visible within both Jewish and Islamic medieval legal texts, as well as in Geniza documents. We have seen that rabbinic texts from late antiquity never consider the effects of child marriage on the minor bride herself. In contrast, a range of Jewish and Islamic sources from medieval Egypt and Iraq directly or indirectly cast sex before puberty as damaging and physically dangerous for young girls. These texts reflect a social ideology of pedophilia different from that reflected in late ancient sources, and that falls somewhere between their approach to this subject and our own. These medieval sources assume that most parents would prefer not to subject their daughters to the trauma of prepubescent marriage; but they also assume, without censure, that most men would naturally prefer to consummate an inchoate marriage as soon as possible, whether or not their wives have reached puberty.

Permitted but Reprehensible: Rabbanite Resistance to Child Marriage

This new perception of child marriage was not a conscious flash point for Rabbanite legal authors. Medieval rabbinic discussions of child marriage are typical of gaonic and postgaonic legal discourse more broadly, in that they preserve only muted traces of tension between their author's social expectations and rabbinic laws surrounding child marriage. Indeed, at first glance these texts seem to yield little insight into their authors' beliefs about child sexuality. No medieval rabbinic jurist denied that child marriage was permitted, and few directly address children's sexual identity. Those who do mostly content themselves with briefly citing one or another of the sometimes contradictory classical rabbinic passages on the subject.[62]

61. Medieval jurists interpreted Rav's statement as "good advice" rather than binding law; see Grossman, *Pious and Rebellious* 67, idem, "Child Marriage," 110–111. See also Ashur, "EBD," 168; Libson, "Betrothal of an Adult Woman," 181–182, n. 13. I discuss Islamic legal approaches below; for Karaite ones, see below, n. 63, and for Syriac Christian law, see Weitz, "Syriac Christians in the Medieval Islamic World," 345–346.

62. For example, the early gaonic *Halakhot Gedolot* explains the Talmudic passage about young girls acting as chaperones cited above (n. 21) by noting that a man who tries to seduce an unchaperoned young girl "will be confounded" by her lack of interest (*Halakhot Gedolot, Yibbum ve-Ḥaliṣa* [no. 31], 335; cf. Maimonides, commentary on the *Mishna*, Qid. 4:11; idem, *MT*, *Issurei Bi'a*, 22:9). On the other hand, an anonymous Judeo-Arabic legal treatise preserved in the Geniza invokes the difficult rabbinic passage discussed above, n. 21, as proof that "a girl of three years and a day enjoys intercourse." (Bodl. MS Heb. c. 23.29b. M.A. Friedman tentatively identifies this text as a fragment of the *Ḥāwī* of David b. Se'adya *ha-ger*, late eleventh-century Andalusia: idem, "Halakhah as Evidence,"

But on closer view, this seemingly passive reception of classical rabbinic tradition proves deceptive. Although medieval Rabbanite authors discuss child marriage only within the narrow channels carved out by late ancient precedent, they nonetheless push these channels in new directions. To begin with, both Rabbanite and Karaite jurists cite classical rabbinic traditions about child marriage selectively, casting them in a more negative light than do the classical texts themselves. Medieval authors invoke the few rabbinic passages that criticize child marriage as regular refrains whenever the subject is mentioned. These include Rav's dictum that a girl should marry only once she can choose her own husband, as well as the classical rabbinic concern that child marriage legalizes procreative sex—respectively invoked, for example, in these two statements by Maimonides, the first in his commentary on the Mishna and the second in his legal code, the *Mishne Torah*:

> It is among our general principles that a man should not marry a woman until he has seen her, because we worry lest she not please him, and he will stand with her, not loving her. . . . It is for this (same) reason that we said, 'A man should not marry his daughter as a minor, *until she matures and states, 'I want so-and-so.'* . . .
>
> It is forbidden to expend semen to no purpose; therefore a man should neither practice *coitus interruptus* nor marry a minor who cannot yet bear children.[63]

97.) Other Rabbanite texts suggest that female sexuality begins in mid-childhood, e.g., Shemu'el b. Ḥofni, commenting on the Dina story in Genesis: "It is not possible that a child of four (years) should know to come in and go out and should seek to look at women, nor that intercourse should befall her" (he concludes that Dina must have been eight when she was abducted; *Biblical Commentary*, ed. Greenbaum, 36, p. 34).

63. Maimonides, Mishna commentary, *Qid.* 2:1 (and cf. idem, *MT*, *Ishut*, 3:19); Maimonides, *MT*, *Issurei Bi'a*, 21:18 (and cf. ibid., *Ishut* 15:7). Rav's dictum is also echoed by Se'adya b. Yosef: "It is better for everyone that (the father) not betroth (his daughter) until she matures, so that the outcome will be successful" (*Shetar mi'un*, ed. Ben-Sasson, "Fragments" 240, ls. 21–24), and in a fragment of an anonymous Karaite work preserved in the Geniza: "It is well-known that a girl cannot exercise choice in marriage—'so-and-so, not so-and-so'—until (she) is mature and intellectually capable" (ENA 2445.1–2). Karaite authorities likewise object to child marriage because it is nonprocreative. Binyamin al-Nahāwandī (ninth-century Iran) reportedly forbade families to marry daughters before they menstruate, "since marriage is permitted only in order (to produce) a child" (cited by Ya'qūb al-Qirqisānī, *Kitāb al-Anwār*, ed. Nemoy, VI:77:6; Qirqisānī himself calls this opinion "absurd," ibid., VI:77:7). Cf. the same anonymous Karaite fragment, which also states: "How can these people (i.e., the Rabbanites) permit one to marry a three year old, and to consummate with her! . . . This is contrary to God's . . . statement . . . that it is shameful to expend seed for a purpose other than that for which it was created" (ENA 2445.1–2).

Conversely, medieval Rabbanite authors only rarely invoke classical rabbinic passages that normalize consummated child marriages, or those (like 'Aqiva's dictum about the *bogeret* as prostitute) that represent adolescent sexuality as dangerous.[64] Moreover, both responsa and documents suggest that in practice, Rabbanite courts in both Fatimid Egypt and Abbasid and Buyid Iraq actively attempted to limit child marriages even while admitting that they were legal.

The longest and clearest of these sources is an anonymous Iraqi gaonic responsum probably composed in the late tenth or early eleventh century. It answers a query (preserved only in citation within the *ga'on*'s response) that betrays the questioner's own cultural difficulties with child marriage: how, he had asked, can minor orphans be permitted to marry, if their marriage can later be voided through *mi'un* and without a proper divorce? And how can marriage with a prepubescent bride be justified in the first place, if the Talmud states that "those who play with little girls delay the Messiah"? In reply, the *ga'on* offers a nuanced legal analysis that both defends child marriage as legally unassailable and betrays his own discomfort with it. He furthermore describes a long-standing gaonic policy discouraging local judges in Iraq from betrothing orphan girls as minors:

> (Because) the Merciful One did not forbid (child marriage), the Sages likewise did not forbid it; but one who marries a woman when she is a minor, for the purpose of sexual intercourse and not of (procreation), is reprehensible (*mekho'ar*); *the spirit of the Sages is displeased with him*[65] and he is considered as *delaying the Messiah.*
>
> When a father betroths his daughter, the betrothal is valid, and there are no biblical grounds to forbid him from betrothing her—as is written, *I give my daughter to this man* (Deut. 22:16).[66]. . . But an orphan is inherently unfit for betrothal. Our regular custom and that of our

64. Maimonides, *MT, Issurei Bi'a*, 21:25, cites bYev. 62b in praise of "marrying sons and daughters close to puberty" (*samukh le-firqan*). But Geniza letters suggest that this phrase was commonly associated with economic rather than sexual anxiety. See, for example, ENA NS 21.11, a thirteenth-century petition in which a man seeking help with his daughter's dowry informs his would-be benefactor: "My intention is to acquire for you *the merit of one who marries off women close to puberty* (*samukh le-firqan*)" (ls. 16–17); T-S 13 J 8.17, twelfth-century Fustat, a document that notes that two orphaned daughters require a dowry "so that they may marry close to puberty (*samukh le-firqan*)." (In its original context, *samukh le-firqan* seems to refer to the period slightly before legal maturity, and was understood as such by many medieval interpreters, but not all; Maimonides seems to understand it to mean slightly after maturity.)

65. For this phrase, see, e.g., mBB 8:5, mShevi'it 10:9.

66. This is the basic rabbinic proof-text for the principle that a father may unilaterally marry off his minor daughter. See Schremer, *Male and Female*, 103.

> fathers follows the words of the Sages: when an orphan comes to be betrothed, we seek proof that she is mature, and we rebuke and censure a judge who betroths a minor orphan—but we do not term this forbidden nor remove her from her husband.[67]

This response invokes a distinction drawn in the Babylonian Talmud that views a father's authority over his minor daughter as a biblical absolute (based on Deut. 22:16) but does not view other guardians' authority as similarly biblically required. But even while expressing himself in an entirely rabbinic idiom and claiming authority from "the words of the Sages," the *ga'on* inverts the internal logic of this classical tradition as he cites it. The Talmud itself distinguishes child marriages contracted by a father from those contracted for fatherless orphans in order to *praise* child marriages for orphans, which protect them socially and sexually: the rabbis legalized marriage with a minor orphan even though they could have chosen not to, it explains, "so that people would not treat her as ownerless property."[68] In contrast, our *ga'on* uses this distinction in order to cast minor orphan marriage as undesirable: biblical law does not allow us to prevent a father from betrothing his daughter, but absent this biblical necessity, minor orphans are "inherently unfit" to be married. In effect, this maneuver represents the rabbinic legitimization of child marriage as an embarrassing but necessary evil, to be circumvented wherever possible—a stance made even clearer by the *ga'on*'s description of child marriage as permitted but "reprehensible," *mekhoʿar*, a term rarely used in rabbinic literature and that likely gestures to the parallel Islamic legal concept *makrūh*.[69] (Indeed, although it explicitly invokes Talmudic categories, this responsum's focus on the difference between paternally and guardian-contracted minor marriage may well reflect the influence of Islamic legal discourse, which focuses extensively on this distinction in its discussion of child brides.[70])

This gaonic responsum thus departs from the rabbinic models on which it ostensibly relies. And it concludes by revealing that this shift was more than

67. Bodl. MS Heb. e 58 (= Lewin, *OHG, Yev.* no. 544, Friedman, "*Teshuvat ha-Rav*," 333–334). The responsum is undated, but its length and style are typical of Iraqi gaonic responsa from the late tenth and early eleventh centuries.

68. bYev. 112b. This discrepancy caused some medieval commentators to misunderstand this responsum as seeking to restrict *mi'un* rather than minor orphan marriage proper; see Lewin, *OHG, Yev.* 220, inset, and cf. Dinari, "*Hishtalshelut*," 225–226.

69. As Friedman notes, "Marital Age," 166. This term appears very rarely in medieval Rabbanite texts. Our author nonetheless manages to assimilate it to a fitting rabbinic proof-text: "A judge who takes payment for his judgment is *mekhoʿar*, but his ruling is valid" (bKet. 105a). (For Maimonides' use of the term *makrūh*, see Friedman, "Two Maimonidean Letters," 197 n. 29.)

70. See below, n. 80.

rhetorical. According to this *ga'on*, he and his predecessors actively discouraged rabbinic judges from permitting minor orphans to marry, although they stopped short of forbidding them to do so—a judicial move that is typical of gaonic approaches to legislation, which tended to be conservative and extremely shy of legal innovation, preferring whenever possible to effect legal change through alterations in court procedure.[71]

Several texts suggest that Rabbanite courts in other regions followed this gaonic policy. For example, a short letter that may have been composed by the Egyptian *ra'īs* David b. Dani'el (r. 1091–94) instructs a judge that he must permit a local father to betroth his prepubescent daughter, although in the past a similar case had caused unspecified problems. That earlier case, he explains, had involved a minor bride who was an orphan, but "this one, whom you state has not yet grown pubic hairs, has a father who betroths her. There is thus no way to forbid her betrothal, and it must be upheld."[72]

The live cultural concerns reflected in medieval responsa can be hard to detect, since they often address even pressing questions through set patterns of inherited proof-texts and legal categories. Nonetheless, pursuing what Haym Soloveitchik calls the "angle of deflection" sometimes visible in even the driest Jewish legal texts, it is easy to see that the author of this responsum's own views of child marriage differed from those held by the late ancient rabbis on whom he draws.[73] By the same token, the stock rabbinic objections that he and other medieval Rabbanite authors use to critique such marriages may perhaps also obscure the basic social perceptions underlying their own resistance to it.

Indeed, neither the Geniza nor surviving Rabbanite responsa provide much reason to think that the main charges leveled against child marriage in either classical or medieval rabbinic sources—namely, disapproval of nonprocreative intercourse and concern for girls' marital freedom—would have held much resonance for Jews in the medieval Middle East. Geniza evidence for birth control has not yet been systematically studied, but contraceptive prescriptions preserved among the corpus suggest that at least some Geniza Jews may have viewed nonprocreative sex with equanimity, as did many of

71. See Chapter 2, at n. 52.

72. ENA 1822A.23. (Gil, *Palestine*, 3:335, identifies the handwriting as that of David b. Dani'el. See also Ashur, "EBD," 169–70, and Friedman, "On Marital Age" 165–166, n. 18.) Although other responsa from Andalusia mention marriages consummated with very young girls (see above, n. 59), a responsum composed by the Andalusian authority Ḥanokh b. Moshe (d. 1014) goes even further in this direction, rejecting minor orphan betrothals as invalid even post facto. (Mueller, *TG Mizraḥ u-Ma'arav*, no. 187. I read this responsum differently from Grossman, *Pious and Rebellious*, 73; see Krakowski, "Female Adolescence," 107 n. 76.)

73. Soloveitchik, "Halakhah, Hermeneutics, and Martyrdom," 77–78.

their Muslim contemporaries.[74] Similarly, Rav's objection that child marriages deprive young women of marital autonomy would have made little sense to Jewish readers who, as we will see, widely assumed that older relatives would control a daughter's choice of first husband both before and after puberty.[75]

How then can we uncover the real cultural anxieties underlying the aversion to prepubescent marriage reflected in both gaonic and postgaonic texts? Geniza documents themselves provide only slight hints that can help us do so. But several more remote Islamic legal and literary sources parallel these documents in ways that may explain their meaning.

Reconstructing a Social Ideology of Pedophilia

In a historical chronicle dedicated to the fifteenth-century Mamluk *sulṭān* al-Ashraf Qāytbāy, the Ḥanafī judge al-Ṣayrafī describes his own involvement in a sensationalistic case spanning both the *qāḍī* and *maẓālim* courts that centered on the marriage of a physically prepubescent twelve-year-old girl.[76] Three years earlier, her parents had left her in care of a maternal aunt and disappeared from Cairo. The aunt had approached al-Ṣayrafī and asked him to find her a husband, and he had accordingly married her off to a man named Fāris, a soldier in the retinue of one of Qāytbāy's *mamlūks*. Fāris promptly consummated the marriage—"although," al-Ṣayrafī notes, "I had not authorized him to have sex with her"—and then just as promptly divorced her, refusing to pay her any of her deferred dower.[77] Later in the story, al-Ṣayrafī ex-

74. E.g., T-S K 14.20, T-S AS 169.150 (see Isaacs, *Medical and Para-Medical Manuscripts*, 2, 87). On medieval Islamic approaches to contraception (which were mainly neutral or positive), see Musallam, *Sex and Society*. Medieval Rabbanite authorities emphasize this issue in the context of child marriage but are similarly lenient in other contexts. The *ga'on* Hayya b. Sherira, for example, encourages young wives physically endangered by pregnancy to use a contraceptive sponge (*mokh*), even if they are reluctant to do so (see Harkavy, *Zikhron Kamma Ge'onim*, no. 338, a discussion of tNid. 2:6/bYev. 12b; and cf. *Halakhot Gedolot, Hilkhot Mi'un*, no. 32). This ruling parallels medieval Arabic medical texts that discuss contraception in precisely such cases; see Musallam, *Sex and Society*, 69–71, Bos, "Ibn al-Jazzār," 309. (However, some proto- and early Karaite jurists are stricter about nonprocreative sex. 'Anan b. David forbade intercourse with a pregnant wife: *Sefer Miṣvot*, ed. Pinsker, *Liqqutei Qadmoniyot*, 60. Ya'qūb al-Qirqisānī claims that the "'Ananites" equated sex during pregnancy with masturbation and homosexual relations: *Kitāb al-Anwār*, ed. Nemoy, VI:77:6, and cf. ibid., VI:77:1. Dani'el al-Qūmisī terms intercourse with a barren wife "prostitution": commentary on Hosea, ed. Markon, *Pitron*, 4:10.) See above, n. 63.

75. See Chapter 6.

76. *Inbā' al-Haṣr bi-Abnā' al-'Aṣr*, 227–230. The passage is translated in full in Petry, "Conjugal Rights" (Petry renders the line I cite below slightly differently). On the *Inbā'* generally, see idem, "Scholastic Stasis."

77. On the deferred dower, see Chapter 4.

pands this account to explain that the girl had run away from him after he and his *mamlūk* patron had "overpowered" and raped her; he also adds that the two men had been terrorizing the neighborhood and looting the marketplace. The girl's aunt raised a mob who stormed the palace to demand justice, and al-Ṣayrafī was called before a government official (*dawādār*) to explain his actions: was it appropriate to marry a girl of this age? Al-Ṣayrafī defended the marriage as legally valid, citing a famous *ḥadīth* attributed to Muḥammad's wife ʿĀ'isha: "The Prophet married me when I was six or seven, and had intercourse with me when I was nine." The *dawādār* accepted this argument, but nonetheless ordered both Fāris and the *mamlūk* flogged and put on public display as an example to anyone "who deflowers girls and takes from them what he is not entitled to."

Yossef Rapoport describes this account as a textbook illustration of differences between the legal methods employed by military *maẓālim* and religious courts in fifteenth-century Egypt, a period when the Mamluk state increasingly began to intervene in family matters that had previously been administered mainly by *qāḍīs*.[78] Rapoport notes that military judges enjoyed the advantage of freedom from the complex technical rules of substantive law and legal procedure to which religious judges were bound: "They argued, and chroniclers sometimes agreed, that theirs was the common sense approach." In this case, when Ḥanafī law provided no grounds for punishing Fāris, the *dawādār* was able to step in and impose a punishment that fit popular perceptions of his crime.

Beyond its political interest, another aspect of this passage is worth noting: the view shared by all participants in the story that a minor girl should be protected from sexual intercourse. Rapoport contrasts the *dawādār*'s "common sense" rejection of this marriage with al-Ṣayrafī's recondite legal justifications; but for our purposes it is significant that even al-Ṣayrafī feels the need to justify himself to readers by pointing out that he had forbidden Fāris to consummate the marriage immediately. Even though it would have been technically licit by any standard, both judges seem to have assumed as a matter of course that this girl should not have been deflowered before she reached puberty.

Despite the distance of four centuries and over a thousand miles between them, this late Mamluk account and the Gaonic responsum discussed above resemble each other in several respects. Both texts describe judicial officials negotiating between a legal tradition that mostly sanctioned prepubescent intercourse and an ordinary cultural sense that it should be avoided, and both depict court officials therefore permitting but attempting to regulate the

78. Rapoport, "Marriage and Divorce," 279–282 (cited text, 280). On flogging as a punishment for rape in Islamic law, see Serrano, "Legal Practice," 199–200.

marriage of minor orphan girls, who as we shall see were more likely to be married off earlier than other girls, and for whom court officials often bore some measure of responsibility.[79]

Islamic prescriptive legal literature elsewhere suggests some of the underlying social ideas that this "common-sense" rejection of child marriage may reflect. Like rabbinic law, Islamic law broadly permits child marriage, although it recognizes a relatively later minimal threshold for consummation, at nine years (a benchmark derived from the *ḥadīth* about ʿĀʾisha cited above).[80] Alongside this age-based standard, however, medieval Islamic legal texts frequently invoke another criterion as relevant to the timing of consummation: the individual bride's physiological capacity to tolerate intercourse, regardless of her chronological age. For example, a passage in Shāfiʿī's *Kitāb al-Umm* states:

> If the wife is mature or close to maturity, or physically large (*jismiyya*), such that she is in the category of those who can tolerate intercourse, (the husband may consummate). But if she cannot tolerate intercourse, her family may prevent (him from) consummating until she can.[81]

Fiqh literature alludes to this standard using a wide variety of terms, chiefly variants on "one who can tolerate intercourse" and "one whose type may be bedded."[82] Although Islamic legal texts mention this concept pervasively, they

79. Islamic legal discussions of minor orphan marriage focus on whether a guardian other than the father may compel his ward to marry; see the next note. The Fatimid chronicler al-Muṣabbiḥī describes a similar confrontation between the *qāḍī* Muḥammad b. al-Nuʿmān and the caliph al-ʿAzīz, in 985: "An orphan known as bt. al-Dībājī (was married) under Muḥammad b. al-Nuʿmān's authority. . . . One of the witnesses protested and alleged that the marriage was invalid, because she was a minor. . . . She was brought to the palace and her case was submitted to al-ʿAzīz, who examined her and found her to be a minor. He ordered the *qāḍī* to invalidate the marriage" (Sayyid, "*Nuṣūṣ*," 33; see Cortese and Calderini, *Women and the Fatimids*, 210–211). On Jewish court officials' involvement in orphans' marriages, see Chapter 4.

80. On this *ḥadīth*, see Spectorsky, *Chapters on Marriage and Divorce*, 10, n. 28. Jurists from all Sunnī *madhhab*s allowed a father to unilaterally marry off his minor daughter, but differed about whether other guardians could marry off a minor ward. Most Ḥanafī jurists permitted minor orphan marriages but allowed the girl to opt out once she reached maturity (*ikhtiyār* or *khiyār al-bulūgh*, a concept parallel to rabbinic *mi'un*). Ḥanbalī doctrine permits minor orphan marriage without *ikhtiyār* after the age of nine, as long as the girl consents; Shāfiʿī and Mālikī jurists categorically forbade such marriages. See Spectorsky, "*Sunnah* in the Responsa of Isḥāq b. Rāhwayh," 57; idem, *Chapters*, 93–96, 143–146; Ali, "Marriage in Classical Islamic Jurisprudence," 17–18; Baugh, "Compulsion in Minor Marriages."

81. al-Shāfiʿī, *Kitāb al-Umm, Kitāb al-nafaqāt, al-ikhtilāf fī al-dukhūl.*

82. *Taqdiru ʿalā/taṣluḥu li- / taḥtamilu / tuṭīqu al-jimāʿ / al-waṭʾ / al-rijāl; allatī yujāmiʿu mithluhā.* This criterion is consistently distinguished from puberty as defined by menarche. See Baugh, "Compulsion in Minor Marriages," 150–158, 254–259, 297–301, 320–324, and Ali, "Money, Sex, and Power," 170–183. (For developments in the Ottoman period, see Motzki, "Child Marriage," 138.) Court-appointed women: see Tillier, "Women before the

do not define it very precisely; as here, "tolerance for intercourse" appears primarily connected to a girl's physical size (either that of her body, or of her vaginal opening; medieval Islamic literary sources describe court-appointed women charged with determining whether individual girls were ready). Like al-Shāfiʿī, other Muslim jurists consistently assume that parents will naturally wish to delay the consummation of a daughter's marriage until she has grown enough to reach this benchmark.[83]

Legal discussions of girls' "tolerance for intercourse" assume that sex is physically traumatic and therefore harmful to very young girls, in ways roughly consistent with al-Ṣayrafī's story about Fāris. At the same time, they do not seem to understand a man's *desire* to consummate marriage with a prepubescent girl as unexpected or taboo. By al-Ṣayrafī's account, Fāris incurred ill-will through his particularly harsh treatment of his young wife, not to mention his public thefts and bad behavior; had an another man merely consummated marriage with a minor bride less violently, even against a *qāḍī*'s instructions, it is not clear that he would have been judged as harshly. Indeed, Islamic legal discourse takes for granted that a groom will be prepared for conjugal relations with his bride whenever her family makes her available to him; the twelfth-century Ḥanbalī jurist ibn Qudāma describes this impulse as natural and inevitable, cautioning that if a bride is not yet "capable of intercourse," her family should not surrender her to her husband even if he promises to take pains to care for her: "He cannot trust his evil desire (*shirrat nafsihi*) for intercourse with her, such that he may deflower her or kill her."[84]

Children's Incapacity for Intercourse as a Cultural Norm

These Islamic legal texts provide a template for understanding the ordinary cultural expectations that may have likewise motivated medieval Rabbanite resistance to child marriage. The very few Geniza documents that directly discuss the consummation of a child marriage support this suggestion. These documents parallel Islamic legal texts in ways that suggest that the concept of "capacity for intercourse" itself reflects basic cultural assumptions about the ethics of sexual activity with very young girls shared broadly among both Jews and Muslims in parts of the medieval Middle East.

Qāḍī," 285, citing al-Khaṣṣāf (ninth-century Iraq); Shaham, *Expert Witness*, 87–88, citing Maghribī sources that discuss whether developing breasts indicated a girl was ready.

83. Some Islamic marriage contracts include clauses stating that consummation will be delayed. See Rapoport, *Marriage, Money and Divorce*, 74, for a clause of this type in an Egyptian Mamluk contract, and cf. for the Maghrib Idris, "Le Mariage," I:59, no. 71; ibid., II:71, no. 91.

84. *Al-Mughnī*, 9:623, cited (with a slightly different translation) by Baugh, "Compulsion in Minor Marriages," 90.

One of these documents is an undated letter likely sent by a local judge to a communal official in Fustat. It describes a man who had sued his wife for divorce on the grounds that after two years she still refused to consummate their marriage:

> I make known to his honor that there is a man with us appealing for help, saying, "I have been with my wife for two years, and she will not permit me of herself." Then we invited her (to testify), and she said, "What he has said is correct; I am unable to have relations with a man." This girl is more than thirteen years old, and she is an orphan. He wishes to divorce her, and she also requests a divorce. Thus I ask that my honor let me know: does this man have to pay the deferred payment (specified) in (her) *ketubba*, or not? Or may he marry another (woman) alongside her, or not?[85]

This query raises a question directly addressed in rabbinic legal literature: may a husband whose wife refuses to have sex with him divorce her without paying her the dower that he had pledged to her at marriage? In most cases the legal answer to this question is clearly yes, but the judge who wrote this letter took pains to note the particular circumstances—both legal and practical—that might complicate its outcome.[86] Among other details, he notes that the young wife is not merely resistant to this husband in particular, but constitutionally incapable of sexual intercourse, *despite having already reached the age of thirteen*. What does this detail add to his account? Most simply, it seems to mean: she is already old enough to be "able." This remark, then, implies that like Muslim jurists, the author of this query understood girls' sexual capacity to depend on their age.

This is one of only two known Geniza texts that document a marriage formalized through *nisu'in* with a minor bride. The other, a court record composed in Fustat in 1047, summarizes the court's response to a remarkably similar lawsuit, filed by a man named Yaʿaqov b. Avraham b. Mukhtār against his young wife. (In fact, the details supplied in these two documents are so similar that it is conceivable they describe the same case.)[87] The document is torn

85. T-S 12.242.

86. As is often the case, the legal ideas reflected in this query are murky. The answer to the question that it raises is straightforward; rabbinic law views a woman who refuses to have sex with her husband as a "rebellious" wife (*moredet*) who forfeits her claim to a financial settlement at divorce. But the judge's primary concern seems to be to find a legally justified means to provide this young wife with financial support, which is probably why he suggests that her husband take a second wife rather than divorce her.

87. T-S Ar. 47.244. The judge's letter (T-S 12.242) is undated; Friedman dates it to the early thirteenth century (idem, "Marital Age," 165, n. 17), but does not explain why. Both documents involve orphan brides married at eleven who have now matured and who

across the middle, so that we can reconstruct its meaning only from the final section of each line. Still, enough is left to allow us to see that it, too, implies that officials viewed the young wife's age as relevant to her sexual capacity.

This document begins by citing Ya'aqov's claim that his wife had failed to fulfill the "obligation to him that God has imposed upon her [. . .] in terms of sexual intercourse." It then notes that witnesses had testified that she had been a minor, "less than eleven years old," at the time of her marriage. This testimony seems intended to provide context for her reluctance; further in the document, however, both spouses make clear that her refusal is not a function of her age, since she remains incapable of consummating the marriage despite having now passed legal maturity: the wife is cited as stating, "I do not have [. . .] that I am able to, regarding [. . .] this, intercourse with him," and the husband as confirming this statement with a statement that ends, "God to me from her, and she is mature."[88] Like the judge's letter, this fragmentary document implies that all parties concerned understood a wife's sexual availability as normally contingent on puberty.

Both of these documents thus associate girls' expected sexual capacity with the beginning of adolescence. This idea is never expressed in medieval Jewish legal sources. Even so, its presence both in Islamic prescriptive texts and in Geniza documents may help explain the underground aversion that prompted medieval Rabbanite authors to marshal whatever classical precedents they could to oppose child marriage, and that prompted gaonic and other Rabbanite officials to attempt to restrict judges from marrying off orphan girls before puberty.

Yet Geniza evidence also suggests that Jews, again like their Muslim neighbors, did not necessarily extend this idea to a more fundamental taboo against male *desire* for prepubescent sex. A letter sent from Alexandria to Eliyyahu b. Zekharya, the chief judge of Fustat in the early thirteenth century, echoes Muslim jurists' descriptions of tensions between men and their in-laws over the timing of consummation.[89] Like the prototypical husbands described by these jurists, its author, identified only as Mūsā, reveals himself as unabashedly eager to consummate marriage with a barely pubescent bride whose father did not consider her to be ready. Mūsā had been involved in a disagreement, now

refuse to consummate the marriage. Although its details are hard to reconstruct, this record seems to describe the court's attempt to mediate between the couple, a standard component of divorce proceedings (see Chapter 7). In l. 14, the wife is termed *nāshiz*, the Arabic equivalent of the rabbinic *moredet* (see Chapter 7; Islamic law defines the *nāshiz* as a wife who withholds sex from her husband: Ali, "Sex, Money, and Power," 183–203).

88. The word "mature" has gone unnoticed in previous discussions of this document and does not appear in Ashur's edition (idem, "EBD," no. 28-א).

89. Mosseri IV.3.

resolved, with a man named Abū Zikrī b. Netan'el. As a means of cementing their reconciliation, he betrothed Abū Zikrī's minor daughter and was prepared to marry her almost immediately, but Abū Zikrī insisted that he wait a year. Mūsā reluctantly agreed to these terms; now, however, he asked that Eliyyahu intervene to ensure that the marriage would not be delayed even further:

> Abū Zikrī and I agreed that I would marry his minor daughter. Before her betrothal, I had intended to grant them a month until—[90] and her mother was promising me this. But when everyone gathered to perform the betrothal, he said, "I will not decrease (the delay) below one year," and I was unable to oppose him.
>
> [. . .] the saying (of the Sages): "(*One should not arrange to marry a minor when she is still a minor, but one may arrange*) *to marry a minor once she has matured*." I ask you to remonstrate with Abū Zikrī on my behalf . . . that he should not delay me more . . . as the delay is painful.

Mūsā does not explicitly spell out his father-in-law's reasons for postponing the wedding. But the rabbinic proof-text that he cites provides a clue. The dictum "One should not arrange to marry a minor when she is still a minor, but one may arrange to marry a minor once she has matured" appears in the Talmudic tractate *Ketubbot*, in one of the only classical rabbinic passages to even hint that the prospect of sex might be worrisome for a prepubescent bride.[91] Nonetheless, the Talmud goes on to explain, there is no need to worry that a minor girl will be anxious about being pledged to marry at puberty. By invoking this proof-text, Mūsā implies that Abū Zikrī was directly concerned about his daughter's sexual readiness for marriage. In this context, his own straightforward urgency that the marriage be consummated—because "the delay is painful"—seems to reflect a cultural universe in which parents, guardians, and communal officials might view it as their duty to protect very young brides from having to endure sex, but in which no shame adhered to a man's urge to overcome their reluctance.[92]

90. The author clearly omitted a word here, likely either *balaghat* ("she matured"), or *al-dukhūl* ("consummation"). Friedman suggests the former, "Marital Age," 164, n. 15.

91. bKet. 57b. See above, n. 22.

92. An undated Judeo-Arabic legal query likewise describes a man who refused to let his daughter's fiancé consummate the marriage. The text is fragmentary but suggests that their disagreement centered on her physical development; it notes that she is already "physically mature (*bāligh*) [. . .], she has (completed) thirteen years and entered her fourteenth year . . . and her mother and maternal uncle have vouched that she is pubescent." T-S Ar. 50.198; see n. 50 above.

This chapter has reviewed two different approaches to the early female life course. The first is a legal model recognized by both late ancient and medieval rabbinic texts, which conditions young women's legal identity on a combination of physiological development, chronological age, and marital status, allowing for a period of adolescence between early puberty and marriage. Between these two events, the mature unmarried daughter (*bogeret*) is socially and economically independent, free from either a father's or husband's control. At the same time, rabbinic law remains mostly agnostic with respect to women's age at marriage: a girl's father may marry her off well before she reaches maturity, in which case she skips over adolescence entirely—an outcome that some rabbinic authors in late antiquity viewed as ideal.

The second is a less formal model of women's adolescence, reflected in the ordinary ideas through which Geniza Jews managed girls' lives. Here I have described these ideas with respect to women's age at marriage. The Rabbanite Jews reflected in the Geniza faithfully maintained rabbinic laws about child marriage, permitting fathers who wished to do so to marry off their daughters as minors. Yet at least in Fatimid and Ayyubid Egypt and Syria, social assumptions external to these laws—and different from those that had originally informed them—shaped their reception and limited their effects. Despite their legal right to do so, few fathers or guardians documented in the Geniza entered girls into consummated marriages as minors; this may have been because unlike the rabbis of late antiquity, many medieval Jews viewed sex before puberty as deeply undesirable for girls themselves. Like the Muslims among whom they lived, these Jews thus invested early puberty with a social meaning that it does not hold in rabbinic law, as the minimal threshold for physically consummated marriage.

The next two chapters will examine how Geniza Jews understood and structured women's adolescence socially and economically, and how they negotiated other aspects of the rabbinic *bogeret* model that conflicted with their own ordinary ideas about young women.

CHAPTER FOUR

The Economics of Female Adolescence

WOMEN WHO HAD NOT YET entered a first marriage appear more often in Geniza documents devoted to money than to any other subject. This is partly because marriage involved significant property transfers that could take years to prepare and negotiate. It is also because Geniza Jews seem to have distinguished adolescence most sharply from other parts of women's lives when it came to money. What it meant to be an unmarried girl, both socially and legally, emerges above all from documents composed to manage girls' support and property and to prepare them financially for marriage.

Central to these preparations was the dowry with which most girls married. The marriages documented in the Geniza, like those throughout the medieval Middle East, were established with a bidirectional exchange of property: among Jews, Muslims, and Christians alike, the groom pledged a cash dower (Arab. *mahr*, Heb. *mohar*, Syr. *mahrā*) to his future wife, while her parents or other kin also granted her a dowry bound up in movable property, real estate, and slaves (Arab. *jihāz*, *qumāsh*, or *shiwār*, Aram. *nedunya* or Heb. *parnasa*, Syr. *pernītā*).[1] But for Jews as well as Muslims in medieval Egypt, the bride's dowry rather than the groom's dower functioned as the primary and most important marriage payment. The values of both types of marriage gifts recorded in Geniza marriage contracts vary widely. A few very poor brides' dowries are smaller than their promised dower; a woman married in rural Egypt in 1081, for example, was promised twelve dinars as dower and brought in as dowry a cloak and three pillows, worth a total of five

1. This model has late ancient roots. See Friedman, "Minimum Mohar"; idem, *JMP*, 1:267–288; Goitein, *Med. Soc.*, 3:364–393; Rapoport, "Matrimonial Gifts"; Weitz, "Syriac Christians in the Medieval Islamic World," 116–117.

and 1/3 dinars.[2] Most Geniza women, however, owned dowries larger than the *mahr* (dower) promised by their husbands, sometimes by several orders of magnitude.[3] Even the wealthiest brides documented in Geniza marriage contracts were seldom promised a dower higher than 150 dinars; the richest bride identified to date—a merchant's daughter in early twelfth-century Fustat (c. 1128–1153) whose dowry contained more than one hundred pieces of jewelry, textiles, and copper utensils, four slaves, and a library of books, worth 2,100 dinars in all—was promised only 140.[4] Moreover, even this relatively smaller sum often went unpaid. Both Jewish and Islamic dowers were divided into two portions: the groom paid his wife a small preliminary sum in cash before or when they married and pledged to pay her a larger deferred sum if he divorced or died before her. Among Jews, at least, recent research suggests that many husbands ended up paying this deferred portion only partially or not at all.[5]

The dowry that a Jewish girl brought into first marriage thus contained most of the assets that she would own throughout her lifetime. For this reason, dowries also mattered a great deal *before* marriage, when the need to accumulate and preserve dotal property cast a long shadow over girls' economic lives. This chapter examines how and why relatives and communal officials gave dowries to women at marriage, and how they managed girls' property, labor, and support in the years before marriage. It argues that Geniza Jews' dowry regime helped shape women's adolescence in ways different from the rabbinic legal model, at least with respect to economic matters: rather than becoming independent actors at puberty, women could become socially adult only once they married—a model closer to the basic frameworks of Islamic than of Jewish law.

Women's Property and the Dowry

Why did Geniza Jews give dowries to their daughters at marriage?

The simplest way to understand assets given to either spouse at marriage is as an endowment for the marriage itself—a base of property that a new couple may use and profit from as they begin their life together. The items contained

2. T-S 16.53, from the village of Ṣā. (The total value noted includes another item that has been effaced.)

3. See the relative amounts listed in Goitein, *Med. Soc.*, 3, Appendix.

4. T-S J 1.29. Her dowry was likely worth even more than this, since dowry lists often omit brides' real estate; see below, n. 60. Dowry lists are an essential source of data for material and economic history; see Goitein, *Med. Soc.*, 4:105–190, Stillman, "Female Attire," Frenkel, "The *Ketubba*," and Molad-Vaza, "Clothing in the Mediterranean Jewish Society," esp. 226–230. Most remain unpublished, apart from those contained in the marriage documents published by Friedman, *JMP*, Olszowy-Schlanger, *KMD*, and Goitein, "Three Trousseaux."

5. Zinger, "Women, Gender, and Law," 130–176; see further Chapter 7.

in Geniza dowries must have served this purpose in some ways. Once married, a woman not only wore the clothing and jewelry listed in her dowry list (*taqwīm*); both she and her husband ate from dishes, sat and slept on sofas, pillows, and mats, were served by slaves, and sometimes lived in an apartment that she had brought to the marriage in her dowry.[6]

But while this is the main purpose of marriage gifts in communal property regimes, dowries in separate property regimes like those typical in medieval Egypt also serve other long-term functions. Throughout much of northwestern Europe in the later Middle Ages, for example, marriage property was communal: husbands and wives pooled their property into a shared conjugal fund at marriage, used it jointly to run and support a nuclear household that they had established, and each inherited all or much of it after the other died.[7] In contrast, among Geniza Jews and the Muslims around them (and likely Christians too, although this is not certain), marriage property was held separately; husbands and wives kept their individual assets formally distinct from each other during the marriage and after. Separate property regimes tend to support more complex household economies in which women and their husbands may receive, use, control, and eventually retain and inherit dotal property in a range of ways.[8]

Scholars have generally understood dowries of the kind exchanged among Geniza Jews—those that are the primary payment made by either side at marriage—to serve two possible aims. First, dowries may permit a form of *diverging devolution*, the anthropologist Jack Goody's term for inheritance systems in which parents transmit significant property to both daughters and sons.[9] This model views dowries as premortem bequests, given when a daughter marries rather than when one or both of her parents die. Alternatively, economists have tended to understand dowries as incentives to grooms that help clear marriage markets efficiently, by matching wealthy wives with productive husbands in societies where men are more economically productive than women.[10] Both of these ideal motives can coexist in practice, as more recent work in economics has begun to acknowledge.[11] Still, women generally

6. See Chapter 1, n. 56.

7. Howell, *Women, Production, and Patriarchy*, and cf. eadem, *The Marriage Exchange*.

8. A sizable literature examines how women's dowries functioned within separate marriage property systems in Renaissance Italy. See, e.g., Guzzetti, "Dowries in Fourteenth-Century Venice," Chojnacki, "Getting Back the Dowry," and Kirshner, *Marriage, Dowry, and Citizenship*, esp. Chapters 6 and 8.

9. See especially Goody, "Bridewealth and Dowry," 17f., and idem, *Production and Reproduction*, 9–22.

10. Building on the work of Gary Becker; see idem, *Treatise*, 80–134. See, for example, Botticini and Siow, "Why Dowries?"; Anderson, "The Economics of Dowry and Brideprice."

11. E.g., Anderson and Bidner, "Property Rights over Marital Transfers," Chan, "Marital Transfers and the Welfare of Women."

control and benefit from their dowries more directly when those giving and receiving these assets understand them as inheritances rather than incentives for husbands.

Rabbinic texts recognize both of these explanations for dowry gifts. A passage in the Talmud describes the dowry both as a woman's patrimony and as a lure for grooms.[12] It begins by citing a tradition attributed to the second-century rabbi Shim'on b. Yoḥai, who explains the Mishnaic law of *benin dikhrin*, which allows a woman's sons to inherit her dowry, as encouraging a form of female inheritance: men will be more likely to transmit property to their daughters if they know it will not end up consumed by their sons-in-law, but will eventually pass to their grandsons. But the Talmud's anonymous narrator then revises Shim'on's explanation, adding that the law aims not to promote women's inheritance for its own sake, but to help them attract a husband:

> R. Yoḥanan stated in the name of R. Shim'on b. Yoḥai: Why was *ketubbat benin dikhrin* established? So that a man would jump to give to his daughter as to his son. But can it be that the Merciful One stated that sons inherit and daughters do not, and the Sages came and established that daughters should inherit? . . . (Rather,) this is what (R. Shim'on's statement) teaches us: That a father must clothe and outfit (his daughter) and give her something, so that (men) will jump to marry her.

This addendum reflects its author's unhappiness with the idea that dowries permit a form of female inheritance different from the biblical order of succession,[13] a problem that he then rationalizes by redefining dowries as a means to marriage.[14] The Talmud here also emphasizes that dowries, to the

12. Ket. 52b. Cf. pKet. 4:29a, 10:33a.

13. Which prevents daughters from inheriting unless they have no living brothers (or brothers' descendants): Numbers 27:8–11; see Rivlin, *Inheritance*, 17–21. Islamic law famously differs from Jewish law in this respect, granting daughters half of a son's inheritance. See Coulson, *Succession*, Powers, "Islamic Law of Inheritance," 3–15. "Jewish" rather than "rabbinic," because most Karaite jurists agreed with the rabbis. Although the proto-Karaite 'Anan b. David and Dani'el al-Qūmisī both granted daughters equal inheritance rights to sons (*Sefer ha-Miṣvot*, ed. Harkavy 120; T-S Misc. 35.199, ed. Ginzberg, *Ginzei Schechter*, 2:470–474, f. 2a, both cited Olszowy-Schlanger, *KMD*, 243 ns. 11–12; on Dani'el as the author of the latter treatise, see Ginzburg's comments ibid., and cf. the opinion attributed to Dani'el cited in S. Poznanski, "Karaite Miscellanies," 691, n. 3), later Karaite jurists ruled differently. Both Ya'qūb al- Qirqisānī and Levi b. Yefet (the son of the great tenth-century Karaite exegete Yefet b. 'Eli) state that orphaned daughters should be granted a dowry from their father's estate rather than an inheritance: *Kitāb al-Anwār*, ed. Nemoy, 13:6; *Sefer ha-Miṣvot*, ed. Algamil, 5:173–174, 196–197.

14. This dictum reinterprets earlier sources so as to limit dowry size, reflecting concern that dowries may serve as a form of female inheritance: Schremer, *Male and Female*, 267–268; cf. Friedman, *JMP*, 1:290.

extent that they do serve as women's inheritance, should remain small. This passage goes on to state that a man should give each daughter no more than one-tenth of his property as a dowry.[15]

As this text suggests, rabbinic law promotes a mixed model of the dowry, in which women's dotal assets function partly as their own inheritance but more primarily as a benefit to their husbands: a wife owns these assets in the sense that her husband must return them to her when the marriage ends, but he controls them, may consume their profits as long as the marriage lasts, and absent *benin dikhrin* (which was abolished by the *ge'onim* sometime before the ninth century) inherits them if she dies before him.[16] Classical rabbinic texts explain this privilege both as compensation for the husband's support of his wife and as a means to protect her from divorce, but it also reflects obvious concern for patriarchal control.[17] While rabbinic law permits married women to maintain property outside their dowries (termed *nikhsei melug*, in contrast to dotal property, which is termed *nikhsei ṣon barzel*),[18] by the end of late antiquity the rabbis had granted men functional authority over their wives' nondotal property as well, leaving little incentive for women to maintain assets outside their dowries when entering marriage—especially since husbands were responsible for safeguarding their wives' dowries, but not their *nikhsei melug*.[19]

15. tKet. 6:1 represents the daughter's dowry as an alternate inheritance: "One who dies leaving sons and daughters—when the estate is large, the sons inherit and the daughters are maintained and provided with a dowry (*nizonot u-mitparnesot*)" (although bKet. 68a reads this phrase as referring to the daughter's maintenance rather than her dowry). See further tKet. 6:2–3, pKet. 6:30d, bKet. 68a-69a, and cf. Maimonides, *MT, Ishut*, 20:3. Most medieval Rabbanite authorities allowed a father to deprive his daughter of a dowry if he wished, but see the variant opinion attributed to Hayya b. Sherira, Lewin, *OHG, Ket.* 207. On parallels in Zoroastrian law that carried over into medieval east Syrian Christian law, see Payne, "Christianity and Iranian Society," 213–215, Weitz, "Syriac Christians in the Medieval Islamic World," 119–121.

16. For the rabbinic sources, see Gulak, "*Ṣon Barzel*," Epstein, *Marriage Contract*, 91–100, and cf. Maimonides' summary, *MT, Ishut*, 16:1–2. For Karaite legal custom, see Olszowy-Schlanger, *KMD*, 219–220, 239–240.

17. On this theme in classical rabbinic texts (and its implications for patriarchal control), see Satlow, *Jewish Marriage in Antiquity*, 209–215, reading "*ketubba*" as "dowry"; cf. Maimonides, *MT, Ishut*, 12:4.

18. On these terms, see the sources cited by Friedman, *JMP*, 1:291, n. 8.

19. Rabbinic law increasingly limited women's control of their *nikhsei melug* over the course of late antiquity, granting the husband rights to income generated by any of his wife's assets, whether formally within her dowry or not, and preventing her from permanently selling, gifting, or bequeathing her *nikhsei melug* without his consent. See Epstein, *Marriage Contract*, 107–120. Classical rabbinic texts focus on married women's ability to sell or gift their extradotal property, but gaonic sources limit women's testamentary bequests as well; see, e.g., *TG Sha'arei Ṣedeq*, 4:3:7, ibid., 4:4:53, and cf. Maimonides, *MT, Ishut*, 22:6.

Geniza Jews' motives for dowry gifts seem to have been equally mixed, although in ways that differed from the rabbinic ideal. To begin with, most Geniza dowries were proportionally larger than the Talmud recommends. Maimonides echoes the Talmud by defining the dowry as "a small amount (the father) gives to his daughter so that she may marry with it," and some Jews in medieval Egypt followed this minimal approach.[20] A man appearing in an undated court record from Fustat, for example, testifies that his late father had charged him to give each of his "unmarried virgin sisters," Munā and Sittūna, precisely one-tenth of his entire legacy.[21] But this is unusual. More typical is a petition addressed to an unnamed *ga'on* (based on the formulae it employs, perhaps Maṣliaḥ b. Shelomo, *ra'īs al-yahūd* from 1127–1139) that describes a man who left his wife half of a *dār* to cover her deferred dower and the value of her dowry, and split the other half equally between his minor son and daughter.[22] He was able to do so because rabbinic law permits individuals to use several kinds of wills that circumvent the biblical order of inheritance.[23] Dozens of these wills were preserved in the Geniza, including some that, as in this case, specify bequests to unmarried daughters similar to those given to sons.[24] Although Geniza wills rarely describe these bequests to daughters as dotal, they clearly functioned as a form of dowry allocation, because they are almost always left for unmarried rather than married daughters.[25] When a daughter listed as a beneficiary in her father's will ended up marrying before his death, she received the assets intended for her bundled into a dowry and his will was revised accordingly.[26]

20. *MT*, *Ishut*, 20:1.

21. Halper 335.

22. Bodl. MS Heb. d. 74.39.

23. The two basic types are wills made in good health (*ṣava'at* or *mattenat bari*), through which a testator transfers his or her assets immediately to the beneficiaries, but may keep using them until he or she dies; and those made directly before death (*ṣava'at shekhiv me-ra'*), which take effect only if the testator dies, and are otherwise nullified. Yaron, *Gifts*, Rivlin, *Inheritance*, 135–150, 161–181, Edrai, "A Gift 'From Now and After Death.'"

24. For example, a will from Fustat, 1241: "Bear witness . . . that I have given my daughter Karam, the mature virgin, two-thirds of the building (*dār*) that belongs to me in the "Alley of the Sun" (*zuqāq al-shamsh*, spelled thus) . . . as a complete gift, which cannot be revoked." T-S 8 J 6.14. See further Goitein, *Med. Soc.*, 3:281–3, Rivlin, *Inheritance* 48–49, idem, "Women and the Law of Inheritance." Other Geniza documents mention fathers' verbal instructions about their daughters' dowries: T-S 18 J 1.4, 1006; Halper, 335, 1041.

25. Large bequests accorded to still unmarried daughters are sometimes accompanied by smaller gifts of clothing or petty cash to their married sisters. Goitein, "Dispositions," 175.

26. A query sent to Maimonides describes the problems caused by a case like this: a father wrote a will giving his daughter a dotal bequest, lived long enough to give her a slightly different dowry directly, but then died before revising the will. *Responsa*, no. 108.

Although fathers do not explain their motives in these wills, the very fact that they gave their daughters dowries in this way—through generic bequests similar to the ones they gave their sons—suggests that they understood these assets as their daughters' equivalent patrimony. So do documents in which women's relatives try to modify rabbinic law in order to limit their husbands' short- or long-term hold on their dowries. Geniza contracts do not include the Mishnaic *benin dikhrin* clause, but Palestinian-formula Rabbanite marriage contracts from the late tenth and early eleventh centuries do stipulate that the wife's dowry will eventually be inherited by her sons alone (and not by her husband's children from another marriage).[27] Karaite contracts from the same period contain a clause obliging the husband to return his wife's dowry to her paternal relatives if she dies before bearing children; many Rabbanite marriage agreements from the twelfth century and after likewise promise that half of the dowry will be returned in this case.[28] These Rabbanite clauses became relatively standardized by the mid-twelfth century, but in some early ad hoc versions women's relatives seek to curb husbands' access to their dowries even within marriage. For example, a deed composed in 1117 records Ḥalfon b. Yosef *ha-levi*'s promise that he will not remove any dowry items belonging to his wife, Turfa bt. Eli'ezer, from Fustat, "even with her approval and consent."[29]

But if these documents thus represent dowries as a form of equal female inheritance, other texts make clear that they could also be a prerequisite to marriage. That girls could not easily marry without a dowry should already be clear from the dowry's ubiquity across economic classes. Incidental remarks in Geniza documents and responsa confirm that this was the case. For example, an early eleventh-century letter composed in Ramla says about a girl whose father had died unexpectedly poor: "Her fiancé entered the union only on the condition that she have some dowry; then when the situation was explained

27. A number of gaonic responsa state that *benin dikhrin* is no longer an automatic condition of the *ketubba*; see Assaf, "*Bittulah*." Palestinian contracts: Friedman, *JMP*, 1:379–391.

28. Friedman, *JMP*, 1:391–418, Olszowy-Schlanger, *KMD*, 241–247, and see below, Chapter 7. Friedman and Olszowy-Schlanger disagree about the origins of the Karaite clause; see Friedman, "Relationship," 153–156.

29. T-S 24.75. Cf. Harkavy, *Zikhron Kamma Ge'onim*, nos. 197–198, an early eleventh-century query (addressed to the *ga'on* Hayya b. Sherira) about a father who granted his daughter a trousseau on the condition that she treat its contents as a sort of permanent loan: "If she wished to give them (away) as a gift, or to sell them, she could not. . . . The husband also (formally agreed) that he would not treat them as his own property, by selling, gifting, or altering them, except with the father's permission." See also Maimonides, *Responsa* no. 191, about a man who asked the local *qāḍī* to prevent his married daughter from giving part of her dowry to her husband. (For the possible Islamic legal context, see Shatzmiller, *Her Day in Court*, 76–86; Rapoport, *Marriage, Money and Divorce*, 18.)

to him . . . he became reluctant to take her."[30] On the flip side, men willing to marry a girl without dowry were rare enough to be seen as exceptionally virtuous: "Words cannot describe (such a) man, who neglects worldly concerns and seeks the Creator . . . he had intended to marry a girl orphaned from her mother for the sake of God, may He be exalted—not for any other possible reason, because she owns not even a garment."[31]

Grooms' interest in dowries could create highly competitive marriage markets that required some parents to give their daughters not the modest endowments the Talmud recommends, but disproportionately large dowries that decimated their own estates, leaving little or nothing for other siblings. A query addressed to Maimonides describes this kind of case: "A man died leaving a wife, a young son, and three young daughters. . . . When the time came to write a marriage contract (for one of the daughters), his widow outfitted the girl with a dowry. . . . It later emerged that she had outfitted the girl with the deceased's entire estate, and had left the boy and the (other) daughters nothing on which to depend."[32] Among medieval Jews, this phenomenon was not limited to twelfth-century Fustat—jurists in eleventh-century Aleppo and Fez received similar queries. Nor was it confined to the Geniza populations. Earlier and further afield, a gaonic responsum claims that the Iraqi *yeshivot* stopped imposing *benin dikhrin* sometime before the ninth century because the law had become superfluous: "The purpose of this decree was only so that 'a man would jump to give to his daughter as to his son'; today, if only a man would give to his son as to his daughter! For most people abandon their sons without food and outfit their daughters, and several times it has been necessary to ban all those who increase their daughters' gifts and dowries beyond what is necessary."[33]

30. Bodl MS Heb b. 13.54. Cf. Yiṣḥaq al-Fāsī, *Responsa*, ed. Leiter, no. 177, about a dispute over a plot of land included in a girl's dowry; the plaintiffs note that their father (the alleged owner) had not protested the land's insertion in her marriage contract "because he did not wish to spoil this girl's betrothal," and had therefore waited to press his claim until after she was married; and Maimonides, *Responsa* no. 238: "If (her father) does not give her a dowry, (the groom) will not take her."

31. T-S 12.289, a letter of recommendation for a disciple of Avraham Maimonides, Minyat Ziftā, Egypt. Cf. similar rhetoric in an eleventh-century letter from Egypt: "I said, 'I want nothing from her but wish only to act *for the sake of heaven*.'" T-S 13 J 23.10; see Goitein, *Med. Soc.*, 3:307.

32. Maimonides, *Responsa*, no. 58.

33. *TG Sha'arei Ṣedeq*, 4:4:17; for the date, see Lewin, *OHG*, *Ket.*, nos. 351–352. Cf. *Teshuvot Rav Natronay*, ed. Brody, no. 368, for a case of this kind referred to a ninth-century *ga'on*. Aleppo and Fez: "A man died intestate . . . and his estate remained in his wife's hands. He left three daughters—the youngest of whom died—and a son. The older daughter married, and her mother outfitted her with two-thirds of her husband's estate; then the other daughter became betrothed and she granted her more than to the son" (Bodl. MS Heb. d. 66.9, addressed to R. Barukh b. Yiṣḥaq of Aleppo); "Re'uven died leaving orphans, two girls

A letter composed in mid-eleventh-century Tripoli vividly illustrates the strain that this demand could place on girls' relatives.[34] Writing amid political and economic chaos (perhaps caused by the Norman conquest of Sicily in the 1060s), the widowed sister of Yeshuʿa b. Ismaʿīl al-Makhmūrī begs him to help her repay crippling debts she has assumed to marry off her young daughter:

> My brother, I have become embroiled in a quagmire from which I do not think we can be freed—I and a young orphan girl (i.e., her daughter).[35] What occurred was that my son-in-law (i.e., the girl's fiancé) wintered in Salerno and returned only with the Egyptian ships; then he said to me, "I will take the girl." I said to him, "What are you thinking? As I was this year, I have nothing." Then people advised me that I should borrow and incur debt and give her to him, because the *Rūm*[36] have burnt the world. Now . . . if free persons could be sold for dirhams, I would be the first to be sold, for I cannot describe my predicament to you . . . (I swear) by these lines[37] that when Passover came I had not even a farthing's worth of chard,[38] nor even a dirham; instead I cut a nettle from the ruins and cooked it. . . . My brother, help me with some portion of this debt engulfing me—do not abandon me and do not forsake me.

Yeshuʿa b. Ismaʿīl is known from many documents as a successful and well-connected merchant.[39] Before this crisis, his sister probably belonged to the sub-elite merchant and professional class that Goitein termed the "upper middle bourgeoisie."[40] She may have followed "people's" advice (that is, common wisdom) to accept debt in exchange for a prosperous son-in-law as a way to maintain her own and her daughter's social standing. But other documents suggest that less elite parents could experience significant dowry pressure too. In a lengthy petition addressed to the *raʾīs* Mevorakh b. Seʿadya, an anonymous indigent scholar without means of income ("neither from teaching, from

---

and a minor boy. He left them nothing but one dwelling and a field. The orphans' relatives saw fit to divide the dwelling and the field between the girls . . . leaving nothing for the boy" (Yiṣḥaq al-Fāsī, *Responsa*, ed. Rothshtein, no. 104). That these cases all concern orphans is probably incidental; disporportionate dowries granted by a living father create no obvious legal problems and so would have been less likely to surface in responsa.

34. T-S 10 J 14.20. For the letter's date, cf. T-S 16.163, and T-S 25.124, both written in the early 1060s, which mention Yeshuʿa's severe illness, also discussed in this letter.

35. "Orphan" because her father was dead.

36. That is, the Normans.

37. On this expression, see Goitein/Friedman, *India Traders*, 684 n. 26.

38. A difficult phrase: סלק וסלקהא. Gil tentatively renders this as "chard and cooked chard"; it may also refer to the plant and its leaves.

39. Goitein, *Med. Soc.*, 5:144–145.

40. Goitein, *Med. Soc.*, 1:79.

the *parnas*, nor from the community") complains that the merchant Nahray b. Nissim, having arranged a marriage to the scholar's daughter, expects the scholar to provide her with a substantial dowry: "He said to me, 'Send ten dinars' [. . .] because he believed I was able to do this, and (I) have not [. . .] years (ago) I s[pe]nt the small sum on myself and //upon// clothing . . . and my family are arrogant merchants, who disdain to do this."[41]

How far did these two motives overlap? Did fathers and mothers compelled to offer crippling dowries to their sons-in-law also take measures to protect their daughters' stake in this property? Or did dowries work differently in different marriages, functioning sometimes more as bequests that benefited the wife, and sometimes more as marriage incentives that benefited the husband, depending on why and how they had originally been accumulated?

Surviving Geniza evidence for dowry *gifts*, on which I have focused here, is too piecemeal and thinly spread to answer these questions, or to reveal obvious differences in dowry motives across classes, over centuries, and between regions. (The difficulties themselves do suggest, however, that these differences were likely messy and complex, occurring at the micro rather than macro level, and that both models persisted side by side among at least some Jews around the eastern Mediterranean throughout the Fatimid and Ayyubid periods.) Nor is it clear how far rabbinic law set Jewish dowries apart from Islamic ones. Dowries were customary among Muslims but not recognized by Islamic law, which meant that Muslim husbands did not formally control their wives' dowries.[42] Yet Jewish and Muslim women's dowries contained such similar kinds of assets—clothing, jewelry, household utensils and textiles, and among wealthier women, slaves and parts of *dār*s—that they may well have been used in similar ways in marriage.[43]

Better answers to these questions likely lie within the hundreds of texts—legal documents, commercial letters, and responsa—that mention dowry *use* within marriage. These texts have not yet been studied systematically. Even at this stage of research, however, it is clear that in marriage as well as before it, husbands and wives understood dotal property in a range of different ways.

At least some wives controlled their dowries more directly than rabbinic law recommends. Wives appear throughout the Geniza record buying and selling real estate, maintaining houses and apartments that they rented out, investing in commercial enterprises, and loaning cash at interest.[44] This evidence is so striking that it has been taken to suggest that the dotal status of women's

41. ENA NS 9.15. Cf. T-S 12.780, by the same author to Nahray. "Family": *ahl*, here seemingly referring to the writer's extended kin. See Chapter 1, n. 69.

42. On this point, cf. Rapoport, "Matrimonial Gifts," 23–24.

43. The available evidence dates mainly from the early Mamluk period; see Rapoport, *Marriage, Money and Divorce*, 14–16.

44. For a preliminary survey, see Goitein, *Med. Soc.*, 3:326–332.

assets meant little in practice—that Jewish women routinely controlled their own dowries without concern for their husband's formal authority.[45] I view this as unlikely, since the documents that describe these transactions are not only thoroughly rabbinic in other respects, but often explicitly acknowledge husbands' legal rights over the property involved. In these cases, husbands authorized their wives' transactions or granted them blanket permission in writing to manage their dowries on their own.[46] Like wills used to enlarge women's patrimony, these documents worked to increase individual women's property rights beyond the constraints imposed by rabbinic law, while still preserving its technical requirements. (Clauses in Geniza marital agreements that gave brides independent labor rights served the same function.)[47] But the practical outcome was indeed the same: the women who appear in these documents seem to have managed their dowries independently of their husbands in all but name.

Other texts describe a different kind of departure from the ideal rabbinic model: men who appropriated and squandered their wives' dowries so that little or nothing remained of them at divorce.[48]

Husbands who sold off dotal property sometimes did so against their wives' will. For example, in an undated petition to a communal official, a wife complains that she has been fighting since her wedding day to make sure that her in-laws "would not take anything from me," but that her husband has now secretly removed her sofa and pillows—household textiles common in Geniza dowry lists—and sold them.[49] This sale was described as abusive (and as a direct precursor to physical abuse; the husband in this document went on to beat his wife and evict her from the household). Yet in other cases where husbands claim to have no money with which to repay their wives' dowries, it is not clear how the assets themselves had been consumed—or whether it was sometimes considered socially acceptable for husbands to

45. Yosef Rivlin has suggested that Geniza women regularly controlled their own dowries within marriage: idem, "Women and the Law of Inheritance"; cf. idem, "The Contribution of the Geniza." See further Krakowski, "Female Adolescence," 51–53.

46. These contracts empower the wife to administer, sell, or give away her dowry. See *Med. Soc.*, 3:181–3, and for the rabbinic legal context, mKet. 9:1, bKet. 83a-84a, pKet. 9:32d-33a, Maimonides, *MT*, *Ishut*, 23:1–7. Rabbinic law also permits a married woman to receive a gift granted on the condition that she will control it (see Maimonides, *MT*, *Zekiyya*, 3:13–14, 12:12), or to avoid her husband's authority by giving away some of her property before marriage, on the understanding that she will recover it if the marriage ends (*havraḥa*: ibid., 6:12, *Ishut* 22:9. For a possible example of *havraḥa* in a Geniza document, see PER H 89).

47. See Chapter 7.

48. See the many cases discussed in Zinger, "Women, Gender, and Law," 130–180.

49. ENA NS 31.21.

appropriate or trade with their wives' property.[50] Wills in which more responsible husbands left their wives replacement property to cover the value of their dowries, suggesting that their original contents had been sold, raise the same questions.[51] More detailed work on this corpus of texts may help to answer them, and to further suggest how dowry practices developed over time, as well as how they varied across regions, classes, and in differently shaped households.

Unmarried Women as Economic Actors

If more work is needed to untangle how dowries worked within marriage, some of their effects on unmarried women are more discernable.

A legal query sent to Maimonides provides an unusually complete picture of one young woman's economic life in the years before she married.[52] It describes a complicated financial argument between a recently orphaned man and his unmarried half-sister (the author describes her as legally mature but does not give her age). Her father had engaged her to a groom who gave him forty dinars to keep for her as a preliminary dower. She then embroidered a batch of textiles to use in her dowry. But before the marriage had been consummated, both her father and her groom died. Eager to increase his own inheritance, the girl's half-brother claimed ownership of the forty dinars that her groom had given to their father, and proposed repaying the groom's heirs with the textiles that she had embroidered. He argued that he had every right to do so, since the raw materials that she had used rightfully belonged to him: they had belonged to their father, not to her, and he could even claim rights to her labor (that is, to her embroidery work), since she remained dependent on him despite having legally come of age.

Women who had not yet married occupy three main economic roles in the Geniza record, all illustrated in this query: as potential and actual property owners, whose upcoming marriages required financial investments from both their future husbands and their relatives; as economically productive workers; and as financial dependents who required the support of others. Rabbinic law defines each of these economic roles precisely, in ways that this query also illustrates. Freed from her father's authority and not yet subject to a husband's, the mature (*bogeret*) daughter is financially independent. She can own property and profit from her own labor; by the same token, she is expected to support herself.

50. Zinger, ibid., esp. 143.

51. Zinger surveys some such cases, ibid.; see also Goitein, *Med. Soc.*, 3:250–255.

52. Maimonides, *Responsa*, no. 84. For the sake of clarity, I have left out some aspects of this extremely complicated story, related to the girl's later engagement to her late groom's brother.

Texts like this responsum allow us to see not only how this rabbinic legal idea was maintained in practice, but also its limits. Rabbanite legal documents and responsa uniformly recognize the technical economic aspects of the *bogeret* model. This brother, for example, assumed that since his sister was legally mature, she was responsible for supporting herself and should thus repay him for having maintained her after their father's death. The Geniza record also makes clear, however, that this legal model mapped very imperfectly onto the real social structure of women's adolescence among Jews in Fatimid and Ayyubid Egypt—as Maimonides' response seems to acknowledge. He rejected the brother's claims on other grounds, but did not even engage this part of his argument. In the rest of this chapter, I will argue that outside the courtroom, Geniza Jews viewed unmarried girls as inherent dependents whose main economic interests lay in accumulating the dowry that they would receive at marriage and who required active financial support from others until they did so.

WOMEN'S PROPERTY BEFORE MARRIAGE

This is most obvious with respect to property rights. Most Jewish women who would eventually enter marriage with a dowry of any meaningful size—that is, everyone above the very poorest stratum of brides documented in the Geniza—had no control over assets of their own before they married and received their dowry.

This was not only a social fact, but one that paralleled rabbinic laws separate from those surrounding the *bogeret*. While rabbinic maturity laws emphasize unmarried women's economic independence, rabbinic property laws point in the opposite direction, by privileging the dowry as a vehicle for women's assets not just within marriage but also before it. As we have seen, rabbinic law follows the biblical order of inheritance in permitting most daughters no inheritance rights beyond their dowry (a point on which most Karaite jurists agreed).[53] Moreover, both late ancient and medieval rabbinic texts assume that unmarried daughters will have no access to the property intended for their dowries before they marry. They describe these assets as passing directly from father to groom: a man who promises his son-in-law to give his daughter a certain sum as dowry must do so, but the daughter retains no claim to this money if she does not marry the man to whom the promise was made.[54] The eleventh-century rabbinic author Yiṣḥaq al-Fāsī sums up this approach: "The

53. See above, n. 13.

54. bKet. 102b; cf. pKet. 5:29c, Maimonides, *MT*, *Ishut*, 23:13–16. Hayya b. Sherira's formulary for a dowry allocation deed begins: "When a girl's father assigns money and utensils to give to his daughter at her marriage, and the husband betroths her, the father is responsible for what he promised to give her" (Assaf, "*Sefer ha-Shetarot le-Rav Hayya*," no. 25).

father prepares a dowry for his daughter in such a manner that if he finds a man whom he approves, he gives it to him; and if one comes who does not please him, he decreases it."[55]

Rabbanite Jews in Fatimid and Ayyubid Egypt seem most often to have followed this rabbinic model, packaging most or all of the property that they gave to their daughters as a dowry that was assembled around the time of marriage and transferred directly to their husbands' control. The process is reflected in the hundreds of itemized dowry evaluations (*taqwīms*) preserved in the Geniza, as stand-alone documents, recorded in court notebooks, and within the bodies of marriage contracts. The *taqwīm* formally ratified the contents of a girl's dowry alongside the dower her husband had pledged to her; it was thus drawn up only once she became engaged or betrothed.[56] These lists describe most of the property women ever received, with the exception of dotal real estate that they often omit—as is clear both from Geniza wills, which rarely include bequests for married women, and from the many documents about disputes over wives' property, which rarely describe them as owning assets outside their dowry.[57]

Some of the movable items named in these documents may have previously belonged to brides' relatives, most often their mothers (including objects that had belonged to the mother's own dowry). [58] But many were purchased just before a girl's first marriage. For example, in a court record composed in 1156, the brother and grandmother of the minor orphan Sitt al-Kafā'a bt. Abū al-Faḍā'il b. Baqā withdraw 238 dinars held in her name by a trustee of the court "so that they might use them to buy the girl's trousseau (*jihāz*)." Sitt al-Kafā'a's betrothal contract, drawn up just two months later, but which no longer identifies her as a minor, includes a record of the "precious items" that they had purchased for her with this money.[59]

55. Harkavy, *Zikhron Kamma Ge'onim*, nos. 128–129 (and cf. the version included in Yiṣḥaq al-Fāsī, *Responsa*, ed. Leiter, no. 232), following mKet. 6:2: "One who assigns money to his son-in-law, and he (the groom) dies: the Sages said, he may say to his (the groom's) brother, 'I was willing to give to your brother, but I cannot give to you.'" According to pKet. 6:30c, the father's promise depends on the marriage being consummated; cf. Maimonides, *MT*, *Ishut*, 23:15; *TG*, ed. Assaf (1942), no. 17.

56. In Egypt the *taqwīm* was sometimes ratified at engagement, but more often at betrothal or marriage: Goitein, *Med. Soc.*, 3:86–87, 124–125. The dowry was usually listed again in the marriage contract; see Olszowy-Schlanger, *KMD*, 124, Friedman, *JMP*, 1:293. Several Egyptian contracts note that the dowry list has been produced separately "for fear of the consequences of time," apparently meaning, in order to keep its contents private; see Goitein, *Med. Soc.*, 3:126, Friedman, *JMP*, 1:293–294, Ashur, "EBD," 88–90.

57. Zinger, "Women, Gender, and Law," 130–200. Dotal real estate: see immediately below.

58. See, e.g., T-S 8 J 5.1: "We asked her if either of them owned jewelry from among what was written in her marriage contract. . . . She replied, 'Those things that I had, I gave to my daughter as a dowry when I married her.'" Cf. T-S 8 J 6.12 (see below, n. 63).

59. Court record: RNL Yevr. Arab. I 1700, 14a; ibid., RNL Yevr. Arab. I 1700, 25b-26b is a slightly revised copy. Betrothal contract: RNL Yevr. Arab. I 1700 I, 25b-26b. Cf.

Dotal real estate seems often to have been gifted directly to young women before they married. Most *taqwīms* list only movable assets, which has led some scholars to conclude that Geniza women did not usually own immovable property. But more women's dowries likely included buildings or apartments than is apparent from these lists, because many real estate transfers to brides were evidently recorded separately in documents that were drawn up before Muslim *qāḍīs* and that did not make their way into the Geniza.[60] Several surviving Judeo-Arabic documents, however, do record parts of *dārs* gifted to daughters as part of their betrothal arrangements; for example, in a short record from Fustat dated 1124, Ṣadaqa "known as b. Warda" gives his engaged daughter Sitt al-Khawāt half of a newly built *dār*, and then sets the dates for her betrothal and dowry evaluation in Sivan of the same year.[61]

Not everyone did things this way. To guarantee their daughters' access to a substantial dowry, some fathers chose to formally set aside assets for them in childhood, long before they were engaged or betrothed to a particular groom. A few documents describe gifts to minor girls that were specifically designated as future dotal property. Outright gifts of this type served to safeguard a girl's dowry against future disaster or losses by preventing other members of her family, including the donors themselves, from using this property for any other purpose.[62] But because it was marked as dotal, the girl herself was also unable

Maimonides, *Responsa* no. 7, about a girl seeking to sell a *dār* to spend the proceeds on her dowry, and CUL Or 1080 J 271, a letter sent by Avraham b. Abū al-Ḥayy that discusses his difficulty buying items for his sister's trousseau. For a similar Islamic source from Mamluk Jerusalem, see Rapoport, *Marriage, Money and Divorce*, 19, n. 46.

60. Most bequests left to unmarried daughters in Geniza wills include *dārs* or portions of *dārs*, yet marriage contracts and dowry lists from medieval Egypt rarely include real estate. M. A. Friedman suggests that Egyptian Jews may either have considered it redundant to list *dārs* in the *taqwīm* because real estate transfers were typically registered in Islamic courts; or that this property may have been excluded from dowry lists specifically to give it nondotal status (*JMP*, 1:302–304). I consider the first suggestion more likely, because dowries that include *dārs* or apartments are extremely common in other genres of Geniza documents and in contemporary legal queries. But this problem merits closer attention.

61. T-S Ar. 51.103. Another deed composed the following year affirms a father's unconditional gift of a house to his daughter together with her dowry (*qumāsh*), at her fiancé's request (T-S NS J 460 + NS J 112 + NS 211.8 + NS 323.11 + T-S 8.138 + T-S AS 152.19.). An undated Judeo-Arabic legal query discusses a man's conditional gift to his daughter of one-fourth of a compound, to take effect at her betrothal (T-S 10 J 7.6a). A responsum composed by Avraham b. Yijū, mid–twelfth century, also discusses a *dār* given within a dowry at marriage (T-S 10 J 9.24). Cf. also T-S 12.668, in which Sasson *ha-levi* brings his future father-in-law to court to record the father-in-law's promise that he has given a small portion (slightly less than one-eighth) of a *dār* to his daughter Sitt al-Dār, "effective from the time that (this gift) is written in her marriage contract."

62. This custom is mentioned by Yiṣḥaq al-Fāsī: "One who gives his daughter an outright gift . . . that she may use it to marry a husband, and does not mention whom (she will marry), cannot retract it" (Yiṣḥaq al-Fāsī, *Responsa*, Bilgoraj ed., no. 70; cf. Harkavy,

to use it before she married. For example, an undated contract (likely from the latter eleventh century) ratifies a commenda partnership between Ṣedaqa *he-ḥaver* b. Muvḥar and Abū Manṣūr Aharon al-Ziyāt permitting Abu Manṣūr to invest seventy-five dinars that Ṣedaqa has granted as an "immediate gift" to his two minor daughters.[63] After specifying how potential profits and losses will be divided between the two men, the contract concludes by stating that the capital belongs exclusively to the two girls: "These dinars are in Abū Manṣūr's possession as a trust of the court for (Ṣedaqa's) two daughters . . . when these two daughters reach full maturity, all of (this money) will be spent on their dowries." Ṣedaqa's daughters may have owned this property, but they did not control it.[64]

More often, parents wishing to earmark dotal property for young unmarried daughters did so by bequeathing it to them in wills. As we have seen, these bequests functioned as a form of dowry allocation but were framed as generic gifts.[65] This is likely because unlike explicit dowry gifts, which remained in trust until a girl's first marriage, assets received as unrestricted bequests could be legally transferred to an orphaned girl as soon as she reached legal maturity. A number of documents reveal Rabbanite courts upholding rabbinic maturity law by allowing girls formal control of their inheritances when they came of age, even if they had not yet married. For example, in a fragmentary court record from Fustat dated 1217, an orphan named Sitt al-Thanā', identified as a "mature virgin" (*al-bikr al-bāligh*), appears in court and testifies that she has received all of her paternal inheritance, consisting of "clothing, rent from property, and other things," and thus holds no further

Zikhron Kamma Ge'onim, no. 133, cited in the next note). A deed written in Fustat, 1121, verifies the orphan Sittūna bt. Abū al-Riḍā's claim to 25½ dinars from her father's estate (in addition to the bequest specified for her in his will) as repayment for "precious objects" he had taken "from that which her mother had prepared for her, to serve as part of her dowry" (T-S NS J 185.12 + T-S NS J 185.8). Cf. RNL Yevr.-Ar. I 1700, 18, Fustat, 1156, testimony that a "binding debt" of 50 dinars to the unmarried orphan Sitt al-Ḥasab, to be returned if she died before marrying, has been discharged (meaning that this sum, too, had been formally set aside for her dowry).

63. T-S 12.461. Ṣedaqa b. Muvḥar appears in several documents from the mid–eleventh century: Goitein, *Med. Soc.*, 1:442, n. 25. Cf. T-S 8 J 6.12, a deed contracted in Qūṣ, Egypt, in 1215, in which the doctor Abū Manṣūr gives his late wife's entire dowry, consisting of "gold, silver, copper, and other items worth two hundred Egyptian dinars" to his two minor daughters Nasab and Kufū, and Bodl. MS Heb. a. 2.23, a deed from Qayrawān, 1050, ratifying Abī al-Ma'ālī b. Yefet's gift to his half-sister Mawlāt of half of an upper story of a house, "on the condition that she go out with it to her husband when she marries."

64. Harkavy, *Zikhron Kamma Ge'onim*, no. 133, discussing this type of dotal gift: "(The gift) endures until she marries one who consummates (marriage) with her, and then she receives it" (a responsum of R. Yiṣḥaq al-Fāsī). The Talmud denies that a still-unmarried girl can control dotal funds deposited for her with a trustee (bKet. 69b; cf. Lewin, *OHG*, *Ket.* no. 538, a responsum of Hayya b. Sherira, and Maimonides, *MT*, *Ishut*, 20:14).

65. See above, at n. 24 and after.

claim against the trustee who had maintained the property for her in the years since her father's death.[66] The timing of this transaction benefited both Sitt al-Thanā' and her relatives: as we will see, she could be supported from her own dotal property until she married,[67] while the trustees of her father's estate and his other heirs could discharge their debts to her without having to wait until that point.[68] In one of a series of documents resolving an argument over the inheritance of the India merchant Yehuda Abū Zikrī b. Yosef *ha-kohen* (d. 1156), Yehuda's son Abū al-Rabīʿ Shelomo agreed to pay four hundred dinars from his father's estate to his two young half-sisters, Sitt al-Ḥasab and Sitt al-Naṣr, on the condition that their mother stopped prosecuting him in Islamic court on her daughters' behalf.[69] The deed had originally said that Abū al-Rabīʿ would grant each of them two hundred dinars when they married. To resolve the case, however, this clause was then crossed out and replaced with a marginal note indicating that he would give each girl this amount "at the time of her maturity, according to the time that Islamic law permits her to release her brother from this (obligation) and receive it from him,"[70] apparently so that she might absolve him before a Muslim *qāḍī* as well as in Jewish court.

Alone among unmarried girls, paternal orphans could thus gain formal control of personal property at puberty, fulfilling their rabbinic legal status as independent economic agents. But documents that discuss this property suggest that in these cases too, girls controlled their property in name only.

66. T-S NS 226.12. Other documents that discuss transfers of inherited assets to unmarried but legally mature girls include (1) AIU VII D 4c, 1027, Fustat: the orphan Mulk bt. Moshe and her brother Ghulayb appoint their maternal uncle Yosef b. Yeshuʿa to retrieve their portions of their father's estate (this case is also discussed in T-S 16.275 + Halper 412 and T-S 18 J 2.16). (2) T-S 8 J 4.14d, possibly later eleventh century: three orphaned sisters will receive ten dinars willed to them by their paternal uncle. (On the dating, see Goitein, *Med. Soc.*, 2:78, about the witness ʿEli *ha-kohen* b. Yaḥya.) (3) Halper 335, 1041, Fustat: Naḥum b. Faraḥ gives a dwelling in the town of Ṣahrajt to his two "unmarried virgin" sisters Munā and Sittūna, to satisfy his promise to his late father that he would give each one-tenth of the father's legacy. (4) T-S 20.152, a query addressed to the *ra'īs* Dani'el b. ʿAzarya from the court of Fustat about goods owned in partnership by two men, one of whom died leaving a daughter: may the remaining partner retrieve his goods, or must he wait until she "matures and can negotiate with him before the court"? (5) T-S 13 J 9.7, a fragmentary gaonic responsum by Shemu'el b. Ḥofni about an estate: "A good portion should be chosen for the orphan girl . . . and it should be transferred to her."

67. See below, at ns. 101–103.

68. Both considerations were important because once a girl matured, she was no longer entitled to support from her father's estate. See below, n. 99.

69. RNL Yevr.-Arab. I 1700, 3.

70. Presumably meaning that she should get the money at menarche, which ushered in maturity (*bulūgh*, the term used here) in Islamic law, rather at rabbinic maturity; see Chapter 3, at n. 10.

Orphan girls' economic authority was taken seriously as a technical rule but not as a social norm; in practice, it meant only that they were asked to formally approve the financial decisions that their older relatives continued to make on their behalf.

A series of documents drafted by the court scribe Ḥalfon b. Menashe in 1129 illustrates this clearly. They describe a complicated financial settlement between a man named Hillel and his two half-sisters after their father's death. In two separate deeds, Hillel and the girls' mother agreed to form a partnership using capital belonging to the two girls, which would be used to provide them with a monthly allowance and eventually a dowry. Although both daughters were legally mature, their mother spoke for them throughout and guaranteed their participation in the partnership. Finally, a third document affirmed that the girls themselves had formally agreed to the arrangement before witnesses.[71]

A few texts offer counterexamples in which orphan girls appear to have been directly involved in their own financial affairs. These accounts mostly appear in legal queries about property disputes.[72] For example, a query addressed to Maimonides says of two orphaned sisters who owned a portion of a building (*dār*), "As the time for one of them to marry approached, they looked for someone to purchase their portion, that its value might be spent on her dowry."[73] Passages like this may simply reflect the conventions of legal query-writing, which tended to foreground legal categories that might advance the interests of the party submitting the case (although not always on legal grounds alone; queries often throw in sympathetic supporting details, including some framed in legal terms, that forward no obvious legal argument). In this case, the query's author may have described these sisters as acting on their own in order to highlight their status as mature orphans needing a dowry,

71. T-S NS 320.46; T-S 12.618; Bodl. MS Heb. b. 12.2. Cf. Bodl. MS Heb. a. 2.3, from tenth- or eleventh-century Egypt: a widow and her daughters appear in court to affirm that her husband's creditors have discharged their debts to his estate. The mother represents both daughters throughout, although the text seems to indicate that one of them is mature.

72. A deed from Fustat, 1121, affirming a debt of 25 five dinars to the unmarried orphan Sittūna bt. Abū al-Riḍā by her father's estate, is an exception. The text is fragmentary, but suggests that Sittūna represented herself in court: "We wrote a deed of possession regarding this (debt), according to the text that testified to it, and gave it to her; then she stated that she also had a witness [. . .] regarding this (debt), and she now brought in before us . . ." (T-S NS J 185.12).

73. Maimonides, *Responsa*, no. 7. Cf. ibid., no 42: "A woman owned one-fourth of a dwelling . . . which she had purchased as a young girl (*ṭifla*) from her mother. . . . She became betrothed, and possessed nothing with which to outfit herself. Thus she wished to sell this fourth"; ibid., no. 4: "Re'uven married Le'ah (and had) a daughter with her; then Le'ah died, and Re'uven married Raḥel after her, and had a daughter with her. Then Re'uven died, leaving land insufficient to support both two girls until they matured. Raḥel's daughter said, 'I am entitled to this land . . . and my sister Le'ah's daughter has no claim to it.'"

who were viewed as especially socially vulnerable (as I discuss below). But it is also possible that girls who had no relatives able or willing to act for them did sometimes manage their own financial affairs. The only Geniza document narrated by an unmarried girl that I have identified is an undated complaint, meant to be read aloud in the synagogue, written in the voice of a destitute orphan girl who appeals to the local community about her inheritance rights:

> I am an orphan girl, (alone) in the house together with a young sister. Yesterday (our) two married sisters came and laid claim on the dwelling and evicted us. . . . May our sin overtake any who hear our plea and fails to impose the inheritance laws of the Torah on behalf of us both.[74]

This form of appeal was the last refuge of the desperate. Like older women forced to appeal to communal authorities because their kinship bonds had failed them, these sisters turned to the community for help because they were otherwise socially alone. Unmarried girls who dealt directly with their own property did so not as a social achievement, but because they lacked the resources that both permitted and compelled better-protected girls to remain economically passive.

THE WORK OF HER HANDS: GIRLS' LABOR AND VOCATIONAL TRAINING

Although unmarried girls exercised little to no economic agency when it came to property given to them by others, they were economically active in other ways. The orphan described in the query discussed at the start of this section, who had embroidered fabric intended for her dowry and thus increased its value, was not unusual. Geniza documents and responsa alike suggest that girls could perform economically significant work from a young age, contributing to their household economies through housework and textile production, and in the case of textile work, to their own future assets as well. If evidence for adolescent girls' property illustrates how legal norms could differ from social ones, texts that mention their labor illustrate the distance between social ideas about unmarried girls' economic agency and their actual economic capacity. It also further underscores the central importance of dowry preparations to their economic lives.

Learning to Work

The Geniza tells us a great deal more about marriage payments than it does about women's labor either before or after marriage. This is not because female labor was unimportant, but because its domestic and often exclusively

74. ENA 2348.1, narrated by the daughters of Dosa.

female contexts rendered it less visible in documents and narrative sources alike. The urban economy of medieval Egypt was heavily gendered, with women performing housework and working for pay in a limited subset of specialized occupations. Many of these involved caring for other women's bodies: women appear in Geniza documents serving as midwives, hairdressers, and corpse-dressers. Other women worked in service jobs that could also be performed by men, as brokers, peddlers, and elementary religious teachers.[75] But by far the most important field of remunerative female labor was textile production. Middle Eastern cultures from antiquity onwards viewed spinning as women's work, an association echoed in both Jewish and Islamic religious traditions.[76] Among the Geniza populations, women of all classes seem to have helped produce clothing and household textiles for household consumption; an unknown number also performed specialized textile work, particularly spinning and embroidery, for wages or sale. The number of women working in textiles for pay seems to have increased among both Jews and Muslims in Egypt in the late twelfth century and after, as textile industries became more technologically sophisticated and increasingly economically important.[77]

Whether or not they received payment for their labor, women in medieval Egypt seem nearly always to have worked within private homes. Most references to female textile laborers describe them as working alone, either in their own residences or in their employers'; a few texts that mention groups of women working together likewise describe them as congregating in homes.[78] This may explain why neither the Geniza nor contemporary literary Arabic sources provide us with detailed descriptions of women's textile work, despite its clear economic importance.[79]

75. See Goitein, *Med. Soc.*, 1:127–131. For comparable evidence from medieval Islamic sources, see Shatzmiller, *Labour*, 350–357; eadem, "Wage Labour," 189–192; Rapoport, *Marriage, Money and Divorce*, 32–33; and Cortese and Calderini, *Women and the Fatimids*, 199–200. Unlike Muslim women, the Jewish women reflected in the Geniza do not seem to have commonly worked as wet-nurses (although this was not the case everywhere; for Jewish wet-nurses in Andalusia, see Giladi, *Wet-Nurses*, 111).

76. On textile work as women's work in classical rabbinic literature, see Peskowitz, *Spinning Fantasies*; for Islamic sources, see Brunschvig, "Métiers vils," 45.

77. Goitein identifies a rise in women's paid labor during this period, based on the fact that thirteenth-century marriage contracts increasingly include clauses granting wives control of their labor: *Med. Soc.*, 1:132–135, and cf. Friedman, *Polygyny*, 103 n. 40. In my view it is not clear whether these clauses reflect a change in women's labor, or merely in the norms of legal document writing; see further Chapter 7, n. 13. Still, there is some evidence that paid female labor became more common in Egypt generally at this time, as the textile industry expanded (Rapoport, *Marriage, Money and Divorce*, 36–38).

78. See Shatzmiller, *Labour*, 357–359, and cf. Rapoport, *Marriage, Money and Divorce*, 34–35; Lutfi, "Manners and Customs."

79. See Shatzmiller, *Labour*, 347–348.

Because so little evidence survives for the social settings and organization of female labor, it is difficult to uncover much about how girls learned textile crafts and other trades in early life. Female vocational training of all types seems to have been mostly informal. Many girls probably learned to spin and embroider within their households, from their mothers or other female relatives. We have no direct evidence for this among Jews in Egypt, but maternal instruction in textile work does appear as a trope in both medieval Karaite and Rabbanite legal sources composed elsewhere in the Islamic world. For example, the twelfth-century Andalusian Rabbanite authority Yosef ibn Migas writes that daughters whose parents have divorced should remain in the mother's care, in part because mothers provide their daughters with domestic education: the mother "teaches her and trains her in that which girls need to learn and become used to, such as weaving and supervising the needs of the household, and all similar matters."[80] Goitein speculated that alongside this kind of informal training, some young girls also learned textile arts from specialized female instructors (*muʿallimāt*). This is certainly possible, but the references to *muʿallimāt* that I have found in Geniza documents allude to women teaching in religious elementary schools, mostly attended by boys, rather than to vocational teachers of girls.[81] The letter cited at the beginning of this book arranging for the care of two orphaned sisters, one ten years old and the other just past puberty, states that they will receive religious instruction from a tutor but will learn embroidery from a local childless woman who has volunteered to care for them as a sort of surrogate mother:

> The wife of R. [Yosef] the cantor, the student of the deceased *ḥaver* ben al-Kāmukhī, is here. She has no child, and she wishes to take these two girls and teach them embroidery . . . she will take charge of their affairs, with regard to (their) craft (*ṣanʿa*) and other matters.[82]

I have found no direct evidence for the process by which women trained for other types of skilled labor, such as midwifery or hairdressing, although here, too, it seems plausible that women who practiced these trades may have taught their daughters to do so. Some women may also have developed specialized skills later in life. A woman whose life story is told in great detail in two separate queries sent to Maimonides became an elementary religious

80. Yosef ibn Migas, *Responsa*, no. 71. Likewise, the ninth century Persian Karaite Binyamin al-Nahāwandī remarks: "A girl (whose parents are divorced) should remain with her mother, for she teaches her spinning and women's matters" (excerpted in Lewin, *OHG, Ket.* 359). For similar passages in medieval Islamic legal literature, see Spectorsky, *Women in Classical Islamic Law*, 189.

81. *Med. Soc.*, 1:128. See, for example, T-S 8 J 28.7.

82. T-S 12.493.

teacher when she was around twenty-five years old.[83] She had learned to read the Bible many years after she married, partly from her husband and partly on her own, and began teaching it from economic necessity after her husband abandoned her for several years and left her without any means of support.

Unmarried Girls' Labor

Who profited from the work that young women performed before first marriage? Legally, the answer is clear. Until a daughter reaches legal maturity, her father owns her labor and anything that she produces; after that point, she becomes autonomous and acquires rights to her own labor.[84] More than in the case of property rights, this rabbinic legal framework seems to partly match the social norms that Geniza Jews recognized.

Minor daughters' labor did not always benefit the father who technically owned it, but there is evidence that young girls did work to benefit relatives they lived with, even if this evidence is too slight to suggest their work's absolute value. Minor daughters probably contributed significantly to their households simply by assisting with domestic tasks such as cleaning and serving food.[85] Several documents allude to minor slave girls performing household labor from as young as five or six years old. Since only an elite minority owned domestic slaves, and paid domestic servants are very rarely attested in the Geniza, minor daughters probably performed similar work in less wealthy households.[86] Medieval rabbinic legal texts describe minor daughters' housework as a valuable commodity. For example, a gaonic responsum preserved in the Geniza cites a father who complained that because his minor daughters lived with their mother (his ex-wife), her new husband improperly benefited from their work: "People shame me, saying, 'Look, your daughters live with that man, who makes use of their labor.'"[87]

Although we have little direct evidence for young girls' vocational education, it is also likely that many girls learned textile crafts in early or middle childhood and were capable of real economic production even before reaching

83. Maimonides, *Responsa*, nos. 34, 45.

84. mKet 4:4, MNid. 5:7, bKet 46b, Maimonides, *MT*, *Ishut*, 3:11–12.

85. But not necessarily cooking; it remains unclear whether Geniza Jews routinely cooked their own food at home. Goitein's treatment of this question is somewhat inconsistent, and also contrasts with the archaeological evidence. See *Med. Soc.*, 3:113–115, 4:140–144, Lewicka, *Food and Foodways of Medieval Cairenes*, 88–92, Harrison, "Fusṭāṭ Reconsidered," 149–154.

86. Minor slaves: e.g., T-S 13 J 21.18, T-S 8 J 4.14a. See Perry, "Daily Life of Slaves," 82–90. See Goitein, *Med. Soc.*, 1:129–130, on servants, slaves, and the extended family's contribution to housework (cf. also *Med. Soc.*, 5:341–342, where in my judgment Goitein unduly minimizes the hardships of women's domestic labor).

87. T-S NS 169.26 (no. 47), printed in *TG Sha'arei Ṣedeq*, 4:4:46.

puberty.[88] A query sent from Alexandria in the tenth century to the Rabbanite authority Yosef ibn Avitur describes a custody dispute between a father and his ex-wife's relatives that hinged on the value of his nine-year-old daughter's spinning:

> She spins in their house every day, enough to offset the cost of her maintenance and more, and they deny me all of it. . . . I wish to remove my daughter from subjection to others and from their service, that she may serve me.[89]

It is not clear from this passage whether the girl's maternal relatives sold the thread she produced, or merely took it to use themselves. I have found no evidence that indicates whether young girls engaged in paid textile work or produced material only for their own households.

For the most part, young women probably continued to perform the same kinds of domestic labor in much the same ways after they became legally mature. Most daughters almost certainly performed chores within their households until marriage, regardless of their legal status. But mature daughters' formal economic independence was taken seriously in one respect. I will argue below that unmarried girls who lacked paternal support were not normally expected to work to support themselves; but girls of marriageable age *do* seem to have commonly performed textile labor in order to increase the value of their own dowries.

A cluster of classical rabbinic sources indirectly suggests that mature daughters' labor autonomy had already served this function among Jews in late antiquity. A passage in the Mishna states that a virgin bride approaching marriage may delay marriage for up to twelve months so she may "furnish herself" with a dowry; the Babylonian Talmud limits this grace period to the twelve months after she has reached legal maturity, that is, from the point at which she becomes financially independent from her father.[90] Leaving aside the more technical aspects of this legal paradigm, it works by assuming that unmarried girls who work for themselves do so primarily to increase their own dowries.

Maimonides' response to the query cited at the start of this section suggests that this was also true among Jews in medieval Egypt. Rebuking the brother who tried to seize the fabric that his half-sister had embroidered for her dowry, Maimonides states that women's dowries routinely include textiles that they made or embellished themselves:

88. Medieval Islamic sources support this assumption; see Rapoport, *Marriage, Money and Divorce*, 34, Shatzmiller, *Labour*, 351 n. 27.

89. Marks, "*Shalosh Teshuvot*," no. 6 (62–64). On the responsum's author, see Assaf, *Qiryat Sefer* II, 183–184.

90. mKet. 5:2, bKet. 57a-b.

> Everything that the father prepared for his daughter's dowry belongs to her, and similarly any women's notions that she herself has embroidered or woven belong to her absolutely. . . . Indeed, it is known that every father increases his daughter's (dowry) by adding as much as he is able to that which she has produced with her own hands.[91]

Besides producing textiles for direct use in their trousseaux, some girls may also have increased their dowries with money earned through wage labor. A query sent from an unknown location to the Rabbanite jurist Yiṣḥaq al-Fāsī turns on a woman's claim that two-thirds of the dowry she had brought into marriage had been paid for with wages she had earned as an unmarried girl "by the toil of her own hands."[92] This is the only source I have found that clearly describes a girl working for pay before marriage. There is no way to know whether this case was exceptional or whether it reflects a social milieu in which young brides regularly earned wages to increase their dowries. In either case, this text further underscores adolescent girls' real financial capacity: it describes the property in question as worth two hundred *mithqāl*s (equivalent to dinars), a sum that Geniza evidence indicates could support a family of moderate means in Fustat for about eight years.[93]

Food, Clothing, and Shelter: Unmarried Women as Economic Dependents

Geniza Jews thus managed young women's property and labor in ways that kept them economically passive, except when contributing to their future dowries. How did this approach determine a girl's immediate financial position in the years before she married?

Geniza documents routinely pay lip service to the idea that unmarried women should be supported by their relatives, particularly by their fathers. Paternal responsibility for unmarried daughters held pride of place among the kin obligations recognized by Geniza Jews. This was a social rather than a strictly legal idea. Classical rabbinic law demands surprisingly little of fathers; they are expected to support their children until age six, and after that only if they can easily afford to do so.[94] But it was a social idea strong enough to force

91. Maimonides, *Responsa*, no. 84.

92. Harkavy, *Zikhron Kamma Ge'onim*, no. 495.

93. Assuming each *mithqāl* was worth a full dinar. Even if an issue of lesser value is intended, the total value would still have been substantial. See Goitein, *Med. Soc.*, 1:359–360.

94. bKet. 49b, derived from mKet. 5:9; cf. pKet. 28d, bKet. 65b, Maimonides, *MT*, *Ishut*, 12:14–15. See also Shemu'el b. Ḥofni in Assaf, "*Shelosha Sefarim*," 126–132. mKet. 4:11 requires fathers to support their daughters until marriage, but mKet. 4:6 reinterprets this to mean only after the father's death, a ruling uniformly adopted by gaonic and

its way into medieval Rabbanite literature, which reflects a much more robust sense of paternal duty, particularly when it comes to unmarried daughters. Rabbanite jurists consistently rule that fathers who are at all solvent must support their daughters until marriage, even if they do not wish to do so, and even if they no longer live together.[95]

Despite the strength of this social ideal, we most often hear about it in the Geniza because it had failed. All evidence suggests that a great many fathers did *not* support their minor and adolescent children, either sons or daughters. Impoverished children appear in many petitions written on behalf of women whose husbands had died or left them, as well as in alms lists naming the recipients of public distributions of bread and clothing.[96]

There is often no way to know who was supporting or living with these children, especially when a mother is not mentioned. (This qualifier is necessary because Geniza letters reflect strongly gendered social expectations about young children's daily care. Whereas fathers frequently abandoned their minor children, we rarely hear about mothers doing so.) Our sources do partly describe the economic circumstances of one class of children, however: girls whose fathers died before they married, and who were therefore formally recognized as lacking paternal support.

The paternally orphaned daughter (Arab. *yatīma*, Heb. *yetoma*) appears as a common figure in both legal literature and Geniza documents. This is both for specific legal reasons, and because girls whose fathers were deceased posed the most obvious and easily addressed challenge to social ideas about paternal support. Despite asking relatively little of living fathers, rabbinic law requires that a man's estate be used to support his minor daughters, who are assumed to have inherited no property of their own beyond their future dowries.[97] This obligation precedes even sons' inheritance rights, and Rabbanite courts took it seriously.[98] But even as a legal mechanism, it provided imperfect security to unmarried orphans, because it was directly undermined by a different aspect of rabbinic law: the principle that mature daughters are financially independent. Because it views adolescent girls as independent,

medieval Rabbanite authorities (in spite of other rabbinic passages to the contrary, e.g., tKet. 4:8). See Friedman, *JMP*, 1:356–360.

95. See, e.g., Lewin, *OHG*, *Ket.* 360 no. 797; Marks, "*Shalosh Teshuvot*," no. 6; Maimonides, *Responsa*, no. 367 (cf. *MT*, *Ishut*, 21:18). For an example of a legal document that follows this model, see CUL Or. 1080 J 141, a divorce settlement dated 1114, in which Se'adya b. Avraham pledges to give his daughter clothing and 10 dirhams a month until she marries.

96. Goitein, *Med. Soc.*, throughout Vols. 2–3; Cohen, *Voice of the Poor*; idem, *Poverty and Charity*, esp. 139–155.

97. See above, at n. 13 and after.

98. Court records about orphans' maintenance include T-S NS 321.4, Bodl. MS Heb. c. 28.54 (Fustat, 1203), and Bodl. MS Heb. d. 66.32 (twelfth century).

classical rabbinic law permits daughters to claim ongoing support from a father's estate only until they reach legal maturity: "Whether girls marry before maturing or mature before marrying, they lose their maintenance but retain their dowry."[99] Rabbanite courts' loyalty to this rule left many adolescent orphan girls without guaranteed means of daily support. Orphans who remained unmarried past maturity were legally required to support themselves, an idea that medieval Rabbanite jurists uniformly affirmed in both legal codes and responsa.[100]

In practice, many mature orphans likely faced problems not much different from those that confronted the many young women whose fathers were still living but unable or unwilling to support them. But because much of our evidence comes from legal texts, and because the *yatīma* evoked special sympathy even in nonlegal sources, orphan girls are particularly visible in the Geniza record. Letters, legal documents, and responsa all address problems raised by female orphans who reached maturity and no longer qualified for support from their fathers' estates. These texts reveal the range of social options open to adolescent girls who could not rely on their fathers for material support. In the process, they help bring into focus how adolescent girls were understood as social persons with respect to economic matters.

SUPPORT FROM RELATIVES

In many ways, the economic options open to adolescent orphans were identical to those available to women in general. As was also the case for married, divorced, and widowed women, unmarried orphans appear in the Geniza record as most economically protected when they possessed strong ties with birth relatives, while girls whose kinship ties failed them faced serious difficulties. But here the parallels diverge subtly but surely, in ways that suggest that Geniza people viewed adolescent girls as socially distinct, different from women at later stages of life. The key difference lies precisely in the distance between legal and social expectations. While mature unmarried orphans were legally expected to maintain themselves, in social terms they were understood to need support from others.

99. tKet. 4:17. Cf. pKet. 29b, bKet. 53b, 68b, Maimonides, *MT*, *Ishut*, 19:10. Some Palestinian *ketubbot* preserved in the Geniza contain variants of a clause termed *benan nuqban* requiring the husband to support his daughters until marriage; see Friedman, *JMP*, 2:360–365.

100. Maimonides, *Responsa*, nos. 33, 58; cf. also no. 4 and idem, *MT*, *Ishut*, 19:15, where Maimonides notes that a girl betrothed as a minor "is not mature, *such that she maintains herself*." Cf. also the query addressed to Yosef ibn Avitur, in Marks, "*Shalosh teshuvot*," 63: "They do not need her to serve them (in exchange for her maintenance), since she is only nine years old." See above, n. 89.

The Geniza record suggests that adolescent orphans could realistically provide for themselves in only one sense: by using personal property that they had inherited from a father, either through a bequest or (if they had no brothers) as his legal heir. We have seen that girls took formal control of inherited property at maturity, although they did not administer it directly. Several documents reveal one benefit of this arrangement: guardians could then use a girl's own property to maintain her once she was no longer allowed to receive direct support from her father's other assets. For example, in a mid-twelfth century deed from Fustat, two orphan sisters loaned fifty dinars to a man named Zikrī b. Ḥalfon; in exchange, he promised to support them for the duration of the loan.[101] Similarly, in a series of legal contracts composed in Fustat in 1129, two girls entered into a formal partnership with their half-brother Hillel, granting him control of the business they had jointly inherited from their father in exchange for a weekly allowance.[102] Along somewhat different lines, an undated Geniza document about a complicated inheritance dispute mentions that two wealthy orphan girls had given a portion of their legacies to the maternal aunt with whom they lived, presumably in exchange for their room and board.[103]

These arrangements take different forms but share a common logic. All structure unmarried orphans' maintenance by providing them with externally managed support, rather than expecting them to be directly self-sufficient. The relatives who appear in these documents never allow an unmarried heiress to simply live off her own assets, but prefer to manage her property so as to generate a small income for her current support while preserving the balance for her dowry. In other words, they position adolescent girls as inherent economic dependents whose relatives or guardians must maintain them until marriage, even when the property being used to do so is their own.

101. T-S NS J 465. A third party would decide how much support the girls would receive, and the money would be returned when one of them became betrothed (i.e., so that her share could be spent on a dowry). To ensure that the girls' legacies would not be lost, Zikrī pledged to sell his own properties to provide them with trousseaux if he defaulted on the loan.

102. T-S NS 320.46, T-S 12.618, Bodl. MS Heb. b. 12.2. The joint property included a perfume shop and a warehouse containing merchandise. The girls would receive an allowance of eight dirhams a week, and then half the capital when the partnership dissolved. Unfortunately, these documents are fragmentary and leave many details of the arrangement unclear. Cf. Bodl. MS Heb a. 3.5, a similar agreement involving two minor orphan boys.

103. T-S 12.714: "Their mother died and the two daughters remained with (their father's) sister . . . and they gave all of the money // and the property// that they had inherited from their father and mother to their paternal aunt as a gift, . . . leaving themselves each 1,000 dinars." Orphan girls who inherited houses or apartments may also have rented them to support themselves; for example, T-S NS J 292v and T-S NS J 342v list monthly revenues for the "orphan girl's dwelling" (*dār al-yatīma*).

This is all the more true for poorer girls, who owned only a small base of property or no property at all. Letters and responsa alike describe a range of economic options open to orphans with meager or no assets. These texts likewise assume that girls in this position would need to depend on others, first and foremost on their kin.

To begin with, many orphans whose fathers had left significant assets probably continued to be supported from their estates—that is, by the brothers who were his legal heirs—even after they had reached legal maturity and formally lost the right to do so. Even legal literature recognizes this possibility. A gaonic responsum notes, "Although (mature orphan girls) may not consume (their fathers' property), their brothers are permitted to feed them and to make arrangements for them, in order (to avoid) shaming them."[104] It is hard to know how common these informal arrangements may have been among Geniza Jews, because they left documentary traces only when they gave rise to conflict, as in the query to Maimonides discussed above, in which a brother seeking to seize his orphaned sister's trousseau complains, "She is mature, but has been consuming her father's property."[105]

Mature orphans also appear in several documents as being supported by their widowed mothers. For example, in a letter sent from Tripoli in 1065, a widow mentions that she has been barely supporting herself and her daughter, a young girl about to be married, by her embroidery work.[106] Girls whose mothers remarried could also be supported by their stepfathers. Some Geniza marriage agreements contain grooms' promises to maintain their wives' daughters from a previous marriage until they marry, or for a specific number of years.[107]

104. Lewin, *OHG*, *Ket.* no. 512. Cf. also Maimonides, comm. on the Mishna, Ket. 6:3, idem, *MT*, *Ishut*, 20:13.

105. Maimonides, *Responsa*, no. 84. Rather than leave matters to chance, some fathers left instructions requiring their sons to maintain their sisters until marriage. For example, the deathbed will of Maṣliaḥ b. Ḥasan (1006) notes that his son Shemarya should "take care of the needs of his two sisters, Jamīl and Qurrat al-ʿAyn, and of their marriages and dowries, according to the orders I have given him" (T-S 18 J 1.4). RNL Yevr.-Ar. I 1700, 28, one of a series of documents from 1156 about an inheritance dispute between Abū al-Rabīʿ Shelomo and his two half-sisters (discussed above, at n. 69), notes that Abū al-Rabīʿ will pay the two girls two and a half dinars a month as maintenance, "in line with what their father willed them at the time of his death."

106. T-S 10 J 14.20. A deed from Fustat, 1038, mentions the financial difficulties of a widow responsible for her orphan daughter (ENA NS 18.26). A letter from Tripoli, 1136, notes that the author's brother has died, leaving "a pair of daughters who have reached the period of maturity (*ḥadd al-bulūgh*), a young son, and a wife with little strength"—that is, who would not be able to help support her children as might otherwise be expected (T-S 10 J 15.26; for the expression *ḥadd al-bulūgh*, cf. Maimonides, *Responsa* 2:406).

107. Some such pledges explicitly discuss girls past legal maturity. See Goitein, *Med. Soc.*, 3:309; Ashur, "EBD," 105–106 and doc. 6-א; Friedman, Polygyny, 67–68 (= Olszowy-Schlanger, KMD, doc. 56).

Finally, other documents allude in passing to female orphans being sheltered and supported by more distant kin. A letter sent from mid-eleventh-century Tripoli al-Shām to the merchant Nahray b. Nissim asks him to inform his colleague Barhūn b. Moshe al-Tāhirtī that "the *yatīma*" was being well cared for.[108] As "the old woman" (perhaps the girl's grandmother) had recently died, an aunt by marriage had assumed responsibility for the girl, "and she has spared no pains on her behalf; the girl has been protected in all comfort, better off than she was in her father's lifetime."

But not all orphans could rely on their relatives to provide for them. The kin networks on which women depended at every stage of life were fragile and changeable, one consequence of a social system in which kinship was centrally important but not embodied in predictable family or household units. Here, too, our sources underscore adolescent girls' perceived economic dependency. Throughout the Geniza corpus, we find kinless women at further stages of life both receiving help from others and working to support themselves. In contrast, unmarried orphans without active kinship ties appear in Geniza documents only as recipients of charity, either private or public.

CHARITY FROM NONKIN

Who provided for orphan girls when their own relatives could not or would not support them? There is no evidence that Geniza Jews maintained regular funds for supporting female (or male) orphans, whether minor or adolescent. But orphaned young women do appear scattered throughout the range of sources that testify to the circulation of charity within the Jewish community of Fustat more broadly.

Administrative records listing donors and recipients of public alms, as well as petitions addressed to private benefactors, provide abundant evidence for communal responses to poverty among Jews in Fustat. These sources reveal a complex and atomized system of both public and private charity, which maintained the same basic form throughout the Fatimid and Ayyubid periods. Public charity, financed by donations to communally maintained funds and administered by the *bet din* and by communal functionaries termed *parnasim*, provided subsistence and emergency relief to the very poor or those hit with catastrophe; funds from the *heqdesh* (communal chest, also termed *waqf*) were used to distribute bread and clothing, pay off poor Jews' *jāliyya* taxes (owed by non-Muslims to the state), and ransom captives.[109] Those who needed or wanted help beyond this minimal threshold had to seek out private benefactors who might be willing to give money to particular individuals—usually

108. Bodl. MS Heb. d. 66.60.

109. Goitein, *Med. Soc.*, 2:91–142, 413–510; Gil, *Documents of the Pious Foundations*; Cohen, *Poverty and Charity*, 198–242.

those of higher social status who had fallen temporarily on hard times—to gain their social loyalties.[110]

This system made women especially dependent on their birth relatives. Because private patronage served primarily to create social ties between a patron and his beneficiary, it was mostly inaccessible to women, who almost never established recognized social relationships with people other than their own kin. Women at later stages of life usually had to fend for themselves if their relatives abandoned them. Remarkably, this seems not to have been the case for adolescent girls. Our sources suggest that both communal officials and individual patrons took special pains to ensure unmarried orphans' economic security, even those not related to them.

They did so in two ways, both of which created replacement kinship-like ties for young women socially abandoned by their own relatives. The most immediate approach was to place orphan girls as dependents within domestic households, sometimes in exchange for their labor. Maimonides praises this form of domestic patronage in his great legal code, the *Mishne Torah*, noting, "A man's household dependents should include the poor and orphans in place of slaves. It is better that he make use of these . . . and benefit them by his property, rather than benefiting the offspring of Ḥam."[111] The Geniza suggests that this passage describes a social ideal active in medieval Egypt. Orphan girls, in particular, appear living as companions and servants within nonkin households of all economic classes.

These arrangements were usually not formalized in court, or at least have left no traces in the Geniza legal record. But they are mentioned in passing in documents of other kinds. Among the very poor, girls identified as *yatīma* appear in several alms lists accompanied by poor widows or divorced women other than their own mothers. A letter of appeal addressed to the community of Fustat in the mid-eleventh century provides some context for these pairings. Its author, a woman desperate to be divorced from her husband, complains that he not only fails to support her, but has also physically abandoned her; in his absence, she notes, "I have an orphan girl with me who keeps me company."[112] Other sources describe female orphans acting as servants in larger and wealthier households. A business letter sent from Palermo in the mid-eleventh century describes an orphan in this position as sharing quasi or replacement kinship ties with her patrons. Reporting a colleague's marriage

110. Cohen, *Poverty and Charity*; on charitable patronage, see also Rustow, "Benefaction."

111. That is, slaves. *MT*, *Matanot ʿAniyyim*, 10:17, an expansion of the Mishna: "let the poor be your household dependents (*benei betekha*)" (mAvot 1:5). Cf. bKet. 50a: "*Fortunate are the guardians of justice, who perform righteousness* (*ṣedaqa*) *at all times* (Ps. 106:3). . . . This (refers to) one who raises an orphan boy or girl within his household and marries them (off)."

112. T-S 18 J 3.2. Alms lists: see Cohen, *Voice of the Poor*, 107–163.

to an orphan dependent, its author complains, "I said to him, 'Why did they marry you to an orphan girl who was serving them in their home? You have made them your in-laws!'"[113]

Most of these sources do not reveal how these orphans ended up in the particular household that they lived in. But the brief letter I cited at the start of this book suggests that in at least some cases, Jewish communal officials may have orchestrated and funded these arrangements. Writing to a Head of the Jews in the early twelfth century, a woman pressed him to send her two dinars for two orphan girls (one ten years old and one just past puberty) so that she could rent them living space and they could buy themselves food and embroidery thread; a local woman would keep an eye on them.[114] This letter suggests that in providing these orphans with a domestic framework and surrogate kin, its author saw herself as acting on behalf of the official she addressed.

Whatever form they took, arrangements of this kind were inherently temporary. The second and most visible way in which Geniza Jews responded to orphan girls' economic problems was by working to marry them off, usually the sooner the better. Writing from al-Mahdiyya in the mid–eleventh century, the merchant Yūsuf b. Mūsā al-Tāhirtī describes marriage as the only solution for his niece after her father's death left her without any immediate relatives to support her:

> I spent money to adorn her, and married her to my sister's son 'Ammār b. Dā'ūd. . . . Her brother married and she was left an orphan from father and mother. Necessity compelled us to do what we could, and we sent her out.[115]

Yūsuf responded to his niece's predicament not by supporting her himself, but by spending money to "adorn" her, that is, to provide her with assets that would allow her to get married. This response was typical. Geniza texts recognize giving a dowry to an orphan as an important act of charity, one that

113. T-S 20.122. An undated administrative letter may allude to a similar arrangement: a widower's sister-in-law, "an orphan who has no one to feed her a piece of bread," is caring for his infant children (T-S 13 J 19.2). In a deed from Fustat, 1117, a woman gives property to an orphan named Sitt al-Dār bt. Sha'ul, "who will serve me and stay constantly with me" (although it seems possible from the wording that Sitt al-Dār may have been a divorced woman or widow; T-S 20.3). In a different vein, a short and fragmentary letter sent from Tripoli describes a sort of temporary marriage with an orphan: "(Your son) had a terrible (illness) that caused him pain, and had no one to serve him; he thus saw fit to take a young orphan girl to attend to him, and he married her on the condition that if he wished to be free to move (back to) his country, he would write her a bill of divorce" (T-S 8 J 19.29).

114. T-S 12.493.

115. T-S 20.71.

receives far more attention than do efforts to provide female orphans with ongoing maintenance in the period before marriage.[116]

References to dotal charity appear in letters, wills, and court records. Most of these gifts came from girls' extended relatives. But communal officials involved themselves in this form of charity too. While the Jewish communities documented in the Geniza do not seem to have maintained institutional dowry funds for orphans, as rabbinic literature describes for Jews in late ancient Roman Palestine, the communal apparatus of charity was sometimes used to fund orphans' dowries. An undated, unsigned letter from the Geniza asks a local official to "appoint someone to make the rounds of the honored community" to raise a dowry for a poor orphan girl about to marry an equally destitute man.[117]

THE SOCIAL MEANING OF ECONOMIC SUPPORT

Why was rapid marriage seen as the best economic solution for orphaned girls who lacked supportive kin? In theory, marriage provided a young woman with legally guaranteed support (*mezonot*) from her husband as soon as the marriage was consummated, and sometimes even before; men occasionally began supporting their future wives at betrothal, while many others paid them the preliminary portion of their dower (*mahr*) at that point.[118] Besides these tangible benefits, marriage might also grant a kinless orphan a recognized position in her husband's household and allow her to form social connections within his family network.

Yet none of these advantages convincingly explains Geniza Jews' focus on marriage as a path to economic security. It is abundantly clear that in practice,

116. See, e.g., T-S 10 J 14.20; Bodl. MS Heb. b. 13.54, a letter from Shelomo b. Ṣemaḥ (Ramla) to the communal leader Efrayim b. Shemarya (Fustat), asking him to petition the aunt and uncle of a newly orphaned girl to give her a dowry; T-S 13 J 9.4, a family letter sent from Palestine to Toledo, which states incidentally, "I was delighted that you provided the young girl with a dowry." Requests to purchase specific items of clothing for orphan girls (likely for their trousseaux) appear in business letters: AIU VII E 4, T-S 16.13, T-S 8 J 16.22. Wills also contain pious bequests intended to provide poor and orphaned girls with dowries: see, for example, T-S 16.115, an anonymous woman's deathbed will from 1006, which grants portions of a compound to a girl named Fāʾiza bt. *ha-levi* "on the condition that she marries with them," and T-S 8 J 4.14d, a court record affirming three orphan girls' receipt of ten dinars left to them by their paternal uncle. For similar evidence in Mamluk texts, see Rapoport, *Marriage, Money and Divorce*, 15–16.

117. T-S 10 J 15.27. Cf. mKet. 6:5, and see Goitein, *Med. Soc.*, 2:135. People other than communal officials sometimes also pressured orphans' relatives to help them. For example, a business letter sent from al-Mahdiyya to Fustat in 1063 asks the recipient to entreat the writer's cousin, the merchant Barhūn b. Ismaʿīl al-Tāhirtī, to send his widowed sister "something she may spend on the young girls, her children" (T-S 13 J 23.18).

118. Ashur, "EBD," 72–84.

marriage did not always make women financially stable. Many married women were deeply economically insecure, and many husbands failed entirely to provide their wives with *mezonot* of any kind. Nor did most women abandoned by a husband retain strong social ties to their in-laws. The relatives and communal officials who worked to marry off kinless orphans surely knew this. Their efforts, then, cannot reflect straightforward calculations about the benefits offered by any particular marriage. Instead, this response betrays a deeper emphasis on the role that first marriage itself played in young women's lives.

We can begin to understand this emphasis by parsing the terms that these texts use to describe orphan girls' financial problems. To begin with, Geniza texts consistently represent unmarried orphans as uniquely pitiable, regardless of their particular circumstances. Ḥanan'el b. Shemu'el, chief judge of Fustat in the early thirteenth century, alludes to this concept when he appeals to a young woman's relative to support her, remarking, "She is a *yatīma*—and there is no need to say more."[119]

More specifically, accounts of dotal charity to orphans use two rhetorical tropes that highlight the social perils of the *yatīma*'s economic position. First, several letters compare the act of giving a dowry to an orphan girl to the ransom of a captive.[120] In rabbinic tradition, the ransom of captives is the most pressing form of charity, a "great obligation" that trumps all other claims to aid.[121] Medieval Rabbanite authors explain this in light of the captive's extreme vulnerability: "The ransom of captives precedes providing for the poor and clothing them . . . for the captive is included among the hungry, thirsty, and naked, and stands in mortal peril."[122] By comparing the *yatīma* to a captive, petitioners for dotal charity not only conveyed an ethical imperative to help her, but also cast her as a uniquely helpless victim in need of salvation.

119. T-S 16.293. Goitein, "Chief Judge," 389–394, assumes that the orphan mentioned here is a newlywed orphan discussed earlier in the letter, but it seems to me more likely that two different girls are intended.

120. A letter from Jerusalem to Fustat, mid-eleventh century, asks the recipient to help an orphan girl retrieve her inheritance so that she may marry: "May you merit (to perform) this ransom (*fidya*), and do not delay your response a moment" (Bodl. MS Heb. b. 3.24). In a letter discussed above, a sister asks her brother to help pay for her daughter's dowry by saying "Consider me . . . a captive . . . and ransom me" (T-S 10 J 14.20, see above, at n. 34). A late eleventh-century letter suggests that this association was common; its writer asks for assistance with his daughter's dowry by noting elliptically, "You know that people redeem captives—and this daughter of mine is orphaned from her mother" (ENA NS 9.15).

121. bBB 8b. Geniza people took this injunction seriously. See Goitein, *Med. Soc.*, 2:137–138, Friedman, "Community Responsibility," Frenkel, "Proclaim Liberty to Captives."

122. Maimonides. *MT*, *Mattenot 'Aniyyim*, 8:10, an injunction illustrated by no fewer than seven biblical quotations emphasizing its importance. Maimonides here significantly elaborates the generic Talmudic formulation of the captive's suffering: "Captivity is harder than all (other forms of suffering), because it includes them all" (bBB 8b). Cf. Friedman, "Charity Begins at Home?" 60–63.

Second, Geniza documents often describe an orphan's dowry as a "veil" (*satr*), using various forms of the root *satara*, "to conceal."[123] In a detailed study of poverty and charity in the Geniza documents, Mark Cohen notes that this term holds special meaning in private charity petitions.[124] These petitions often take pains to describe their bearers as victims of "conjunctural" poverty, that is, as normally self-sufficient people who have fallen temporarily on hard times—as distinct from the chronic or structural poor, who regularly received help from public funds. These passages describe dependence on public charity as shameful and publicly humiliating, a form of *kashf al-wajh*, "uncovering one's face"; in contrast, private patronage and self-sufficiency alike are described as "veils" that protect a person from this form of public exposure. We can easily understand Geniza texts that call an orphan's dowry her "veil" in similar terms: this usage likewise serves to portray female orphans as especially vulnerable because of their economic need.

A letter sent by Barukh b. Yiṣḥaq, the head of the rabbinic academy of Aleppo in the late eleventh century, to the uncle of an orphan named Raḍiyya bt. Faḍīla, indicates this explicitly.[125] Barukh urged the uncle to give Raḍiyya a small building worth about 30 dinars to use as a dowry, reminding him of his kinship obligation to protect her from the social exposure caused by her father's death:

> It is not hidden from you that this type of merit ranks first of all the favors you are known to graciously bestow—because she is, first of all, an orphan, and your relative, and God commands (us) to conceal (*yasturu*) the family before strangers. The Creator knows that if I could, I would not render her indebted to any person, nor permit anyone to assist her in any respect. In all that I have done, since your niece came to my notice, to make arrangements for her needs, I have not made her indebted to anyone for anything.

This letter directly invokes the cluster of ideas about poverty and shame that Cohen has noted in other contexts, portraying Raḍiyya as vulnerable because she is an impoverished and unmarried orphan.[126]

123. Besides the example cited below, see Bodl. MS Heb. b. 13.54; T-S 10 J 15.27; T-S 13 J 20.20, and cf. Blau, *Dictionary*, 288.

124. Cohen, *Poverty and Charity*, 35–48.

125. Bodl. MS Heb. d. 66.3.

126. Similarly, a father's letter from Jerusalem to his estranged daughter, c. 1040, uses *yatīma* to denote an unmarried girl socially exposed by her lack of paternal support: "May God (judge) between you and she who has harmed you and made you an orphan while I yet live—you, my daughter, are *at the mercy of other people's kindness* because of your mother's deeds" (CUL Or 1080 J 21). As Cohen notes, this use of *satr/kashf al-wajh* is common in medieval Arabic, but classical rabbinic sources also emphasize unmarried girls' economic vulnerability, e.g., Ket. 53b: a man who betroths a minor orphan (causing her to

Both of these rhetorical themes reveal a common concern that transcends simple anxiety for orphan girls' immediate material welfare. They imply that girls who could count on paternal support were also *socially* protected. Contrary to what we might expect, especially given these texts' potentially suggestive use of the term "veil" (*satr*), this protection does not seem to have been understood in sexual terms; these passages make no mention of young girls' modesty or sexual chastity.[127] Nor did this ideal simply reflect concern for women's economic protection in general, since Geniza documents do not use this kind of rhetoric to discuss women who have already entered a first marriage. While wives, widows, and divorced women who lack spousal support are often described as objects of pity who deserve charitable help, they are also assumed to have some capacity to provide for themselves, if only at a minimal level.[128] Instead, texts about the *yatīma* suggest that she was socially exposed not just by her gender but by her stage of life; as a figure in Geniza texts, she reflects Geniza Jews' view of unmarried girls as helpless economic dependents in a way that women past first marriage were not.

Conclusions: The Economic Importance of First Marriage

Geniza evidence for young women's economic lives is anecdotal, widely diffused across time and space, and impenetrable in some respects. One of the most important questions that it raises seems unanswerable: how the nearly universal dowry regime that prevailed among urban Jews in Egypt (and perhaps elsewhere in the eastern Mediterranean) throughout the tenth to thirteenth centuries affected marriage timing.

Work on regional marriage systems across late medieval and early modern Europe has found consistent class differences in women's age at first marriage. Although the range of ages at which women married varied within and between regions, *within* these ranges wealthier women generally married earlier than poorer ones. But the reasons for this gap differed under different marriage regimes. In much of northern Europe—where women could inherit property independently of marriage, husbands and wives held marriage

lose support from her father's estate) will wish to maintain her, because "having betrothed her, he would not permit her to be degraded," that is, by allowing her to rely on charity. Cf. Maimonides *MT*, *Ishut*, 19:15: "No man wishes his fiancée to demean herself by going and asking for charity at doors"; and above, at n. 104.

127. See further Chapter 5.

128. Although widows and orphans appear together as the archetypal objects of charity in the Hebrew Bible, Geniza texts do not typically apply the same kind of rhetoric to widows as to orphan girls. See, for example, the petitions sent by widows translated in Cohen, *Voice of the Poor*, 83–94; none invoke their widowed status alone as grounds for assistance. Cf. Cohen, *Poverty and Charity*, 142.

property communally, and young women routinely worked for pay before marrying—poor and middling-class women often delayed marriage until their late teens or early twenties so that they could first accumulate a base of property with which to build their households (a trend that accelerated during the early modern period as wage labor markets expanded, the context for Hajnal's European Marriage Pattern).[129] In contrast, Italian women entered marriage with dowries held separately from their husbands' property, were less likely to work before marriage, and married earlier than their northern European counterparts.[130] But the exceptionally rich records preserved for Florence's early fifteenth-century communal dowry fund (the *Monte delle doti*) suggests that there, too, women with larger dowries married earlier—in this case because this property made them more attractive in an intensely competitive marriage market.[131] Even this basic disparity was not universal, however. The *Monte* register documents marriages among Florentine patricians and upper-middling class artisans, notaries, and entrepreneurs. In contrast, a study of marriages in the Tuscan town of Cortona and its surrounding countryside during the same period finds that women's dowries increased as they aged, perhaps to offset their declining reproductive capacity and potential to perform housework and agricultural labor.[132]

Geniza evidence attests to disparate elements of all these marriage regimes. As in Renaissance Italy, women's property was mainly dotal, remained formally separate from their husbands', and was inflated by a competitive marriage market in at least some times and places. Yet, as in northern Europe, some women also worked before marriage to help accumulate their own dotal property (although through textile labor likely performed in their own homes rather than through domestic service). Unfortunately, the extremely limited evidence that survives for women's ages at first marriage and for class differences in both dowry motives and dowry preparations makes it impossible to know how these elements may have combined to affect marriage timing. The most consistent data we possess for this question lies in the rich array of sources reviewed in this chapter that describe relatives and communal officials urgently seeking to endow and marry poor orphan girls after their fathers died.

129. See above, n. 7, and on poorer women's labor before marriage, see also the scholarship reviewed in Kowaleski, "Single Women in Medieval and Early Modern Europe." A large literature examines young women in domestic service in early modern England; see, e.g., the studies surveyed by Froide, *Never Married*, 88–89, and McIntosh, *Working Women in English Society*, 46–48.

130. On young women's relatively less frequent domestic service in late medieval and early modern Italy, see Klapisch-Zuber, "Women Servants in Florence," Chojnacka, *Working Women of Early Modern Venice*, 4–7, and Lynch, *Individuals, Families, and Communities in Europe*, 49–51, and the studies cited there.

131. Kirshner and Molho, "The Dowry Fund and the Marriage Market," 430–431.

132. Botticini, "A Loveless Economy?" 110.

These passages may suggest that the girls documented in the Geniza worked to increase their own dowries only above a minimal level of prosperity—that is, that unlike in early modern northern Europe, delaying marriage in order to accumulate a larger dowry was a luxury of the financially secure, whereas poorer and more unstable families simply did whatever they could to marry off their girls as quickly as possible. A query sent to Maimonides supports this possibility. It quotes a man from Alexandria who explained his daughter's hasty betrothal by arguing, "I cannot detain (her), because I am a poor man."[133] Yet even this modest thesis may not have held true at all times and in all places represented in the corpus. It is clear that not all girls who married young were poor. A court record composed in Fustat in 1156 describes the purchase of a very large trousseau, worth 238 dinars, for a minor orphan.[134] And one of the cases of child engagement discussed in Chapter 3 involves a nonorphan from early thirteenth-century Bilbays whose relatives and in-laws appear to have been local elites.[135]

If we cannot be sure whether dowry pressure increased or decreased women's ages at marriage, Geniza evidence does demonstrate other ways in which Jews' marriage regime affected young women financially. Most importantly, the texts discussed in this chapter make clear that whenever girls married, the act of marrying itself transformed their economic lives. Comparison with European examples again proves useful here. A range of work on single women in the European past concludes that women's marital status often helped to determine their social status.[136] In early modern England, for example, women who had married at least once faced better economic opportunities and commanded greater prestige than women who had not, whether the marriage itself endured.[137]

Lifelong single women were rare among the Geniza populations, or at least remain nearly invisible in our sources.[138] But first marriage seems to have changed women's economic positions in similar ways. I do not mean to suggest, of course, that this change happened overnight, or all at once. Different women lived in a range of different circumstances in the years after marriage, as they had in the years before it; women's standing within households, access

133. Maimonides, *Responsa*, no. 88. (As Goitein points out, *Med. Soc.*, 3:68, the bride's relatively large dowry belies this remark.)

134. Court record: RNL Yevr. Arab. I 1700, 14a, RNL Yevr. Arab. 1700 I, 15a-b (a revised copy). Betrothal contract: RNL Yevr. Arab. I 1700, 25b-26b.

135. T-S 8.112.

136. These include, for England, Beattie, *Medieval Single Women*, Froide, *Never Married*, and Phillips, *Medieval Maidens*, esp. 43–60, for France, *Madame ou Mademoiselle?* (ed. Farge and Klapisch-Zuber), and Lanza, *From Wives to Widows in Early Modern Paris*. See also *Singlewomen* (eds. Bennett and Froide).

137. Froide, *Never Married*, 1–43.

138. See Chapter 3, n. 35.

to property, and labor must have evolved in varying ways over time and with other events, including the births of children and the deaths of older relatives. Still, unmarried girls and married (or formerly married) women appear different enough from each other in our sources to make first marriage a visible economic milestone in young women's lives.

Marriage changed how young women were perceived as well as their real economic possibilities. Although unmarried daughters could perform economically valuable labor, Geniza Jews expected them to remain passive financial dependents until first marriage. Adolescent girls were not encouraged to provide for themselves, and those who lacked means of external support were considered socially vulnerable. Only once a young woman had married could she begin to be expected to provide for herself when necessary—no matter how difficult it might actually be for her to do so.

Social emphasis on the dowry also meant that most women acquired personal property only by marrying. Unlike in many dotal regimes, Geniza women could inherit and nominally own personal assets if their parents died before they married. But unmarried orphans almost never administered their property directly, and their relatives and guardians worked to preserve as much of it as possible for eventual use as a dowry. Unmarried girls' autonomous labor was also used exclusively to increase their dotal assets. This ubiquitous focus on the dowry meant that the rare women whom our sources describe as remaining unmarried into later adulthood might have had trouble acquiring personal property at all. A query sent to Yiṣḥaq al-Fāsī describes a legal case brought by an orphaned woman whose brother wanted to take over the dwelling in which she had lived for eleven years.[139] Although she received the property as a dotal gift, her claim to it was rejected because the betrothal foundered and she never married: "I gave it to you only on the assumption that you consummate marriage with him, but since you divorced (i.e., from betrothal), it remains mine." After marriage, matters were different; although married women's property and labor were subject to formal legal disabilities, in practice many wives exerted direct control over their own assets.

Geniza Jews thus structured young women's economic lives differently from the rabbinic model that they maintained in legal practice, which grants girls complete financial independence at maturity. Their expectation that a young woman's relatives, or their substitutes, should protect her property and labor until she married—and in ways that would best help her to marry—more closely resembles the basic framework of Islamic maturity law, where women become legally adult in most respects at first marriage, not puberty.[140]

139. Yiṣḥaq al-Fāsī, *Responsa,* ed. Leiter, no. 172 (= Bilgoraj ed. no. 140).
140. See above, Chapter 3, at ns. 10–13.

This is not to say that Geniza Jews who took pains to shelter unmarried adolescent girls financially were somehow following Islamic law. On the contrary, control of personal property was the one right that most Muslim jurists allowed unmarried girls at puberty (even if it is not yet clear how far or in what ways medieval Muslims followed this rule).[141] Geniza Jews' ordinary ideas about young women, their capabilities, and their place in the social order seem not to have been grounded fully in formal law, and were not fully or faithfully reflected in either Islamic or Rabbanite legal discourse. Still, on the whole these ordinary ideas are better captured by the Islamic legal distinction between the passive and protected *bikr* (virgin) and the autonomous *thayyib* (nonvirgin), central to Islamic jurists' treatments of most aspects of women's adolescence, than by the autonomous *bogeret* of rabbinic law.

For this reason, it seems likely that these ordinary ideas—the norms through which Geniza Jews managed and understood young women's property, labor, and support—resembled those held by their Muslim (and probably Christian) contemporaries, at least in some respects. Although legally Rabbanite girls differed from Muslim ones in being most autonomous in the period from puberty (when they left their fathers' authority) until marriage (when they fell subject to their husbands' financial control), socially the reverse was true: it was only at first marriage that Jewish girls (perhaps like Muslim and Christian ones) could become financially independent, both for better and for worse.

141. Ibid., n. 11. To my knowledge, no study has yet addressed adolescent girls' economic agency in any medieval Islamic context. But at least one document suggests that Geniza Jews were familiar with this aspect of Islamic law as a lived reality: see above, at n. 70.

CHAPTER FIVE

A Virgin in Her Father's House

MODESTY, MOBILITY, AND SOCIAL CONTROL

NISSIM B. YA'AQOV IBN SHĀHĪN'S *al-Faraj Ba'd al-Shidda*, a story collection composed in eleventh-century Qayrawān but hugely popular among Jews in Fatimid Egypt, contains a story about a butcher who was rewarded after death for having performed a single good deed.[1] He had rescued a young girl from captivity, intending to marry her to his son. But at the wedding feast, a stranger who had been let in as a charity guest suddenly announced that the girl was already formally married, to him; they had been betrothed two years earlier in her native city. He produced both legal proof in the form of a betrothal contract, and a more intimate type of proof: as he had "once seen her in her father's house," he knew that she had a distinctive birthmark in "a certain place" on her body. Faced with this evidence, the butcher canceled his son's wedding and married his intended daughter-in-law to the stranger instead.

This story provides a different kind of evidence for young women's lives from the economic documents and family letters examined in the previous chapter. To begin with, it is a literary tale rather than a record of actual events. It is thus historically useful only insofar as it suggests how ibn Shāhīn and his readers might have expected its characters—the young bride, her father, and her intended husbands—to act toward each other. So much is obvious; but even approached on these terms, this story is frustratingly opaque. It hints at aspects of ibn Shāhīn's social universe that legal texts and letters often leave unmentioned—providing further evidence, for example, that a young Jewish

1. Abramson, *R. Nissim Ga'on*, 5:479–483 (= Brinner, *Elegant Composition*, 80–85). The *faraj ba'd al-shidda* was an Arabic literary genre that developed at least as early as the ninth century (see Moebius, "Narrative Judgments," 91–146), which ibn Shāhīn adapted for a Jewish audience, incorporating narratives characteristic of Arabic *faraj* works with tales and ethical homilies drawn from rabbinic literature.

girl in Zirid Ifrīqiyya, unlike most in Fatimid or Ayyubid Fustat, might expect to be married off immediately at puberty,[2] and suggesting that she might expect to have some form of intimate contact with her intended groom before marriage. But the precise meaning of these hints remains elusive. Were childhood betrothals really commonplace in eleventh-century Ifrīqiyya, or is this an unusual detail that renders the story more interesting precisely because it is peculiar? What about physical marriage with barely pubescent brides? And what exactly would the stranger's knowledge of the bride's hidden birthmark have signaled to the story's readers, either in Qayrawān or in Fustat?

These difficulties are characteristic of the evidence that Judeo-Arabic literary texts and Geniza documents alike offer for young women's private lives before marriage. The Geniza record makes it relatively easy to examine unmarried women's economic circumstances (or at least certain aspects of them, for certain classes of women), because their finances were managed in ways naturally captured in writing. We are much less fortunate when it comes to other aspects of female adolescence, which our sources rarely mention, and then often in brief and elliptical terms. Uncovering even the basic shape of young girls' social lives thus requires digging deeply around the meager hints at our disposal. Reading these clues closely alongside each other, and alongside more far-flung points of comparison offered by earlier and later Jewish and Islamic texts, offers the best hope we have of understanding them.

In Chapter 3, I used this approach to examine one set of questions raised by ibn Shāhīn's story: the ideas about sexual ethics that may have helped to determine marriage timing. This chapter does the same for another topic: attitudes about young women's sexuality and physical mobility in adolescence, before they entered a first marriage.

Virginity

The young bride at the center of ibn Shāhīn's story is more a plot device than an actual character. She is barely present in the story, takes no action, and never speaks about her own wishes or desires. This is typical. Geniza documents and literary sources rarely attest, even indirectly, to young girls' subjective sexual experiences—nor, for that matter, to those of married women. But incidental references in texts of both kinds give some sense of how Geniza Jews understood adolescent sexuality from the outside, as it was or should be managed by others.

We might well expect this understanding to be charged and negative. Many historical Mediterranean and Middle Eastern societies have viewed unmarried daughters' sexuality as a serious moral threat. The Hebrew Bible, for example,

2. See Chapter 3, at ns. 58–60.

prescribes harsh punishment for a bride found to have lost her virginity before marriage: having "committed an abomination in Israel, by whoring in her father's house," she is brought to the doorway of her father's household and stoned to death (Deut. 22:20–21).[3] Much ink has been spilled on the idea that a broad range of Mediterranean cultures, modern and premodern, have shared (and continue to share) a similar form of gendered ideology about "honor and shame" that conditions men's social status on their female relatives' sexual purity.[4]

But one of the great pleasures of working with Geniza documents lies in the ways that they confound and complicate our assumptions about the Middle Eastern past. Detailed fieldwork has helped anthropologists to realize that not all modern Mediterranean societies view women's sexuality as a source of either honor or shame for their male relatives, and that even those that do may do so in quite different ways.[5] Geniza documents suggest that this was probably just as true of the premodern Islamic Mediterranean. They reflect a medieval society that limited at least some unmarried women's physical freedoms, but not always or only for the reasons that we might expect.

Our sources touch on this topic in two ways: occasionally through explicit allusions to virginity, and more often through discussion of women's freedom of movement in public space. Both kinds of references suggest that adolescent girls' sexuality did not attract heightened anxiety different from that provoked by women further along in the life course. I argued in the last chapter that Geniza documents reflect particular concern for protecting young women's financial interests during the period between puberty and first marriage. Documents discussing women's property and support implicitly portray adolescence as a distinct phase of women's lives, a phase in which they held a different social position than they would after marrying for a first time. Remarkably, this seems not to have been the case when it came to young women's socio-sexual protection—or, viewed from another angle, control: unmarried girls were not viewed as requiring particular social safeguards merely by virtue of their virginity. Instead, the concerns that Geniza Jews express about women's physical freedom center more on social status than on immediate sexual activity. Physical modesty and seclusion emerge from the Geniza documents mainly as *class* categories that set some elite women of all ages apart from their lower-class peers, rather than as forms of protection reserved for girls or women of a particular age or marital status.

3. On the patriarchal ideology reflected in this passage and its relationship to other biblical chastity laws, see Frymer-Kensky, "Virginity," Kawashima, "Could a Woman Say 'No'?"

4. For a thoughtful discussion of this literature and of its limits (focusing mainly on anthropology), see Horden and Purcell, *The Corrupting Sea*, 485–523; see further Introduction, n. 16.

5. Horden and Purcell, ibid.

VIRGINITY CLAIMS: CHASTITY AND THE LAW

Unmarried girls' sexual chastity inspires less moral panic in rabbinic legal tradition than in the Hebrew Bible. Whereas Deuteronomy requires a supposedly virgin bride found guilty of sex before marriage to be put to death by stoning, the rabbis assign her a far less dire outcome. Rabbinic law deems virginity charges unprovable in most cases; when they are proven, the wayward bride loses not her life but her marriage payment (that is, her dower).[6] (The rabbis read Deuteronomy here as discussing a bride who had sex *after* her betrothal, in which case she is guilty not of fornication but adultery, a crime that they viewed much more severely.)[7]

Medieval Rabbanite authorities went further. Citing long-standing precedent, several gaonic responsa state that a child born out of wedlock bears no legal stigma. As long as an unmarried mother claims that she was impregnated by a Jewish man of valid lineage, her child may "enter the community" and freely marry other Jews.[8] As for a woman accused of nonvirginity after marriage, a responsum issued by Avraham Maimonides reveals that she faced only a negligible legal penalty even if the claim were confirmed. He rules that a husband who charged his wife of lacking a hymen on their wedding night should be believed, but must nonetheless pay her the deferred portion of her dower if he divorces her; she forfeits only her basic nominal *ketubba* of twenty-five dirhams, a minor sum.[9] This relatively relaxed legal approach to fornication seems to reflect a broader legal tolerance for sexual transgression

6. Indeed, the *bogeret* is not liable to criminal nonvirginity charges, on the rabbinic reasoning that her hymen may have disappeared naturally; see Bamberger, "Qetanah." (Medieval authorities disagreed about some aspects of this principle, apparently due to textual variants in their copies of the Talmud. See Lewin, *OHG, Ket.*, 36–77, Assaf, *Mi-Sifrut ha-Ge'onim* no. 6, and cf. Maimonides, *MT, Ishut*, 11:12–13.) But rabbinic literature is not entirely complacent about the *bogeret*'s sexuality; compare 'Aqiva's dictum discussed above, Chapter 3, at n. 17.

7. See, e.g., bKet. 11b, 45b–46a. For virginity claims as a financial matter, see esp. mKet. 1:1–9, 2:1, and both Talmuds there. Satlow, *Jewish Marriage in Antiquity*, 176–177, points out that the Babylonian Talmud seems ambivalent even about civil-law virginity suits.

8. See Ginzburg, *Geonica*, 2, no. 592, and Harkavy, *Zikhron Kamma Ge'onim*, no. 228, which describes this position as a "tradition . . . from our fathers and our forefathers, (going back) many generations." Cf. Maimonides, *MT, Issurei Bi'a*, 15:11. For the Talmudic background, see mKet. 1:7–9, bQid. 74a. Nonetheless, the well-known story of Wuḥsha (Karīma bt. 'Ammār), a female broker (*dallāla*) described in several Geniza documents from the eleventh century, suggests that legal paternity remained socially important; T-S 10 J 7.10 describes her as convening people to witness her secluded with a man she had married in Islamic but not Jewish court, so that they could testify that he was her baby's father. See Goitein, "Jewish Business Woman," Frenkel, "Charity in Jewish Society," 363–364.

9. Avraham Maimonides, *Responsa*, no. 105. On 25 dirhams as the minimal *ketubba* payment, see Goitein, *Med. Soc.*, 3:119, Friedman, *JMP*, 239–257.

in general. Medieval Rabbanite jurists were reluctant even to punish women for adultery. For example, responding to a legal query about a very young bride who had confessed to an affair, Yehuda b. Yosef (a prominent jurist in eleventh-century Fustat) not only seeks out every conceivable legal means to find her innocent, but blames the court for having pursued the matter in the first place; its judges should have left well enough alone. In any case, he concludes, her husband was not required to divorce her, and if he chose to do so, should pay her a full settlement.[10]

The Geniza legal record suggests that in practice, virginity lawsuits were rare among Geniza Jews. I have identified only three references to legal cases involving a woman's chastity before marriage. The first appears in a query seemingly addressed to Dani'el b. ʿAzarya, *ga'on* of the Palestinian academy in the mid–eleventh century.[11] It describes a man who accused his wife of nonvirginity several years after their marriage, in the middle of a heated dispute with her relatives:

> Sarī b. Ḥasan *kohen* married a woman as a virgin, and she bore him a son. After a time this Sarī quarreled with this woman's relatives, and in the course of arguing with them, he said, "This woman of yours that I married was not a virgin!" After they reconciled he said, "I lied when I said this about my wife; she was a virgin."

Despite Sarī's quick retraction, the accusation led to a convoluted series of events. A local judge caught wind of the claim and used it to blackmail him, by threatening to seize and enslave the couple's son on the grounds that as Sarī was a *kohen*, his wife's nonvirginity at marriage rendered the boy a *ḥalal* (a *kohen* disqualified on grounds of impure lineage).[12] This part of the account is, frankly, bizarre. I am unaware of any legal or ideological tradition that might explain the judge's threat (although a ninth-century Shīʿī text does describe the Jewish exilarch in Iraq as raising illegitimate children to be his personal slaves).[13] However, it is easier to parse the basic social conception of virginity implicit in this story. By representing Sarī's claim as an

10. In theory, a woman convicted of adultery should have been divorced without her dower, and if she became pregnant, her child ostracized as a *mamzer* unmarriageable by ordinary Jews. bYev. 24b-25a; cf. Maimonides *MT*, *Ishut*, 24:10, 24:15; on the *mamzer*, see Satlow, *Tasting the Dish*, 56–62, 137–139. On this query, see Friedman, "*Teshuvat ha-Rav.*" Cf. Yiṣḥaq al-Fāsī, *Responsa*, ed. Leiter, no. 73 (a similar ruling about a woman caught sleeping with her brother-in-law). See also GW 9, a family letter sent from Alexandria in 1176, which mentions a woman who gave birth to a baby fourteen months after her husband had left town: "We suppressed the matter, and did not let anyone know a thing."

11. T-S Ar. 49.166. Gil, *Palestine*, 2:704, identifies the handwriting as that of Dani'el b. ʿAzarya.

12. For the rabbinic background, see Poppers, "Declassé."

13. See Gil, *Jews in Islamic Countries*, 89, citing al-Qāsim b. Ibrāhīm b. Ṭabāṭabā.

attack on his wife's relatives, the author does suggest that a daughter's chastity before marriage might affect her male relatives' social honor, a point reinforced by the fact that Sarī's accusation became sufficiently well-known to come to the judge's attention. Yet the query also represents Sarī's allegation as one salvo among many in an ongoing fight, and one that could comfortably be forgotten once the dispute had ended—not as a uniquely scandalous charge whose mere mention might leave a permanent stain on his wife's character.

The other two cases are described in documents composed some two centuries later, in the early thirteenth century. One is the query behind Avraham Maimonides' ruling mentioned above, and it does not describe the suit that prompted it. The other is a letter sent c. 1200–1240, probably within Egypt.[14] Addressed to an unnamed communal official, it documents the abuse that a man named Sulaymān b. Hānī and his relatives inflicted on his young wife, as background for her divorce suit against him. The author alleges that Sulaymān, his father, and his sister had been tormenting and degrading his wife, cursing her, beating her with a shoe, and routinely evicting her from her living chamber (all actions that are not merely cruel, but intentionally socially humiliating). Moreover, the author adds, this mistreatment began at the very start of the marriage, when the family subjected her to a physical examination to establish that she was a virgin:

> He wished from the start to *slander* her,[15] by God! They brought the midwife, Umm Baqā, and she examined[16] her and informed them that she was pure.

These people were probably much poorer than Sarī b. Ḥasan and his wife.[17] And unlike Sarī's wife, this unfortunate bride seems not to have possessed strong ties to relatives of her own who might protect her, or whose honor might be undermined by sexual slander against her. Sulaymān's accusation thus appears as a direct attempt to personally humiliate her, underscoring the damage that charges of this type might inflict on a woman's public reputation. At the same time, this account suggests that it was unusual for a man to question his wife's honor in this way. Virginity examinations conducted by midwives are frequently attested in medieval Islamic legal texts, sometimes as

14. ENA NS 16.30.

15. The phrase used is the Hebrew *le-hoṣi 'aleha shem ra'*, citing Deut. 22:14 about a bride falsely accused of nonvirginity.

16. *Bāsharathā*, a term connoting intimate physical contact.

17. Sulaymān was a pauper, who appears as a recipient of public charity in a Geniza alms list from the early thirteenth century, from which this document can be dated (BL Or. 5549.7). On this case, see further Chapter 8, n. 34f. In contrast, the query about Sarī b. Ḥasan describes his children and grandchildren as important communal leaders.

a standard component of the wedding night.[18] In contrast, this is the only reference to this practice that I have encountered in the documentary Geniza.[19] It portrays this inspection not as a routine product of intense social focus on women's virginity at marriage, but as an extraordinary event that helps demonstrate Sulaymān's severe animosity toward his wife.

Despite the very different social milieux in which these two accounts were written, and despite the two centuries between them, they portray the accusations that they describe in roughly similar ways. Both documents present Sarī's and Sulaymān's claims against their wives as unusual acts requiring explanation. Each is primarily concerned with describing this act and the broader social conflict that motivated it, rather than with resolving or even addressing the empirical question of either woman's virginity. And although both cases were known to legal officials, neither appears to have been formally lodged in court. Both accounts, then, produce a similar impression: virginity claims were legally possible but not common practice in Geniza Rabbanite courts. By the same token, accusing a woman of having had sex before marriage might damage her reputation, but would not necessarily destroy it—much less the reputations of her male relatives.

SOCIAL APPROACHES TO VIRGINITY

Sources from outside the legal arena parallel and provide further context for this handful of accounts of legal cases. From a variety of angles, they suggest that the Geniza populations were at most moderately rather than intensely concerned about defending and demonstrating women's sexual purity before first marriage. The strongest evidence for active interest in brides' virginity comes from the ritual sphere. Liturgical texts preserved in the Geniza describe a wedding custom, first mentioned in early gaonic literature, in which the groom publicly exhibited a bloodied sheet while reciting a virginity blessing over wine and spices (*birkat betulim*).[20] Responsa issued by both Maimonides and his son Avraham reveal that some Jews in Ayyubid Egypt continued to recite the *birkat betulim* at weddings, but neither responsum makes clear whether it was usually accompanied by an actual display of bloodied

18. See Shaham, *Expert Witness*, 85–87, Tillier, "Women before the *Qāḍī*," 285–286, Spectorsky, *Women in Classical Islamic Law*, 194; for examples of virginity suits filed by new husbands in medieval Andalusia and the Maghrib, see Zomeño, *Dote*, 89–94. On midwives as legal witnesses in Islamic courts more generally, see Giladi, "Liminal Craft."

19. Although a gaonic responsum mentions (and rejects as unreliable) midwives' testimony about women's virginity in the context of impotence claims: T-S G 2.67 (=*TG Sha'arei Ṣedeq*, 4:4:30), attributed to Hayya b. Sherira.

20. The fullest description appears in the early gaonic text *Halakhot Gedolot* (no. 36, *Ketubbot*). See further Langer, "Birkat Betulim."

proofs.[21] In either case, Avraham Maimonides suggests that the practice may not have held great social meaning; he describes it as persisting mainly out of cantorial habit.[22]

On the other hand, the Geniza provides little indication that men preferred to marry a *formally* virgin (that is, previously unmarried) bride. In his commentary on Genesis, Avraham Maimonides describes Yiṣḥaq's marriage to Rivqa, "a virgin whom no man had known" (Gen. 24:16) as a mark of the lofty "modesty" practiced by the Patriarchs—a comment that gestures toward marriage with a virgin as ideal, while also suggesting that most people were not so particular.[23] Goitein points out that courtship letters from the Geniza never single out virgin brides as more desirable than sexually experienced widows or divorced women.[24] The very high rates of female remarriage, as documented in Chapter 1, make it unlikely that a stigma could have attached to marriage with a divorced woman or a widow.

None of this is to suggest that adolescent girls normally engaged in uncontrolled sexual activity. It seems likely that most brides married their first husbands without having experienced prior sexual contact with any other man. Yet ibn Shāhīn's story points to a further sign that many medieval Middle Eastern Jews were less than intensely preoccupied with premarital chastity. The tale's denouement, which hinges on the long-lost groom's special knowledge of his bride's body, echoes numerous gaonic sources indicating that some men expected to have sexual access to their future wives before they stood together under the wedding canopy. Several gaonic responsa refer to grooms who seclude themselves with an intended bride "in her father's house" before formal consummation at *nisu'in* and sometimes even before formal betrothal.[25] Some gaonic authorities take a dim view of this practice, labeling it "debauched" (*periṣut*); others accept it as relatively unproblematic provided the groom does not

21. A query submitted to Maimonides describes the *birkat betulim* without mentioning a bloodied sheet: "When the community gathers in the groom's house on the Sabbath for prayer or blessing, the one reciting the blessing takes the cup in his hand and recites the blessings over wine and spices and this blessing." But some variants of this blessing preserved in the Geniza call *birkat* or *qiddush dam betulim* ("virginity blood": Langer, Langer, "Birkat Betulim," 88–89).

22. *Min tartīb al-ḥazzanim*: idem, *Responsa*, no. 90. Se'adya b. Yosef, Maimonides, and Avraham all opposed the custom as "immodest" (*min qillat al-ṣiyāna*: see Maimonides, *Responsa*, no. 207, Brody, "Saadya Gaon on the Limits of Liturgical Flexibility," and cf. Ta-Shma, "Maimonides' Responsum").

23. "Modesty": the word is *ṣiyāna*, the same term he uses for women's seclusion in the passage on Dina cited below, n. 76. Avraham Maimonides, *Commentary*, ed. Sasson, Gen. 24:16 (54–57).

24. *Med. Soc.*, 3:274.

25. The Mishna describes this as the "custom of Judea," Ket. 1:5, and describes it as intended to preempt potential nonvirginity claims. Cf. tKet. 1:4, bKet. 12a, and for the possible historical context, Ilan, "Premarital Cohabitation."

subsequently renege on his promise to marry the girl.[26] These passages make clear that young women's relatives often willingly sanctioned this form of premarital intimacy; for example, an anonymous gaonic responsum addresses the obligations incurred by a groom whose bride's family had "designated a space for her in her father's house and handed her to him there" (that is, before the wedding).[27] A reference to a lost responsum catalogued in an index of gaonic responsa preserved in the Geniza describes this practice as common among Jews in many parts of North Africa: "It is the custom in many cities of the Maghrib that a man who wished to do so might have sex with his fiancée in her father's house."[28]

I have not identified similarly clear evidence for premarital sex between betrothed couples in the Geniza. But a few texts hint at it. A small, undated fragment of a legal document contains testimony that a young woman was "protected" (*mastūra*) and had not been secluded with her groom, "neither at night nor in the daytime," neither with her father's knowledge "nor in his dwelling."[29] This fragment suggests that premarital seclusion could tarnish a girl's reputation (one line calls the charge that must have prompted this testimony "nothing but slander"), but that it must have been permitted in at least some households. Another deed of testimony, composed in Fustat in 1134, suggests the same. It cites a woman named Milāḥ bt. Ḥalfon who sought to divorce her fiancé because she was disgusted by his attempts to commit "obscenities with her, the like of which are not permitted."[30]

Seclusion and Female Honor

If the Jews documented in the Geniza seem to have been only moderately interested in monitoring adolescent girls' virginity, some men (and women)

26. *TG Sha'arei Ṣedeq*, 3:3:14: "There are *peruṣim* who rely on the *erusin* blessing, seclude themselves with their fiancées, and have sex" (attributed to the eighth-century Yehuday Gaon); cf. Mueller, *TG Mizraḥ u-Ma'arav*, no. 37 (ninth century). See also Assaf, *TG ve-Liqqutei Sefer ha-Din* nos. 45 and 113, both attributed to Hayya b. Sherira (early eleventh century), criticizing men who marry without a written contract.

27. *TG Sha'arei Ṣedeq*, 4:4:62. In such a case, the responsum continues, the woman should be considered "like a wife in every respect" and entitled to her deferred dower at divorce, specifically to discourage "*peruṣim*" from having sex with a fiancée and then abandoning her. Cf. *TG Sha'arei Ṣedeq*, 4:4:25: such men should be lashed and excommunicated. See also Ginzburg, *Geonica* 2, no. 569, which simply condones intercourse before *nisu'in* as unexceptional.

28. T-S Misc. 35.90 + 103 + 104 + 105, ed. Ginsburg, *Gaonica* 2, no. 52; see Ben-Sasson, *Qayrawan*, 114, n. 24. Maghribī and Andalusian responsa also describe this practice as common: Mueller, *TG Mizraḥ u-Ma'arav*, nos. 187, 197.

29. ENA NS 19.23.

30. Obscenities: "*al-fawāḥish*"; it is not clear whether this implies something beyond premarital consummation. JNUL Heb. 4 577.7/3.

among them did seek to maintain other forms of control over women's bodies. A much larger base of legal texts and agreements attest to active negotiations over women's modesty, defined in terms of their physical mobility and visibility in public. Most of this evidence pertains not to still unmarried women, but rather to women at later stages of life, particularly within marriage itself. But precisely for this reason, it helps illuminate by contrast how adolescent modesty was understood as well. In what follows, I will discuss married women's mobility at some length before moving on to the few references that shed light on the movements of still unmarried girls.

MODESTY AS A CLASS CATEGORY

The idea that women's physical mobility presents a moral threat, either to their relatives or to the public order more broadly, would likely have been familiar to many Geniza Jews.[31] Both Jewish and Islamic legal traditions connect women's presence in public space to their sexual control. Later Islamic didactic works composed in Ayyubid and especially Mamluk Egypt express strong concern for this issue, harshly criticizing women's relative freedom of movement and visibility in the shops and streets of Cairo and Fustat. "This is a great affliction nowadays," the Mamluk jurist ibn al-Ḥajj complains, "for one rarely sees the shop of the cloth merchant empty of women dressed in delicate clothes that expose their adornment, and behaving as if they were with their husbands, or members of their family."[32]

These texts reflect what Marion Katz describes as Muslim jurists' growing emphasis, in the twelfth century and after, on the dangers of *fitna* (sexual temptation) created by women in public space.[33] But medieval Arabic historiographical texts suggest that even in earlier periods, similar ideological concerns sometimes spilled over into state policy. Early Fatimid and late Mamluk accounts alike describe specific cases in which either a caliph or a *muḥtasib*—the state official charged with maintaining public order—prohibited women from appearing in public or in particular public locations. Most famously, the Fatimid caliph al-Ḥākim, who ruled from 996 until he mysteriously disappeared

31. Several previous studies have examined Geniza evidence for women's mobility and veiling. This section builds on Goitein, *Med. Soc.*, 3:153–156; Friedman, "Ethics," 87–95, idem, "Halakhah as Evidence," 91–99; and Ashur, "*Haggana*."

32. Ibn al-Ḥajj, *al-Madkhal*, 4:32, cited Lutfi, "Manners and Customs," 103. On *al-Madkhal*, see eadem; on earlier works of this kind, see Cortese and Calderini, *Women and the Fatimids*, 193–194, Afsaruddin, "Early Women Exemplars."

33. Katz, *Women in the Mosque*, 24–26, 40–41, 74–75, 103–104. On women's seclusion and veiling in the Qur'ān, see Spectorsky, *Women in Classical Islamic Law*, 44–51; cf. also Mernissi, *The Veil and the Male Elite*, 85–101, Stowasser, *Women in the Qur'an*, 91–92. On modesty regulations in classical Islamic law, see eadem, 90–97; Alshech, "Out of Sight"; Tucker, *Women, Family, and Gender*, 177–184.

in 1021, banned women from visiting cemeteries and bathhouses, and eventually from leaving their households altogether, a restriction that he reinforced by also banning the manufacture of women's shoes.[34] Some four centuries later, in 1438, the Mamluk *sulṭān* Barsbāy similarly forbade women to go to the marketplace or to the bathhouse at night.[35] A coherent history of these sporadic crackdowns has yet to be written; further research may reveal more such episodes and help explain the particular historical contexts in which they occurred. But they have left no apparent traces in the Geniza corpus. I am unaware of any document that mentions state efforts to control women's mobility.

Nor do Geniza documents describe Jewish communal officials routinely policing women's movements or sexual behavior. A few documents do suggest that communal authorities sometimes intervened to disrupt suspected interactions between Jewish women and non-Jewish (Muslim or Christian) men. For example, a fragmentary undated court record describes a case in which Muslims observed a Jewish woman spending time with a Christian doctor in the store he worked in and reported them both to the Muslim authorities.[36] The text is fragmentary and it is unclear exactly which officials were involved, but the document's existence demonstrates that the matter somehow ended up before the Rabbanite court.

More visibly, however, Geniza documents attest to a different mode of patriarchal control over women's movements, imposed not from above by public

34. See Cortese and Calderini, *Women and the Fatimids*, 192–196, who note a similar decree by al-Ḥākim's successor al-Ẓāhir. Cf. Lev, "Aspects of the Egyptian Society," 16–18. More regularly, women's public behavior was theoretically regulated by the *muḥtasib* (market inspector, an official who came to function as a general guardian of the public order; see "Ḥisba," *EI²*). Mamluk-era sources describe *muḥtasibs* occasionally trying to curb women's circulation in public (see Stilt, *Islamic Law in Action*, 101–106), but less is known about this office under the Fatimids and Ayyubids, and it is rarely mentioned in Geniza documents; see Lev, *State and Society*, 160–161, idem, "Suppression of Crime," and Goitein, *Med. Soc.*, 2:369. Both Islamic texts and Geniza documents also mention sanctions on unaccompanied women traveling long distances; see Khalilieh, "Women at Sea," and cf. Goitein, *Med. Soc.*, 3:336–341. Husbands sometimes appointed traveling companions for their wives; see, for example, T-S 10 J 26.1 + Bodl. MS Heb. d. 66.4, a legal deed composed in Fustat, 1065; T-S 10 J 7.2, an early thirteenth-century letter that mentions a similar deed.

35. See Rapoport, *Marriage, Money and Divorce*, 36, Cortese and Calderini, *Women and the Fatimids*, 193.

36. CUL 1080 J 93. See Goitein, *Med. Soc.*, 5:315–316, and on the official called the *ṣāḥib al-rub'*, ibid., 2:369. Islamic narrative sources similarly suggest that Muslim state and communal authorities were especially anxious about interactions between Muslim and non-Muslim men and women; see Lev, "Aspects of the Egyptian Society," 9–10, citing the Fatimid historian al-Musabbiḥī. A thirteenth-century Geniza deed describes a communal controversy over a provincial judge's weekly sermon condemning the local women for "adorning and embellishing themselves" and mixing with non-Jews in the marketplace (ENA 2727.31; see Zinger, "What Sort of Sermon is This?").

authorities, but by husbands within the semiprivate sphere of marriage. Most of our evidence for these efforts comes from a small group of Geniza marriage contracts and reconciliation agreements that dictate when the wife may leave her living space (perhaps meaning the entire *dār* that she lived in, but perhaps meaning even her personal chamber within the *dār*)[37] and where she may go when she does so. These clauses begin appearing in Geniza Rabbanite marriage documents in the early twelfth century, alongside other stipulations regulating both spouses' rights and responsibilities in marriage (including the residence clauses examined in Chapter 1 as evidence for household formation).[38]

Like these other stipulations, mobility clauses do not follow a standard formula. By definition, however, they all present a woman's physical freedom as a problem of spousal authority. The more restrictive clauses grant the husband control over his wife's movements (e.g., "she will go out only with his consent"),[39] whereas others deny him such control (e.g., "he will not lock her in the *dār* nor prevent her from visiting her family").[40]

These clauses' assumption that a husband may control his wife's mobility is supported in slightly different ways by both Jewish and Islamic legal literature. The major schools of Sunnī Islamic law predicate a man's marital support (*nafaqa*) of his wife on his control of her movements: a woman who physically leaves her husband, even with his consent, is no longer entitled to maintenance.[41] Late ancient rabbinic texts, for their part, describe husbands as not only permitted but obliged to regulate their wives' movements.[42] A passage in the Tosefta (likely compiled in third-century Palestine) outlines a hierarchy of degrees of restriction:

> As there are opinions regarding food, so regarding women:
>
> One man, when a fly enters his cup, throws (his drink) away without drinking it; this is like Pappus b. Yehuda, who locked the door against his wife and left.

37. This point is never specified; at least some of the very secluded women discussed below, beginning at n. 57, seem not even to have interacted with other neighbors in their *dār*s, and it is clear that the woman described in the passage that I discuss at n. 58 did not do so. On wives' personal chambers, see Chapter 8.

38. See Chapter 7 for more on these clauses.

39. Mosseri VII 10.1.

40. RNL Yevr.-Arab. I 1700, 17b.

41. See Ali, *Marriage and Slavery*, 71–72, eadem, "Money, Sex, and Power," 183–203. Cf. Katz, *Women in the Mosque*, 26–28, 42–43, 45–46, 95 (on husbands' authority over their wives' mosque attendance).

42. Besides the discussions of husbands' authority mentioned in the following note, classical rabbinic literature does not systematically regulate women's modesty; for rabbinic approaches to women's nudity as it affects men's behavior, see Satlow, "Jewish Constructions," 440–442.

> Another, when a fly falls into his drink, throws (the fly) away and drinks; this is the measure of any man who sees his wife speaking with her neighbors or her relatives and permits her.
>
> Another, when a fly falls into his plate—takes it, sucks it, throws it out and eats (the plate's) contents; this is the measure of an evil man, who sees his wife going out bare-headed, with her shoulders exposed . . . spinning in the marketplace, washing and sporting with every man. It is a good deed (*miṣva*) to divorce her, as is said, *If a man should take a wife and marry her (and she did not please him, because he found in her some lewdness, he should . . . send her from his house)* (Deut. 24:1).[43]

This passage describes three types of husband. The first attempts to seclude his wife entirely, the second permits her basic social contact with her neighbors and relatives, and the third allows her complete liberty to move through public space—a degree of freedom that it presents as inherently sexually licentious. Ishay Rosen-Zvi has suggested that this and related texts reflect an internal rabbinic debate between two different models of patriarchal control.[44] One requires a husband to limit his wife's behavior in order to ensure her sexual chastity; this model is represented here in cautionary terms by the third husband, who fails to keep his wife out of the marketplace and thus allows her to "[sport] with every man." The other model, embodied here by the first husband (the authoritarian Pappus b. Yehuda), promotes physical control of women as a value in and of itself. As Rosen-Zvi notes, most classical rabbinic sources reject the latter model in favor of a more moderate patriarchal ideal, fulfilled by the second husband in this passage, which asks men to limit their wives' public movements without completely secluding them. Commenting on a related passage, the Babylonian Talmud criticizes a husband who "locks the door" on his wife for socially isolating her: "She might die tomorrow and not a single soul would mourn her."[45]

Most mobility clauses in Geniza marriage documents closely echo the intermediate, "moderately patriarchal" model promoted in these rabbinic texts. For example, a fragmentary premarital contract, undated but likely from the early twelfth century, records the wife's pledge that she will leave her chamber

43. tSot. 5:9 (=bGit. 90a-b). mKet. 7:4–6 parallels this passage, and establishes that a husband may not prevent his wife from visiting her relatives or houses of celebration or mourning; if he does so, he must divorce her and pay her a full divorce settlement (*ketubba*). Conversely, a wife who acts lewdly in public forfeits her right to a *ketubba*. Cf. pKet. there, bKet. 72a-b.

44. Rosen-Zvi, "'Tractate Kinui,'" esp. 24–25.

45. bKet. 72a.

(*bayt*)[46] only to visit places permitted to "proper Jewish women."[47] In another marriage agreement from the same period, a woman named Ẓāfira bt. Yefet specifies that her husband must permit her to freely attend the synagogue, the bathhouse, celebrations and places of mourning; to circulate in order to buy and sell flax; and to visit her sister whenever she wishes—all outings, the document notes, "permitted to a proper Jewish woman of her type."[48]

Whether they outline the restrictions that a husband imposes on his wife, as in the first of these examples, or the mobility rights that she claims from him, as in the second, these clauses define socially acceptable female mobility outside the home in similar terms. Both ratify a married woman's freedom to leave her household, but only to visit a specific roster of licit venues.

This standard was almost certainly not shared by all populations or social groups represented in the Geniza. Even in early twelfth-century Fustat, where most of these clauses were composed, married women much poorer than the "proper" Ẓāfira regularly attended public charity distributions sponsored and recorded without comment by Rabbanite communal officials.[49] Yet if their usefulness as a general index of women's movements is uncertain, mobility

46. In Geniza documents this term refers not to a house but to an individual living space or chamber; see Goitein, *Med. Soc.*, 4:57, and see further Chapter 8.

47. *Benot yisra'el ha-kesherot*, T-S NS 226.48. The handwriting is that of Ḥalfon b. Menashe, the most active court scribe in Fustat, whose dated documents span 1100–1138. On the term "*keshera*," see Goitein, *Med. Soc.*, 3:166.

48. "Proper," etc.: *mithlihā min benot yisra'el al-kesherot*. T-S 8 J 29.13, a reconciliation agreement between a couple on the verge of divorce. Goitein identifies INA D 55/2 as their bill of divorce, *Med. Soc.*, 3:217. Other reconciliation agreements that stipulate the wife's acceptable sphere of movement include T-S NS 226.29, also composed by Ḥalfon (the wife is authorized to visit the bathhouse and her family); T-S 6 J 2.2, mid-thirteenth century (fragmentary, but seems to note that the wife may go to the market to purchase flax); possibly T-S NS J 185 (also fragmentary, but the husband may not prevent his wife from doing something, and the word "places" appears). Cf. Mosseri II 195, a twelfth-century letter: a man begs his estranged wife, a Karaite woman from Tripoli, to join him in Cairo on the condition that she remain "safeguarded" (*muḥtaraza*, seemingly a synonym for *maṣūna*, see below, n. 67), "minimizing her coming and going except for the Karaite synagogue and the bathhouse." Premarital contracts that define the wife's freedom of movement include Mosseri VII 6.1 (also drafted by Ḥalfon; the husband "may not prevent (his wife) from any [. . . *benot*] *yisra'el ha-kesherot*, nor from coming and [going]"); T-S Misc 26.61 (a fragmentary *ketubba*, also in Ḥalfon's hand; the husband may not prevent his wife from visiting her family); RNL Yevr–Arab. I 1700, 17b (a Karaite-Rabbanite betrothal contract, Fustat, 1156; the husband may not lock his wife in the *dār* nor prevent her from visiting his family). Most of these documents are noted and partly edited and translated into Hebrew in Ashur, "EBD," 119–121, idem, "*Haggana*" 20–23; see further Chapter 7. Maimonides *Responsa*, no. 45 (and cf. ibid., no. 34, likely on the same case) describes a female teacher of young boys whose husband tried to force her to stop teaching because he was afraid she would socialize with her students' fathers.

49. On women in charity lists, see Cohen, *Poverty and Charity*, 148–155.

clauses do reveal something meaningful about social ideas surrounding female mobility. The concept of wifely propriety that they reflect appears to have been relatively durable and widespread beyond the immediate context of twelfth-century Fustat. It is paralleled both in Geniza documents of other types and in a variety of medieval prescriptive Rabbanite texts. Maimonides, for example, programmatically states:

> Every woman has the right to go and come to her father's house to visit him, and to houses of mourning and feasting, in order to behave kindly towards her friends and relatives so that they will come to visit her. For she is not in prison such that she may not come and go. But it is shameful for a woman to be constantly going out . . . and a husband should prevent his wife from doing this and permit her to go out only once or twice a month, as needed.[50]

This approach also appears roughly compatible with ideas shared by other religious groups in medieval Egypt. Early Mamluk Islamic prescriptive texts represent men's ideal control over their wives' movements in basically the same way: a husband should supervise his wife and ensure that she did not behave lewdly in public, but it was not accepted practice to lock her in the house.[51]

Both documentary and literary evidence thus suggests that many of the Jews documented in the Geniza likely expected a "proper" woman to leave her home at least occasionally. It is impossible to know how often such women actually ventured outside the household. Maimonides' recommendation of "once or twice a month" may perhaps describe actual Jewish practice in Ayyubid Egypt, but it is equally possible that this statement is simply a textual gloss on his classical rabbinic source material.[52] In this same passage, Maimonides also states that women in some (unnamed) places appeared in public only in an

50. *MT*, *Ishut*, 13:11. Cf., e.g., a passage from the *Siddur* of Shelomo b. Natan of Sijilmāsa (eleventh or twelfth century, cited in Friedman, "Government Intervention," 218–219), which echoes mKet. 7:4–5 by stating that a wife whose husband prevents her from visiting her "father" (i.e., her relatives) or visiting "people at times of mourning and celebration" must divorce her and pay her deferred dower. An undated letter about a woman distraught by her recent divorce defines women's normal outings in similar terms, emphasizing her depression by noting that she no longer "enters the bathhouse, except at the new month (*rosh ḥodesh*) and the like, nor attends wedding nor participates in celebrations" (DK 238.4).

51. See Rapoport, *Marriage, Money and Divorce*, 71–72.

52. *MT*, *Ishut*, 13:11. Friedman, "Ethics," 91, suggests this may allude to mKet. 7:4, which allows a husband to keep his wife away from her family for a month but not two or three. On the other hand, Maimonides' commentary on this *mishna* does not mention this point. Maimonides states elsewhere that many women in Egypt refrained from leaving the *dār* (or perhaps their private living chambers) during their menstrual periods. Maimonides, *Responsa* no. 320, and see Friedman, "Menstrual Impurity," idem, "Social Realities," 231–232.

enveloping cloak (Heb. *radid*, possibly intended as a translation of the Arabic *radda*): "In places where a woman does not customarily go out to the marketplace . . . unless covered by a *radid* that covers her whole body like a prayer shawl, (a man must minimally) provide (his wife) with the meanest type of *radid* among her clothing." This comment is more likely to reflect actual social norms, given that Maimonides explicitly describes it as a local custom, rather than as a recommendation. In fact, the *radda* and numerous types of facial veils appear in many Geniza trousseaux lists.[53]

Yet even if many or most Geniza women really were subject to these constraints—emerging only at infrequent intervals to visit certain designated places, and then physically covered from head to toe—they likely came into regular contact with people beyond their own households, including nonkin men. In theory, men and women stayed physically separated at weddings and at prayer, but it seems unlikely that this segregation was upheld consistently among all social groups throughout the entire Geniza period. In an early thirteenth-century letter, a man reminds the woman to whom he is writing about something that occurred "the day you met me in the synagogue."[54] Legal documents and letters alike describe married women meeting privately with men other than their husbands in order to conduct business transactions.[55] Men and women may also have mingled to some extent in the common areas of the *dār*s in which they lived. (It is surely no coincidence that most pre- and extramarital affairs mentioned in medieval Middle Eastern Rabbanite responsa are described as having occurred between neighbors.)[56]

STRICT SECLUSION AND ELITE STATUS

Alongside this evidence for partial restrictions on women's mobility, however, other Geniza documents describe women who practiced or submitted

53. Also *MT*, *Ishut*, 13:11; on the *radda* and other veils, see Stillman, "Female Attire," 116–203, and on women's veiling more broadly, see Friedman, "Halakhah as Evidence," 91–99.

54. T-S 8 J 17.3. On this letter and gendered space in the synagogue, see Goitein, *Med. Soc.*, 2:144–145, and on weddings, ibid., 3:116. (On the synagogue at Dammūh mentioned ibid., 2:144, see also Kraemer, "Jewish Cult.")

55. See, e.g., T-S 13 J 18.8, T-S NS 338.75, Maimonides, *Responsa*, no. 60. Bodl MS Heb. e. 94.25, early twelfth century, describes a woman who secluded herself with a man before hidden witnesses, to obtain their testimony about her business conversation with him; see Goitein, *Med. Soc.*, 3:328–331, and cf. ibid., 1:129.

56. See, e.g., Coronel, *TG*, no. 17, about a betrothed girl who became pregnant by another man, a "youth in the *ḥaṣer* (= *dār*), who was constantly coming and going into her house"; Ginzburg, *Geonica* 2, no. 592, about a pregnant unmarried woman who identified a neighbor as the father; cf. al-Fāsī, *Responsa*, ed. Leiter no. 73, a soap operatic account about a woman whose husband caught her sleeping "under one cloak" with his brother (who was also their upstairs neighbor).

to a stricter form of physical seclusion. In contrast to marital agreements like Ẓāfira's, which promise wives limited freedom of movement, a few marriage contracts grant husbands total control over their wives' mobility. In a betrothal agreement composed in 1127 in Fustat, a bride authorizes her future husband to behave exactly like Pappus b. Yehuda, the rabbinic archetype of overbearing patriarchy: "She will come and go only by his will and when he permits her to do so; whenever he wishes, he may lock her in . . . and she may make no claim against him about this at all."[57]

What explains the very different approach to female autonomy ratified in this contract? Modesty clauses that appear in marital reconciliation agreements were presumably composed only after some kind of struggle between spouses—in which most wives, it seems, wanted to retain personal freedoms that their husbands wished to deny or limit. It is less clear what motivated couples and their families to include modesty clauses in premarital contracts, but they, too, serve to define the scope of the husband's authority. Legal agreements that severely limit a woman's mobility, then, may simply reflect her husband's desire for particularly strict control.

But other Geniza documents suggest that not all stringently secluded women were kept indoors by a husband's demands. Some women instead secluded themselves without any man directly demanding that they do so, not only within but also outside of marriage. Consider, for example, an eleventh-century letter sent from Jerusalem that eulogizes one of the most severely isolated women to appear in the Geniza corpus, an old woman named Ester.[58] The letter's author, Avraham b. ʿAmram, does not make his own relationship to Ester clear, but he describes himself as her primary caretaker and was most likely a relative. He laments that her strict refusal to socially expose herself in the slightest degree, even within the *dār* where she lived, had prevented him from caring for her properly during her illness:

> I was unable to care for her as was needed, because . . . our master Barhūn and his father were staying in the room (*bayt*) . . . adjacent to the room in which she lived. She was exceedingly modest (*ṣenuʿa be-yoter*), that no noise be heard from her; but there was a small door between the rooms, where she used to sit companionably with me, and

57. T-S 8 J 5.7. Cf. Mosseri VII 10.1, an early twelfth-century premarital contract in which the bride promises to "go out only by his word." Restrictive conditions like this appear more often in reconciliation agreements drawn up during marriage itself: see PER H 82, 1007, Egypt (among many other conditions, the wife "will not go out of his house except by his leave"), T-S 16.246, early twelfth century ("she will not exit the *bayt* except by his word"); T-S 13 J 2.22, also early twelfth century ("she will not go and come except by his word"); T-S NS 321.100 ("she will not go out [. . .]"). Cf. Chapter 7.

58. Bodl. MS Heb. b. 3.24. The name "Ester" is unusual for Geniza women, and may indicate that this woman was originally from Europe or the Byzantine empire. I am grateful to Oded Zinger for pointing this out to me.

I provided whatever she needed. . . . She asked me to stop doing this, out of concern for the men (i.e., Barhūn and his father), that they not hear a word from her.

This account describes Ester as practicing not only physical but also auditory seclusion, restraining even the sound of her voice from intruding into the public sphere—even as represented by the next room over.[59] Avraham describes this degree of "modesty" as unusual. Certainly it radically contracts the geography of proper female movement staked out by women like Ẓāfira. But perhaps more importantly, it reveals Ester to have viewed her own mobility in different terms: rather than a restriction imposed on her by others, a husband or anyone else, Avraham presents Ester's seclusion as her own personal stringency, which she insisted on maintaining despite his protests.

Here again, prescriptive legal texts help shed light on Ester's "exceeding modesty"—not, in this case, because they advocate the degree of seclusion that she practiced, but because they describe it as a recognized *social* custom that often had legal implications, specifically for court procedure. Both Jewish and Islamic legal works composed in various parts of the medieval Middle East, beginning first in Abbasid and Buyid Iraq, mention a class of women who never appeared in public, a practice that required courts to develop special protocols for communicating with them.

Medieval Muslim jurists call these women "secluded" (*mukhaddara*), or simply "(those) who do not go out" (*lā takhruju*).[60] Rabbanite texts typically term them "modest" (*ṣenuʿa*), the same word that Avraham uses to describe Ester. According to the late tenth-century Iraqi *gaʾon* Sherira b. Ḥananya, Rabbanite court officials in Iraq who wanted to summon a woman to court would first work to determine whether she was "accustomed to go out in order to conduct business, buy and sell, and speak with men," or a "*ṣenuʿa* who dwells inside."[61] An undated Geniza fragment seems to allude to a similar protocol in a rabbinic court in Fustat. It describes two court representatives as having visited a woman "to investigate her circumstances, since

59. Cf. bBer. 24a: "A woman's voice is a form of nudity."

60. On the *mukhaddara*, see Tillier, "Women before the *Qāḍī*," 295–300, based on references to specially protected women in both legal and narrative Islamic texts. Muslim jurists single out court as the one place where a woman may be legally required to unveil herself before men not related to her; see Spectorsky, *Women in Classical Islamic Law*, 51, 191–195, Tyan, *Le Notariat*, 56, and Tillier, "L'identification" (who cites narrative sources that corroborate this). Many Geniza court records accompany women's names by a clause indicating that their identity had been confirmed (*baʿd ṣiḥḥat al-maʿrifa bihā*), but by what means is unclear. Unlike medieval Islamic legal documents, Geniza legal documents do not include physical descriptions of the litigants (as noted by Goitein, *Med. Soc.*, 3:332).

61. Assaf, *TG ve-Liqqutei Sefer ha-Din*, no. 3; on this responsum, see Friedman, "Ethics," 92–95, Libson, "Status," 239, idem, *Jewish and Islamic Law*, 107–110. Cf. Musafia, *TG*, no. 9.

she is a veiled woman."[62] Other legal documents suggest that this was not an isolated incident; while many mention women appearing personally in court, others describe women who communicated only by proxy from their homes.[63]

Whether imposed by others or upheld by women themselves, strict seclusion probably had complex motives only partly captured by any of the sources at our disposal. Still, it is worth noting how these sources typically describe strict female "modesty": not as a marker of individual piety or sexual chastity, but rather of elite social status. In a recent study of women appearing before Abbasid *qāḍīs*, Mathieu Tillier points out that Muslim jurists negatively correlate women's mobility with their social status; the secluded woman's refusal to circulate in public signifies her nobility (*sharaf*).[64] Tillier points out that this social conception may extend back to late antiquity: for example, Syriac accounts describe veiling and seclusion as elite practices among the sixth-century Christian population of Najrān in southwest Arabia.[65] Taking an even broader view, the link between women's seclusion and social status can be seen as a Middle Eastern cultural idea of extremely *longue durée*, which has been noted in studies stretching from ancient Mesopotamia (where veiling in public denoted a woman's high rank) to late Ottoman Istanbul and Cairo (where designation as a *mukhaddara* continued to serve as a mark of social honor).[66] Unsurprisingly, Geniza Jews also understood women's seclusion in these terms. For example, an early twelfth-century court record from Fustat awarding a woman alimony while her husband was away on business notes that she required provisions not only for herself, but also for her slave, since

62. ENA NS 298.38. I am grateful to Oded Zinger for pointing out this document to me.

63. On women in court, see Goitein, *Med. Soc.*, 3:332–336. Legal documents describe some women appearing in court and others as communicating from home by proxy (see ibid., 3:214). I have not found a Geniza document that describes a protocol for identifying a woman as a *ṣenu'a*, but it seems clear that women could not automatically refuse to come to court. See Friedman, "Ethics," 95, discussing T-S 13 J 16.11, an early eleventh-century document about a divorce: the wife refused to come to court because she was ill (not out of modesty), and the court declared that if the couple could not come to terms, she would be declared "rebellious" (*moredet*) against both the court and her husband and would forfeit her financial claims on him. (On the *moredet*, see Chapter 7.)

64. Tillier, "Women before the *Qāḍī*," 297–300. See also Katz, *Women in the Mosque*, 107–108, and see below, n. 69.

65. This argument draws on Doumato, "Hearing Other Voices," 183–185.

66. For the ancient Near East, see van der Toorn, "Significance of the Veil." On women's seclusion as a mark of elite status in a range of medieval and early modern Islamic contexts, see Thompson, "Public and Private," esp. 56; see also Peirce, "The Law Shall Not Languish," eadem, *Morality Tales*, 154–161, on the *muhaddere* (*mukhaddara*) in sixteenth-century Turkey, and for Cairo, see, e.g., Tucker, "Problems in the Historiography of Women in the Middle East," 330.

she was among "the elite of the city who remain secluded in their homes (or, perhaps, rooms: *buyūtihin*)."[67]

These passing references do not reveal the precise fault lines that separated women who "went out" from those who did not. Did the most strictly secluded women described in the Geniza refrain even from visiting the bathhouse?[68] Maimonides refers to women who customarily ventured outside only at night, a practice also mentioned in a range of medieval Islamic sources.[69] As with other aspects of Maimonides' treatment of this subject, it is not clear whether he is here referring to an exceptional level of modesty or whether he means that even less restricted women ordinarily avoid daytime excursions. Nor do available sources reveal precisely how extreme seclusion mapped onto social status. Commercial legal documents, for example, make clear that not

67. *Tovei ha-ʿir al-maṣūnāt fī buy*[*ūtihin*], T-S NS J 401k (the term *maṣūna* is a common female honorific in Mamluk texts; see Marmon, *Eunuchs*, 18–19, and Lutfi, "*Iqrārs*," 292.) This remark underscores the structural basis of elite women's seclusion, which depends in practice on the presence of a lower class of nonsecluded women who can mediate and provide services for their sheltered counterparts. Cf. ENA 2808.52: "Sutayt (likely a slave) is the only one among us who comes and goes (that is, who circulates in public), therefore I sent her [. . .]." On women acquiring domestic slaves, see Perry, "Daily Life of Slaves," 95–98. Goitein notes generally that women's seclusion varied by class, *Med. Soc.*, 3:324–325, 5:308. The common use of the term *mastūr*/*mastūra* ("protected," but also "veiled") to describe financially secure individuals may reflect a similar association between seclusion and class; see Chapter 4.

68. We might assume that even the most "modest" women visited the ritual bath (*miqveh*) to purify themselves after menstruation, but in fact this is uncertain; Maimonides famously tried to enforce women's use of the *miqveh* in Egypt because many women instead purified themselves by washing their bodies with "drawn" water at a regular bathhouse (*ḥammām*). See Maimonides, *Responsa*, no. 242, and Friedman, "Social Realities," 180–182, idem, "Menstrual Purity." (It is unclear where the *miqveh* of Fustat was located, or if one existed at all before Maimonides assumed leadership; see Goitein, *Med. Soc.*, 2:154–155).—Maimonides suggests that some extremely modest women did attend the bathhouse under specific constraints: "If it were their custom to obscure (i.e., veil) themselves and hide even in the bathhouse, such that the girl washes (herself) at night or alone in a small room (*bayit*, likely an equivalent for *bayt*) in the bathhouse, so that she is not seen" (*MT*, *Ishut*, 25:2).

69. See the previous note, and from the same passage: "In places where girls do not customarily go to the marketplace at all, and when a girl goes to the bathhouse at twilight, she obscures (i.e., veils) herself" (*MT*, *Ishut*, 25:2). Islamic sources: this distinction also comes up in early legal discussions of women appearing before a *qāḍī* (where "the woman who does not go out during the daytime" is eventually replaced by the *mukhadarra*; see above, at n. 60), as well as in mosques (where jurists eventually promoted nighttime attendance as an ideal for all women, not merely a preference held by elite ones). See Katz, *Women in the Mosque*, 22–23, 29–30, 107–108. The Mamluk *sulṭān* Barsbāy, who banned women from the marketplace in Cairo after an outbreak of plague in 1438, also decreed that they could go to the bathhouse only at night; see Cortese and Calderini, *Women and the Fatimids*, 193.

all wealthy and well-connected women stayed indoors, since some describe women contracting substantial business transactions with nonkin men outside their households.[70] Nor, finally, does the prescriptive legal material that I have reviewed reveal how these fault lines themselves may have shifted over time and between regions, either within Egypt or throughout the broader medieval Islamic world—nor whether they fell along different axes for Jews and Muslims. Further work on Islamic literary and documentary sources may help answer these questions more fully.

But even given the limitations of our evidence, recognizing that strict physical seclusion served as a sign of female status allows us to better understand why women like Ester physically isolated themselves even without a husband compelling them to do so, and even at considerable personal cost. Women who confined themselves to their chambers and who did not often receive visitors must have been painfully lonely. In a thirteenth-century letter, a man writing to his mother-in-law in Fustat laments his wife's social isolation: "(Your daughter) has known neither day nor night since you (left); the world closes in on her, in her desolation and loneliness. . . . As you know, when you are not here, not a single person comes in nor goes out" (meaning, no one from the outside world enters her living space).[71] Those who willingly endured such deprivation, as well as the husbands and birth relatives who compelled or encouraged them to do so, must have done so in part because they valued the social honor that women's confinement conferred on women and their relatives alike.

SECLUSION BEFORE MARRIAGE

I have spent considerable space discussing married women's freedom of movement because, like other aspects of women's lives, restrictions on women's mobility are directly defined in marriage contracts and rarely spelled out elsewhere. But this source bias does not mean that young women who had not yet married were free to circulate wherever they pleased; it simply means that their relatives or other de facto guardians felt no need to codify limits on their movements in writing. What, then, can Geniza documents tell us about physical controls on adolescent girls?

The evidence for this question is not abundant, but it is consistent. All available clues suggest that women who had not yet married were subject

70. See above, n. 55.

71. T-S 13 J 24.10, about the daughter of Eliyyahu b. Zekharya, the chief Rabbanite judge of Fustat in the early thirteenth century. Cf., for example, T-S 12.495, an early eleventh-century letter: the death of a woman's father "has cut us (the woman and her mother) off; we have no one who comes and goes" (that is, who visits us); T-S 12.386, Tinnīs, 1068: "What will become of this small child and his mother . . . who have no one who comes in nor goes out to them?"

to precisely the same types of restrictions, imposed for the same types of reasons, as their older counterparts. Adolescent girls whose mothers, sisters, and other female relatives circulated freely in public likely did so as well. Unmarried orphaned girls appear frequently on alms lists, meaning that like older women who lived in chronic poverty, poor girls routinely appeared in the unsegregated crowds of men and women who gathered to receive public distributions of bread and clothing.[72] Similarly, lower-status girls seem to have ventured into the marketplace without raising eyebrows. The undated letter about two orphaned sisters with which I opened the book notes that while a local childless woman would oversee the girls' education, they lived by themselves and used money provided for them from communal funds to manage their daily needs: "A place should be rented for somewhere close to my chamber . . . and these two dinars should be given to the older girl, (who may spend them) on maintenance, silk (for embroidery), and other things."[73]

Unmarried girls higher up the social ladder likely went out to visit the same types of public and semipublic venues as their older female relatives. For example, in a letter sent from mid-eleventh-century Tripoli, a woman distraught by the illness of her brother, a prosperous merchant, informs him that she has vowed that neither she nor her daughter, a young woman about to enter her first marriage, would enter the bathhouse—as was, she implies, their ordinary habit—until he recovered.[74] And while unmarried girls are often represented by proxy in court records, this seems to reflect Geniza Jews' perception that girls were unable to act for themselves, rather than concern that their physical appearance in the courtroom would be improper: not only do unmarried girls sometimes formally speak for themselves in legal documents, in some cases they also seem to have been present during legal proceedings conducted on their behalf.[75]

72. For example, alms lists from Fustat published in translation by Mark Cohen include several orphan girls as sole recipients of rations, as well as "a *yatīma* and her brothers" (T-S NS J 41 Col. II l. 1, T-S Misc 8.9 Col. III l. 12, T-S K 15.50 Col. I l. 12; see also T-S Ar. 15.85r, Col. II l. 19, T-S Ar. 52.247r, Col. 1 l. 13). Others record food distributed to orphan girls accompanied by older women, e.g., "the teacher and the orphan who is with her" (T-S K 15.97, ls. 9–10, ls. 20–21).

73. T-S 12.493. Several other documents describe orphan girls living alone: see ENA 2348.1, likely early eleventh century, Palestine, a communal appeal by two orphaned sisters whose older married sisters had evicted them from the house they had been living in; T-S 13 J 18.27, a letter about two young girls living in a ruined house in Alexandria; Maimonides, *Responsa*, nos. 37, 90, both about two unmarried orphan sisters who lived without adult supervision in Fustat.

74. T-S 10 J 14.20.

75. E.g., CUL Or. 1080 J 59, a betrothal agreement composed in court in Cairo, 1191, in which both the bride and her agent (*wakīl*) appear.

By the same token, unmarried girls whose own female relatives did not regularly leave their households likely remained secluded as well. The gaonic responsum cited above that distinguishes "modest" women from those "who go out" explicitly notes that the former designation applies "not only to a wife, but also to a virgin in her father's house who does not customarily come and go."[76] Several legal queries submitted to Maimonides describe girls who veiled themselves when appearing before nonkin men even in childhood. One discusses a teacher of "little girls" who had quarreled with his pupils' father and vowed never to teach them again.[77] To make the case that he might violate this oath and return to his post, the query's author notes that he was uniquely suited for the position: the girls were willing to unveil themselves before him, as he was blind. Another describes a father who refused to permit his minor daughter to unveil herself before her intended husband, unless the groom confirmed the match through a binding betrothal:

> A man sought (to marry) a girl . . . and agreed with her father to become engaged to her through *shiddukhin* . . . and they composed a deed to this effect. Then some women advised the girl's mother, "Your daughter is young (*ṣaghīra*); make a ceremony for her and unveil her before the boy." After they had agreed to this, her father said, "I will do no such thing unless (she is betrothed to him) through *qiddushin*." So they went to R. Yosef b. al-Maqdisī and returned betrothed.[78]

Because we know relatively little about the ceremonial aspects of either *shiddukhin* or *qiddushin*, the details of this account are difficult to parse.[79] But ritual unveiling appears to have been a standard component of the betrothal ceremony.[80] The women's advice to the bride's mother—that as her

76. Assaf, *TG ve-Liqqutei Sefer ha-Din*, no. 3 (p. 27). Note also that in his commentary on Genesis 34:1, Avraham Maimonides criticizes Dina's excursion *to see the daughters of the land* as inappropriate: her story "serves as instruction for religious people, that they not be lax in secluding women" (*ṣiyānat al-nisā'*, from the same root as *maṣūna*). Yet he does not emphasize Dina's virginity as a cause for secluding her in a different manner from other women. *Commentary*, ed. Sasson, 114–117.

77. Maimonides, *Responsa*, no. 276; see also the less detailed alternate version of this query published by Friedman, "New Fragments," 118–120, repr. Maimonides, *Responsa*, Vol. 4, pp. 9–10 (not numbered).

78. Maimonides, *Responsa*, no. 85.

79. On the wedding festivities generally, see Goitein, *Med. Soc.*, 3:114–118. Betrothal agreements generally record only the parties' testimony and the groom's transfer of a ring or other jewelry to the bride's representative; see Ashur, "EBD," 54–71.

80. For the rabbinic context, see, e.g., *Midrash Tanḥuma*, *Ki Tisa*, 16. In the Geniza context, see the sources cited by Blau, *Dictionary*, 93, s.v. جلو, form VII. (Some medieval Muslim jurists also note that a man should look at his bride's face before marrying her; see Spectorsky, *Women in Classical Islamic Law*, 191.) See also ENA NS 19.23, a fragmentary twelfth-century betrothal contract that seems to indicate that as a mark of special modesty,

daughter was "young," she might reveal herself to her groom even while merely engaged—thus seems to imply that physical seclusion may have been taken somewhat less seriously in childhood than in adolescence; on the other hand, the father's outraged reaction suggests that this viewpoint had its limits.

None of these brief references permit us to trace the geography of young women's movements with any specificity. None provide even a hint, for example, whether young girls usually attended synagogue services, or attended elementary schools together with boys. Goitein asserted that they sometimes did both, but as far as I can tell the documents that he cites to demonstrate this mention only boys, not girls.[81]

But as with the evidence for women's mobility in later life, even this small group of sources helps to suggest how physical restrictions on adolescent girls were understood, particularly by those who managed their movements. The material that I have just reviewed suggests that unmarried daughters' status as virgins did not directly affect their mobility. Of course, it is difficult to demonstrate this kind of negative claim conclusively, especially since the available evidence is so fragmentary. But several medieval Rabbanite legal texts do suggest more directly that Geniza Jews did not view it as a father's duty to control his unmarried daughter's movements.

These texts explicitly describe fathers as typically careless about their daughters' modesty. For example, in a responsum about a custody dispute, Maimonides notes that after a divorce, a daughter should live with her mother, since her father is unlikely to pay much attention to her movements: "It is not customary for a father to sit and guard his daughter . . . a girl's modesty (*ṣeniʿut*) depends on her remaining with her mother."[82] An undated Geniza letter sent by a dying woman to her sister partly supports Maimonides' assumption by revealing that at least some women took care to restrict their daughters' public visibility. She implores her sister to educate her young daughter after she has died, to retain a female slave who had been caring for her, and finally to keep the little girl strictly secluded: "Do not let her appear before anyone."[83]

---

the bride was not unveiled at the time of betrothal: "she (remained) veiled (*mastūra*) [. . .] Jewish [women] at the time of her betrothal ceremony."

81. For the synagogue, see *Med. Soc.*, 2:183, n. 1, citing Bodl. MS Heb. d. 66.6, which says only, "Your children (no gender specified) are well, going to school every day and to the synagogue on the Sabbath"; ibid., 3:60, ns. 52–53, citing T-S 13 J 28.15, which describes groups of young men congregating in the synagogue. For school, see 2:183, n. 3, citing T-S 8 J 28.7, a letter by a schoolteacher that seems to mention a boy's sister present in the school; but the document is partially effaced and torn at this point, and this reading is uncertain.

82. Maimonides, *Responsa*, no. 367. Cf. Yosef ibn Migas, *Responsa*, no. 71 (and for the legal context, cf. bKet. 102b-103a, Maimonides, *MT*, *Ishut*, 21:17, and see Assaf, "Appointment").

83. ENA NS 48.6, possibly early twelfth century (see Goitein, "Side Lights," 87).

What does it mean that these sources represent mothers rather than fathers as concerned to seclude their daughters? It goes without saying that women as well as men can exert patriarchal control over other women.[84] It is nonetheless worth noting that many women who took pains to restrict their daughters' (or nieces' or sisters') movements may not only, or even primarily, have been seeking directly to control their sexuality. Instead, women like the author of this letter may have sought to keep their daughters secluded because seclusion was an elite status symbol important to their own social identities, which they wished their daughters to reproduce. If rabbinic literature promotes female seclusion *only* to the extent that it prevents sexual misbehavior, Geniza evidence suggests that medieval Middle Eastern Jews implicitly understood things inversely: young girls and older women alike remained secluded to varying degrees for reasons only indirectly related to sexual activity, either real or imagined.

Social vs. Economic Protection of Adolescent Girls

What, then, can we make of ibn Shāhīn's story about the captive bride, cited at the beginning of this chapter? Based on the comparative evidence that the Geniza and gaonic and later Rabbanite sources provide, it is possible to read this story's conclusion, in which the stranger proves his claim to the girl by identifying a hidden birthmark on her body, in two entirely different ways. This plot twist might suggest that as she was usually veiled and secluded, he was able to prove his special familiarity with her simply by knowing anything about her appearance at all; however, it might also mean that he identified a mark in a place that revealed him to have had sexual contact with her. Ibn Shāhīn's Egyptian readers might plausibly have accepted either interpretation depending on what they assumed about the fictional bride's social status, given that some girls and women remained wholly isolated from nonkin men, while others circulated in the public sphere, and that some men did have sex with their intended brides before marriage.

This evidence complicates the picture of female coming-of-age presented in the previous chapter. I argued there that first marriage acted as the primary threshold to economic adulthood for women in Geniza society: Jews in medieval Egypt viewed even physically mature adolescent girls as intrinsic economic dependents, who required special economic oversight and protection as long as they remained unmarried.

It would be reasonable to assume that this emphasis on adolescent girls' protection derived at least in part from anxiety about sex. Anthropologists

84. This point informs Deniz Kandiyoti's idea of the "patriarchal bargain" made by Middle Eastern women (among others), who internalize patriarchal norms that eventually grant them power over younger women. See eadem, "Bargaining with Patriarchy."

and historians alike identify unmarried daughters' sexual chastity as holding central importance within a wide range of Mediterranean and Middle Eastern patriarchal systems. But the evidence reviewed in this chapter suggests otherwise. Adolescent sexuality appears as a relatively minor social concern in the documentary Geniza, and there is good reason to believe that young women's virginity was not always guarded very jealously, especially once they had become betrothed. On the other hand, girls and women of all ages could be bound by varyingly severe social restrictions that served as markers of social class—a patriarchal model that cut across age lines and could apply equally to unmarried girls, wives, widows, and divorced women alike.

In the last three chapters, I have examined the legal and social boundaries of adolescence and its distinctive social characteristics among Geniza Jews. The next three will consider how adolescent girls' economic and social position, particularly their dependence on their birth relatives, shaped their entry into first marriage and helped determine their lives beyond it.

PART III

Becoming a Wife

CHAPTER SIX

Marriage Choices

AN UNDATED GENIZA LETTER composed in Bilbays, Egypt, describes a complaint from a man named Ibrahīm b. Abū Dā'ūd al-Ashqar against his former fiancée's family.[1] Her relatives had broken their long-standing betrothal after Ibrahīm lost most of his assets. The letter suggests that they were wrong to do so, because Ibrahīm had maintained a close relationship with his future in-laws that should have earned him their enduring loyalty: "He had been betrothed to this girl for years, and everyone in Bilbays tells me that he had given gifts to his in-laws throughout this period, of food and other things—many things."

This letter offers a rare glimpse of the lengthy social process surrounding the formal agreements recorded in Geniza marriage documents. Few Geniza documents mention unofficial groom's gifts of the kind that Ibrahīm gave to his future wife's family. But such gifts are described as customary in classical and medieval rabbinic legal literature, where they are termed *sivlonot*. While late ancient rabbinic texts sometimes describe *sivlonot* as personal presents given to the bride herself, medieval Middle Eastern ones invariably describe them as gifts to her birth relatives.[2] This shift is unsurprising: the relationships that a groom like Ibrahīm developed with his in-laws mattered more

1. ENA 1822A.4.

2. On *sivlonot* in classical rabbinic literature, see Schremer, *Male and Female*, 280–285, and in the medieval Middle East, Maimonides, *MT, Ishut*, 4:20. Maimonides states that these gifts' timing varied by local custom and could be given either before or after betrothal (ibid., 9:28; cf. Yiṣḥaq al-Fāsī, *Responsa*, ed. Leiter, no. 185, and Mueller, *TG Mizraḥ u-Ma'arav*, no. 100. See also T-S NS 309.106, a gaonic responsum that describes *sivlonot* given at *shiddukhin*, and Shemu'el b. Ḥofni's *Commentary*, which describes them as given to the bride's family after the *mohar*: ed. Greenbaum, 52–53, and cf. Se'adya's commentary on Genesis, ed. Zucker, *'Al Targum Rasa"g*, 155, Heb. trans., 420). T-S NS J 183, a legal agreement from Cairo, 1231, also describes a groom's gifts to his in-laws at betrothal.

than any contact he might have with his future bride—especially if this was her first marriage. The marriages described in the Geniza were very much family affairs, and especially so for first-time brides. Geniza documents that discuss these relationships thus suggest the overlapping social interests surrounding a young woman's first marriage, which connected her to relatives by marriage as well as her own kin, and eventually helped to shape her marriage itself.

Marriage was, of course, not only a social bond but also a legal one. The distinction is important, because its social and legal aspects diverged significantly. Virgin brides' passivity about their own marriages, as described in Geniza documents and in Islamic legal discourse alike, contrasts sharply with their formal status as autonomous agents in rabbinic law. Rabbanite legal texts and documents struggle with this discrepancy, further demonstrating how Geniza Jews balanced Jewish legal tradition against their own Islamicate cultural assumptions—and in some cases, bringing to life the unexpected roles that technical rabbinic law could play not only in internal Jewish disputes, but also in Jews' interactions with Muslim state officials.

In this chapter I examine marriage choices from both angles: as social decisions and as an element of rabbinic legal practice. I have argued that women began to enter social adulthood when they married. Here I examine that transition more closely, as it illuminates what had come before and how adolescence set the stage for what came after.

Marriage Choices as Social Choices

How did ordinary men and women pair off as husbands and wives in the towns and cities of Fatimid and Ayyubid Egypt? Arabic narrative literature tells us almost nothing that might answer this question; the Geniza corpus, while more helpful, is still limited in important ways. Geniza documents seldom mention the details of matchmaking negotiations. When they do so, it is mainly in passing, through brief references that provide only general hints about the process: that it was complex, involving multiple stages of deliberations, and that the groom, rather than the bride or her relatives, was usually supposed to lead the way. In most letters it is the prospective groom (or his relatives) who brings suit, either directly or through an intermediary.[3] Geniza

3. His relatives: Unlike girls (on whom see further below), men's marital autonomy seems to have varied, likely depending on their age and perhaps other social factors, e.g., class and occupation. Some documents and responsa describe men "married off" by older relatives (e.g., T-S AS 147.2, mid-eleventh century, Jerusalem: "I betrothed my young son Abū Naṣr on Passover; he had a beautiful betrothal"); many others, like Labrāṭ's letters to his brother Yehuda (cited below at ns. 55–56), describe men who arranged their own marriages independent of their relatives.

letters mention communal leaders and professional matchmakers, male and female, involved as mediators in courtship agreements.[4]

But if most of these details are too slimly documented to be entirely reliable, the material we have is consistent on one point: it was the woman's male relatives that a hopeful suitor courted, not the bride herself. A letter of recommendation composed by Avraham Maimonides recommends a hopeful groom by noting his "enduring love" for his intended father-in-law and urges the latter, who had apparently been drawing out his reply, either to accept him or reject him humanely: "Inform him clearly and do not give him evasive responses; explain to him your ultimate intention and opinion."[5] In response, any one of a broad array of relatives (or in their absence, communal officials) managed decisions for a marriageable girl. Uncles and other extended male kin most often speak for orphans, but brides with living fathers also appear represented by other relatives, because the father is either traveling or living elsewhere ("Abū Kathīr . . . writes me that my daughter is about to become betrothed to the son of Abū al-Muʿammar," notes the eleventh-century Mediterranean trader Natan b. Nahray in a business letter), or even in his presence.[6] Avraham Maimonides explains the biblical account of Rivqa's marriage, in which her brother Lavan rather than her father marries her off, as typical of social norms in his own day: "A father is embarrassed by his daughter's marriage, as is well-known."[7]

What values and concerns guided these relatives' decisions? Goitein identified two types of marriage in the Geniza, prompted by seemingly different impulses: marriages between genealogical kin already bound by mutual loyalty and perhaps personal affection, and marriages that served to create

4. Courtship letters composed or dictated by grooms include T-S 13 J 18.22, T-S 13 J 35.14, and T-S 13 J 8.27. In a few letters fathers do offer their daughters to prospective sons-in-law, particularly in endogamous matches, e.g., Avraham b. Yijū, discussed below, and T-S 10 J 18.10. Communal leaders: see the following note. Professional matchmakers: in T-S 13 J 14.3, a father seems to blame "the accursed broker (*wakīla*) Umm Sawdā'" for a miscommunication with his daughter's groom (see Goitein, *Med. Soc.*, 3:73, 3:442). The cantor Ṣedaqa b. Nufayʿ appears as a broker of both marriage and divorce, the former in T-S 13 J 35.14, the latter in *Megillat Evyatar*, T-S 10 K 7.1. (On Ṣedaqa, see Gil, *Palestine* 1, sect. 905 n. 177.)

5. T-S 10 J 30.11. Cf. the *ra'īs* in the document discussed below, beginning at n. 79.

6. T-S 10 J 20.17. See also T-S 12.262, an early eleventh-century letter from a woman in al-Mahdiyya to her brother Ismaʿīl b. Barhūn al-Tāhirtī in Fustat, which reports the recent marriage of a girl named Mawlāt, possibly Ismaʿīl's daughter.

7. Idem, *Commentary*, ed. Sasson, 56–57. Cf. Seʿadya b. Yosef's similar comment on this passage: "a father is more ashamed in this matter than a brother" (Zucker, *Al Targum*, 420, Heb. trans. 154). The *ga'on* Shemu'el b. Ḥofni explained nonbinding engagements (*shiddukhin*) as intended to give a groom and his in-laws time to nurture their relationship, "so that each may determine whether marriage with the other will succeed." (T-S 8 Fa 2.2, 2v, a fragment of Shemuʿel's "Book of Marriage," *Kitāb Aḥkām al-Zawjiyya*.

alliances between previously unrelated families.[8] A similar distinction—between endogamous marriages joining descendants of a common lineage and exogamous marriages between spouses of different lineages—loomed large in twentieth-century anthropology, where it informed anthropologists' ideas about how kinship creates social orders. Structuralist anthropologists, following Claude Lévi-Strauss, understood kin exogamy as a central form of social exchange that creates ties between different lineage groups and thus integrates them into a common social system.[9] Evidence that Middle Eastern societies have often favored endogamous marriages *within* lineages poses a well-known challenge to Lévi-Strauss' alliance theory, which anthropologists have most often resolved by viewing close-kin endogamy as fostering a distinct form of social organization focused around self-contained lineage groups.[10]

Geniza letters discuss both types of marriage, using a repetitive vocabulary that conveys widely shared social ideas about marriage choices. These letters draw on a recognized set of biblical and rabbinic tropes to praise both endogamy and exogamy: the former for allowing patrilineal kin to demonstrate their mutual loyalty, the latter for joining nonkin equivalent in piety and religious learning. Attending to how Geniza documents deploy these tropes not only helps us understand how both forms of marriages created social alliances, it also collapses much of the apparent differences between them. In a social universe where kinship loyalties paralleled social loyalties between nonkin, endogamous and exogamous marriages often furthered similar motives: whether they married her to a relative or not, the individual kin who controlled a woman's first marriage could strengthen their personal social networks—and thus demonstrate and increase their own social honor—through the decisions that they made for her.

8. *Med. Soc.*, 3:26–33, 55–61; cf. also ibid., 5:256–257.

9. Formally, endogamy refers to prescriptive marriage with members of a particular group, exogamy to *prohibitions* on marriage with members of a particular group, e.g., incest taboos. Lévi-Strauss distinguished "elementary" kinship structures predicated on rules of endogamy from "complex" kinship structures, in which exogamous rules compel marriage between groups and thus create alliances based on reciprocal exchange of women; Lévi-Strauss identified cross-cousin marriage (between the children of a brother and sister) as the most basic exchange of this type, which serves to connect distinct patrilineal descent groups (Lévi-Strauss, *Elementary Structures*, 42–51, 119–135). Throughout this chapter, I use "endogamy" and "exogamy" more loosely, to distinguish marriages between close relatives, whether matrilineal or patrilineal, from marriages between nonkin.

10. On the Middle Eastern preference for patrilateral parallel cousin (FBD, for father's brother's daughter) marriage, see immediately below. See Kuper, "Changing the subject," for a succinct discussion of anthropological approaches to both types of cousin marriage.

ENDOGAMOUS MARRIAGE IN THE GENIZA

The final lines of the biblical book of Numbers conclude the story of Ṣelofeḥad's five daughters, who in an earlier passage were named his heirs after he died without sons.[11] In this epilogue, the women's relatives approach Moshe and complain that this arrangement will deprive their clan of Ṣelofeḥad's land when the women marry. Moshe responds by ruling that any woman who inherits land from her father must preserve his clan's patrimony by marrying within it: "Every daughter who inherits a portion among the tribes of the children of Israel must marry within her father's tribe's family, so that each of the children of Israel may inherit his fathers' portion." Ṣelofeḥad's daughters obediently marry their paternal cousins.

This story reflects and explains a tendency toward patrilineal endogamy widely understood as characteristic of Middle Eastern kinship systems. Many societies in the Middle East, from antiquity until the modern era, have favored or prescribed marriage between close paternal relatives, particularly parallel patrilineal cousins (cousins whose fathers are brothers, termed FBD—for *father's brother's daughter*—marriage, or in Arabic *bint ʿamm* marriage). This preference plays a central role in most accounts of the cohesive Middle Eastern patrilineal family.[12] These accounts explain FBD marriage both as a way to consolidate family property within inheritance systems in which daughters can inherit property, as in the Ṣelofeḥad story, and as a sort of structural glue that helps maintain and reinforce group solidarity within extended patrilineal families.

Yet both the prevalence and the cultural meanings of endogamous marriages have varied across time and space in the Middle East.[13] Classical rabbinic literature composed in late ancient Palestine and Iraq, for example, promotes a different understanding of family marriage from the one emphasized by the biblical story of Ṣelofeḥad. Rabbinic texts explicitly minimize the economic arguments for endogamy forwarded in this biblical passage, dismissing Moshe's order to Ṣelofeḥad's daughters as nonbinding "good advice" that does

11. Numbers 36:1–13 (cited text: 36:7–8), continuing the story begun in Numbers 26:1–11.

12. See Holy, *Kinship, Honour and Solidarity*, and the literature cited there, especially 16–23, and ibid., 93–103 for explanations of FBD marriage centered on patrilineal solidarity. For the ancient Near East, see, e.g., Marsman, *Women in Ugarit and Israel*, 56–72, Schloen, *House of the Father*, 121–122.

13. To my knowledge, rates of endogamy in the Islamic Middle East before the eighteenth century have not been systematically studied. Meriwether, *The Kin Who Count*, 132–140, finds that approximately one-quarter of marriages among elite families in eighteenth- and nineteenth-century Aleppo were between close cousins—but that most of these marriages occurred within a small subset of families within her larger sample.

not dictate how family property should be transmitted.[14] Instead, rabbinic literature promotes close-kin endogamy primarily in the context of maternal uncle-niece marriages (between a man and his sister's daughter), which they frame not as a means to consolidate property, but as a form of charitable fraternal duty.[15]

Several dozen Geniza documents mention marriages contracted between close relatives, particularly parallel patrilineal cousins. These references have been taken to demonstrate that many or even most Jews in Fatimid and Ayyubid Egypt married their own kin—a conclusion that in turn underpins a view of extended Geniza families themselves as robust and durable social units. But there are both quantitative and interpretive reasons to revisit this conclusion. A range of evidence suggests that marriages between close relatives were not only less common among Geniza Jews than has been supposed; they also held more permeable social meanings for the people who entered them.

How Common was Close-Kin Endogamy?

Goitein identified almost all the references to close-kin marriage found in the Geniza corpus to date, including more than two dozen instances of FBD marriage mentioned in eleventh- to thirteenth-century Geniza contracts, court records, deeds and letters (mostly from Egypt and Syria), and an additional dozen documents that mention marriages between maternal cousins.[16] While also noting substantial Geniza evidence for marriages between non-relatives, Goitein concluded that Geniza Jews were normally endogamous: "If a more or less suitable close relative was available and amenable, the matter was decided."[17] This conclusion has been widely accepted in subsequent scholarship.[18]

But these references may be understood differently. To begin with, what do they mean for normal practice? As with the handful of Geniza texts that mention child marriage (discussed in Chapter 3), there is no way to know. These references may reflect a widespread norm that other texts simply fail to mention; or they may describe relatively unusual cases, which these documents' scribes noted precisely because they were unusual. (It should also be

14. bBB 120a.

15. See, e.g., bYev. 62b-63a/San. 76b, and the discussion in Satlow, *Jewish Marriage in Antiquity*, 156–158; Schremer, *Male and Female*, 159–168. Satlow and Schremer both see this trope as aiming to justify the rabbis' validation of uncle-niece marriages (see also Friedman, *JMP*, 1:47 n. 112), and locate such marriages partly in the context of ideologies about lineage purity among Jews in late ancient Iraq.

16. *Med. Soc.*, 3:26–33.

17. *Med. Soc.*, 3:55, alluding to the cases detailed in ibid., 3:26–33.

18. E.g., Motzkin, "Judge Elijah," 26; Baskin, "Marriage and Mobility," 238; Kraemer, "Women Speak," 211; Ashur, "EBD," 92. In nonspecialist literature, see, for example, the recent survey by Sacchi and Viazzo, "Family and Household," 373–375.

noted that a number of these cases derive from Goitein's conjectural readings of difficult and fragmentary letters.)[19] Thankfully, once again the general corpus of Geniza marriage documents provides a more systematic means to judge an otherwise unanswerable question. Geniza marriage documents, whether formal *ketubbot*, or betrothal, engagement, or other auxiliary marital agreements, very rarely specify that a bride and groom are kin, and never point out that they are *not* related. Yet as with the other demographic questions examined in Chapter 1, they do contain clauses (originally included for unrelated reasons) that incidentally cast light on the frequency of endogamy.

This accidental data appears in the patronymics typically accompanying both the bride's and groom's names. In a subset of Geniza marriage documents, these patronymics suggest whether the spouses' fathers may themselves have been paternal relatives—either because they provide the two men's own lineages or places of origin, or more commonly, designate one or both by a patrilineal priestly caste marker, as a *kohen* or *levi*. Among the entire corpus of currently accessible Geniza marriage documents, I have found ninety-nine documents that describe one or both spouses' fathers by these markers, and thus indicate whether they may ratify a patrilineally endogamous marriage.[20] Like the larger group of marriage documents surveyed in Chapter 1, with which it partly overlaps, this corpus seems to represent a relatively random sample of the documentary marriage corpus overall—itself likely the most systematic record we have of the urban Jewish populations of Fatimid and Ayyubid Egypt and Syria. While elite figures sometimes invoked priestly status as a mark of distinction, neither *kohanim* nor *leviyyim* constituted a distinct social or economic class by the Middle Ages; at the same time, Geniza scribes appear to have always or almost always identified *kohanim* or *leviyyim* as such, so this sample is not likely to be skewed by varying scribal conventions.[21]

These ninety-nine documents describe couples across a range of economic classes, as gauged by the values of their dowries and dowers. Seventy-four of them (75 percent) can be securely dated (an unusually high percentage, explained by the fact that all documents in this sample were well enough preserved to contain both the bride's and groom's full names). As with the corpus discussed in Chapter 1, most describe Rabbanite marriages contracted in eleventh- to thirteenth-century Fustat (here, in particular, the greatest concentration of these documents come from the twelfth century), with much smaller

19. See Krakowski, "Female Adolescence," 154 n. 13.

20. In fourteen of these documents, endogamy is either explicitly noted or excluded by comparison of both fathers' names; the remaining eighty-five documents suggest or exclude possible cases of patrilineal endogamy through one or both spouses' priestly caste markers.

21. On Jewish priestly status in the medieval Middle East, see Franklin, *This Noble House*, 111–114, and passim.

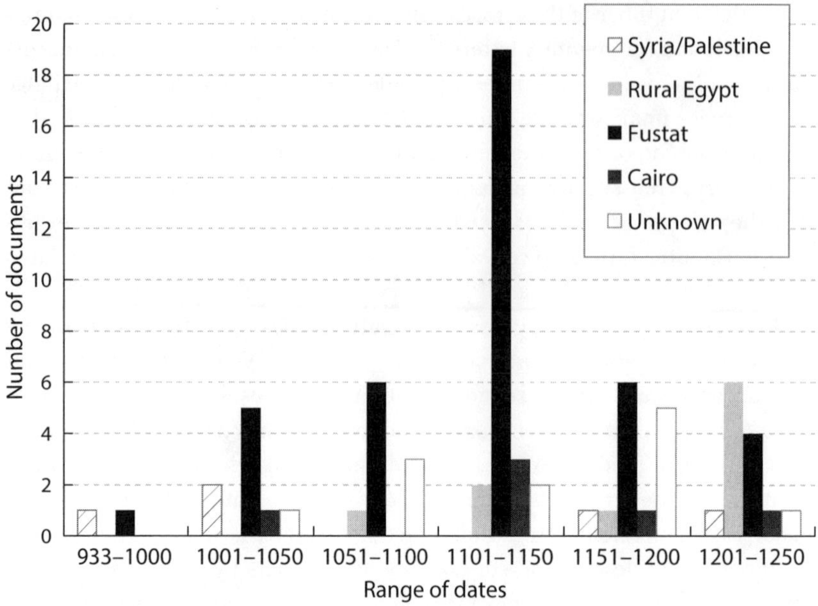

FIGURE 6.1. Datable marriage documents with data about endogamy, 933–1250

subgroups from eleventh- through thirteenth-century Cairo and rural Egypt, and tenth- through thirteenth-century Syria.[22] (See Figure 6.1 and Table 6.1.)

This corpus suggests that cousin marriage was less common among Geniza Jews than the references collected by Goitein might seem to indicate. Only eleven of these ninety-nine contracts may even possibly reflect cases of direct patrilineal endogamy. One explicitly identifies the bride and groom as niece and uncle; two represent likely cases of FBD marriage (the spouses appear to share a common paternal grandfather); and eight involve couples who share matching priestly designations and thus may possibly—although not necessarily—have been patrilineal kin (e.g., Natan b. Avraham *ha-kohen* betroths the daughter of Yosef *ha-kohen* in the Egyptian town of Minyat Ziftā, 1140/41).[23]

The remaining eighty-eight contracts (89 percent) involve couples who *cannot* have been direct patrilineal relatives, as they attach different priestly caste markers, extended lineages, or places of origin to the bride's and groom's fathers: e.g., Natan *ha-levi* b. Yiṣḥaq betroths Sitt al-Bayt bt. Natan, no priestly designation given, Cairo, 1108; Abū Manṣūr Ṣemaḥ b. Yefet b. Tiqva becomes engaged to Sitt al-Khāṣṣa bt. Abū al-Barakāt b. (Yosef) al-Lebdī, 1146, Fustat; the Karaite El'azar b. Shemen Tov, a fifth-generation Egyptian,

22. Five of the ninety-nine documents (5 percent) are Karaite marriage or betrothal contracts.

23. T-S NS J 475.

Table 6.1. Datable marriage documents with data about endogamy, 933–1250

	Syria-Pal.	Fustat	Cairo	Rural Egypt	Unknown	**Total (by region)**
933–1000	1	1				**2**
1000–1050	2	5	1		1	**9**
1050–1100		6		1	3	**10**
1100–1150		19	3	2	2	**26**
1150–1200	1	6	1	1	5	**14**
1200–1250	1	4	1	6	1	**13**
Total (by date)	**5**	**41**	**6**	**10**	**12**	**74**

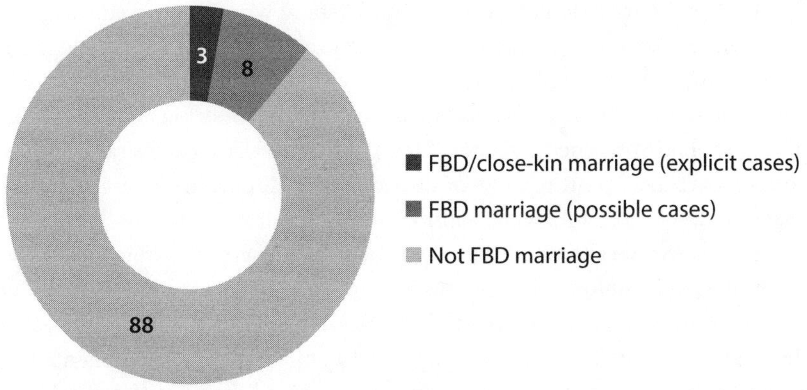

FIGURE 6.2. Endogamous marriages in Geniza marriage documents, 933–1250

marries Rivqa, the daughter of Yosef "who was from Byzantium," Cairo, 1201.[24] (See Figure 6.2.)

These documents thus indicate a rate of close patrilineal endogamy somewhere between 3 percent and 13 percent. Because Geniza marital contracts never provide matronymics, this finding does not capture marriages between maternal relatives. But there is no reason to suppose that matrilineal cousin marriages were significantly more prevalent than patrilineal ones.[25] Even if we assume that they were equally common, the most maximalist possible reading of this corpus thus predicts that around one-quarter of the marriages documented in the Geniza occurred between close cousins; but the real figure may be as low as 6 percent, or around one-seventeenth. (To put this figure in perspective, among contemporary Middle Eastern populations who practice

24. Natan *ha-levi*: T-S 8 J 4.22v; Abū Manṣūr: Bodl. MS Heb. d. 66.48; El'azar b. Shemen Tov: T-S 16.67.

25. Preferential FBD marriage systems typically include a secondary preference for other types of cousin marriages. See Holy, *Kinship, Honour and Solidarity*, 31.

prescriptive FBD marriage, consanguineous unions can account for upwards of half of all marriages.[26]) Endogamy, this evidence suggests, was at most a significant minority practice, not a dominant social norm.

Endogamy as a Marriage Strategy

Judging from this sample, most Geniza marriages did not occur between patrilineal cousins. How, then, can we explain the many explicit cases of FBD marriages that Goitein identified? The most obvious answer is that while cousins did not regularly marry each other, those who did so attracted special attention; writers and scribes who mentioned such couples in documents took pains to note their blood relationship.

We do not have to look far afield to understand why. Even if marriages between close relatives were relatively rare, Geniza Jews seem to have held them up as a cultural ideal, at least in theory. Jewish religious literature from this period does not reflect a well-developed ideology affirming kin endogamy; following rabbinic precedent, medieval Rabbanite and Karaite texts rarely praise cousin marriage.[27] But a range of documentary Geniza texts describe marriages between close relatives as admirable and desirable.

It is impossible to trace this cultural idea, or the personal choices underlying either endogamous or exogamous marriages, across the entire range of socioeconomic classes documented in the Geniza. This is because detailed discussion of marriage choices tends not to appear in legal documents but in letters. And unlike legal documents—which for all their limits, provide the closest approximation we have to a bird's-eye view of marriage among Geniza Jews at large—letters reveal marriage choices over a broad chronological period but among a limited set of sub-elites: the mobile and literate eleventh- through early thirteenth-century merchants and scholars who wrote most of the personal correspondence preserved in the Geniza. While our evidence for adolescent girls in other contexts thus emerges mainly from moments of crisis, through references to socially insecure girls, marriage choices are instead best documented for their more protected peers: girls sheltered and supported by well-positioned kin who stood to benefit from their marriages.

Perhaps the strongest expression of pro-endogamous ideology contained in the documentary Geniza appears in the letters of one such man, the twelfth-century India trader Avraham b. Yijū, who married his daughter Sitt al-Dār to his brother Yosef's son Peraḥya. In a series of letters between the two men arranging this match, Avraham stresses its economic suitability. Writing from Aden in 1149, he urges Peraḥya to "come quickly and take possession of this

26. See Khlat, "Endogamy in the Arab World," 70–75.

27. Although Maimonides codifies rabbinic praise of uncle-niece marriage (*MT, Issurei Bi'a*, 2:14; he extends this praise to the brother's as well as the sister's daughter). Cf. also Maimonides, *Guide*, 3:42.

money (his daughter's dowry); this is better than strangers taking it." Writing from Fustat in 1152, he notes, "My brother's son comes before strangers."[28] For his part, Yosef directly invokes the story of Ṣelofeḥad's daughters to praise the marriage as a "great commandment" (*miṣva kabīra*):

> For you have taken your paternal cousin (*bint ʿamm*) and done as Scripture testifies concerning the tribe of Yosef: . . . an inheritance may not move from one tribe to another, for each of the children of Israel must cleave to his fathers' inheritance.[29]

While it appears mainly in merchant letters, and despite its absence from contemporary Judeo-Arabic literary texts, this attitude was sufficiently diffused to have been promoted at times by communal officials. For example, a query sent to Maimonides notes that when an orphan girl's betrothal was challenged by a relative claiming to be her fiancé, court officials encouraged her to marry him even though she did not want to—not out of conviction that the alleged betrothal was genuine, but "because he is her relative" (the query also makes clear that her mother and other relatives likewise did not want her to; see more below).[30]

Do these Geniza passages reflect an ideal of family solidarity reinforced by cousin marriage? Do they describe a form of "cousin-right," the idea that a man holds an a priori claim to his *bint ʿamm* (a phenomenon documented in many modern Arab societies)?[31]

On closer view, it seems to me that they do neither.

To address the second of these questions first: A marriage proposal offered by Shelomo b. Eliyyahu (the son of Eliyyahu b. Zekharya, the chief Rabbanite judge of Fustat in the early thirteenth century) indicates the limits of Geniza

28. 1149: T-S 10 J 10.15; 1152: T-S 12.337.

29. T-S 16.288, citing Numbers 36:7–9 slightly imprecisely. Similarly, an undated letter sent by an India merchant to his cousin (who was also a brother-in-law) in Egypt proposes that the writer's daughter should marry the recipient's son (even though there was considerable bad blood between the two men) to preserve her dowry for a relative: "He should come and take her . . . rather than another devour me. You have a better claim." (T-S 10 J 18.10; see Goitein, *Med. Soc.*, 3:35). A legal query sent to Maimonides describes a family marriage prompted by a cruder economic motive: a woman had included part of a building owned by her mother in her dowry; the mother's cousins later claimed ownership of it, forced her husband to divorce her by threatening his life, and married her to one of their own sons (idem, *Responsa*, no. 362).

30. Maimonides, *Responsa*, no. 196. See also T-S Ar. 53.37, a late eleventh-century letter from a long-estranged father in Salonika to his son in Fustat: "[Man]y youths have sought (to marry) her, but she accepted none of them, until your letter and that of your in-law Abū al-Ḥasan arrived." Cf. T-S 13 J 20.20, a family letter sent to Qalyūb, Egypt, that may also presume a man's claim to his cousin: "We have detained the girl for Abu al-ʿAlā (presumably a relative). If he is going to follow through, he should inform us."

31. See Holy, *Kinship, Honour and Solidarity*, 72–92; Patai, "Cousin-Right."

Jews' notion of "cousin-right." Writing to his paternal aunt Umm Dā'ūd about her daughter Sitt al-Yumn, Shelomo affects a self-understood claim to marry his cousin:

> I have decided without a doubt . . . to come to you . . . to take the lucky daughter who is so dear to me—that is, Sitt al-Yumn, may God grant her success and bring us together. . . . I shall stay only ten days, because at home I have some children whom I am instructing.[32]

Yet the letter also makes clear that in reality, matters were hardly so simple; Shelomo betrays obvious anxiety that his suit will be rebuffed, repeatedly exhorting his aunt not to "create obstructions" to the match, emphasizing his own financial security and expressing his willingness to send a preliminary dower (*mahr*) in the amount of her choosing. His concern proved justified; a later letter written by her mother makes clear that Sitt al-Yumn ultimately married a different man.[33] For all his bluster, Shelomo clearly understood that his kinship with his cousin did not guarantee him an automatic right to marry her.

What about the ideal of family solidarity that Avraham b. Yijū's letters to his brother Yosef seem to invoke?[34] Although Yosef's reply cites the story of Ṣelofeḥad's daughters, these two men did not belong to a robust extended family group, and the match they were arranging did not strengthen such a family's existing bonds of loyalty. Like other appeals to kinship in Geniza letters (discussed in Chapter 1), Avraham's emphasis on his loyalty to his brother, embodied in this marriage, was instead intended to *create* family ties that had previously been inactive. Avraham wrote to suggest the match upon arriving in Aden, after he had spent almost twenty years away in India without apparently maintaining any contact with his relatives (the letter makes clear that they did not know about any of the children born to him during this period). His marriage proposal appears in a letter clearly intended to rekindle these dormant relationships. The brothers' hometown of al-Mahdiyya had been decimated by the Norman invasion in 1148, and they had fled to Sicily; urging his siblings to join him in Aden, Avraham stresses their precarious state, promises to provide for them, and offers to marry both his son and daughter to their cousins as a means of enriching them:

> I have abundant property, enough for us all to live on . . . Sulaymān b. Gabbay . . . told me that you have been reduced to a single loaf of bread. I ask you, O my brother, to come to me by all means and without delay. *Come down to me, do not delay, and I will provide for you there*

32. T-S 13 J 18.22.
33. T-S 13 J 34.9.
34. Discussed above at ns. 28–29.

> (Gen. 45:9–11). I have with me a son and a daughter; take them, and take with them all (my) money and favor![35]

Here and elsewhere, Avraham frames this proposal as a benefaction to his impoverished family inspired by disinterested loyalty to them. But we need not take this rhetorical pose at face value; however poor his siblings may temporarily have become, Avraham may have had good reasons to want to renew his social ties with them, as he sought to reestablish himself in the Mediterranean arena. Indeed, Avraham's subsequent actions as they emerge piecemeal from later letters suggest a complex and shifting set of social motives: having settled in Aden, he proceeded to engage Sitt al-Dār not to her cousin but to the son of the local merchant Khalaf b. Bundār (whose prominent uncle Maḍmūn had helped Avraham to relocate from India), only to break off this match and again pursue her marriage with his nephew when he left Aden for Egypt some three years later.[36]

If Avraham couched his motives in biblical rhetoric, not everyone seeking to marry a relative for social gain was so demure. A legal document describing another family betrothal between an India trader's daughter and her cousin (in Fustat, 1118) makes a very similar strategy transparent.[37] Witnesses testify that the groom, Abū Iṣḥāq Avraham b. Yiṣḥaq, had sought the match specifically to regain his lost social intimacy with his uncle's family:

> When this *shaykh* Abū Iṣḥāq's mother died, he came to us and said, "It is not hidden from you that when my mother was alive . . . I came and went freely in their household. Now I am alone, and I have no way to regain the intimate association that I had with them [. . .]. Thus, I wish to marry my cousin."

In both these cases, cousin marriage served not to affirm and reify existing social loyalties, but to create an essentially new connection between socially distant relatives—to transform what Pierre Bourdieu called official kinship ties into practical ones.

35. T-S 10 J 10.15. (My translation differs somewhat from Goitein's, *India Book*, Vol. 3, no. 29).

36. Sitt al-Dār's engagements and marriage can be reconstructed from the three letters cited above, ns. 28–29, and from five other documents, all published in Goitein/Friedman's *India Book*; see ibid., 69–89, and Vol. 3, nos. 39, 48, 50, 52, and 54; Goitein, *Med. Soc.*, 3:55–56. On a much later letter from Peraḥya b. Yosef (the cousin Sitt al-Dār eventually married) to his wife (either Sitt al-Dār or another woman whom he married later), see Goitein/Friedman, *India Book*, Vol. 3, no. 56, and Friedman's comments there, 792–793. For Maḍmūn's assistance to Avraham b. Yijū, see CUL Or. 1080 J 263. My reading of this story differs from Goitein's, who views Avraham's offer as reflecting "deeply (rooted) . . . sentiments about the prior rights of the cousin" (*Med. Soc.*, 3:55).

37. T-S NS 184, fols. 58, 62, 50, 71, 70, 74, 72, 98. For the continuation of this document, see below, at n. 77.

Bourdieu famously challenged structuralist anthropology by suggesting that endogamy is best understood as a marriage strategy pursued, like any other, for tangible motives, rather than as a static, self-reproducing social institution.[38] Rather than seeing endogamy and exogamy as reflecting qualitatively different social orders, Bourdieu argued that both marriage types are fungible and open to manipulation, by anthropologists and their subjects alike. Ideologies of *official* kinship, including endogamy, thus tend to be mobilized only to the extent that they are *practically* useful in other ways; even family marriages apparently dictated by firm prescriptive conventions reflect relatives' disparate personal interests in each other. If, as Bourdieu argued, this is true even in widely endogamous societies, it is all the more likely to be the case among Geniza Jews, who marshaled arguments about endogamy only sometimes and in moderation.

Some family marriages described in the Geniza were arranged between closer relatives than these. For example, a woman's deathbed request (dictated in 1143, Fustat) that her son marry her fraternal niece appears in a will saturated with expressions of physical and social closeness to her own relatives.[39] And regardless of their immediate causes, endogamous marriages doubtless held meaningful structural consequences for the kin who entered them, particularly when the personal ties they created were fortified by overlapping marital, economic, and affective associations between other members of a broader family network.[40]

Still, both of these stories about marriage—the one told by Avraham b. Yijū's letters and the one narrated in the legal document concerning Abū Iṣḥāq Avraham b. Yiṣḥaq—suggest that Bourdieu's observations match the Geniza evidence neatly: family marriages could further ends similar to those that prompted marriages between nonkin. And indeed, both of these stories highlight the aims of marriage most prominently discussed in the documentary Geniza, among cousins and nonkin alike: not to fortify group loyalties, but to create social ties between individual men.

Letters that discuss these alliances and their role in determining women's marriages bring us full circle to the parallel between natal kinship and other forms of social loyalty described in Chapter 1. These letters reveal that

38. "Marriage Strategies," *Outline*, 58–71, *Logic*, 162–199.

39. T-S 13 J 3.3, the deathbed will of Sitt al-Ahl bt. Abū al-Munā, Fustat, 1143. The will reflects Sitt al-Ahl's allegiance to her parents and brother, who lived with her (and who of course may have dictated its contents to her); she stipulates that they should remain in their apartment (which had been part of her dowry) after her death, orders her son to remain under her mother's care, and states: "I would like the daughter of my brother al-Surūr for my son Mūsā."

40. For examples of multiple marriages within a single family group or between two families, see Goitein, *Med. Soc.*, 3:28, no. 4, ibid., 3:30, nos. 3–4, 12, and ibid., 3:32.

marital kinship likewise served to create personal social loyalties between individuals—not only husband and wife, but also the male in-laws whose interests largely determined their union.

DAUGHTERS AS SOCIAL CAPITAL

The Babylonian Talmud treats kin endogamy ambivalently, but strongly commends *class* endogamy, in the form of marriage among members of the rabbinic movement:

> Our rabbis taught: A man should always sell all that he has to marry the daughter of a sage (*talmid ḥakham*). This may be compared to (grafting) vine-grapes with vine-grapes—a pleasing and acceptable thing.[41]

A number of Geniza letters quote this Talmudic passage to praise a proposed or recently concluded marriage. For example, a thirteenth-century letter sent by the Fustat judge Ḥanan'el b. Shemu'el congratulates a relative on his son's recent marriage, "through which he attains great achievement, for this alliance (*ittiṣāl*) is one between *vine-grapes and vine-grapes*."[42] But whereas in its Talmudic context, the phrase "vine-grapes with vine-grapes" casts class endogamy as a means to build group solidarity against outsiders (this passage goes on to decry marriage to the daughter of a non-rabbi [a "person of the land," or *'am ha-areṣ*] as "repulsive and unacceptable"),[43] Geniza Jews invoke it to express a different conception of marriage strategy, which assumes that marital alliances create exogamous relationships between individuals embedded in a broader social network.

Courtship and congratulatory letters preserved in the Geniza describe the advantages of such alliances. Besides procreation,[44] Geniza letters mention the promise of socially affiliating with a woman's male relatives more often than any other benefit of marriage. (Pleasant companionship and men's need for a caretaker rank third and a distant fourth; the dowry, though certainly a

41. bPes. 49a.

42. T-S 16.293. See below, n. 69, for other letters that invoke this passage.

43. This passage leads into some of the most violent rhetoric against the *'am ha-areṣ* found in classical rabbinic literature; see Oppenheimer, *The 'Am Ha-Aretz*, 172–179.

44. Marriage contracts and congratulatory letters ubiquitously wish new husbands a fertile union, especially one that produces sons, most often by citing the biblical blessing given to Rut at marriage: *May the Lord make the woman who enters your house like Raḥel and like Le'ah, who built the house of Israel. . . . May your house be like the house of Pereṣ whom Tamar bore to Yehuda* (Ruth 4:11–12). For this theme in Geniza letters, see, e.g., ENA 4020.33; T-S 12.246; T-S 18 J 4.11; T-S 13 J 14.6; and T-S 18 J 3.19. For its use in contracts, see the indices of biblical verses in Friedman, *JMP*, and Olszowy-Schlanger, *KMD*. Karaite marriage contracts also employ 2 Chron. 26:5, *God made him prosper*; Palestinian-style contracts use 2 Chron. 14:6, *They built and prospered.*

driving concern, is almost never openly mentioned.[45]) These passages suggest how alliances formed through women could yield benefits for men.

Marriage Alliance in Geniza Letters

Marriage not only made a couple man and wife, it also created a recognized social bond between a man and his wife's relatives, especially her father and brothers.[46] Geniza texts use a special term to denote this in-law relationship: *ittiṣāl*, used in other contexts for intimate unions, e.g., between man and God or between man and wife.[47] Marriage proposals and congratulatory letters that discuss *ittiṣāl* between male in-laws typically center on both parties' social standing, as represented by their lineage,[48] religious scholarship and piety,[49] or, most commonly, reputation within a shared social community, a value best rendered by the Arabic (originally Persian) term *jāh*.[50]

45. Wishes for a companionable marriage appear less often than wishes for sons, but are also expressed through a standard biblical allusion, to Prov. 18:22: *One who finds a wife finds goodness* (for letters, see, e.g., ENA 4020.24; ENA 4100.6b; for contracts, see again the indices in Friedman, *JMP*, and Olszowy-Schlanger, *KMD*, and cf. Friedman, "Ethics," 84–86, idem, "Marital Age," 173–177). More pragmatically, a mid-eleventh-century letter seems to explain the writer's marriage as a means of securing nursing care for himself: BL Or. 5542.20; cf. T-S 8 J 19.29, cited Chapter 4, n. 113. Several men note that they married to have someone to look after their children, e.g., T-S 10 J 12.1: "I married her for several reasons . . . (among which,) I wanted my son to be brought up, and not to stand in need of (other) people"; T-S Ar. 50.197: "Your intent . . . is to give her to the husband of her sister who died months ago, so that she may watch her children." The only Geniza letter I have identified that directly mentions the dowry as an incentive for marriage is T-S 13 J 29.2: "I married, in al-Mahdiyya, one who provided for me."

46. Male in-laws' precise relationship can be hard to discern; the term *ṣihr* is used interchangeably for fathers-, brothers-, and sons-in-law, and also for more distant relations through marriage, e.g., T-S 12.252: "'Alī b. Faraj b. Raḥmān, who is my *ṣihr*, because we married his daughter to b. Maḥfūẓ b. Yosef, who is my sister's son."

47. *Ittiṣāl* is usually mentioned in letters, but appears in at least one marriage document: T-S Ar. 54.78 (Fustat, 1042), which describes itself as recording the groom's "alliance" (*ittiṣāl*) to his father-in-law "through (the latter's) daughter."

48. E.g., Bodl. MS Heb. c. 28.60, an early twelfth-century merchant letter: "I have heard of (your) union with the honored and lofty house (*bayt*), and your alliance (*ittiṣāl*) with it, and I was exceedingly overjoyed by this." Cf. CUL Add. 3343, cited Chapter 1, n. 7.

49. Bodl. MS Heb. a. 2.17, right margin (eleventh century, congratulating a man on his recent marriage): "Send best greetings to your in-law (*ṣihr*) Abū Ghālib, for I know him and his paternal uncles and their piety." Cf. T-S 10 J 5.10 + 10 J 11.13 (also eleventh century, from Avon b. Ṣedaqa to Nahray b. Nissim): a man quarreled with his daughter's fiancé and the match was dissolved, but "God has compensated the girl with a fine replacement, in terms of piety, money, and *Torah*, and she is now entering her house." For this theme in twelfth- and thirteenth-century letters, see below, n. 69.

50. On *jāh* in general, see Goitein, *Med. Soc.*, 5:254–259; on its significance in in-law alliances, see idem, 256–257, and below.

Allusions to this theme appear across the entire range of eleventh- through thirteenth-century letters preserved in the Geniza: most often in merchant letters, but also in correspondence sent by religious officials both prominent and petty,[51] doctors,[52] schoolteachers,[53] and even shopkeepers.[54] This theme finds its most lucid expression, however, among a group for whom it exerted particularly potent meaning: the set of eleventh-century Mediterranean traders from Fustat who left an extensive paper trail of correspondence in the Geniza.

A series of letters written by Labrāṭ b. Moshe b. Sughmār, a merchant and Rabbanite judge in eleventh-century al-Mahdiyya, epitomizes this theme. Sometime in the mid-1050s, Labrāṭ's brother Yehuda emigrated to Fustat and married a young woman from a prominent local family. In letters composed in 1056 and 1057, Labrāṭ congratulates Yehuda effusively, repeatedly emphasizing the high standing of his bride's relatives and the social advantages of the alliance, and urging him to preserve and nurture his social relationship with his new in-laws:

> You have allied yourself (*ittaṣalta*) with the exalted and revered, through whom East and West are glorified. . . . God has allotted your portion among the first in *Israel*. . . . You have allied yourself with people through whom we are glorified. . . .[55]

> Know how you are situated (and) woe if you quarrel with your father-in-law! Make him a substitute for your late father and a substitute for me. . . . May God make this a most fortunate alliance for you, through which you assist one another.[56]

These remarks echo other eleventh-century congratulatory letters that emphasize the social rank of a groom's new in-laws (e.g., "You mentioned your betrothal *with the best people*; may God make this a most prosperous time

51. E.g., T-S 13 J 9.4, a letter from Shim'on b. Sha'ul, Jerusalem to his sister in Toledo: "I have already informed you of the reasons for my marriage; I, thank God, rejoice that I allied myself (*ittaṣaltu*) with them."

52. E.g., T-S 10 J 12.1, a letter from a physician in al-Maḥalla, mid-twelfth century; the author notes that he married to secure childcare (see above, n. 45) and because of the "respectability (*sutra*), *jāh*, and medical knowledge" of his wife's family (the letter has גהאה for *jāh*).

53. E.g., Shelomo b. Eliyyahu, cited above, Chapter 1, n. 7.

54. E.g., T-S 13 J 8.27, a courtship letter whose writer suggests to his prospective father-in-law that he will open a store. He also urges the latter to keep the proposal secret, so as to protect his (the writer's) *jāh*; see Goitein's discussion, *Med. Soc.*, 3:59–60, 5:256–257.

55. Bodl MS Heb. b. 13.49.

56. ENA NS 18.35. Labrāṭ expresses similar sentiments in Mosseri II 133.

for you").[57] Labrāṭ describes alliance through *ittiṣāl* as a dyadic relationship between individual men that contributed to both parties' public honor, and by extension, to that of their associates—in this case including Labrāṭ himself.

Ittiṣāl and Social Status

The ideal bond between male in-laws that Labrāṭ describes resembles other social affiliations invoked throughout the Geniza corpus. I have argued that kin relationships resembled such acquired loyalties. Discussions of *ittiṣāl*, a form of quasi-kinship acquired by choice rather than by birth, further demonstrates the similarities between family ties and other forms of affiliation. It also helps explain how men could draw broader social strength from all forms of kin relationships—acquired and inborn.

From different angles, recent work by Marina Rustow and Jessica Goldberg demonstrates how personal affiliations contributed to individuals' statuses within eleventh-century Geniza social networks. Rustow's analysis of *ni'ma* and related terms in the Geniza corpus suggests that an ongoing "calculus of benefit" within relationships of many kinds—formed through political patronage, charity, apprenticeship, and business alike—allowed men to enhance and demonstrate their own social honor through benefactions to each other (including gratitude for the other's benefactions).[58] Goldberg reaches an analogous conclusion working with eleventh-century commercial Geniza correspondence.[59] Expanding on earlier studies by Goitein and Abraham Udovitch, she concludes that Geniza commercial letters from this period reveal a highly individualized mercantile system, in which a merchant's practical access to long-distance markets depended on his immediate personal relationships with local officials and fellow merchants. Because they determined the scope and value both of his own labor and of the indirect leverage he could exercise on behalf of others, such relationships directly informed a trader's reputation and standing within the broader business community. Goldberg notes that merchant letters employ the term *jāh*, which typically denotes social status, rank, or honor, as a literal referent for the vitality of a merchant's personal network of business associates.

57. Bodl. MS Heb. a. 2.17, from Yaḥyā b. Mūsā al-Majjānī, Mahdiyya, to Zakharya b. Tammām, Fustat. Cf. ENA 4100.6b, to Nahray b. Nissim: "I was delighted to hear that you entered your house (i.e., got married); I ask [God to . . . you] the best people, and the happiest 'find,' and make you *like Raḥel and like Le'ah*." (For the latter two phrases, see above, ns. 44–45.) Cf. T-S Ar. 53.37, an eleventh-century letter sent by an indigent scholar to his son in Fustat: "Your in-law Abū al-Ḥasan . . . is of the best people; your association (here, *'ishra*) with him is good."

58. Rustow, "Benefaction," esp. 379–380; eadem, "Formal and Informal Patronage." See further my discussion in the Introduction and Chapter 1.

59. Goldberg, *Trade and Institutions*, 144–150; eadem, "Geographies," 156–163; eadem, "Back-biting," 123, 126.

Both scholars' work illuminates how marriage alliances between male in-laws could help both parties' social status. As portrayed by Labrāṭ b. Moshe and others, *ittiṣāl* worked similarly to the dyadic relationships described by both Goldberg and Rustow. Like business and patronage alliances, in-law affiliations were publicly recognized within the social and communal networks to which both men belonged; like business and patronage alliances, they thus provided male in-laws access to each other's personal networks and contributed to the public identity through which each acquired standing in these networks. Indeed, Geniza letters often designate individuals by their in-law affiliations, e.g., "Please mention to . . . Abū Kathīr the matter of the books that the in-law of Abū Ya'qūb Yosef promised to send me."[60]

Among merchants, these analogous relationships could literally coincide, as male in-laws often functioned as close business partners. A letter that Yehuda b. Moshe b. Sughmār's wife wrote to him some thirteen years after their marriage suggests he had fulfilled his brother Labrāṭ's wishes by becoming deeply and indispensably engaged in his father-in-law's financial affairs; she asks him to intervene to manage a business dispute on the latter's behalf, noting, "No one is more upset by your departure than my father; he now . . . has no one to assist him but God."[61]

But in-law relationships did more than simply facilitate professional cooperation. Several letters describe marriage itself as a form of *ni'ma*, through which a woman's father or other male relatives bestowed on her husband a portion of their own reputational status or *jāh* (not to mention the more tangible benefit provided by her dowry). For example, in an eleventh-century letter, a suitor thanks his future father-in-law for benefiting him by their alliance, whose value he affirms specifically in light of the latter's high social reputation ("I praise God daily for that which you have conferred on me [*mā an'ama bihi 'alayya*], by bestowing on me this alliance [*ittiṣāl*] with you, and honor through you; everything I hear uttered among people—I praise God and thank Him greatly for this").[62]

60. T-S 13 J 10.5, a letter from Yoshiyyahu b. Aharon to Avraham b. Ḥaggay, early eleventh century. Geniza letters and legal documents use in-law affiliations to identify people of all social strata, including even the recipients of public charity named in alms lists (for example, a list from eleventh-century Fustat records a payment of five-eighths of a dinar to "Shelomo *al-Rūmī*, who is the in-law of the son of Binyamin," T-S K 196).

61. CUL Or. 1080 J 71. In-law affiliations bled into professional ones in other spheres as well; cf. the twelfth-century physician cited above, n. 52, who noted that he had married his wife partly because of her family's "medical knowledge."

62. T-S 13 J 35.14. Cf. Labrāṭ b. Moshe b. Sughmār, ENA NS 18.35, who reminds his brother Yehuda that Yehuda's association with "the best and most honored people (*jūh al-nās*) is a *ni'ma*." Cf. also Avraham b. Yijū's comments cited above, at n. 35 ("favor" there translates *ni'ma*).

Similarly but in a different register, *Megillat Evyatar* (a Hebrew polemic against David b. Dani'el, head of the Jews in Egypt in the late-eleventh century) describes David's betrothal to a notable's daughter as a literal patronage relationship, using imagery that vaguely recalls the biblical account of Mordekhay's elevation by Aḥashverosh:

> David b. Dani'el went down (to Egypt, seeking) . . . to ally himself (*le-hityaḥes*)[63] further with a [. . .][64] family, the elite of the Nile . . . and Maṣliaḥ b. Yefet b. Zubʿa found him and allied himself with him and sought to treat him well and kindly. . . . He betrothed his daughter to him and fed him and dressed and clothed him for two years; and after that he appointed embroidered garments for him and installed him in his carriage and set two servants to run before him.[65]

The text goes on to condemn David for abandoning his patron to pursue a better match. As with other forms of benefaction, giving a daughter in marriage created an ongoing (if never assuredly permanent) relationship between benefactor and recipient that benefited both men: variants of Labrāṭ's wish that Yehuda and his father-in-law "assist each other" through their alliance appear as a standard blessing in several letters.[66]

Beginning in the twelfth century, the frank appraisals of status expressed by eleventh-century traders give way to more pious rhetoric, as both merchants and others increasingly extol marital alliances by invoking both sides' religious scholarship or piety, often by citing the Talmudic passage about grafting "vine-grapes with vine-grapes" cited above. This shift may reflect a broader transformation among Jews in the late Fatimid period, toward a mode of social identification predicated less on individual relationships and more on a religiously inflected concept of group solidarity.[67]

63. Perhaps intended as a Hebrew cognate for *ittiṣāl*.

64. The meaning of the text here is unclear to me: ביש נער.

65. T-S 10 K 7.1. On *Megillat Evyatar* and its historical context, see Cohen, *Jewish Self-Government*, 178–212, Gil, *Palestine* 1, sects. 902–915, and Rustow, *Heresy*, 326–329. The chariot and riders signalled David's exilarchal pretensions; see Rustow, ibid., 333 n. 27, Cohen, *Jewish Self-Government*, 187 n. 21. *Megillat Evyatar* is modeled on the Scroll of Esther; I tentatively suggest that Evyatar's description merges this exilarchal motif with the account of Mordekhay's elevation in Esther 6:8–10.

66. E.g., Bodl. MS Heb. a. 2.17, congratulations to Zekharya b. Tammām: "May God help (or: enrich) you through each other"; Bodl. MS Heb. b. 13.49, Labrāṭ b. Moshe to his brother Yehuda: "May (God) help (or: enrich) them through you and you through them, and make you a *blessing* for each other."

67. Marina Rustow points to the growing emphasis on group solidarity among Geniza Jews in the late eleventh and early twelfth centuries, a trend that may have intensified in the late twelfth century with the Sunnī reforms initiated by the early Ayyubids; see Rustow, "Patronage in the Context of Solidarity." This ideological shift may have accompanied tangible changes in Jewish social networks. Thus, Jessica Goldberg notes that whereas

These references are more cursory than their eleventh-century counterparts, and it becomes harder to discern the functions of the alliances they describe, especially since the broader communal dynamics underlying twelfth-century Geniza documents, in which these alliances operated, have not been as carefully studied. But even if marriage came to connect people in somewhat different ways than it had previously, these later letters still disclose a basic concern for how a marriage will enhance each party's social position. Twelfth- and thirteenth-century writers who use rabbinic phraseology to praise marriage alliances not only reveal the same underlying interest in individual social rank as their eleventh-century predecessors (as when Ḥanan'el b. Shemu'el, in the letter cited above, describes marriage between like "vine-grapes" as a "great achievement").[68] They sometimes invoke these rabbinic allusions so perfunctorily, even nonsensically, that they must be understood as a type of metonymic shorthand for treating questions of status, as when a prospective son-in-law emphasizes his own desirability by citing a phrase from this same Talmudic discussion on vine-grapes: "A man who gives his daughter to a boor—this is as if he cut her and placed her before a lion," a statement that in its Talmudic context refers to sexual brutality.[69]

The standard vocabulary that Geniza letters employ to discuss marriage choices obscures significant parts of the process by which these choices were made. Because they represent marriage as a hierarchical benefaction to the groom, these texts do not discuss the qualities that made a groom himself attractive. Thus, while their heavy emphasis on status renders it likely that most

eleventh-century merchants usually acted as agents only for direct associates, twelfth-century merchants relied on unknown friends of friends connected only through their common membership in a broader associate network (that is, merchant affiliations shifted from what Rustow, ibid., terms a "reciprocity-based" to a "solidarity-based" social model; Goldberg, "Geographies," 300–301).

68. See above, at n. 42.

69. T-S 13 J 35.14 (early twelfth century, since it mentions Ṣedaqa b. Nufay'; see above, n. 4). The author notes that this refers to "*ittiṣāl* with an *'am ha-areṣ*," apparently to emphasize his own prestige. But the Talmud explains the saying this way: *just as a lion attacks and eats and has no shame, so an 'am ha-areṣ strikes and copulates and has no shame*, hardly an apt reference to invoke to one's prospective father-in-law (as Goitein notes, *Med. Soc.*, 3:439 n. 45). Other twelfth- and thirteenth-century courtship and congratulation letters that reflect this rhetorical shift include Bodl. MS Heb. c. 28.60 (citing "*This may be compared to (grafting) vine-grapes with vine-grapes*," etc.; T-S 10 J 30.11, from Avraham Maimonides on the suitor's behalf; and T-S 13 J 8.27, an anonymous courtship letter (datable to the twelfth century or later based on the Arabic legal document on the verso; see Khan, *ALAD*, 432), which both cite another phrase from bPes. 49a, *A man should always sell all that he has (in order to) marry a Sage's daughter*.

young women married men of a similar social class, we do not really know how much social mobility this marriage system permitted.[70] Nor can we gauge how competitive marriage markets that disadvantaged women (discussed in Chapter 4) affected this process, although such imbalances may explain several Geniza marital contracts that attempt to regulate the behavior of what Mordechai Akiva Friedman terms "grooms of questionable character."[71]

Still, this material illuminates a central reason for which relatives entered their daughters into marriage. Geniza discourse on *ittiṣāl* represents a daughter's marriage as an important form of social capital for her male relatives. An unmarried daughter's marriage helped the men around her to acquire the social loyalties on which their own status depended, whether they used the opportunity to create new associations or to fortify existing ones, even with their own close relatives. While discussions of marriage alliances inevitably tilt heavily toward the well-protected and well-connected, similar dynamics may have operated to some degree even with marriage choices involving poorer girls from less economically and socially stable families.

Indeed, the social value of a daughter's marriage was sufficiently recognized that some people sought to duplicate its effects with nongenealogical dependents. An eleventh-century letter sent from Palermo (discussed in Chapter 4) complains about an acquaintance's marriage to an orphaned girl serving as a domestic: "You have made them your in-laws!" The objection was not to the bride herself, but to an affiliation with her patrons, people "who have no good in them."[72]

Marriage Choices as Legal Acts: Autonomy and Assent

When Avraham b. Yijū left Aden for Egypt in 1152, he removed his daughter Sitt al-Dār from the household of Khalaf b. Bundār, the prominent Adenese merchant with a son to whom Avraham had engaged her when he arrived in Yemen. At this point Sitt al-Dār had lived for three years in the Bundār home as an intended daughter-in-law (an arrangement not known to me from any other source). Writing to Khalaf from the Red Sea port of ʿAydhāb, Avraham reported that she missed the family bitterly: "She cries day and night over

70. I have not identified Geniza material that invokes the Islamic concept of *kafāʾa*, legally defined class endogamy (see *EI²*, *s.v. kafāʾa*), although the Karaite exegete Yefet b. ʿEli invokes, in his comments on Prov. 18:23, class equality as necessary for a successful marriage; see Sasson, "Methods and Approach," 171–172, eadem, "Gender Equality," 52.

71. Friedman, "Pre-nuptial Agreements," a study of two contracts in which the groom pledges not to behave badly, e.g., "not to associate with corrupt men nor . . . enter the home of anyone who engages in licentiousness (*periṣut*)," T-S 20.160.

72. T-S 20.122. Cf. Chapter 4, n. 113. Gil, *Ishmael*, doc. 651, identifies the groom as the broker Nissim b. Shemarya (which seems to me plausible but uncertain).

your separation from her."[73] He promised to try to return her to them as soon as possible. "May God allow her to reunite with you . . . in the best of circumstances; I am working very hard on this." But only a short time later, he broke off the engagement and arranged to marry her instead to his brother's son Peraḥya b. Yosef b. Yijū, whom neither Avraham nor Sitt al-Dār had met. She married Peraḥya some four years later and probably never saw the Bundār family again.

Where did a first-time bride and her wishes figure in the complex calculus of male alliances that surrounded her marriage? Sitt al-Dār's silence about her fate (at least in the sources at our disposal) was typical of the young women who appear in Geniza documents. Yet in legal terms, Sitt al-Dār may have been[74] perfectly free to reject her father's choices and marry whomever she pleased. Classical rabbinic law recognizes fathers' authority over their daughters' marriages in childhood, but grants adolescent girls full control over their own marital choices once they reach legal maturity.

This is the final component of the rabbinic *bogeret* model discussed in Chapter 3: a girl gains authority to marry herself at maturity, and her father may no longer marry her. I have argued that other aspects of this model had little effect on adolescent girls' real social status in Fatimid and Ayyubid Egypt. Although adolescent girls technically held property and bore financial responsibility, they remained protected and passive economic dependents as long as they remained unmarried. The Geniza evidence makes clear that this was equally true of adolescent girls' autonomy in marriage. Adolescent girls' formal independence did little to lift them out of the thick web of kinship ties within which their first marriages were arranged. In practice, their position more closely resembled that of the Islamic virgin (*bikr*), whose first marriage was formally subject to her father's authority.

But some documents also suggest that this feature of rabbinic legal practice retained potentially concrete effects, albeit unexpected ones. At least theoretically, unmarried daughters retained the power to resist an unwanted marriage. Under certain circumstances, this legal principle could play a role within marriage disputes, not only in Jewish courts but even before Muslim state officials. But there is no evidence that it ever permitted first-time brides to make autonomous decisions about their own marriages.

73. T-S 8 J 21.10; for Sitt al-Dār's marriage to Peraḥya, see above, n. 36.

74. "May have been," because it seems possible that Sitt al-Dār was a minor when she became engaged to Khalaf's son, and perhaps even when she became betrothed to Peraḥya. In a letter composed after Avraham b. Yijū's death and around when he married Sitt al-Dār, Peraḥya calls her a "young orphan *who has reached puberty*," suggesting that she had recently become mature and therefore (following my argument in Chapter 3) become socially marriageable (ENA 4020.1).

MARITAL AUTONOMY: THE BRIDE'S ASSENT AS LEGAL PERFORMANCE

Rabbanite courts carefully maintained adolescent girls' marital autonomy on paper. Geniza betrothal and marriage contracts typically note mature brides' official participation in legally binding betrothal and marriage ceremonies, through explicit assent clauses and through agency clauses in which the bride appoints a representative to act on her behalf.[75] Yet like Sitt al-Dār, most of the first-time brides cited in these documents exercised no real control over their own marriages. Geniza letters and contemporary responsa ubiquitously refer to fathers, mothers, and other guardians as "marrying off" their daughters, without regard to their formal maturity status. An example is this legal query to Maimonides: "A man vowed that he would not marry his daughter to Shim'on unless the latter refrained from moving her away. . . . When her father vowed this, the girl was mature."[76] The evidence I have reviewed throughout this chapter overwhelmingly suggests that a woman's first marriage was decided by social and economic interests to which she herself remained mostly incidental.

In most cases, the bride's moment of active agency recorded in Geniza contracts was thus a pro forma legal performance determined and directed by her relatives and by court or communal officials. A deed of betrothal composed in early twelfth-century Fustat brings such a performance to life in its broader social setting.[77] This deed (partially cited in the section on endogamy above) records Abū Iṣḥāq Avraham b. Yiṣḥaq's betrothal to his cousin Sitt al-Ahl bt. Yosef al-Lebdī. It describes the context of its own composition in unusual detail, providing a complete snapshot of the negotiations surrounding it, from proposal to formal agreement:

> Abū Iṣḥāq appeared before us and said . . . "I wish to marry my cousin, by your hand." . . .
>
> We went together, along with his honor the *ra'īs* Abū Sa'd al-[. . .]ī, and approached Jamī', the wife of this Abū Ya'qūb (Yosef al-Lebdī) about this. She agreed to marry her daughter to this Abū Iṣḥāq Avraham, saying, "None is dearer to me than him, but I will not marry her until her brother arrives." The aforementioned *ra'īs* answered her, saying, "Once I have come, I cannot leave without accomplishing our

75. On these clauses, see Chapter 3.

76. Maimonides, *Responsa*, no. 238. Cf. ibid., no. 88, also describing a daughter legally mature daughter "married off" by her father. This language is pervasive throughout the Geniza and in responsa; I have found only one document that describes a virgin daughter deciding her own marriage (T-S Ar. 53.37, cited above, n. 30).

77. T-S NS 184, fols. 58, 62, 50, 71, 70, 74, 72, 98 (cf. above, n. 37).

> purpose! Betroth her to him with *qiddushin*,[78] and her marriage may wait until your son arrives."
>
> We consulted the girl Sitt al-Ahl about this and she agreed also—because we identified her, in our presence and with sound knowledge of her identity . . . and we performed *qinyan*[79] with her, in her mother's presence and with her assent, and in her brother's presence and with his consent as well . . . (to affirm) that she had betrothed herself to this *shaykh* Avraham b. Yiṣḥaq.

The emphasis that this deed places on Sitt al-Ahl's agency reflects the legal importance of her participation. As Goitein points out, the deed itself was drawn up some fourteen months after the events it describes, likely because the match had foundered and she needed proof that Avraham should give her a bill of divorce. In this context, the text's emphasis on Sitt al-Ahl's assent to her betrothal and direct participation in the *qiddushin* ceremony served to signal that the betrothal had been legally valid and was thus binding.[80] Yet despite its emphasis on this point, the document also reveals the discrepancy between Sitt al-Ahl's official autonomy and the way in which her marriage was arranged: its description of the parley that preceded it reveals her consent as a legally necessary afterthought.

NEGOTIATING RABBINIC MATURITY LAW: THE SOCIAL MEANING OF MARITAL AUTONOMY

Medieval Rabbanite authors recognized that the *bogeret*'s technical marital autonomy was incongruous with medieval Jews' social expectations. A series of gaonic and Egyptian Rabbanite responsa incorporate the pro forma character of most virgin brides' assent into their understanding of rabbinic law itself. These responsa consider whether a mature girl's father may contract a betrothal for her without her explicit permission. To varying degrees, they rule that despite her nominal independence, such a betrothal may indeed be legally valid, given the overwhelming presumption that a father retains practical authority over his virgin daughter's marriage and that her consent is typically automatic:

78. That is, through a legally binding betrothal ceremony.

79. See Chapter 2, n. 102.

80. See Goitein/Friedman, *India Book*, Vol. 1, 240, *India Traders*, 265–266. A betrothal agreement written six and a half years later, in 1124, documents Sitt al-Ahl's betrothal to a different groom and describes her as a "divorcée from betrothal" (T-S NS J 460 + T-S NS J 112 + T-S NS 211.8 + T-S NS 323.11 + T-S 8.138 + T-S AS 152.19). As noted in Chapter 3, engagement (*shiddukhin*) contracts, which did not legally require the bride's participation, rarely feature assent or agency clauses—an omission that highlights these clauses' purely technical function in betrothal and marriage contracts.

> It is the custom of all daughters of Israel—even a mature daughter in her father's house, and even a twenty-year old whose father is still alive—to follow after her father. . . . (She is) not so licentious or impudent as to reveal her will and say, 'I want so-and-so'—rather, she relies on her father. . . .
>
> Such is the law: . . . if (her father) betroths her, the betrothal is entirely valid, unless she reveals herself and disavows her father's betrothal; but if she reveals (herself) and disavows her father's betrothal, it does not bind her.[81]

This responsum rhetorically inverts the rabbinic principle of daughters' marital autonomy, answering the Talmudic dictum that a mature girl may declare, "I want so-and-so"[82] with a dictum of its own: no girl would be "so impudent . . . as to say 'I want so-and-so'—rather, she relies on her father" to select a husband for her.

In an article devoted to gaonic responsa on this subject, Gideon Libson argues that they betray the influence of Islamic law, which gives a father control over his daughter's first marriage regardless of her age.[83] Libson is undoubt-

81. Harkavy, *Zikhron Kamma Ge'onim*, no. 194, possibly from Hayya b. Sherira (see Abramson, "*Aḥat she'ela*," 17–18). Cf. *OHG*, *Qid.* no. 283, attributed to Ṣemaḥ b. Paltoy, ninth century: a father cannot betroth his mature daughter if she objects, but if the groom sends *sivlonot* and she makes no move to reject them, the betrothal is binding; ibid., no. 287, Yosef ibn Avitur, tenth–eleventh century Andalusia, Egypt, and Syria; *TG*, ed. Coronel, no. 97. Cf. also the early medieval Palestinian text *Ma'asim*, ed. Lewin, 91: a daughter who remains silent when her mother (!) betroths her is bound by the betrothal. As Gideon Libson notes ("Betrothal of an Adult Woman," 184), these responsa turn on the social question of whether a daughter may be presumed to accept her father's marriage choices. They reach different legal conclusions, but (unlike Libson) I read them all as expecting virgin daughters to normally do so. (However, some gaonic texts straightforwardly invalidate a father's betrothal of his mature daughter: Lewin, *OHG*, *Qid.* no. 439, *TG Sha'arei Sedeq* 3:3:13, Assaf, *TG ve-Liqqutei Sefer ha-Din*, no. 46.)

82. bQid. 41a/81b.

83. Libson, "Betrothal of an Adult Woman." Islamic discussions of this topic focus on two questions: (1) May a woman contract her own first marriage? Except for some Ḥanafī jurists, all Sunnī authorities say no: all first-time brides must be married by a guardian (*walī*). (2) May a guardian compel a virgin to marry against her will (*ijbār* or *jabr*, *ikrāh*)? Most jurists limited nonpaternal guardians from doing so, but gave fathers far-reaching powers: Mālikī and Shāfiʿī law grant fathers unilateral *jabr* over a virgin daughter; Ḥanbalī jurists recognize such coercive marriages as valid, but criticize them as improper. Again, only the Ḥanafīs permit a mature virgin daughter to deny her father's marriage choices, although (like the Rabbanites discussed below, n. 86) they assume her consent if she does not explicitly object. (Ismāʿīlī law is similar: a *walī* and the bride's consent are both required: Fyzee and Poonawala, *Pillars*, 2:204.) See Ali, "Money, Sex, and Power," 86–108, eadem, "Marriage in Classical Islamic Jurisprudence," 17–18; Spectorsky, *Chapters*, 143; and cf. Baugh, "Compulsion," esp. 217–219, who notes that in contrast to

edly correct that these responsa echo assumptions made in Islamic legal literature, in particular several well-known *ḥadīths* that define a virgin daughter's silence as constituting assent in marriage.[84]

But Geniza evidence casts this parallel in a different light. The material discussed in the previous sections reveals Geniza Jews to have understood young women's first marriages as a resource controlled by their relatives. This attitude seems too pervasive merely to reflect the influence of Islamic legal discourse or court protocol. Instead, despite its expression in Islamic legal texts, it can more properly be termed *Islamicate*—a social norm common to many premodern Middle Eastern societies, including but not limited to medieval Islamic ones, from which rabbinic maturity law departs.[85]

In my view these responsa do not reproduce a characteristically Islamic form of patriarchy so much as they attempt to negotiate and defend a peculiar rabbinic legal principle deeply at odds with their authors' own (Islamicate) patriarchal assumptions. Thus, while these texts display a clear bias toward paternal control of a daughter's marriage, they also attempt to accommodate rabbinic maturity law given that bias. They do so by formulating the *bogeret*'s marital independence as a matter of freedom from compulsion rather than direct agency; in contrast to a minor daughter, who could be married against her will, the *bogeret* possessed the legal power to refuse a marriage distasteful to her. This formulation may itself reflect engagement with Islamic legal discourse about marital compulsion (*jabr*) of a virgin daughter (*bikr*), but it also reflects a plausible reading of classical rabbinic sources.[86] Even within late ancient rabbinic culture, it is extremely unlikely that the *bogeret*'s legal autonomy ever served to grant never-married daughters complete freedom to select their own husbands; rabbinic literature routinely represents parents as supervising their adolescent daughters' marriages.[87]

---

this classical consensus, some early (ninth–tenth century) Islamic legal texts grant daughters marital autonomy at puberty.

84. "The *bikr*'s permission is asked, and her silence is her permission," cited in Libson, "Betrothal of an Adult Woman," 186 n. 20. See further Ali, "Money, Sex, and Power," 86–108. Brides are represented by an agent in many Geniza contracts and contemporary responsa, a convention that Libson suggests derives from the Islamic *walī*; on the other hand, M. A. Friedman notes that it has earlier Jewish antecedents, *JMP*, 1:216–232.

85. See Chapter 3.

86. The core classical rabbinic passage establishing mature daughters' marital autonomy is bQid. 79: "If her father betrothed her on the road, while she betrothed herself in town, and she is mature—Rav said, 'Behold, she is mature before us'" (i.e., her betrothal prevails). The medieval responsa cited above, n. 81, seem to read this passage to mean that paternal betrothals are normative, but a mature daughter may reject her father's betrothal. (Cf. Se'adya b. Yosef, *Sefer ha-Shetarot*: a minor girl is different precisely because her father "can compel her to marry whomever he wishes," Ben-Sasson, "Fragments," 240.) On *jabr*, see above, n. 83.

87. Schremer, *Male and Female*, 126–142.

Even while emphasizing daughters' expected passivity at marriage, gaonic and Rabbanite authorities thus uniformly affirm that a mature daughter may in principle resist her father's marriage choices, however unlikely such resistance may be in social practice: "If she disavows her father's betrothal, it does not bind her." Most Karaite jurists maintain a very similar position, requiring that both a girl *and* her father consent to her marriage.[88]

Viewed from this angle, these texts demonstrate how rabbinic courts' adherence to rabbinic legal forms, however pro forma, might nonetheless expand Jews' imaginable social expectations. The freedom from coercion that Rabbanite jurists prescribed was not axiomatic in the medieval Middle East, even in theory. The primary schools of Sunnī Islamic law disagreed about this; most specifically permitted a father to compel his virgin (*bikr*) daughter in marriage.[89] In this context, Rabbanite fidelity to this principle may have retained tangible, if highly circumscribed, social meaning: by maintaining this legal technicality, however formulaically, Rabbanite courts at least hypothetically protected adolescent girls from marital coercion.

Whether Jewish girls ever actually exercised this right to reject their families' marriage choices is another question. We do sometimes hear of girls protesting engagements and betrothals; discussing several such cases, Goitein romantically noted that they seem to demonstrate that brides as well as grooms "were not entirely inactive with regard to the choice of their hearts."[90] But on closer inspection, these occasional protests cannot be taken as straightforward expressions of adolescent emotion, since they almost always forward the interests of the girl's own parents or guardians. For example, a letter sent from Ascalon in 1085 by a man named Yosef b. Menashe to a Rabbanite judge in Fustat describes a dramatic controversy over Yosef's involvement with a young woman named or nicknamed al-Jawziyya.[91] Jawziyya's father wanted to marry

88. Al-Qirqisānī, *Kitāb al-Anwār*, ed. Nemoy, VI, 69.5: "marriage requires the girl's consent and her father's consent." Cf. 'Anan, *Sefer ha-Miṣvot*, ed. Harkavy, 113; and ENA 2445.1–2, cited Chapter 3, n. 63. However, Binyamin al-Nahāwandī permits a father to unilaterally marry off a virgin daughter (*Mas'at Binyamin*, 39). Brides in Karaite *ketubbot* are represented by formally appointed agents (see Chapter 3), but two Karaite formularies describe fathers marrying their daughters without any formal appointment: T-S Misc. 35.10, c; II Firk. Heb. A 506 + 2222, fol. 1v–fol. 2r.

89. See above, n. 83. Yet it is noteworthy that medieval Egyptian Islamic marriage contracts, like Geniza ones, include standard allusions to the bride's participation and authorization of her *walī*; see, e.g., Grohmann, *Arabic Papyri*, Vol. 1, docs. 38, 40, 41, 42, and 44 (all ninth-century contracts involving virgin brides), and the thirteenth-century document cited by Friedman, *JMP*, 1:231. Cf. Zomeño, "Islamic Marriage Contract," on Andalusian contracts (which typically included such formulae only for orphans, whose guardians could not compel them according to Mālikī law).

90. *Med. Soc.*, 3:73.

91. T-S 13 J a. 1.1. The letter is addressed to Yiṣḥaq b. Avraham, a banker and communal official: Goitein, *Med. Soc.*, 1:238–239. According to Goitein, *jawziyya* was a type of

her to Yosef, and so sought to annul a betrothal he had contracted for her with another man. But the first groom refused to give up his claim to her. When a local court proved unable to force the issue, the father petitioned a Fatimid official, who ordered that the dispute be remanded to a new, "unbiased," Rabbanite court. Yosef's letter urges its recipient to forward his case in this new hearing; in this context, he asserts that Jawziyya herself is desperate to escape marriage to her current fiancé:

> I ask you to be present when the letter (from Sitr al-Dawla, the Fatimid officer) arrives. . . . I heard that Jawziyya said that if he took her by (order of the) government or by force, she would throw herself in a well or kill herself. This matter, which (affects) all of us, compels you, for your family and ours are as one. . . . Her father casts himself before you—please act in this matter as you see fit.[92]

A stronger expression of a young bride's own desires can hardly be imagined. Yet for all its Gothic melodrama, we cannot necessarily take Jawziyya's declaration at face value: Yosef says this to convince the judge reading his letter to support her father's appeal. To my knowledge, no account of a girl similarly resisting marriage against her parents' wishes has been identified in the documentary Geniza.[93]

The complex interaction between individual families, the Rabbanite court system, and the Fatimid state described in this story also merits attention. Jawziyya's is not the only account to invoke a girl's opposition to her own

---

sweetmeat made from walnuts (he renders the name as "Nougat"); see *Med. Soc.*, 3:442, n. 22; cf. Goitein/Friedman, *India Book*, 354, n. 5.

92. "Family": *ahl*; as often, it is not clear whether this denotes an extended family group, or the members of a household, or specific individuals within a family network. See Chapter 1, n. 69. Other examples of girls protesting a marriage in support of their parents' wishes include (1) T-S 13 J 16.5 (Fustat, thirteenth cent.; see Krakowski, "Female Adolescence," 1–2). (2) Maimonides, *Responsa*, 196 (same case discussed ibid., 304): A girl refused to marry a man who claimed her now-dead father had betrothed her to him as a minor: "neither she nor her mother nor any of her relatives" recognized his claim. (3) T-S G 1.18, a legal query possibly sent to Yehuda *ha-kohen* b. Yosef *rosh ha-seder* (Fustat, mid-eleventh century): a fifteen-year-old girl betrothed by her father now "wished to marry another" man. Here the groom himself had traveled to a different region, and the query almost certainly reflects her relatives' efforts to free her from the betrothal. See also the case discussed in the next paragraph.

93. The only Geniza reference I have found to a previously unmarried girl resisting marriage for her own reasons appears in an extraordinary literary narrative about a young female mystic in early twelfth-century Baghdad, who wanted to stay unmarried to maintain her father's pious practices "of fasting and prayer and charity"; communal officials eventually pressured her and arranged a marriage for her. (Bodl. MS Heb. f 56 13v-19r; see Goitein "Report on Messianic Troubles," Frenkel, "Literary Products," 151–154, Gil, *Jews in Islamic Countries*, 421–422.)

marriage in the context of Islamic state involvement in a Jewish marital dispute. A legal query sent from Qayrawān to an unnamed *ga'on*, published by Mordechai Akiva Friedman, describes a similar conflict between a girl's father and her fiancé's family.[94] The father, unhappy with a local judge's response to his suit, sought help from a state official with whom he possessed clout;[95] here, too, the official eventually ordered a new Rabbanite judge to adjudicate the matter, "in accordance with your legal doctrine (*madhhab*)." In the course of this second hearing, a contingent of "trustworthy" women was dispatched to question the bride herself, apparently to verify that she truly wished to end the betrothal.[96] Another aspect of Jawziyya's story—her cited fear that she would be married by order of the state—is paralleled in yet another Geniza document (from beyond our core geographical purview), a letter issued by the Iraqi neo-*ga'on* Shemu'el b. 'Eli (famous as the object of Maimonides' disdain) to an unknown community.[97] The letter cryptically refers to communal agitation over a government order to compel girls to marry against their will. A fragmentary line reads, "girls [. . .] from the *sulṭān* to marry them not by their ch[oice]."

Like the handful of other documents discussed in Chapter 2 that mention state involvement in Rabbanite court proceedings, these accounts remain obscure in many respects. Moreover, both Jawziyya's case and the Qayrawān query involve a technically different set of legal issues from the ones considered in gaonic discussions of the *bogeret*'s marital autonomy: both center on the girl's right to obtain a divorce from an unconsummated but binding betrothal, rather than whether a betrothal contracted without her assent can be valid.[98] Still, these cases suggest a final aspect of the broader social context in which the *bogeret*'s formal autonomy may have exerted social

94. T-S Ar. 50.197. Friedman: "Government Intervention."

95. "The father went away and sought help from the *sulṭān*, because he possessed clout (*'ināya*) with him." On this term as a formula for patronage, see Rustow, "Formal and Informal Patronage," 360–362. The query is undated, but likely dates to Zirid rule, probably sometime between 972 and 1057.

96. The women testify that "they found no subterfuge (*ḥīla*) in her," seemingly meaning that she genuinely did not want to marry him (and that it was not true that her father wanted to break the betrothal so that he could marry her to someone else, as the groom's father claimed). For the legal context, see below, n. 98; on *ḥīla* as "stratagem" in Islamic law, see Horii, "Reconsideration."

97. ENA 4011.75 + Bodl. MS Heb. e. 100.55 + West. Coll. Misc. 11.

98. The legal issue explicitly at stake in the Qayrawān case (and likely in Jawziyya's too) was the bride's right to a divorce against her groom's wishes; the girl's father claimed that "the custom (*sunna*) of Qayrawān" entitled her to a divorce, while the original judge refused to break the betrothal without the groom's assent. On wife-initiated divorce, see Chapter 7.

meaning: the relationships that individual Jewish litigants maintained with Muslim state officials.

Medieval Islamic states played complex roles in Jews' internal political disputes.[99] As we have seen, state involvement did not run one way only; individual Jews under Fatimid, Ayyubid (and later, Mamluk) rule petitioned local Muslim officials for support that would give them power within Jewish courts and communal institutions.[100] While scholarship on this subject has focused primarily on petitions submitted about communal politics, Jews also sometimes appealed to state officials to gain leverage in marriage and family disputes.[101] In this context—and given state officials' occasional interest in ensuring Jewish litigants' conformity to Jewish law—Jews might claim to be obeying rabbinic legal norms in order to sway not only Rabbanite communal officials, but also the Muslim bureaucrats and judges in whose shadow these officials operated.

In both Yosef's letter and the Qayrawān query, a virgin daughter's opposition to her impending marriage is marshaled in just this way, as evidence submitted to a Rabbanite judge who was himself seeking to satisfy a Muslim state official—and who, in both cases, had become involved at the urging of the girl's own father.[102] In other words, these statements of protest serve as their own form of legal performance, enacted to demonstrate the rabbinic validity of a judgment commissioned by a Muslim official on behalf of a Jewish client. Shemu'el b. 'Eli's elliptical reference remains less clear, but may perhaps refer to the opposite situation, in which Rabbanite communal officials attempted to oppose a government action solicited by a disputed groom. By analogy, these cases raise the possibility that Rabbanite courts' concern about the *bogeret*'s formal independence may have been invoked in similar contexts. Either way, they point to the complicated legal arena in which these courts operated: one in which proof of their rabbinic legitimacy could matter not only to Jews, but also to the Muslims among whom they lived—including the Muslim state officials who ruled over them.

99. See Chapter 2.

100. See the sources surveyed in Chapter 2, especially Rustow, "The legal status of *ḏimmī-s*," 316–319, idem, "Limits of Communal Autonomy," 138. Cf. also Ben-Sasson, *Qayrawan*, 310–312, and Frenkel, *The Compassionate and Benevolent*, 177–178.

101. For other family disputes in which a Jew appealed to a Fatimid or Ayyubid *qāḍī* or government official, see Goitein, *Med. Soc.*, 2:399–400, to which may be added T-S 16.231, which discusses a state petition in the context of a dispute over an annulled betrothal.

102. This tactic became more common under the Mamluks, when state policy began to overtly emphasize Jewish and Christian communities' fidelity to their own authentic practice, and appeal to rabbinic law became a standard way to gain leverage with state officials. See Cohen, "Jews in the Mamlūk Environment," 439–440, Rustow, "Limits of Communal Autonomy," 140–141, and cf. El-Leithy, "Coptic Culture," 435–439, on similar evidence among Egyptian Christians.

Conclusions: Stepping into Marriage

The marriage choices documented in the Geniza defy easy categorization.[103] Both the immediate reasons for which a given match was pursued, and the personal circumstances that it created for a young bride, varied in ways that blur the easy distinction between endogamous and exogamous alliances. Sitt al-Dār bt. Avraham b. Yijū's story demonstrates that marriage to a nonrelative could link a girl to people she had come to know well during a lengthy betrothal, whereas marriage to a close cousin might bring her into an unfamiliar home in which she was surrounded by strangers.

In either case, the decisions that a young woman's parents and other relatives made for her had lasting consequences. Not only the man she married, but also the size of the dowry she brought in to him, the contract with which she married him, and the makeup of the new household they formed together were all determined by the choices her relatives made in negotiating her first marriage. This process led to the final and most significant event in a woman's early life, ending the period of complete social subordination to her natal family—or to the communal officials or charitable patrons who substituted for them—that began at birth and lasted for as long as she remained unmarried.

Once a girl entered marriage, things began to change—in part because of the economic aspects of first marriage (discussed in Chapter 4) and in part because it became socially acceptable and even desirable for her to express differences with her new family, in ways that she could not have with her own parents and siblings. This book's last two chapters will examine how the same kinship ties that determined whom she married also shaped this transition, defining a young wife's expected role within her marital household and the terms on which she might maneuver within it.

103. Cf. Goitein, *Med. Soc.*, 3:55.

CHAPTER SEVEN

Defining Marriage

LEGAL AGREEMENTS AND THEIR USES

A MARRIAGE AGREEMENT WRITTEN in Fustat in 1127 severely limits the bride's rights within marriage.[1] The document's top half is missing, and with it her name. What remains is a series of pledges she made to her husband Yeshuʿa on the evening of their betrothal. Once they were married, she would allow him to travel whenever he wanted and would not use his absence as grounds for claiming the deferred portion of her dower (*mahr*). Nor would she ever try to extract a penny more of dower from him than the twenty dinars listed in her *ketubba*. Most extraordinarily, she promised never to leave her living space without his explicit permission, and she agreed that he could lock her inside whenever he wanted; she would have no legal standing to sue him over this.

Another marriage agreement composed in Fustat thirty years later reads very differently. The agreement does not survive in full, but its contents are summarized above a partial inventory of the bride's dowry (*taqwīm*) copied into a court notebook.[2] Here the pledges all extend the other way, strengthening the bride's legal position rather than eroding it. The groom, Yosef b. Netan'el *ha-kohen*, promises his future wife, Sitt al-Kafā'a bt. Abū al-Faḍā'il, that he will trust her financially;[3] that he will neither marry a second wife without her permission nor keep a female slave against her wishes; that if she dies before bearing children, he will claim only half her dowry as inheritance and return the rest to her birth relatives; that she may continue to live in

1. T-S 8 J 5.7.

2. RNL Yevr.-Arab. I 1700, 25b. This summary appears in part of a court notebook from Fustat, 1156.

3. Specifically, that she would not have to take a "widow's oath" after he died, demonstrating that she had not used his property. See below, n. 17.

Fustat rather than Cairo; and that he will not object if she sells off any of her dowry items and buys other property with the proceeds.

Why did these two women begin marriage on such different terms? One obvious answer is economic class. Sitt al-Kafāʾa was much wealthier than Yeshuʿa's anonymous wife, as is obvious from the values of their marriage payments, the most systematic way of gauging individual women's economic status in the Geniza corpus. Yeshuʿa promised his wife twenty dinars as dower, a relatively modest sum that predicts her own dowry was worth no more than 100 dinars and possibly much less. In contrast, Sitt al-Kafāʾa's dower totaled 150 dinars (50 payable at marriage and 100 if Yosef divorced or died before her) while the portion of her dowry listed in this *taqwīm* contained more than 620 dinars' worth of jewelry, clothing, household textiles, and copper utensils.[4]

It is logical to assume that this generous dowry made Sitt al-Kafāʾa an attractive catch who could demand stronger concessions from her groom than Yeshuʿa was prepared to grant his bride. But economics alone do not explain fully why Sitt al-Kafāʾa's marriage contract empowers her as strongly as it does. Some relatively poor women who married around the same time as she did received similar promises from their husbands, while other wealthy women married without them. Nor can the relative poverty of Yeshuʿa's wife explain the legal disabilities imposed on her at marriage, because few Geniza women of any class agreed to subjugate themselves to their husbands this completely. A woman's marriage agreement served as a form of personal equipment in its own right, which alongside the dowry helped to determine how she would live as a wife.

Geniza marriage documents worked as personal apparatuses especially from the turn of the twelfth century, when they began to feature stipulations like those in these two documents: pledges made by both spouses, but especially husbands, to grant the other specific personal and financial rights in marriage. These agreements provide some of the best information we have for individual wives' living conditions, which I have exploited elsewhere in this book. As is often the case with legal documents, it is easier to read them for this kind of ancillary data than as social artifacts with their own history and purpose. But the effort to understand why these documents developed and how they worked is well worthwhile. Read between the lines, they also offer some of our best evidence for how Jewish communal institutions worked to situate women within the wider social field they entered at first marriage.

That is the aim of this chapter. It focuses in depth on the twelfth-century turn in rabbinic marriage documents, as a window onto the legal structures that defined a new wife's standing vis-à-vis her husband and in-laws—how

4. Her dowry may also have contained real estate and slaves, even though neither is mentioned; both were often included in large dowries but not always in dowry lists (see Chapter 4, n. 60). This list also appears to break off in the middle of the section devoted to copper utensils.

much control she held over her person and property, and how far her husband controlled both; whether he supported her, or whether she would have to struggle to survive; how easily she could end the marriage, or prevent him from doing so.

I read these documents primarily as a record of kinship support reified into law, which suggests how women's birth relatives could influence their social positions as wives. This view departs from previous scholars' understanding of these documents as top-down rabbinic products that testify to women's protection by a maturing Jewish communal infrastructure. In what follows, I revisit the new marriage documents' textual origins, political meaning within the rabbinic legal system, and likely uses by husbands and wives in the courtroom, and conclude that they illustrate something different: a socially contingent Jewish legal system that allowed women's male relatives pride of place in determining their rights in marriage—not only when a marriage was arranged, but also after it began.

Marriage Stipulations in the Twelfth Century: From Islamic to Jewish Documents

According to rabbinic law, all women must receive a written contract, a *ketubba*, when they marry.[5] This rule seems to have been followed widely in tenth- to thirteenth-century Egypt and Syria. As far as we know, all or almost all Jewish wives documented in the Geniza did receive a *ketubba* when they married.[6] Hundreds of these contracts were preserved in the Geniza chamber, most in fragments. The vast majority follow a fixed Aramaic formulary similar to that described in surviving Iraqi gaonic formulary books. Some tenth- and early eleventh-century *ketubbot* use a different formulary apparently drawn from Palestinian gaonic tradition; others, written entirely in Hebrew, are not gaonic or even Rabbanite at all but Karaite, since Karaite jurists, too, declared the *ketubba* legally necessary for marriage.[7]

Whether Rabbanite or Karaite, all *ketubbot* share the same economic purpose: to record debts the husband will owe his wife if he dies or divorces her. In Geniza *ketubbot*, these debts include the minimal *ketubba* payment described in late-ancient rabbinic literature (typically valued at 25 *dirham*s for virgins and 12½ for nonvirgins, both economically trivial sums),[8] as well

5. bKet. 57a.

6. At least, all women who married through a Jewish court did so. Jewish women who married before a *qāḍī* are almost invisible in the Geniza legal record, but not entirely; see Chapter 5, n. 8.

7. See Chapter 1, n. 10, for the major edited collections of these corpora.

8. Karaite documents name slightly higher sums: 50 dirhams for a virgin and 25 for a nonvirgin. Olszowy-Schlanger, *KMD*, 194–195.

as two other sets of more substantial assets: the wife's dowry items and the deferred groom's dower, the lion's share of the cash payment—Arab. *mahr*, Heb. *mohar*, Syr. *mahrā*—that all husbands in the medieval Middle East, Jews, Muslims, and Christians alike, typically gave or pledged their wives at marriage. The groom's dower was divided into two portions, an early portion paid before or at marriage and a deferred portion payable later—for Jews, when the marriage ended. Rabbinic jurists technically classed the entire dower, both early and late payments, as extra *ketubba* money, *tosefet ketubba*.[9]

Around the turn of the twelfth century, hundreds of other kinds of marriage documents that are not *ketubbot* also begin to appear in the Geniza corpus: records of betrothal attesting that a couple has contracted binding *qiddushin*, engagement (*shiddukhin*) contracts describing their nonbinding agreement to marry, *taqwīms* listing the contents and value of the bride's dowry, and miscellaneous auxiliary testimonies given by couples and their relatives—recording, for example, a father's promise to give his daughter half a *dār* as dowry, or a groom's that he will pay his bride a fine if he continues postponing the wedding.[10] Unlike *ketubbot*, these documents are written not in standardized Aramaic or Hebrew, but in the fluid mix of Judeo-Arabic narrative passages and Hebrew and Aramaic validating formulae typical of other Geniza legal documents from this period.[11] Most mention the same set of transactions as the *ketubba*: the groom's dower and the bride's dowry. Again unlike *ketubbot*, however, many also contain personalized stipulations like those pledged by Yeshuʿa's wife and Sitt al-Kafāʾa's husband, which define the marriage well beyond this basic financial framework.

These new marriage stipulations mostly address a set repertoire of issues. They include three clause types whose content is fixed (although their language is not): the husband promises (1) that he and his heirs will consider his wife financially trustworthy (which means that after he dies, his heirs cannot force her to swear a "widow's oath" that she had not illicitly taken property from his estate); (2) that he will not marry another wife or own a female slave (sometimes described more directly as a concubine) without her permission, and (3) that he will give half of her dowry back to her relatives if she dies before bearing children. They also include four clause types whose specific content

9. The minimal rabbinic *ketubba* was technically folded into the late portion of the dower. However, Geniza documents themselves often use *mahr/mohar* and *ketubba* imprecisely, employing both terms for both the technical rabbinic payment and the entire promised sum. See Friedman, "Minimum Mohar Payment," idem, *JMP*, 1:239–287.

10. On *shiddukhin*, *qiddushin*, and the *ketubba*, see Chapter 3, ns. 28–29. Ashur, "EBD," discusses these new document forms in detail and provides editions of many of them. Father's promise: e.g., T-S 12.668. Fine: e.g., T-S NS 320.141v.

11. See Chapter 2.

is more fluid, although they center on a fixed set of questions: (4) where the wife will live (either in a specific city, e.g., "in Fustat and not Cairo," or with a specific set of relatives, either her own or her husband's), (5) whether the husband may travel, either with or without her, (6) whether she may control her labor or her own dowry, and (7) her physical mobility outside her living chamber.[12] Once they had been developed in non-*ketubba* agreements, these clauses made their way into some *ketubbot* as well, where they appear translated into Aramaic.[13]

Where did these stipulations come from? Nothing like them occurs in Jewish marriage documents before they begin to surface in the Geniza in the early 1100s. But precedents are not hard to find once we look beyond the Jewish marriage contract tradition to the Islamic one, which features similar stipulations from as early as the eighth century.

This is not to say that the basic idea of spousal stipulations is Islamic. Records of promises exchanged by spouses had appeared in marriage documents from across the Middle East long before Islam, including some produced by Jews in Elephantine in the fifth century BCE and in second-century Judea.[14] Late ancient rabbinic texts mention spousal stipulations as common features

12. Several other clause types appear only once or a few times across the corpus: grooms' promises not to beat or curse their wives (T-S 8 J 5.2c-d, 1132, Fustat; T-S NS J 378, Mosseri VII 16.1, both early twelfth century, Fustat), promises by both spouses to care for or support each other's children from previous marriages (e.g., Bodl. MS Heb. a. 3.42, 1117, Fustat; Bodl. MS Heb. c. 28.14, 1165, Fustat; T-S 20.39, T-S 12.763, both undated); a groom's promise not to associate with "unfit" persons (ENA 2806.11 + ENA 2727.18, 1133, Fustat); and another's to pay for his mother-in-law's medical care and bury her (also Mosseri VII 16.1). I have also excluded a cluster of later *ketubba* clauses from the late twelfth century and afterward promising that the couple will not have sex unless the wife has ritually immersed herself in a *miqveh* after menstruation (some record the wife's promise and some the husband's). These clauses deserve to be studied separately, in context of Maimonides' edict from this period requiring women to immerse or forfeit their deferred dower. See idem, *Responsa*, no. 242; Cohen, "Purity, Piety, Polemic"; Friedman, "Social Realities"; Ashur, "EBD," 126–129.

13. The earliest *ketubba* to include an Aramaic version of any of these clauses (except for the half-dowry return clause, which appears earlier; see below, n. 19) is a Karaite-Rabbanite contract from Fustat, 1117: Bodl. MS Heb. a. 3.42. They reach a critical mass in both non-*ketubba* agreements and *ketubbot* by the 1140s, and continue to be standard features of both through the end of the classical Geniza period. By the early thirteenth century, however, their formulation becomes increasingly generic, e.g., where an earlier agreement might specify that the wife will "live in Fustat and not Cairo," later ones say simply "her (place of) residence is up to her." See, e.g., Bodl. MS Heb. Heb. d. 66.48 (Fustat, 1146); T-S 8 J 5.21 (Al-Maḥalla, 1160); Maimonides, *Responsa*, no. 88 (citing an engagement contract from Alexandria, 1201); T-S 12.121 (Fustat, 1243); ENA NS 1.95a + T-S Misc. 27.4.31 (Fustat, 1244); T-S NS J 363 (thirteenth century); T-S NS J 297a (1290).

14. See, e.g., Fitzmyer, "Elephantine Marriage Contract," Cotton, "Cancelled Marriage Contract," and cf. Stol, "Women in Mesopotamia," 125–126.

of the *ketubba*, as do earlier medieval gaonic texts.[15] The Geniza corpus itself preserves examples of these stipulations, in both Rabbanite and Karaite *ketubbot* from tenth- and eleventh-century Syria and Egypt.[16]

But most of the twelfth-century stipulations differ from these earlier *ketubba* clauses in two ways. First, they seek to define not just the economic foundations of marriage, but also its internal structure—how couples must treat each other and live together as man and wife. The one exception is the half-dowry return clause, which has classical rabbinic roots.[17] Second, many of the terms they impose are variable and change from document to document. In contrast, the marriage stipulations cited by classical rabbinic and gaonic texts mostly impose certain standard economic duties on the husband: he must ransom his wife if she is captured by pirates, or transmit her dowry to her sons if she dies, or permit her to live off his estate if he dies.[18] Tenth- and eleventh-century Geniza Palestinian Rabbanite and Karaite *ketubbot* include some of these same economic clauses, including dowry return clauses.[19] But the only pre-twelfth-century Geniza stipulations to dictate spouses' *behavior* within marriage are religious behavior clauses included in eleventh-century "mixed" Karaite-Rabbanite *ketubbot* (for example, a Rabbanite man promises his Karaite bride not to bring home cuts of meat permitted as kosher in Rabbanite but not Karaite law), and conditions cited in a single record of testimony composed in 1047, in which a groom promises his bride not to associate with debauched men, leave Fustat, or buy a female slave without her consent.[20]

Personalized behavioral stipulations are thus virtually unattested in Jewish marriage documents until the twelfth century, and entirely so before 1047.

15. Rabbinic texts: e.g., mKet. 4:8–12; see Friedman, *JMP*, 1:312–450. Gaonic texts: e.g., Se'adya b. Yosef, *Sefer Shetarot*, ed. Brody and Ben Sasson, no. 15; Harkavy, *Zikhron Kamma Ge'onim*, no. 143; and the query preserved in T-S Misc. 28.186.

16. See below, n. 19.

17. pKet. 9:1, pBB 8:6. Two other clause types have loose antecedents. The "trustworthiness" (widow's-oath) clause is partly anticipated by mKet. 4:12, but the clause cited there differs completely from those that appear in our twelfth-century documents. Conversely, polygamy clauses appear in some ancient Near Eastern contracts (including Jewish ones), but not in late ancient rabbinic texts. See Fitzmyer, "Elephantine Marriage Contract," Stol, "Women in Mesopotamia."

18. mKet. 4:7–13, where these obligations are described as "conditions of the court" that obligate the husband whether or not they are stated in his marriage contract.

19. Half-dowry clauses appear routinely in tenth- and eleventh-century Palestinian-formula *ketubbot* (as do general divorce stipulations), and in some Iraqi-formula *ketubbot* from the later eleventh century: Friedman, *JMP*, 1:327–346, 398–400; Iraqi examples include Bodl. MS Heb. a. 3.43, (1059, Fustat), T-S 24.1 (1081), and T-S J 3.26 (1089, Cairo). Karaite *ketubbot* from the same period contain clauses promising the return of the *entire* dowry if the wife dies childless: Olszowy-Schlanger, *KMD*, 241–243, Friedman, "Relationship."

20. Karaite-Rabbanite *ketubbot*: Olszowy-Schlanger, *KMD*, 252–255. 1047: T-S 20.160.

But they appear much earlier in Islamic marriage contracts. Among the earliest surviving Islamic legal documents are three marriage contracts from late ninth-century Egypt (two from al-Ushmūnayn, late-ancient Hermopolis) in which the husband pledges to respect his wife, permit her to socialize with her relatives, and dismiss any wife or female slave that he marries or buys after her.[21] Islamic legal texts describe similar clauses even earlier; in the eighth century, *ḥadīth* compilations and prescriptive legal works were already debating whether marriage contracts could forbid a husband from moving his wife to a different city or from taking a second wife or concubine.[22] Similar clauses continue to be mentioned in Islamic prescriptive texts and responsa from Egypt under the Fatimids and into the Mamluk period and beyond.[23]

The near-total absence of this genre of clause in Jewish marriage documents until the twelfth century, compared to its long history in Islamic ones, suggests that Geniza scribes adopted these clauses from contemporary Islamic contracts. They thus offer further indication that Jewish court scribes were closely familiar with Islamic document forms and incorporated them into the Jewish legal documents they produced. Unfortunately, in this case we have no way of tracing precisely how the transfer occurred, because very few Fatimid Islamic marriage contracts have survived, and almost none of them contain personalized clauses.[24] But the Geniza does allow us to recover the Jewish institutional settings in which the clauses took root: why communal leaders in the early twelfth century may have encouraged scribes to use them, and why Jewish litigants may have wanted to record and preserve them.

Marriage Agreements and Jewish Communal Politics

Why did rabbinic courts begin producing new forms of marriage documents at the start of the twelfth century? There is an obvious place to seek answers to this question: a body of evidence demonstrating that the Fatimid Heads of the Jews (*ra'īs al-yahūd*) publicly cemented their authority over local rabbinic

21. Grohmann, *Arabic Papyri*, nos. 38, 39, and 41.

22. Spectorsky, *Women in Classical Islamic Law*, 89–90.

23. Fatimid examples: Cortese and Calderini, *Women and the Fatimids*, 212, Ashur, "Protecting," 8. For the Mamluk period, see Rapoport, *Marriage, Money and Divorce*, 74–76. For a rare documentary exception from the eleventh century, see Grohmann, "Arabische Papyri aus den Staatlichen Museen zu Berlin," no. 11; and from Damascus in 1258, Mouton, Sourdel, and Sourdel-Thomine, *Mariage et Séparation à Damas*, no. 47 C. (For Muslim jurists' approaches to these stipulations, see Ali, "Marriage in Classical Islamic Jurisprudence," 21–23.)

24. More may yet be identified and published, including from within the Geniza corpus itself.

courts at precisely this time, in part by cultivating the Fustat court, where many of these documents were produced, as a regional center.[25]

Scholars have assumed a direct link between these two developments, although without reference to the documents' Islamic parallels and chiefly in regard to polygamy clauses. From different angles, Mordechai Akiva Friedman, Mark Cohen, and Amir Ashur have suggested that the Heads (*ru'asā'*) or their associates introduced polygamy clauses into Jewish marriage documents to regulate marriages and protect Jewish wives. Ashur suggests that this may also be true of other aspects of the new marriage documents; for example, communal officials may have encouraged nonbinding engagement agreements because they shielded brides from becoming trapped in unconsummated but binding betrothals (i.e., inchoate marriages) if a groom changed his mind or disappeared.[26] Whether applied narrowly to polygamy clauses or more broadly to the new document forms as a whole, this consensus views these documents as products of top-down communal reforms, evidence that the Heads of the Jews were able to manage Jewish women's lives more effectively as they gained greater control of the courts.

Yet the surviving documents themselves call into question this hierarchical account of their origins, as does the other evidence for how the Heads ruled as communal leaders. Both forms of evidence suggest that the growth of the rabbinic court system in this period affected women differently—not by protecting brides as a class, but by providing their relatives with the tools to reinforce social differences among them as legal ones.

MARRIAGE AGREEMENTS AS A RECORD OF LITIGANT CHOICES

As a group, the new marriage agreements did not help all women equally, but rather redefined individual women's rights in marriage in different ways. This variety has been easy to miss, in part because of scholars' isolated emphasis on the emergence of polygamy clauses. But it is equally easy to see when we step

25. Cohen, *Jewish Self-Government*, reconstructs this history in detail, with reference to earlier treatments.

26. Cohen, *Jewish Self-Government*, 256–259, 294; Friedman, *Jewish Polygyny*, 39–41, 62–65; Ashur, "EBD," 26, 175–176, and cf. idem, "*Haggana*" and "Protecting the Wife's Rights." I should note that Friedman's discussion is cautious and inconclusive, and that he views the polygamy clause as a product of internal rabbinic legal concerns rather than social anxiety about women's welfare. But I include him among these scholars because he, too, assumes that it was developed and propagated by the *ru'asā'* or officials working under them. (Although he suggests elsewhere that the clause may have been adopted in Fustat "by popular demand," he seems to mean by this demand among communal elites, not litigants: idem, "Polygyny in Jewish Tradition," 62–63.) See also idem, "Monogamy Clause," 25, and cf. Krakowski and Rustow, "Formula as Content."

back and return these clauses to the broader cluster of diplomatic innovations among which they developed.

Geniza marriage agreements from the twelfth and thirteenth centuries vary widely by *genre*, comprising different kinds of agreements and testimonies that advance both brides' and grooms' interests in different ways, including records of betrothal, records of engagement, promises about the bride's dowry, promises about the timing of the marriage, and so on. As far as we know, no one couple recorded in writing all the different stages of marriage represented in this corpus, which means that each record represents a deliberate choice by either spouse, or their representatives, to manage a specific aspect of their marriage through the courts.

The agreements also vary in *content*, that is, in the personalized stipulations that are their hallmark feature—polygamy clauses among them. This is obvious when it comes to the four stipulation types that are inherently variable: those regulating wives' place of residence, mobility, property and labor rights and husbands' travel. But even the three types whose content is fixed are unevenly diffused across the corpus: half-dowry return clauses, "widow's oath" clauses, and polygamy clauses. These three stipulations always say the same thing when they appear, but they do not always appear, and can appear in different groupings when they do.

Among the entire group of known Geniza marriage documents datable to the twelfth and thirteenth centuries (more precisely, 1099–1250), I have identified 101 that contain one or more promises about the terms of a couple's marriage: seventy-one non-*ketubba* documents and thirty *ketubbot*.[27] This is only a fraction of the surviving marriage agreements produced during this period. Other twelfth- to thirteenth-century Geniza marriage documents, many of them written by the same scribes, do not include personal stipulations at all.[28] Moreover, these 101 documents contain different sets of stipulations. Not one of the eight basic types of personal clauses represented in this corpus appears in more than about half the documents overall (Figure 7.1). Conversely, no single document has been found that includes all eight clause types.[29] Even the promises in this group most generically beneficial to women, then, did not benefit all Jewish brides as a class, but

27. Many are undated but can be dated to this period on formulaic grounds, in part because the *ru'asā'* began to insert clauses asserting their own authority in rabbinic court documents at this time (see below, at n. 33).

28. For example, T-S 8 J 10.10, T-S NS 226.10, and T-S NS 19.6, all in the hand of Ḥalfon b. Menashe, the early twelfth-century scribe who wrote many of the 101 agreements that *do* contain these clauses.

29. This is true even of the three fixed clauses whose use initially appears more standardized (the half-dowry return, widow's oath, and monogamy clauses); only eight of these 101 agreements include all three.

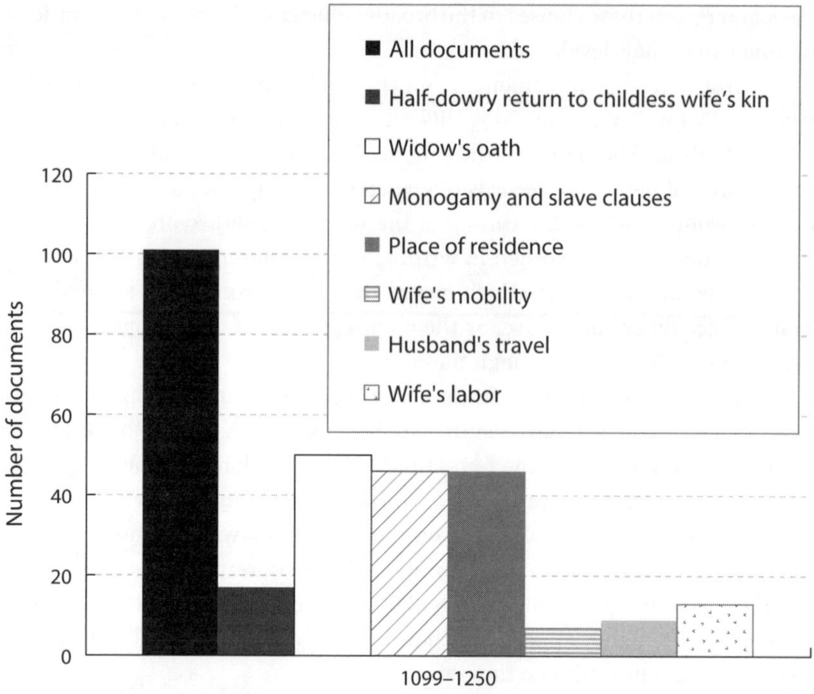

FIGURE 7.1. Stipulations in Geniza marriage documents, 1099–1250

rather equipped some women entering marriage with specific legal advantages that others lacked.

Viewed together, these agreements do not seem to reflect a systematic program of communal reform. They are more plausibly read as personalized legal tools commissioned by the people who appear in them: brides, grooms, and their relatives. This corpus offers, in other words, an index of *litigant choices*—or more precisely in the case of first-time brides, of the choices made by girls' birth relatives, or those substituting for them. It thus suggests a further way that a girl's natal kin determined her adult life as a married woman—not only by choosing her husband and giving her a dowry, but also through their expectations for how her husband and in-laws could treat her.

One important question remains unclear: Did these expectations themselves change in the early twelfth century? That is, do these new agreements reflect new ideas about marriage itself? There is no way to know. The specific concerns at stake in some of these clause types—especially polygamy clauses and half-dowry return clauses—had already been legal flashpoints within marriage in the eleventh century. But it is not clear whether other clauses, such as residence and labor clauses, reflect long-standing points of concern not previously expressed in writing, or instead reflect new concepts of the

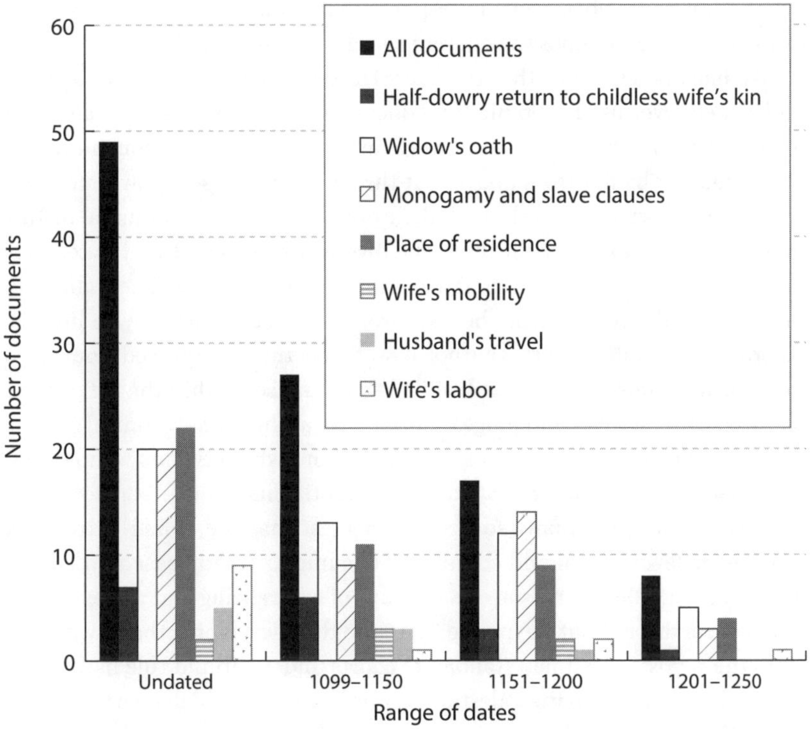

FIGURE 7.2. Stipulations in Geniza marriage documents, 1099–1250, by date

rights husbands and wives owed each other that developed only at this time.[30] Nor can we tell how the practice of inserting these particular clause types and not others shaped how Jews came to understand marriage in the twelfth century and after. What is clear, however, is that rabbinic courts' growing formalization in the early twelfth century allowed relatives to begin to cement their *social* expectations (whether new or old) for their daughters as written *legal* rights—and thus render them visible to us for the first time.

MARRIAGE DOCUMENTS AND RABBINIC LEGAL AUTHORITY

How and why did court officials support their doing so? Here our best evidence lies not in the agreements themselves, but in other legal documents and letters about the Jewish communal leadership of Fustat during this period. These sources, too, suggest that communal leaders more likely promoted new

30. Polygamy: see below, n. 35. Half-dowry return: see above, n. 19.

forms of marriage documents in response to litigant demand rather than because of a desire to impose a coherent social vision from on high.

We have no evidence that the early Heads of the Jews or Jewish courts under them ever used rabbinic legal documents to enforce large-scale social reforms. Cohen's groundbreaking work on the first *ru'asā'* demonstrates that they ruled not by fiat from above, but through a mix of soft power and government support, accrued through their prerogatives over communal institutions, the help of local Jewish elites, and investiture by the Fatimid state.[31] The same is true of the rabbinic courts, as I argued in Chapter 2. Their authority came first and foremost from below, through the legitimacy Jewish litigants accorded them, although this authority was sometimes reinforced from above by *qāḍīs* and state officials. And while legal practices within the *bet din* emphasized court scribes' and judges' hierarchical authority as technical experts, rabbinic officials needed to remain flexible about what litigants wanted their agreements to say in order to attract them as litigants in the first place.

However, a great many sources do suggest that the *ru'asā'* introduced changes to Jewish legal and communal documents (many based on Islamic models) for a different reason—as a means of centralizing and annexing rabbinic courts throughout Egypt and Syria and thus developing their own office. Until the 1070s, Palestinian Rabbanite courts under Fatimid rule had at least nominally answered to the Palestinian *ge'onim* and their high court, although in practice, Geniza evidence suggests the *ge'onim* did not always closely supervise local courts, at least in Egypt.[32] But by 1080, the Egyptian *ra'īs* Mevorakh b. Se'adya had begun authorizing and instructing judges in Fustat and Alexandria. Under Mevorakh's successor, David b. Dani'el (r. 1082–1094), the Palestinian Rabbanite court of Fustat began terming itself a "high court" (*bet din gadol*) in documents, an implicit claim that its authority and David's own equaled or exceeded those of the *yeshiva* court and *ge'onim*. Mevorakh ruled as *ra'īs* again after David (ca. 1094–1111), during a period when the Palestinian *yeshiva* closed temporarily and then moved to Tyre. He further promoted the Fustat court as a high court under his control, appointing three fixed (*qavu'a*) judges in Fustat about whom he received petitions from disaffected litigants (in imitation of Islamic state *maẓālim*), and signaling his political leadership by having court scribes insert his own name at the top of *ketubbot* (in imitation of Islamic chancery practice). Later *ru'asā'* maintained these practices and extended them; by 1127, the Palestinian *yeshiva* had closed, and its last *ga'on*, Maṣliaḥ b. Shelomo, had moved to serve as *ra'īs* in Egypt, where he introduced a "*rashut*" clause signaling his authority at the start of all legal documents, a formula that remained standard for centuries.[33]

31. Cohen, *Jewish Self-Government.*

32. See Chapter 2, n. 17.

33. Cohen, *Jewish Self-Government*, 196–200, 232–237, 245–248, 266.

The Heads thus promoted themselves as leaders in part by expanding the rabbinic court system and encouraging its officials to develop new forms of Fatimid-inspired legal and administrative writing. To the extent that they or their associates encouraged rabbinic scribes to produce new kinds of marriage documents with Islamicate features, they most likely did so for much the same reason: to increase the court's reach and with it their own political position. These documents, rabbinic versions of Islamic products likely familiar to many Jewish litigants, drew more people to the *bet din* and made it more important to marriage and divorce, institutions central to most Jews' lives.

Marriage was an obvious place for this expansion to occur, because it had long been a key source of the *bet din*'s power from below. It is no coincidence that when Mevorakh b. Seʿadya first started placing his imprimatur on legal documents, he began with *ketubbot*. He did so because Geniza Jews seem to have cared more about recording their marriages and divorces in rabbinic courts than any other kind of transaction, perhaps because they wanted to ensure that their children could not be classed as legal bastards (*mamzerim*).[34] Court officials could thus effectively block certain marriages by refusing to produce a couple's *ketubba*—one of the few ways they exerted direct control over the Jewish litigants who appeared before them.[35] Yet at least until Maimonides in the late twelfth century, communal leaders seem never to have systematically intervened more deeply than this to dictate how husbands should treat their wives.[36] This is also what the only known document tying a *ra'īs* to

34. This is suggested both by the sheer number of marriage and divorce documents preserved in the Geniza, more than those about any other transaction, and by the economic diversity of the marriage payments they record, which reflect couples at every level of the social ladder. *Mamzerim*: see the next note.

35. They mostly did so, or threatened to, in two types of cases: (1) To prevent women still bound by an earlier betrothal (or marriage) from marrying again—which would make the second marriage adultery and her children bastards (*mamzerim*). This anxiety mostly left traces in the Geniza when cases were resolved, in documents affirming that a woman was single or of valid lineage and could marry freely: Ashur, "EBD," docs. 1-ג—3-ג, Friedman, *Jewish Polygyny*, Chapters 6–7. See also CUL Or. 1080 J 58, affirming that a woman's divorce was valid and that she could remarry, and conversely ENA 2560.6v, a scribe's or judge's note that a woman is a *mamzeret*. (2) To prevent men from marrying a second wife without the first wife's consent. Documents from the early eleventh century onward describe court officials refusing to ratify polygamous marriages until the first wife agreed: Friedman, *Jewish Polygyny*, esp. Chapters 6–8. This evidence partly explains why scholars have viewed polygamy clauses, which seek to protect individual women from precisely this situation, as products of top-down reform by court officials.

36. This changed somewhat in the reformist atmosphere of the early Ayyubid period (late twelfth century), when Maimonides did try to exploit rabbinic courts' control over marriage and divorce as a tool for religious-social reform, most notably by trying to enforce rabbinic menstrual purity laws (see above, n. 12) and to regulate unwanted polygamy, decreeing that foreigners who marry Egyptian women must swear that they are single and must give their Egyptian wives a conditional bill of divorce before leaving town

the new marriage agreements suggests. It is a request sent by a court scribe to Maṣliaḥ b. Shelomo, asking him to translate a list of personal stipulations from Arabic to Aramaic so they can be inserted into a particular *ketubba*; that is, asking Maṣliaḥ to guarantee that the *ketubba* was linguistically accurate and thus legally viable, rather than to pass judgment on its content.[37] The Heads of the Jews, this document suggests, knew about these agreements and may even have helped to develop them and assimilate them to rabbinic documentary norms. But they did so as part of a general move toward increasing Jews' attachment to written rabbinic records, not because they wanted to transform Jewish marriages.

What Was a Written Promise Worth?

This political history matters to young women's experiences of marriage, because it helps explain not just why the new agreements developed but also how they could be used. The same complex legal culture that produced these documents also determined how they worked to benefit and constrain women within marriage.

What could promises recorded in a marriage agreement accomplish once the wedding was over? Few Geniza documents or responsa directly describe these clauses' afterlives.[38] But from different angles, prescriptive texts and Geniza documents alike make it possible to infer how husbands and wives invoked them against each other within marriage.

MARRIAGE STIPULATIONS AS RABBINIC LEGAL TOOLS

I begin with the view from prescriptive rabbinic law, which explains how things worked in theory. The claim that Geniza marriage stipulations held specifically rabbinic legal functions may seem strange, since I have just argued that they derive from Islamic models. But this synthesis is typical of Geniza legal documents, which routinely assimilate substantive rabbinic law to Islamicate document forms (as I argued in Chapter 2). In this case, while Geniza scribes borrowed these clauses from Islamic contracts, they did not

(Maimonides, *Responsa*, no. 347; see Friedman, "Social Realities"). Even these reforms, however, were narrowly targeted and did not address most aspects of marriage covered by the early twelfth-century agreements. (We also have no way of knowing how, or how successfully, Maimonides enforced them.)

37. T-S J 3.27. See Krakowski and Rustow, "Formula as Content."

38. A few queries and reconciliation documents do describe husbands' efforts to break their promises. See, e.g., ENA 2922.30a and T-S K 27.45 (both queries about men who wanted to violate contract pledges about their wives' place of residence), and T-S 16.35 (a reconciliation agreement about a similar case, discussed in Chapter 8).

simply copy them undigested. Instead, they Judaized many of them—most obviously by translating them into Aramaic for use in *ketubbot*, and more subtly in Judeo-Arabic documents by tailoring them to fit rabbinic marriage and divorce law.

This Judaization is most readily apparent in the stipulations' content. Many of the eight common clause types discussed above engage rabbinic law in some way, most often by directly modifying rabbinic norms, a move that is likewise common in Geniza legal documents. For example, eleven documents in my corpus promise wives rights to their own labor, exempting them from the rabbinic principle that ordinarily grants the husband control of his wife's labor. These stipulations not only directly amend rabbinic law; six of them do so explicitly, by addressing the classical rabbinic idea that the husband gains this prerogative in exchange for supporting his wife.[39] As is typical of this varied corpus, they do so in different ways: one document grants the wife labor rights but requires her to clothe herself—a direct inversion of the rabbinic bargain—while the other five state that the husband must supply her clothes regardless.[40]

Less obviously but more importantly for my purposes, Geniza scribes also changed these stipulations' uses, by embedding them in a rabbinic framework different from the one they inhabit in Islamic marriage contracts. This framework explains how these Islamicate clauses were supposed to work as legal instruments in rabbinic courtrooms.

Rabbinic Divorce and the Dower

Non-*ketubba* Geniza marriage agreements assume the same economic framework as the *ketubba*, in which marriage makes the husband liable both for the value of his wife's dowry and for a dower payment to her (the groom's *mahr*, divided into early and deferred payments).[41] These rabbinic debts resemble their Islamic counterparts in some respects, but not in all. Islamic law does not recognize women's dowries, so although most Muslim wives in medieval Egypt received dowries from their relatives at marriage, they are not listed in Islamic marriage contracts.[42] On the other hand, Islamic law recognizes the groom's dower but defines it differently from rabbinic law. Whereas the rabbinic dower is paid *only* at divorce or a husband's death, many early Muslim jurists opposed linking the groom's dower to divorce, preferring that it be paid straight

39. mKet. 5:9, bKet. 47b, 58b (which notes that a wife may opt out of this exchange, waiving her husband's support in exchange for control of her labor—precisely what one Geniza agreement dictates; see the following note).

40. She must clothe herself: T-S 12.537. She controls her labor but her husband must clothe her: Mosseri VII 16.1, T-S 20.109, T-S 24.9, ENA 2727.5, T-S NS J 363.

41. See Chapter 4.

42. Rapoport, "Matrimonial Gifts," idem, *Marriage, Money and Divorce*, 12–18.

away at the outset of the marriage.[43] This theoretical distinction may not have made much difference socially, since many Muslims used a portion of the *mahr* as a divorce payment despite Muslim jurists' opposition. But it did create concrete differences between Islamic and Rabbanite marriage documents.

Surviving Islamic contracts from ninth- to eleventh-century Egypt are careful to disentangle the *mahr* from divorce, often by naming a preset date by which the husband will have to pay his wife her deferred dower, or by stating that she may ask for it whenever she wants.[44] These contracts likewise avoid linking the personal stipulations they contain either to the groom's *mahr*, or to the couple's divorce. In contrast, non-*ketubba* Geniza marriage agreements connect all three of these dots—marriage stipulations, the deferred dower, and divorce. They most often do so through a formula attached to polygamy and concubinage clauses, which states that if the husband breaks his promise and marries a second wife or keeps a slave concubine, he will have to "pay (his wife's) deferred portion and divorce her, even if it is she who chooses to separate."[45]

This formula links Geniza marriage agreements to a characteristically rabbinic model of divorce—albeit one that may be unfamiliar even to readers well versed in Jewish law, because later medieval rabbinic authors abandoned it. It was commonplace, however, among gaonic and other Rabbanite authors in the Middle East through at least the thirteenth century. At its core, rabbinic divorce is a male privilege tempered by the *ketubba* payment: a husband may divorce his wife at will, even against her wishes, but must pay her *ketubba* if he does so.[46] Classical rabbinic texts qualify this rule in two ways. On the one hand, a "rebellious" (*moredet*) wife who refuses to have sex with her husband loses rights to her *ketubba* and can be divorced freely.[47] On the other hand, a husband who denies his wife support or basic material pleasures also loses his unilateral divorce rights; he must divorce her and pay her *ketubba* even if he does not want to (an outcome expressed through the standard rabbinic phrase *yoṣi ve-yitten ketubba*, "he divorces her and pays her *ketubba*").[48]

43. Rapoport, "Matrimonial Gifts," 5–16.

44. Rapoport, ibid., 9–10, and see, e.g., Mouton, Sourdel, and Sourdel-Thomine, *Mariage et Séparation à Damas*, no. 3.

45. Versions of this formula also appear alongside some residence clauses (e.g., in Mosseri VII 16.1 and T-S Misc. 8.97). A few other agreements state that the groom must pay a fine if he violates a certain pledge, e.g., T-S AS 145.60 (attached to the polygamy clause). Some tenth- and eleventh-century Palestinian-formula *ketubbot* state that the wife may *not* claim her deferred dower before the marriage ends, an explicit contrast to Islamic document conventions. Friedman, *JMP*, 1:279–280.

46. mYev. 14:1: "A woman goes out (i.e., is divorced) willingly or unwillingly, but a man sends (her) out only willingly." On the *ketubba* as divorce payment, see Friedman, "Minimum *Mohar* Payment."

47. mKet. 5:7, tKet. 5:7, pKet. 5:7, bKet. 63b-64a.

48. See mKet. 7:1–5, 7:9–10; tKet. 5:6–7, 7:1–7; bKet. 77a.

Medieval Rabbanite jurists read these texts as creating what is essentially a bilateral divorce system centered on the dower. A wife who wanted to divorce her husband could force him to do so by "rebelling" and forfeiting her *ketubba*.[49] (In practice, the sum that mattered was the much larger deferred *mahr*, technically considered an addition to the *ketubba*.) But she could also try to force him to divorce her without forfeiting this money, by demonstrating that he had oppressed her and was required to "send her out and pay her *ketubba*." Some gaonic jurists broadened this model by stretching the concept of *yoṣi ve-yitten ketubba* to include any form of documented abuse: "If a woman said, 'I don't want this man, divorce me from him' because he had mistreated her—if she had witnesses to this, the law (requires him to divorce her and pay her *ketubba*)."[50]

Marriage Stipulations in Divorce Negotiations

This dual model of the "rebellious" wife and the husband who "must divorce and pay" explains the practical value Geniza marriage stipulations may have held for litigants in rabbinic courtrooms. Geniza documents and responsa alike suggest that throughout the eleventh to thirteenth centuries, rabbinic courts in Egypt and Syria managed divorces through a legal framework substantively identical to this Rabbanite model, even though Geniza documents almost never use rabbinic language to describe it (the terms *moredet* and *yoṣi ve-yitten ketubba* rarely appear in Geniza discussions of divorce).

The "rebellious wife" (*moredet*) side of this equation has been discussed extensively in prior scholarship, most thoroughly by Mordechai Akiva Friedman. Friedman demonstrates that Geniza women often sued for divorce by agreeing to forfeit their deferred dower—in Rabbanite prescriptive terms, by "rebelling" against their husbands to end the marriage.[51] (Geniza documents, however, more often refer to these women as having "ransomed" themselves, using the Arabic word *iftidā'*—a cognate term in Islamic texts for *khul'*, an Islamic form of wife-initiated divorce closely similar to the rabbinic *moredet* model. Geniza documents do not use the term *khul'* itself.)[52] "He must divorce and

49. Later medieval rabbinic jurists viewed this model as a gaonic innovation, a view that modern scholars have sometimes endorsed. But Robert Brody has demonstrated that the *ge'onim* understood the Talmud itself as allowing women to do this. See Brody, "Were the Geonim Legislators?" 290–304. Cf. Maimonides, *MT*, *Ishut*, 14:8–14. For a review of rabbinic jurists in medieval Christian Europe who interpreted Talmudic law differently, see Riskin, *Women and Jewish Divorce*, 93–129, and cf. Westreich, "Compelling a Divorce?"

50. *Halakhot Gedolot*, in Lewin, *OHG*, *Ket.* no. 475; see further Friedman, *JMP*, 1:332. Not all gaonic jurists agreed; for example, *TG ha-Qeṣarot*, no. 135, states that a husband who beats his wife must pay a fine but does not have to divorce her.

51. Friedman, "Termination," "Ransom-Divorce," "Divorce upon the Wife's Demand," *JMP*, 1:312–346, "Government Intervention," 218–222.

52. *Khul'*: Spectorsky, *Women in Classical Islamic Law*, 39–40, 124–128, 171–176; Rapoport, "Matrimonial Gifts," 28–31; Fierro, "Ill-Treated Women."

pay" (*yoṣi ve-yitten ketubba*) divorces have received less attention. Yet they too are visible in the Geniza legal record, when women sued for divorce but claimed their deferred dower nonetheless, on the grounds that their husbands had mistreated them. For example, in a deed drafted in Ramla in 1015, Malika bt. Rawḥ appoints an agent to sue her husband for divorce and "two years' alimony (*mezonot*), dower, and any jewelry he has taken from me," claiming that he had failed to support her and had neglected her sexually.[53] Both types of suit assume the same basic rabbinic model of the dower as a contingent debt, to be paid at divorce depending on how each spouse had behaved and which one of them was divorcing the other.

It is here that spousal stipulations could make a difference to both spouses within marriage, but especially to women. Once written into a marriage agreement, they expanded the range of legal arguments each could use against the other, sometimes by making it easier for husbands to cast their wives as "rebellious" and divorce them freely, but more often by making it easier for women to claim a compensated *yoṣi ve-yitten ketubba* divorce. Only polygamy clauses state this directly (the husband "must pay her deferred portion and divorce her, even if it is she who chooses to separate"), perhaps because they were inherently more enforceable than other types; court officials controlled the production of *ketubbot* and so could prevent a man from taking a second wife,[54] whereas they could not restrain him from traveling abroad or seizing his wife's profits after he had promised not to. But other stipulations implicitly affected claims about the dower in the same way, an outcome that granted them whatever degree of coercive power they possessed. This is suggested by these stipulations' placement; in many agreements they appear within the groom's pledge to give his wife her dower. It is also easy to see from surviving questions sent to Rabbanite jurists, which presume as a matter of course that pledges in a marriage agreement increase women's legal claims to the dower. Take, for example, a query sent to Maimonides in the late twelfth century: may a man divorce his wife without paying her dower because she refuses to move with him to a different city, "if she has no stipulation in her *ketubba* obliging him" not to move her?[55] The question suggests that a woman whose marriage agreement did contain a residence clause could not be discarded so easily. Relatives who worked to insert these stipulations into a daughter's marriage agreement did so for this reason: in hopes of giving her greater bargaining power against her husband during the marriage, but also in case it dissolved.

53. T-S 13 J 1.2.

54. See above, n. 35.

55. Maimonides, *Responsa*, no. 202. Geniza reconciliation agreements about spousal abuse also make this outcome explicit: the husband must stop beating his wife, or he will have to divorce her and pay her *ketubba*. See, e.g., T-S AS 151.24 (Fustat, early twelfth century); Bodl. MS Heb. c. 28.7 (1148); T-S 8 J 6.16 (Fustat, 1252).

MARRIAGE STIPULATIONS AS SOCIAL TOOLS

Beyond the pages of responsa and legal codes, however, even this limited protection was not worth much on its own. Strong marriage agreements gave women greater legal rights to their dowers but not the means to actually acquire them. Women's real power to use these marriage agreements depended not just on legal principles but also on other people: their birth relatives, husbands, and in-laws, as well as court personnel. Human contingency affects how law works in all legal systems, of course. But married women appearing before the *bet din* were especially vulnerable to the social settings of rabbinic legal practice, because Geniza courts' executive weaknesses produced gendered effects that hit women especially hard.[56]

Women and Rabbinic Court Culture

The first hurdle women faced stemmed from rabbinic officials' inability to physically punish or even effectively fine litigants. The *bet din* typically responded to divorce suits by trying to mediate peace between husband and wife (Arab. *ṣulḥ*, Heb. *piyyus*) before either issuing them a reconciliation agreement redefining the terms of the marriage or divorcing them.[57] A woman's marriage agreement held meaning only as long as her husband remained committed to this process. Not all men did. Rather than face the demands rabbinic mediation might involve, many simply abandoned their wives—some by refusing to support *or* divorce them, others by migrating to a different region where local rabbinic authorities did not know them and they could marry someone new.[58]

We read about these cases mainly when wives complained, either to their husbands or to communal officials.[59] An unusually frank Geniza letter from a husband to a communal official named Ḥisday is an exception, and demonstrates that even regular patrons of the *bet din* sometimes left their wives in this way.[60] The letter is undated, but may perhaps be from early thirteenth-century Fustat. Its author was not indifferent to rabbinic law. He had begun negotiating his case in rabbinic court, and cared enough to appeal to Ḥisday and perhaps other Jewish communal officials too, since a surviving query sent to the *ra'īs* Avraham Maimonides seems to describe the same marriage (the

56. These effects are examined closely in Zinger, "Women, Gender and Law," a work that has transformed my thinking about this subject, and without which I would not have arrived at the ideas presented in this section.

57. See Krakowski, "Female Adolescence," 210–211, a tentative reconstruction building on Goitein, *Med. Soc.*, 3:260–272, Friedman's studies cited above, n. 51, and David, "Divorce."

58. Goitein, *Med. Soc.*, 3:189–205.

59. On letters to husbands, see Zinger, "Long-Distance Marriages," 25–30; to communal officials, see immediately below.

60. T-S 8 J 14.2.

basis for our letter's tentative dating).[61] Yet he baldly states that if Ḥisday does not issue him a divorce deed immediately, he will walk away from the case—and from his wife:

> Either you yourself divorce me from her, or I will leave her and travel far away, never to see her again, and she will be left chained in living widowhood. But if you give her a divorce deed from me, and set her deferred dower on me in installments, as you rule . . .

The letter unfortunately breaks off here, but the author's intent is clear. He wants Ḥisday to let him pay off his wife's dower in installments after he has divorced her, effectively allowing him to avoid paying it at all.[62] Otherwise he threatens to leave her without a divorce, trapped in a dead marriage and unable to remarry. This threat illustrates not only how a husband's desertion could harm his wife, but also the power this option gave men in divorce negotiations. Men's freedom to walk away from the *bet din* made it risky for women to press too hard for their dowers, no matter how impeccable their legal claims on paper.

Even when a woman's husband did not run away, she faced further problems from court officials, who were likely to ignore her claims unless a man advanced them for her—usually a male relative, since Geniza women did not socially affiliate with nonkin except through marriage, and could not call on connections they had formed through marriage when divorcing. A wife's legal outcomes thus hinged in large measure on the social position of her own father, brothers, uncles, and cousins, and on the connections she maintained with them.

This hurdle, too, can be understood as a product of the *bet din*'s bottom-up authority. Because Jewish leaders depended on their subjects for political support, they inevitably favored legal outcomes that could help them cultivate social associations with other men: networks of patronage shared among litigants, scribes, and judges alike, in which women could not directly participate. In this climate, court officials were naturally predisposed against women who approached them to sue a husband without another man's support—which is to say, without anything to offer in the "calculus of benefit" on which Geniza society ran.[63] Of course, these two obstacles were not entirely unrelated, since a woman whose kin connections gave her greater pull with court officials could likely exert greater social pressure on her husband too, especially since she was

61. JNUL Heb. 4 577.5/21. The sender in both cases has been identified as Shelomo b. Eliyyahu, son of the chief Rabbanite judge of Fustat in this period; see Chapter 8, beginning at n. 76.

62. On this point, see Zinger, "Women, Gender and Law," 148-152.

63. For this phrase, see Mottahedeh, *Loyalty and Leadership*, 78; Rustow, "Formal and Informal Patronage," 344.

more likely to have married a man who was himself embedded in these same social networks and had more to lose from running away.

Rabbinic leaders' bias against socially isolated women is easiest to see at its limits, in petitions these women sent in hopes of securing a male patron in the one other way available to them—by convincing a *ra'īs* or lower communal official to intervene in court on their behalf.[64] The fact that women could write directly to Jewish officials, alone among all men not related to them, attests to a unique form of gendered political patronage within Jewish communities that deserves fuller explanation than it has received so far. But sponsorship procured in this way, even from the *ra'īs* himself, seems to have yielded a poorer range of outcomes for women than they could obtain with help from their relatives.[65] (Women could also turn to Muslim *qāḍī* or *maẓālim* courts for help, as we know from the many petitions in which they threaten to do just that.[66] But because the Geniza tells us little about how Islamic courts treated women who did so, my focus here is limited to the rabbinic legal sphere.)

A petition sent sometime between 1127 and 1139 by the wife of Adam al-Ṣayrafī (the money-changer) to the *ra'īs* Maṣliaḥ b. Shelomo is typical of these appeals. After describing her fruitless attempts to obtain a divorce without a man to represent her in court, she begs Maṣliaḥ to step in and issue a ruling, even if it means she must give up her claims to a dower:

> For eight months I have been requesting a divorce over and over, without success. . . . By the religious law you cherish! Look into my situation and give me a judgment, whatever it may end up being. I had appointed an agent (*wakīl*) to represent me, but because of all he did for the man, he said he would no longer enter in between us. I am bashful; I have no tongue to speak with. . . . I have no one but God and you in your mercy.[67]

Both the procedural details this letter mentions, and the formulae it uses, suggest how far women's legal rights depended on their male kin. As here, many Geniza documents mention wives appointing an agent to represent them against their husbands—an indication that even at the level of formal legal process, women fared better in divorce when a man spoke for them. But this passage also underscores that some women had no man attached to them who cared enough to do so, much less to throw his weight around behind the

64. These petitions have not yet been studied as a genre. Mark Cohen discusses them together with charity petitions from abandoned wives, widows, and divorced women in *Poverty and Charity*, 143–146; *Voice of the Poor*, 83–94.

65. See more on this point in Chapter 8.

66. Oded Zinger is now working on documents that mention these threats: idem, "Medieval Jewish Women in Jewish and Muslim Courts."

67. Bodl. MS Heb. d. 66.16.

scenes on their behalf. In this case, the man Adam's wife had appointed—probably a relative, but perhaps a distant one—felt a stronger social obligation to her husband than to her, and eventually refused to keep representing her. (This seems to me the only way to read the enigmatic line: "because of all he [her husband] did for the man, he said he would no longer enter in between us.") Without his backing, she was unable to command court officials' attention ("I have no tongue to speak with"), and appealed to Maṣliaḥ to take charge of her case, emphasizing her social helplessness through a loneliness formula that appears in almost all women's petitions of this kind: "I have no one but God and you."

In contrast, documents about women who did have someone besides God and the *ra'īs* show what a difference this made to court officials. These women did not narrate their own appeals. Their stories appear instead in letters exchanged between men, letters that interweave some of the formulae used in women's petitions with a different vocabulary: the language of male reciprocity. A letter sent by Shela b. Mevasser, the chief Rabbanite judge of Alexandria from 1079 to 1103, to a man named Abū al-Ḥasan Surūr b. Ḥayyim in Fustat is a textbook example.[68] It responds to an earlier letter in which Abū al-Ḥasan had thanked Shela for helping his daughter in a marriage dispute with her husband. Shela accepts Abū al-Ḥasan's gratitude (*shukr*) and explains that this was no more than his duty "for many reasons—the first being her loneliness and isolation; and also because I am obliged to help the people of my city with their affairs; and also out of honor (*ikrām*) for (you), my lord—just as (your) . . . favor (*faḍl*) extends over the elite and the common people alike." By mixing terms usually applied to socially isolated women ("her loneliness and isolation") with others typical of patronage discourse in Geniza letters (*shukr, ikrām, faḍl*), Shela highlights his generic moral obligation as a judge to help Abū al-Ḥasan's daughter in her father's physical absence, even while making clear that he has actually helped her as part of an ongoing exchange of benefaction between the two men. In fact, this exchange animates the passage itself; after accepting Abū al-Ḥasan's thanks for promoting his daughter's interests, Shela goes on to thank Abū al-Ḥasan in turn for having represented him in an unspecified matter at the court of the *ra'īs* (that is, the *bet din* of Fustat) even though the *ra'īs* is currently upset with him. This passage and others like it explain why women supported by a father or other male relative also received greater support from rabbinic officials, especially if the man was socially prominent. A well-connected man like Abū al-Ḥasan could assimilate his female kin into his own web of mutual benefaction, transforming their standing with court officials and thus their legal outcomes.

68. T-S 13 J 17.5.

Marriage Documents and Women's Kinship Support

The rabbinic courts' loose hold on litigants and concomitant culture of patronage stacked the deck heavily against women at divorce. Reviewing a wide range of Geniza evidence for marriage disputes, Oded Zinger has concluded that Jewish men rarely paid their wives the whole dower they had promised them at marriage, no matter how badly they had treated them when married.[69] Many women described in the Geniza ended their marriages only by "ransoming" away their dower entirely; others managed to extract some money from their husbands, but not as much as they had been promised. (Medieval Islamic divorces seem to have followed a similar pattern, although not necessarily for the same reasons, since *qāḍīs* wielded different powers from rabbinic judges. Islamic literary sources likewise suggest that *khul'* divorces in which women gave up some or all of their dower were pervasively common in Egypt at least through the Mamluk period.)[70]

Against these odds, what could the promises preserved in a marriage agreement really achieve? In theory, many of these stipulations gave women extra legal privileges in marriage by increasing the financial claims they could make on their husbands at divorce. In practice, they probably held weight in court only to the extent that a woman's male relatives promoted her right to them. Even a girl lucky enough to have entered marriage with a highly favorable agreement stood little chance of enforcing it without help from her natal kin. I have argued throughout this chapter that beginning in the twelfth century, young women's relatives used rabbinic marriage agreements to dictate their future legal rights. But the broader Geniza record thus suggests something more: a woman's ability to enforce these rights depended on her continued affiliation with her birth relatives during her marriage as well as at its start.

What prompted relatives to champion a married daughter or sister in court, long after she had left their formal care? The self-interest inherent in this help is obvious, although Geniza letters rarely mention it. A man who helped his daughter or sister to reconcile with her husband, or extract a dower from him, thereby lessened the likelihood that she would have to turn to him for money. The moral ideas about obligations between kin that Geniza Jews *do* frequently invoke[71] likely played a role too. But some documents suggest a further motive impelling men who intervened to support a married daughter, sister, or niece against her husband and in-laws: their own social honor. Take, for example, the beginning of a legal query sent to Maimonides from Alexandria about a young woman whose husband demanded that she reduce her promised dower by thirty dinars—not because of anything she had done, but to insult her relatives:

69. Zinger, "Women, Gender and Law," 130–173.

70. Rapoport, *Money, Marriage and Divorce*, 69.

71. See Chapter 1.

> A man married a woman in Alexandria, and wrote in her (marriage agreement) that he would give her a deferred dower of 100 Egyptian dinars. She was a daughter of the elite of Alexandria. She bore him a son, and when he was almost three months old, her husband fought with her relatives and took an oath before witnesses that he would divorce her unless she deducted thirty dinars from her deferred dower, intending thereby to triumph over her relatives. When her relatives heard about this, they were furious; how could he decrease her deferred dower when she had done nothing wrong? They viewed this as a great disgrace and prevented her from agreeing. He came before the court, and they informed him that he could not compel her about this.[72]

The original Judeo-Arabic text of this passage has not survived, which means that we cannot map the words it uses to denote prestige and shame ("elite," "disgrace," and so on) against those common in Geniza documents. But even in Hebrew translation, it is clear that its author understood this wife's financial claim on her husband as a point of honor for her own relatives, a view he describes as shared by all parties to this case. This is why the husband tried to force her to decrease her dower: not because he had fought with her directly, but in order to score points in a dispute with her relatives. And it is also why they reacted to this demand with fury, viewing his attempt to reduce her dower when "she had done nothing wrong" (i.e., she had neither "rebelled" against him nor sued him for divorce) as socially humiliating—not only for her but also, it seems, for themselves.

A first marriage expanded most young women's social world, connecting them for the first time not just to their birth kin (or occasionally their replacements) but also to kin by marriage: their husbands and their husbands' relatives. It also made new wives conduits for relationships between people on both sides of this expanded network, especially between their husbands and their fathers and brothers. The book's next and final chapter will focus on this triangular relationship as it shaped women's experiences as young wives.

72. *Responsa*, no 365. The rest of the query concerns a legal stratagem the husband devised to cast his wife as a "rebellious wife" (*moredet*) and thus deny her dower.

CHAPTER EIGHT

In the Marital Household

AVRAHAM B. YIJŪ DIED BEFORE his daughter Sitt al-Dār entered the marriage that he had spent years arranging for her.[1] In 1156, she married her cousin Peraḥya in Fustat without either of their parents present. Peraḥya's father, Yosef, wrote him from Mazara, Sicily, shortly afterward, urging him to bring Sitt al-Dār there, so that he could help guide the couple into married life, and in particular, guide Sitt al-Dār into her new role as a wife:

> I would be uneasy about the two of you if you were absent from me even for a moment. I would like you to leave quickly and come to me, you and your cousin, so that I can finish her training (*tarbiyya*) under my guardianship (*ḥajrī*), and rejoice in you both, and in her.[2]

Having entered marriage as economic and social dependents, it is no surprise that girls like Sitt al-Dār did not achieve full social adulthood immediately after the wedding. Letters and responsa alike continue to term young brides "little one" (*ṣaghīra*) and even "baby" (*ṭifla*) well into their lives as wives and mothers.[3] But if this much seems to have been true for all women, the circumstances in which young brides reached adulthood could differ sharply. Yosef expected to live together with his daughter-in-law and to exercise some form of social authority over her. But not all Geniza Jews shared this expectation, and in any case it could have been demographically possible only for a small minority of couples. Other wives lived with their own relatives rather than their husbands', or alone in nuclear households.[4] And individual wives' standing varied even within similarly shaped households. Yosef's plan to "train" his young daughter-in-law seems benevolent, but this idea could also harden into

1. On this marriage, see Chapter 6.
2. T-S 16.288.
3. Goitein, *Med. Soc.*, 3:162.
4. See Chapter 1.

exploitation and mistreatment, visible in Geniza documents that describe women physically or verbally abused by their husbands' fathers and other relatives.

Between these extremes lay many factors that determined both the shape of the household that a new wife entered and the position she occupied within it: her social class, her dowry and marriage agreements, the physical space in which she lived, her relationships with her birth relatives, these relatives' ties with her husband and his relatives, and her physical proximity to both sets of kin. This chapter follows girls into the marital household through two case studies that bring to life how these variables could interact to shape their position there—especially the kin relationships that I have emphasized as central to women's social positions. The first half of the chapter focuses on a corpus of legal documents regulating wives' living conditions in marriage, the second on the story of a single marriage, captured in a group of personal letters between a husband and his in-laws.

A Bayt *of One's Own: Young Wives in the Marital Household*

My first case study takes place in the courtroom. Among the personalized Geniza marriage agreements from the twelfth and early thirteenth centuries discussed in Chapter 7, a small number dictate the bride's coresidence with family members: with whom she will live once she is married, for how long, and under what conditions. Longer versions of these stipulations also appear in some reconciliation agreements from the same period: documents drawn up for married couples renegotiating the terms of the marriage, usually after either the husband or wife had sued for divorce.[5]

Read as a group, these clauses contain some of the best information about household composition preserved in the Geniza corpus. I discussed them in Chapter 1 as an index of household formation, which suggests that Geniza Jews lived in a wider variety of domestic groupings than has been assumed. But they are equally interesting as evidence for young wives' personal positions within households. Because they address living arrangements seen as potentially contentious, coresidence clauses preserve a shadow portrait of social tensions surrounding women's entry into marriage.

In what follows, I examine a subset of these clauses that grant wives the right to eventually leave a patrilocal household. Although they are framed as legal safeguards against abuse, I argue that these "exit rights" clauses worked most effectively to strengthen some women's domestic autonomy within

5. Marriage reconciliation documents appear in the Geniza from as early as 1007 (PER H 82, a wonderfully intimate agreement from an Egyptian village), but most date to the twelfth century.

patrilocal households as a mark of their social honor—and by extension, that of their own relatives. These clauses thus suggest how the web of extended social relationships created by a woman's marriage could affect her within it; not just her formal rights before the *bet din*, but also her everyday life within her marital household.

DOMESTIC SPACE AS LEGAL PROTECTION AND AS SOCIAL PRIVILEGE

To briefly review the basic forms of the coresidence clauses preserved in the Geniza, I have identified 29 coresidence stipulations in marriage documents, dated mainly between 1100 and 1250.[6] Twenty-three appear in premarital agreements and six in reconciliation agreements. Almost all address the wife's lodging rather than the husband's, a convention that suggests Geniza Jews understood husbands to be responsible for their wives' lodging, although this is not the case in rabbinic law—another instance in which Geniza documents' social assumptions parallel Islamic law more closely than Jewish law.[7] Most require the wife to live in a joint patrilocal household, with her husband's mother, parents, or siblings; a sizable minority require her to live in a joint matrilocal household, with her own mother or parents; and a very small minority (two documents only) state that she will live in a neolocal or nuclear household, without any other relatives at all.

This much is suggested by the specific relatives that coresidence clauses mention, the subject of my discussion in Chapter 1. Here my interest lies in the clauses themselves, especially the social ideas about women, kinship, and households they reflect. Not all women who joined an extended household at marriage had this detail recorded in their marriage agreements. What impelled some couples and relatives to fix these arrangements in writing? This question can be readily answered for about half of these 29 clauses.

Conditional and Unconditional Coresidence Clauses

Taken as a whole, coresidence clauses reflect two sets of competing anxieties: marriage both disrupted physical attachments among kin and dragged nonkin into uneasy proximity in joint households. Almost all the surviving matrilocal clauses, and a subset of the patrilocal ones, mitigate the first of these anxieties by promising relatives on both sides that the marriage will not "separate"

6. See Chapter 1, at n. 38 and after.

7. Islamic law includes lodging within the support that a husband owes his wife (see below, ns. 22–23), but classical rabbinic law does not. (Maimonides, *MT*, *Ishut*, 13:3, responds to this discrepancy by assimilating lodging to the husband's obligation to "clothe" his wife, a further example of the legal adjustments discussed by Cohen, *Maimonides and the Merchants*.)

them from a child or sibling—either stipulating that the bride will live with her own parents or mother, or sometimes that her husband may not move her away from them (e.g., "he will live with her and her parents in the *dār* . . . he will not separate (*yafruqu*) her from them [. . .] as long as they both live"), or that she will live with her husband's parents or mother, sometimes adding that *she* may not separate him from them (e.g., "she will not separate (*tafruqu*) him from his mother").[8]

These promises are easy to understand. While they may well reflect an affective ideal that birth relatives should live together, they also respond to evident economic concerns. The households that they prescribe had almost certainly been formed from financial need—either because the husband owned or paid rent for his mother's and siblings' lodging; or because he lived in space that they owned and could not afford to house his wife elsewhere; or in the case of matrilocal clauses, because the bride's mother or parents had given her their own dwelling as part of her dowry but needed to keep living in it.[9] These unconditional coresidence clauses thus protected relatives' economic interests, compelling a new wife to live with them and so ensuring that their joint household would not dissolve with her marriage.

In contrast, the other subset of these clauses is less transparent. Most privilege the opposite anxiety, protecting the wife from the discomforts of cohabitation by allowing her to "separate" from her husband's extended relatives: she will live with his parents or siblings, but only so long as they do not harm her, or only so long as she remains willing to do so (e.g., "she will live with his mother and with his brother in one dwelling, as long as no harm comes to her from them," "if she hates living with his father and mother, he must lodge her wherever she chooses").[10] The two premarital clauses I have loosely labeled "neolocal" go further, promising the wife she will not have to endure her in-laws at all, e.g., "he must lodge her in a separate place designated for her, and not compel her" (here some text is missing, presumably "to live with anyone," because the next preserved words are "neither a nonrelative or a relative").[11]

8. "He will not separate her": T-S NS J 378; "She will not separate him": ENA NS 21.6 (both undated). Other such documents: Matrilocal: Bodl. MS Heb. a. 3.32, T-S 13 J 6.33, T-S 10 J 27.3a, Mosseri VII 10.1, T-S J 3.27, JTS Marshall 8229 (a reconciliation agreement); Patrilocal: T-S 20.8 + 12.552, RNL Yevr.-Arab. I 1700, 17b; ENA 2727.5; T-S 24.9; ENA NS 21.6, ENA 3792.1; T-S Misc. 25.140 (a reconciliation agreement).

9. See Chapter 1, n. 56.

10. "As long as no harm comes to her": T-S 8 J 5.22 (1162, Fustat); "If she hates living with his father and mother": T-S 13 J 8.24 (undated). Other such documents (all patrilocal): T-S NS 224.104, Mosseri VII 16.1, T-S K 15.65, T-S 20.36, T-S NS J 457, T-S Misc. 8.97, ENA 3755.6. Four reconciliation agreements address wives' residence rights in a patrilocal household; see below, n. 19.

11. T-S AS 151.244 (undated). The other "neolocal" clause appears in T-S 8 J 5.3 + NS 259.37.

These conditional clauses benefited the wife alone, forwarding her interests at the expense of her husband's relatives. Why did some women's relatives negotiate these clauses for them?

Private Space and Social Honor

At first glance, the documents themselves supply an obvious motive, one noted by all scholars who have worked on them. Many of the conditional "exit rights" clauses preserved in this small corpus specify that the bride will live with her in-laws as long as they do not harm her (as in the clause cited above, "she will live with his mother and with his brother in one dwelling, as long as no harm comes to her from them"). Scholars from Goitein onward have read this language straightforwardly, understanding these stipulations as intended to protect young wives from physical or verbal abuse.

But on closer inspection, this language performs a narrower and more specific legal function. Rather than simple expressions of concern, these references to in-law abuse are shorthand legal arguments, framed with direct reference to Rabbanite divorce law. This becomes clear once we compare these clauses to gaonic-Rabbanite discourse about women's residence rights vis-à-vis their in-laws, a topic first addressed in a responsum attributed to the mid-ninth-century Iraqi *ga'on* Paltoy b. Abbaye:

> If the people of the house, such as her[12] mother-in-law or her sister-in-law, constantly fight (with her), he is legally required to bring her out to another place, for "*no man lives together with a serpent in a basket*."[13] And if he does not bring her out, he divorces her and pays her *ketubba*. Such is the law and such is the custom.[14]

Paltoy here permits a wife harassed by her in-laws to sue for a no-forfeit divorce, allowing her to end the marriage without losing her claim to her *ketubba* (an idea rooted in the legal model of divorce discussed in Chapter 7). This ruling extends a broader gaonic view, endorsed by the early digest *Halakhot Gedolot* and some later gaonic jurists, that a husband who "torments" his wife in any way must divorce her and pay her *ketubba*.[15] (Recall that in contrast, classical rabbinic texts required husbands to "send her out and pay her *ketubba*"—*yoṣi ve-yitten ketubba*—only in a handful of specific cases.) Although not all gaonic jurists accepted this expansion of *yoṣi ve-yitten ketubba*, a number of reconciliation agreements from this period suggest that it was

12. Lit. "his," clearly a scribal error.

13. In the Talmud this phrase explains why a husband who refuses to support his wife must divorce her and pay her *ketubba* (Ket. 77a).

14. Cited in Me'ir b. Barukh of Rothenburg, *Responsa*, Crimona ed., no. 291 (Lewin, *OHG, Ket.* no. 474). A variant version appears in Elfenbeim's edition, 4:81.

15. See Chapter 7, n. 50.

recognized by court officials in twelfth- and thirteenth-century Fustat, at least in theory.[16] These agreements promise the wife that she may divorce her husband and demand her *ketubba* if he beats or insults her, a direct echo of *Halakhot Gedolot*.[17] Similarly, our coresidence stipulations echo Paltoy's ruling that a husband whose relatives mistreat his wife must also "send her out and pay her *ketubba*" if he fails to move her away from them.

This parallel explains why so many of these stipulations mention the bride's mistreatment by her husband's relatives. Like many of the Geniza marriage stipulations I discussed in Chapter 7, these clauses increased the wife's legal right to a financially compensated divorce, in this case allowing her to sue for divorce without forfeiting her deferred dower if she could demonstrate that she had been harmed by living with her husband's relatives and that he refused to move her elsewhere. However sincerely intended, their language about harm did not arise only from worry about the young bride's immediate welfare, but also reflects an effort to strengthen her legal position vis-à-vis her husband should she eventually divorce him.

THE WIFE'S BAYT *BETWEEN NATAL AND MARITAL KIN*. If allusions to women's mistreatment in coresidence clauses reflect a prescriptive legal formulation of the wife's domestic rights, other passages in this corpus, and beyond it, hint at a different *social* concern at stake in these agreements: her access to a room (*bayt*, in Geniza texts not a house but a self-enclosed chamber within a *dār*) or set of rooms (*ṭabaqa*) set aside for her exclusive use, usually within a larger *ṭabaqa* or *dār* shared with her husband's relatives.[18]

This theme appears only rarely in premarital documents, in the two "neolocal" documents that promise brides they may live apart from their husbands' kin. But it is prominent in the handful of surviving reconciliation agreements that mention women's place of residence. Among the six

16. Postgaonic Rabbanite authors did, however, accept Paltoy's narrower assertion that a wife may demand to be moved away from in-laws who mistreat her, e.g., Maimonides: "If she says, 'I don't want your mother and sisters to enter my dwelling, nor to live with them in one courtyard (*ḥaṣer*, equivalent to *dār*) because they mistreat me and vex me'—they must heed her." *MT*, *Ishut*, 13:14. Cf. Yiṣḥaq al-Fāsī, *Responsa*, ed. Leiter, no. 235; *TG Sha'arei Ṣedeq* 4:4:42 (by Yosef ibn Avitur); Yosef ibn Migas, *Responsa*, no. 101.

17. See, for example, T-S AS 151.24 (early twelfth century, Fustat), Bodl. MS Heb. a. 3.40 (1128, Fustat), and Bodl. MS Heb. c. 28.7 (1148, Fustat). Two reconciliation agreements in our corpus use similar language: T-S 13 J 2.22, T-S 6 J 2.2. Of course, all of these agreements also suggest the *bet din*'s incapacity to enforce this stance, since they address complaints that women had already brought before the court—meaning that in practice, a wife who sued her husband for abuse may have been less likely to receive her deferred dower than to receive a piece of paper promising she would receive her deferred dower in the future if he continued to beat her.

18. On the terms *ṭabaqa* and *bayt* in Geniza documents, see Goitein, *Med. Soc.*, 4:56–59.

reconciliation documents I have identified, four dictate that the wife would now be granted a *bayt* or *ṭabaqa* of her own within the patrilocal household in which she had been living.[19] Passing references in responsa further suggest this promise was a commonplace goal of marital residence complaints. For example, a legal query addressed to Avraham Maimonides offhandedly describes a woman whose marriage agreement had contained a generic residence clause ("residence is up to her," *suknā bi-yadihā*, common in surviving agreements from the early thirteenth century); shortly after the marriage began, she "requested separation (*infirād*) and a chamber (*bayt*) to herself."[20]

Rather than casting the wife's *bayt* as a protection from domestic abuse, some passages instead link this space to her social autonomy from other relatives in the household, especially from other women. A reconciliation deed composed in 1102 in Tyre (or perhaps Tripoli al-Shām) promises the wife exclusive right to an upper apartment in the *dār* she shared with her father-in-law and his wife; they were now required to "move to the middle (a word is missing here, possibly *ṭabaqa*) and not ascend [to her] . . . nor harass anyone who comes to care for her."[21] (For a more elaborate example that focuses on the wife's independence from her mother- and sister-in-law, see the document about Sitt al-Nasab discussed below.)

The idea that a wife may demand a *bayt* of her own has no parallel in Jewish law. But like other social concepts recognized by Geniza Jews that I have examined in this book, it directly echoes Islamic legal discourse. Unlike rabbinic law, Islamic law considers lodging (*suknā*) part of the basic spousal maintenance (*nafaqa*) a husband owes his wife. This aspect of marriage law was elaborated in greatest detail by Ḥanafī jurists in Iraq and Syria from the eleventh century onward. These jurists universally defined the wife's lodging as a secluded living space set apart exclusively for her—either an entirely separate dwelling (*dār mufrada*) or more minimally a separate room (*bayt*), possibly within a larger household but isolated from its other female inhabitants, e.g., her mother-in-law or her co-wives.[22] Some authorities concretized the separateness of this space by requiring that the wife's *bayt* possess a lock. The parallels between this Islamic legal definition and our Geniza marriage agreements suggest that both reflect a common conception of women's

19. T-S 8 J 4.18c (Tyre or Tripoli al-Shām, 1102), T-S 16.35 (1119, Fustat), T-S 13 J 2.22, and T-S 6 J 2.2 (both undated).

20. T-S K 27.45. "Separation and a *bayt* to herself" seems to function as shorthand here, since in this case the wife was asking not only for a private room, but to leave the patrilocal *dār* entirely.

21. T-S 8 J 4.18c.

22. See Spectorsky, *Women in Classical Islamic Law*, 180–183, Meron, *L'obligation alimentaire*, 202–209.

domestic space diffused among Jews and Muslims across the medieval Middle East.[23]

Among Jews and Muslims alike, it is tempting to view the wife's *bayt* and the social independence it allowed as intended to foster young wives' self-determination—a medieval Egyptian version of Virginia Woolf's "room of one's own" (equipped, Woolf specifies, with "a lock on the door").[24] This idea is appealing, but almost certainly incorrect. Geniza coresidence agreements do not emphasize women's social autonomy as a value in and of itself, but only under certain circumstances: when they lived in a shared household with nonkin. In contrast, matrilocal stipulations, with their unconditional promises to keep the bride together with her mother or parents, kept women socially enmeshed with their birth relatives, whether or not they wanted to be. An undated marriage document listing the conditions of a Karaite-Rabbanite marriage notes explicitly that she may not live apart from her mother even if she wants to: "She will not depart from residing with her mother, nor separate from her. Even if, God forbid, the girl (herself) requests this, she will not be assisted in doing so."[25]

Rather than encouraging married daughters' independence for its own sake, Geniza Jews more likely viewed the wife's *bayt* as a means to emphasize her social standing within her marital household, which her own kin sought to ensure specifically when they had sent her to live among nonrelatives. A formulary written by the court scribe Ḥalfon b. Menashe (fl. 1100–1138) suggests this explicitly.[26] This document lists a set of Judeo-Arabic marriage stipulations together with their Aramaic *ketubba* equivalents, including the standard Judeo-Aramaic formula "if she (the bride) hates living with the groom's mother, he must lodge her separately from her"—rendered in Aramaic in a more elaborate formulation that describes her control of a separate apartment as a status marker:

> If so-and-so, this his wife, wishes to live in an apartment alone, *as is fitting for her*, and not to live with the mother of so-and-so, this groom—he must do as she wishes, and may not compel her in this matter at all.

The phrase "as is fitting for her" suggests that the private apartment available to this bride functioned as a symbol of her social standing, a reading supported

23. The two sets of texts explain this private space differently, however. Whereas Geniza agreements tie the wife's *bayt* to her domestic autonomy and social honor (as I suggest below), Ḥanafī jurists explain it as a way to ensure conjugal privacy and protect her movable property.

24. Woolf, *A Room of One's Own*, 103, 105.

25. T-S 13 J 6.33.

26. ENA 3755.6.

by other clauses in this document that identify her as an elite woman: she is promised a female slave to serve her "all the days of her life," and the groom pledges to "honor" her (*yukrimuhā*). Similarly, the reconciliation agreement from Tyre (or Tripoli al-Shām) dated 1102 cited above that grants the wife an autonomous apartment also states she will have "someone to serve her," and it requires her husband to use an honorific (*al-raḥma*) when mentioning her deceased parents.[27]

THREE IN-LAW DISPUTES AND THEIR OUTCOMES

How did these two foci—Rabbanite legal ideas about protecting wives from harm on the one hand, and an Islamicate social emphasis on married women's private space as a status symbol on the other—affect women once they entered marriage?

The second of these themes provides a better clue to our documents' practical meaning. Young women *were* vulnerable to mistreatment by husbands and in-laws in patrilocal households, but efforts to strengthen women's residence rights through rabbinic marriage documents did not do much to change this. Instead, the primary outcome of these efforts was to allow some women—not necessarily those who had suffered abuse—a measure of physical and social autonomy from the nonkin women among whom they lived. Three very different documents about agreements over the wife's coresidence illustrate this discrepancy. [28]

"None of Them May . . . Take from Her Even a Matchstick"

A detailed agreement composed in Fustat in 1118 describes the outcome of a residence dispute between Abū al-Ḥasan Shelomo b. Menashe *ha-kohen* and his wife Sitt al-Nasab bt. Abū al-Munā Yiṣḥaq.[29] The document opens with a short anonymous narrative describing the history of their disagreement: Sitt al-Nasab had entered marriage on the agreement that she would move into a *dār* with his relatives, but that she could ask Abū al-Ḥasan to relocate her to a private space (*makān mufrad*) "if she hated living with his mother and sisters"—a right she put into action several months into the marriage, demanding "relocation and separation (*furqa*) from them after words passed between them." Abū al-Ḥasan obliged by moving Sitt al-Nasab to a different dwelling, but then found this arrangement impossible: "His heart remained divided, and the rent was too much for him, and it was difficult." He asked Sitt

27. T-S 8 J 4.18c.

28. My discussion of the first two of these three documents builds on Marmer, "Patrilocal Residence."

29. T-S 16.35.

al-Nasab if she would agree to move back to the original *dār* if he placed her in a separate apartment from his mother and sisters.

The body of the document then cites testimony given by Sitt al-Nasab's paternal uncle Abū 'Alī, a rabbinic court trustee.[30] Addressing Abū al-Ḥasan, he presented the terms under which Sitt al-Nasab would be willing to return to the shared *dār*:

> Her paternal uncle Abū 'Alī addressed him, saying, "I do not wish to harm you, nor to separate you from your sisters; but I also do not want to harm my niece. She agrees to return with you to (that) place and to live with your sisters, as long as they and your mother are in the room facing the road, and she is in the inner apartment, in an isolated space of her own, designated for her. None of them may freely come and go into her (space), nor ask her for anything, nor take from her (even) a matchstick, for example. . . . And she will have authority over her living space, exclusive of them, with regard to her food and expenses and the rest of her needs, without associating with them in any way whatsoever."

If the women violated these conditions by intruding on her in any way, Abū al-Ḥasan would have to move her out again. The document ends with Abū al-Ḥasan's agreement to these terms, guaranteed against an enormous fine of fifty dinars payable to the poor of Fustat.

This is one of the most robust defenses of an individual woman's rights within marriage preserved in the Geniza. For my purposes here, it is remarkable for two reasons: first, because the document makes clear that it was a direct product of demands made by her uncle, a man court officials knew and respected. This uncle, or perhaps other relatives of Sitt-al-Nasab's, also seems to have held social pull over her husband, as suggested by his deference to her demands at each stage of this story. Second, because although the document uses the legal discourse of "harm" in passing ("I do not wish to harm my niece"),[31] it makes equally clear that Abū 'Alī made these demands not from fear that his niece had been or would be physically or verbally abused—neither possibility is mentioned—but rather to promote her domestic autonomy from her mother- and sisters-in-law ("she will have authority over her living space, exclusive of them, with regard to her food and expenses and the rest of her needs, without associating with them in any way whatsoever").

30. *Al-ne'eman.* On this office, see Goitein, *Med. Soc.*, 2:80–82.

31. "Harm": *ḍurr*, which like *muḍājara* (discussed below, at n. 36), is used in Geniza legal documents for a husband's legally consequential mistreatment of his wife, e.g., T-S 13 J 22.21, administrative letter, early eleventh century; T-S 12.129, reconciliation agreement, late eleventh–early twelfth century.

"He Will Not Permit Her to be Tormented"

A second reconciliation document written by the same court scribe less than two decades later, in 1135, also promises a wife separate living space from her husband's mother and sister—not to ensure her autonomy but to protect her from harm.[32]

The document's beginning is fragmentary, but enough remains to suggest that Ṣedaqa (his patronymic is effaced) appeared in court after his wife, the daughter of Shabbetay (her first name is effaced), had sued him for divorce. The court mediated an agreement between them, which the rest of the document preserves in full:

> He made her pledge that she would come and go (from the household) only by his command, and improve her relations with him according to what is required from Jewish woman of her station. . . . And he also pledged that neither his mother nor his sister nor any of his family may enter his wife's (living space). He will not permit her to be tormented, nor any of them to harm her. Nor will he raise his hand against her in violence, nor run away, nor hide himself as a runaway.

Ṣedaqa's promises indirectly reveal bt. Shabbetay's charges against him. She had accused him and his relatives of beating and insulting her, and Ṣedaqa of intermittently abandoning her without support, or at least threatening to do so. Beyond this, the document tells us little about bt. Shabbetay's broader life, a silence that is itself suggestive. She appears in court alone, with her husband but without a male representative, even though her patronymic indicates that her father, Shabbetay, was still alive. No earlier coresidence stipulation is mentioned, which means that she had probably married without one.

These details suggest that it was court officials, rather than bt. Shabbetay's relatives, who had urged Ṣedaqa to promise her a private room, and that they did so for legal reasons: Ṣedaqa was in Rabbanite legal terms a husband who "must divorce and pay" (*yoṣi ve-yitten ketubba*),[33] that is, he was legally required either to divorce bt. Shabbetay and pay her dower, or move her away from his relatives—an obligation fulfilled by his promise to keep his mother and sister out of her living chamber. This residence clause thus shows the *bet din* invoking an Islamicate social concept (the wife's private *bayt*) in service of a gaonic legal norm aimed at protecting wives. But stripped of the social motives that had animated Sitt al-Nasab's agreement, it invokes this law as minimally as possible—without any of the elaborate privacy safeguards promised to Sitt al-Nasab, and accompanied by a list of punitive conditions binding bt. Shabbetay to major concessions of her own in return.

32. T-S 13 J 2.22.
33. See Chapter 7.

"His Sister Took to Beating Her with a Shoe"

A third Geniza document from the thirteenth century brings the contrast between these two agreements into sharper focus. It is an administrative letter about a marriage dispute, sent by an unnamed communal official in Fustat to a local judge sometime between 1200 and 1240.[34] The letter describes a long campaign of harassment by the parents and sister of Sulaymān b. Hānī against his young wife (her name is not preserved, but she is termed *ṣaghīra*, "little one"):

> I have heard that his sister took to beating her with a shoe, and his father curses her whenever he comes in. . . . And now he wants to marry another wife. All of this is distressing to her. He evicts her from the room (*bayt*, here seemingly the family's common living space) every day. . . . Now, my lord, summon her opponent (her husband). If he wants to reconcile with her, he should pledge to treat her as common decency[35] requires a husband to treat his wife. And if he hates her, he should pay her what he owes her, if he is not destitute. His father and mother and sister have already ganged up on her . . . to the point that they have cast her out without support.

I understand the seemingly absurd understatement "All of this is distressing to her" to bear a technical meaning: the word *muḍājara* (distress or vexation) appears as a term for abuse by a husband in other reconciliation documents.[36] Its use here identifies this account as a formal charge of complaint against Sulaymān, written by an official clearly sympathetic to his wife, possibly because she had sent him a petition asking for help; like bt. Shabbetay, she seems to have lacked any supportive relatives. Despite this sympathy, the options he prescribes for her are limited: she may either divorce Sulaymān without compensation (as suggested by the caveat, "he should pay her what he owes her, *if he is not destitute*") or return to live with his abusive relatives, in which case Sulaymān should pledge in writing (i.e., in a reconciliation agreement) to treat her with "common decency."

This letter offers a glimpse beneath the surface of an abused wife's reconciliation document, revealing some of the conditions under which it might have been produced—and how little its protective language may have meant

34. ENA NS 16.30. For the date, see below, at n. 37, and cf. Chapter 5 at n. 14 and after. M. A. Friedman describes this document as a letter sent by the wife's father, because he reads the fragmentary first line as *azūju bintī*, "I married my daughter" (idem, *Jewish Polygyny*, 261). I read instead *azwaja bint*, "He married the daughter of . . ." See Blau, *Dictionary*, 277–278.

35. "Common decency": *ādāb*.

36. E.g., T-S 8 J 22.27, a petition to Maṣliaḥ *ha-kohen*, Head of the Jews in Egypt from 1127 to 1138 (I read this document differently from Goitein, *Med. Soc.*, 3:186; rather than demanding her delayed dower, the woman seems to agree to surrender it if her husband will return her dowry).

in practice. We do not know what happened to Sulaymān's wife, but if she ultimately reconciled with him, the "common decency" that he was supposed to promise her might well have included a nominal pledge about private space similar to the one that appears in bt. Shabbetay's agreement. Yet the letter nowhere stresses this point, and we can easily understand why. Sulaymān b. Hānī was a pauper; he appears as a recipient of public charity in a communal list from the early thirteenth century (from which this letter can be dated).[37] The residence he shared with his parents and sister was probably too small to contain a secluded living chamber, much less an extensive apartment like the one in which Sitt al-Nasab lived.

Excavations of Fatimid Fustat suggest what each of these two women's dwellings might have looked like. Sitt al-Nasab may conceivably have lived in a lavish building like the one depicted in Figure 8.1. The dwelling inhabited by Sulaymān, his relatives, and his wife more likely resembled the "dwellings of the poor" pictured in Figure 8.2, described by the excavators as two or three cramped rooms in which a family slept, above an equally packed ground floor open directly to the street, which was likely used for commerce or as a workshop or warehouse.[38] This likely contrast between these two women's living spaces reflects the general contrast between their overall circumstances—a contrast that also afforded them different legal rights in practice, if not on paper. Unlike Sitt al-Nasab's husband, Sulaymān would have had no practical way to give his wife a *bayt* of her own, even if he had wanted to. Nor did he have any real motive to do so; no matter how he and his relatives continued to treat her, she would remain unable to do much about it besides divorce him without receiving any dower.

Each of these three documents shows court officials responding to a woman's complaints about her life in a patrilocal household, with results inverse to those a literal reading of Rabbanite law would predict. Two of these women lived with in-laws who had humiliated, cursed, or thrown things at them—conditions that without question legally entitled them to be moved elsewhere. In at least one and perhaps both cases, the court upheld Rabbanite law by making the husband promise to physically isolate his wife. But neither promise is very convincing. One man (Ṣedaqa) agreed only if he were allowed to control his wife's physical mobility; the other (Sulaymān) could not realistically have afforded to provide his wife with separate space and had no incentive to do so. Not coincidentally, both of these women were also socially

37. BL Or. 5549.7.
38. Kubiak and Scanlon, *Fustat Expedition Final Report*, 2:10.

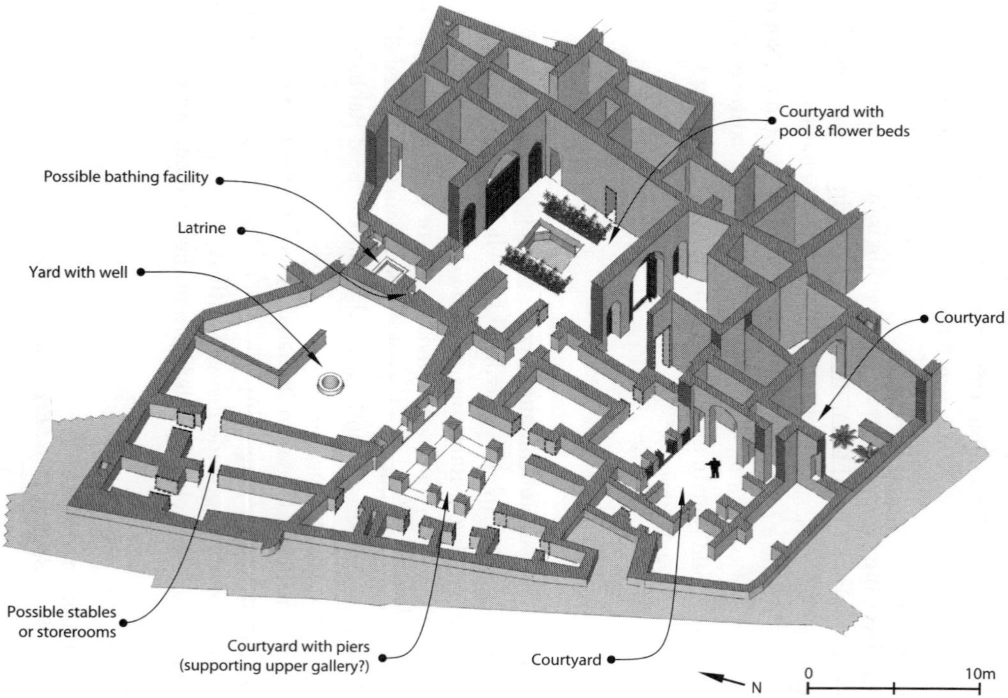

FIGURE 8.1. House 10, Fustat B. This illustration depicts a large *dār* of the kind that Sitt al-Nasab might have lived in. It was prepared by Dr. Matthew Harrison, who explains: "This building, House 10, was excavated under the direction of George Scanlon in 1965 at the site of Fusṭāṭ-B, on behalf of ARCE. This partial reconstruction is based on this season's preliminary excavation report, as a final report was never published (Scanlon, 'Fustat Expedition: Preliminary Report,' 87–100; Plans II and Iv; Section A-A). The report is brief for such a vast and complex building, and so the reconstruction should be read with due caution. Scanlon suggested that the house resulted from the jointure of two earlier Ṭūlūnid-era houses centred on courtyards—one centred on the courtyard with a pool and flower beds, another on the arcaded courtyard to its west—amalgamated in the Fāṭimid period. Hypothetical arches have been added to the entrances of rooms that may be interpreted as examples of *majālis* (sing. *majlis*), and their flanking chambers, *kummayn* (sing. *kumm*). Folding doors have been added to *majālis*, following Geniza descriptions [see Goitein, 'Mansion']. Several speculative entrances have also been added (marked with dashed lines) where a room had no surviving threshold. . . . No entrance from the street has been proposed as its location remains unclear, [although Scanlon suggested] that it was located in the south-west corner. As with House 4-4, wall-flues indicate an upper-story existed in at least some parts of the complex, though no staircase was recovered." Source: Matthew Harrison, personal communication, Nov. 1, 2016.

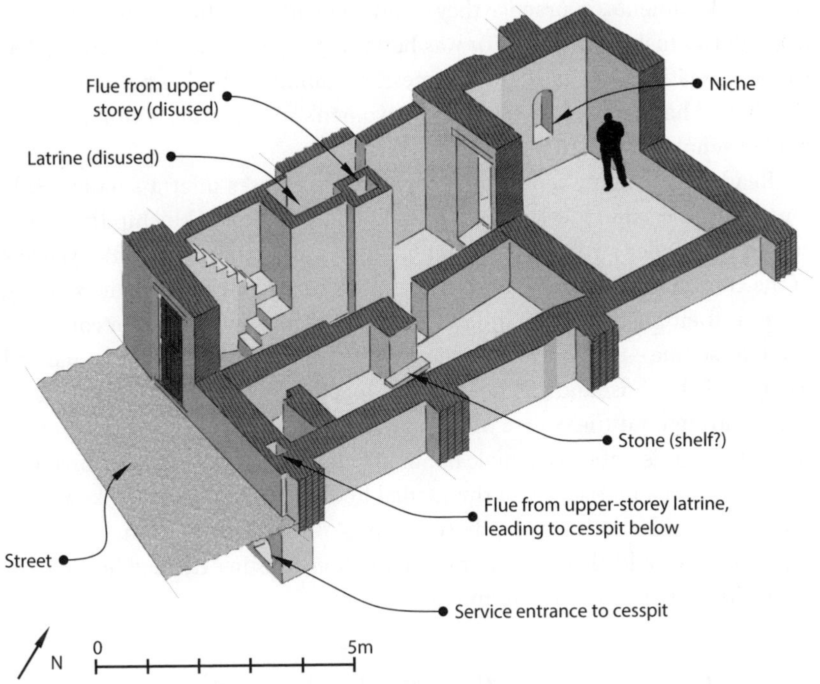

FIGURE 8.2. House 4-4, Fustat C. This illustration depicts a poorer dwelling. It was prepared by Dr. Matthew Harrison, who explains: "This building, House 4-4, was recovered during excavations directed by George Scanlon in 1980 at the site of Fusṭāṭ-C, under the aegis of the American Research Center in Egypt (ARCE). This partial reconstruction is based on the description given in the final excavation report (Kubiak and Scanlon, *Fustat Expedition Final Report*, 21–15; Plans II and III; Sections 4-4, 7-7, and 8-8). The recovered walls and floors indicate several phases of adaptation and use; this reconstruction represents the final phase before abandonment. Notably, the long dividing wall (running NE-SW) is proposed to be a later addition, meaning there were originally only two ground-floor rooms. The wall-flues (for evacuation of waste-water and sewage) and three surviving stairs indicate that at least one upper storey existed. Finds indicate that the house was occupied in the ninth and tenth centuries." Source: Matthew Harrison, personal communication, Nov. 1, 2016.

disadvantaged; at least one of them was very poor, and neither seems to have had relatives willing or able to champion their residence rights in court. In contrast, the third woman (Sitt al-Nasab) had suffered no legally compelling mistreatment. Her husband's mother and sisters seem not to have hurt her so much as annoyed her. But because she appeared in court supported by a locally prominent uncle, she obtained a detailed and credible guarantee of domestic privacy.

These documents thus suggest that although Rabbanite court officials routinely invoked rabbinic legal ideas about women's mistreatment when crafting documents, in practice they could do relatively little to protect women from abuse. Instead, the *bet din* was better equipped to help well-connected women's relatives safeguard their domestic autonomy for other reasons—most clearly, as I have argued, to signal these women's social status within the nonkin households they had joined at marriage.

Read in this light, conditional coresidence clauses offer a smaller-scale portrait of the same ideas surrounding honor and female kinship that I discussed in broader strokes in Chapter 7. There I argued from a bird's-eye view of the Geniza legal record that some women's relatives viewed their standing vis-à-vis their husbands and in-laws as a point of personal honor, or commensurately, shame—the logical outcome of a system in which a woman married partly to tie her husband and her relatives together in a social affiliation maintained throughout the course of the marriage. Most Geniza legal documents suggest how this notion of female honor affected a woman's legal and financial position when a marriage had threatened to unravel. Agreements like Sitt al-Nasab's go further, illustrating how relatives' investment in a daughter's domestic status could also shape her social relationships in extended households even when divorce was not imminent.

Sitt Ghazāl bt. Abū al-Faraj: The Story of a Marriage

The legal documents I have just examined reflect one limited means through which Geniza Jews negotiated the web of social relationships created by a couple's marriage—by producing and retaining rabbinic legal agreements. The second part of the chapter moves beyond the narrow arena of rabbinic document production to a more chaotic and intimate form of evidence: the prosopography of a single marriage, traced through a series of letters between the husband and his wife's relatives.

Most women who appear in the Geniza corpus appear only once, or at most in a handful of disconnected documents. It is rarely possible to trace an individual woman's personal history through this material, much less her experience of a marriage over time. One especially unhappy young wife, however, appears directly or indirectly in at least sixteen letters and legal queries focused on her brief, miserable marriage to her paternal cousin.[39] The marriage between Sitt Ghazāl bt. Abū al-Faraj b. Ḥasan of Alexandria and her cousin Abū al-Barakāt Shelomo b. Eliyyahu of Fustat is likely the most deeply documented in the Geniza corpus. Because this was Sitt Ghazāl's first marriage, and because it did not last very long—these texts were all written within a span of

39. For the full list, see Krakowski, "Female Adolescence," Appendix B. Most of these letters were published in Motzkin, "Judge Elijah," "Young Couple," and "Thirteenth-Century Teacher"; several remain unpublished, including two that M. A. Friedman has recently suggested adding to this dossier: idem, "Marital Crisis," 73–81.

about three years—these letters also provide the clearest picture we have of any young woman's transition from unmarried daughter to wife. Several previous studies have described aspects of these letters, but not as evidence for women's experiences in early marriage.[40] Here I will revisit the Sitt Ghazāl dossier with an eye to understanding how the relationships between her birth relatives and her husband shaped her own relationship with him and with his relatives, as a means of breathing life into the often abstract account of this question that I have offered thus far on the basis of more formal legal texts.

Inevitably, Sitt Ghazāl's story is a tragic one. A happier marriage would not have left behind such significant written traces. It is also exceptional. Shelomo emerges from these letters as an unusually difficult person whose behavior struck his own contemporaries as shocking. In tracing the history of their marriage, it is not always possible to distinguish which of his statements and actions reflect socially normative ideas and practices and which stem from his particular personality. Nonetheless, many of the social dynamics documented in these letters should sound familiar; they echo the arguments I have made throughout the previous chapters about how and why women's relatives supported them in marriage and the difference made by their support, besides adding new dimensions that rarely surface directly in either legal or personal documents. This corpus demonstrates in vivid detail how the broader social and family relationships in which marriage was embedded could affect a couple's private life.

SHELOMO TAKES A WIFE

Shelomo b. Eliyyahu was the younger of two known sons born to Eliyyahu b. Zekharya, chief judge of the Rabbanite *bet din* of Fustat in the first half of the thirteenth century (fl. 1210–1241), a period in which a series of earthquakes, famine, and plague seem to have shrunk both the city of Fustat and its Jewish population.[41] His older brother Abū Zikrī was a physician to the Ayyubid court in Cairo. Shelomo held an assortment of less exalted jobs in Fustat, working simultaneously as a children's religious teacher, cantor, court scribe, and petty communal functionary. Some portion of the family's papers seem to have been preserved and deposited as a group in the Geniza; Shelomo is therefore known from several dozen letters besides those related to his marriage. As previous scholars have noted, he emerges from this archive as a complicated

40. See the articles by Motzkin and Friedman cited below, ns. 42 and 77; Goitein, *Med. Soc.*, 3:30, 60, 186, 263.

41. Eliyyahu also had at least two daughters, and possibly a third son who died young: Motzkin, "Judge Elijah," 27, Goitein, *Med. Soc.*, 5:175–177. On Fustat and its Jews in the early thirteenth century, see Goitein, *Med. Soc.*, 2:103, 124, 128, 141; Russ-Fishbane, "Between Politics and Piety," 34–66.

and unpleasant man, consumed by anxiety about his health, finances, and personal status.[42]

Shelomo and Sitt Ghazāl were both children of an extended family network bound by an unusually dense cluster of endogamous marriages connecting them as both patrilineal and matrilineal kin. Her mother was his maternal aunt and her father his paternal cousin.[43] We know less about her immediate family, since they did not leave their own papers in the Geniza; but Abū al-Barakāt b. Ḥasan, Sitt Ghazāl's paternal uncle, who represents her in several of these letters, appears to have been a communal leader in Alexandria.

The story of their marriage begins in 1228 with a letter from this uncle to Shelomo's father, Eliyyahu b. Zekharya, praising him as a desirable bridegroom.[44] Most of the letter describes the resolution of a communal dispute in Alexandria over the appointment of a foreigner from Byzantium or Europe as the local *muqaddam* (appointed over local Jewish institutions in a given region by the *ra'īs al-yahūd*).[45] But before delving into this story, Abū al-Barakāt first apologized for having neglected to keep up his end of their correspondence ("your servant has been unable to correspond as my lord does, but my lord forgives his servant for his boorishness"), sent greetings to various relatives, and noted in particular that he had heard great things about Eliyyahu's younger son:

> I rejoice greatly in Abū al-Barakāt (i.e., Shelomo) . . . for everyone who comes from Fustat speaks well of him, on account of his acumen and devotion to knowledge; may God assist him in his pursuit of knowledge.

This comment has been seen as evidence that despite his unpleasant personality, Shelomo was a well-respected scholar.[46] I suggest that we should take Abū al-Barakāt's praise with a grain of salt—not because it is necessarily untrue that Shelomo was rabbinically learned, but because Abū al-Barakāt had a specific purpose for saying so, indicated in the letter's next line: "My reason for (writing) these lines is to inform you of my complete agreement with your suggestion to me . . . please honor me with a letter; perhaps the heart will show the way, because the matter requires reflection." Taken together, I read these lines as Abū al-Barakāt's way of expressing interest in Shelomo

42. Motzkin, "Judge Elijah," 45–72, idem, "Thirteenth Century Teacher."

43. Maternal aunt: T-S 10 J 18.6, T-S 13 J 8.23. His precise relationship with Abū al-Faraj is harder to trace; Motzkin identifies them as paternal cousins based on T-S 12.69, where Shelomo addresses Abū al-Faraj as "my *ibn 'amm*": idem, "Judge Elijah," 59, n. 1. Goitein instead identifies Abū al-Faraj as Shelomo's uncle, but does not explain why: idem, *Med. Soc.*, 3:434.

44. T-S 18 J 3.15.

45. Several waves of Jewish immigrants from France and the Byzantine empire settled in Egypt in the early thirteenth century. See Russ-Fishbane, "Between Politics and Piety," 67–97.

46. Motzkin, "Judge Elijah," 48, "Thirteenth-Century Teacher," 51.

as a prospective husband for his niece, Sitt Ghazāl, in response to an earlier proposal ("your suggestion to me") made by Eliyyahu or by Shelomo himself. By answering Eliyyahu's suggestion with compliments about Shelomo's scholarship and public reputation, Abū al-Barakāt was using the idiom of early thirteenth-century matchmaking correspondence to affirm Shelomo's desirability as a groom.[47]

Sitt Ghazāl had not been Shelomo's first choice of wife. The Geniza also preserves an earlier letter (discussed in Chapter 6) in which he proposes marriage to his paternal cousin Sitt al-Yumn.[48] But that proposal was rejected. In a letter to another paternal cousin (a different Abū al-Barakāt, the son of Abū al-Manṣūr al-Ḥarīrī), Shelomo mentions Sitt al-Yumn's recent marriage to a nonrelative with some bitterness:

> Hibat Allāh b. al-ʿAmmānī has married . . . my aunt's daughter (Sitt al-Yumn). Inform him that she is not honored by him, but he by her.[49]

This letter also contains our next piece of evidence for the story of Shelomo's marriage to Sitt Ghazāl. He had already become engaged or betrothed to her when he wrote it, and affirms in passing his intent to marry her soon: "I dearly miss . . . the little one . . . and wish to spend Passover only with her, that I may take her and go out."

Shelomo did eventually come to Alexandria to marry Sitt Ghazāl. He then brought her to Fustat and lodged her in his parents' home. A letter written to Eliyyahu by his son-in-law Simḥa uses standard congratulatory formulae to describe the couple's recent betrothal or marriage: "may God grant him male children and *may the woman who comes to his house be like Raḥel and Le'ah*."[50] But the next relevant document in the dossier suggests that their union began to fail almost immediately. In a long letter written shortly after their arrival in Fustat, Shelomo complains to Sitt Ghazāl's father, Abū al-Faraj, about her disappointing character, blames him for having foisted her on him, and asks Abū al-Faraj to write and chastise her, since he is too far away to discipline her in person:

> I wish (that you would write) us a letter, to admonish her . . . you have not written since we left you. . . . Tell her she must submit [. . .] to her about things, and she disobeys all of it. . . . She is your daughter, and I your brother, or son, or servant [. . .] me a girl who does not obey at all; rather, everything people [ord]er her (to do), she immediately disobeys. . . .

47. See above, Chapter 6.
48. T-S 13 J 18.22; see Chapter 6, at ns. 32–33.
49. CUL Add. 3343.
50. T-S 18 J 4.10. On this formula, see Chapter 6, n. 44.

> This is not hatred for her, but for her character. I say to her, "This thing—don't do it." She says, "No, I will not do it"; then she forgets and does it. May God improve her and her blessed character and characteristics; may He change them for the better. By God, O my cousin! If I were living with you, in one city, I would never separate from you, and *you* would improve her.[51]

The conflict between husband and wife that this letter captures appears to have been entirely genuine, and is echoed and fleshed out in later letters. But buried beneath Shelomo's litany of complaints against Sitt Ghazāl, he hints at two other issues, equally or perhaps more important, related to his relationship not with Sitt Ghazāl herself but with the letter's recipient: her father.

The first of these is reflected in Shelomo's request that Abū al-Faraj write him a letter; the second in his (insincere) expression of longing to live with Abū al-Faraj. Both questions emerge from later letters as driving concerns in the relationship between the two men.

SHELOMO AND ABŪ AL-FARAJ

Five later letters written by Shelomo to or about Abū al-Faraj survive.[52] None are dated, but they hint at a series of important events in the couple's life that serve as a rough guide to their chronological order. In what seems to be the first of these letters, Sitt Ghazāl is pregnant and receiving a visit from her mother (Shelomo's maternal aunt), Umm Abū al-'Izz: "My aunt mentioned that she came only . . . to visit on account of the cherished event, may God make it successful."[53] A second letter mentions Umm Abū al-'Izz's eventual departure without mentioning Sitt Ghazāl's childbirth;[54] but in a third, Shelomo states that the baby had died after three months—a loss that he mentions in a strikingly callous way, as a footnote to a detailed complaint about a minor financial loss: "Now . . . (this makes) four dirhams I have lost, together with what I have incurred over the baby girl—for she lived three months, and I lost, by the law of Moses, close to one hundred and fifty dirhams on her . . . because she died."[55]

51. T-S 12.69. Two details suggest that this letter was written at the start of the marriage: it is dated 7 Nissan, a week before Passover (around when Shelomo had said he intended to marry Sitt Ghazāl; see immediately above); and Shelomo mentions that the couple has recently left Fustat.

52. CUL Or. 1080 J 28, T-S NS J 97, T-S 20.174, T-S 10 J 18.6, and PER H 85.

53. T-S 20.174.

54. T-S 10 J 18.6.

55. PER H 85. This was not a typical way to respond to a daughter's death; for more standard responses, see Goitein, *Med. Soc.*, 3:227–228.

Yet none of these events receive nearly as much attention in Shelomo's letters to Abū al-Faraj as does his anxiety over the correspondence itself. This anxiety emerges full-fledged in the first of these letters, written during Sitt Ghazāl's pregnancy, which describes a humiliating incident.[56] An acquaintance had stopped Shelomo in public and accused him of mistreating Sitt Ghazāl, a rumor apparently started by a letter her uncle Abū al-Barakāt had sent to Shelomo himself:

> I went out of synagogue on the Sabbath and met . . . Abū al-Faḍl b. ʿAṭā b. Ḥasan . . . who said to me that Abū al-Barakāt . . . had sent me a letter. He said that he was inquiring into my wife's we[lfare], because I have greatly degraded her. . . . This pained me, and caused me very profound heartache, and I became extremely ill. . . . How did this distressing story reach him, such that (this) letter circulated to a stranger—what business is it of his?

This passage suggests that Shelomo and Sitt Ghazāl continued to have serious marriage problems; that her relatives were upset by the way he was treating her; and that they tried to retaliate by using letters to harm his reputation. (The anecdote suggests that Abū al-Barakāt or someone close to him had written to associates in Fustat describing his correspondence with Shelomo, likely to provoke the very type of social shaming he describes here.) But Shelomo's reaction is unexpected and revealing. While he is embarrassed by his encounter with Abū al-Faḍl, he expresses little concern for his social reputation as a husband; the rest of the letter says nothing more about his alleged "degradation" of Sitt Ghazāl. Instead, he goes on to complain at length about his own correspondence with Sitt Ghazāl's relatives—first, that he never received Abū al-Barakāt's letter, an omission that he understands as a deliberate slight; and second, that Abū al-Faraj, Sitt Ghazāl's father, has not written him either: "You no longer consent to correspond with me, for which I am diminished, abased, and degraded, *a reproach among men, despised among people, a lowly worm.*"[57]

This diatribe sets the tone for the rest of Shelomo's preserved letters to Abū al-Faraj, which focus almost exclusively on his escalating distress that Abū al-Faraj is not writing to him. "Many Alexandrians have come (i.e., to Fustat), yet not one of them bore a letter (from you)—and I was worried . . . for I did not suppose that you would delay (writing to) me unless there were a compelling reason," he complains in one of these. Another, addressed to "Abū al-Faraj, with whom I am incensed," notes acerbically: "When our lord the *nasi* came, I was consumed with anxiety that he might have brought a letter

56. T-S 20.174.

57. Psalms 22:7. This self-abasing rhetoric is characteristic of Shelomo's letters: Motzkin, "Thirteenth-Century Teacher," 57.

from (you)—yet (you) did not send a letter with him. But he said that you were well—I was delighted to hear it!"[58]

The same agitation also spills over into his correspondence with others. For example, a letter sent to another relative, Abū al-Barakāt al-Ḥarīrī, directs him to pressure Abū al-Faraj on his behalf: "Greet my in-law . . . Abū al-Faraj al-ʿAṭṭār, and inform him that I strongly censure his cutting off of his letters. I have already sent him many letters, and have received nothing by way of reply."[59] Like the letter written during Sitt Ghazāl's pregnancy, these letters focus less on the marriage itself than on Shelomo's anxiety about his correspondence with his father-in-law. They invoke Sitt Ghazāl only occasionally, and primarily as moral ballast to convince Abū al-Faraj to write to Shelomo; e.g., "Your daughter is extremely well, and lacks for nothing except to see you, and that you not cut off care for her through your cherished letters."[60]

Shelomo's obsession with his father-in-law's letters may seem petty and peculiar. But it reflects a real social concern that would have been clear to both men. The letters preserved in the Geniza were written not just to communicate information, but as a means of creating, signaling, and maintaining personal relationships, and hence the personal honor that these relationships could generate. Political, commercial, and purely social letters alike represent themselves as a miniature form of *niʿma*—benefactions the writer conferred upon the recipient that affirmed and maintained their affiliation with each other.[61] For one party to deliberately sever an established written correspondence (*inqiṭāʿ*) was thus a highly charged act, one that weakened or even ended the relationship itself.[62] Shelomo's anxiety about Abū al-Faraj's missing letters was thus not really about the letters themselves, but about the strength of their in-law alliance (*ittiṣāl*)—an alliance that had likely helped motivate him to marry Sitt Ghazāl in the first place. As we have seen, many Geniza documents stress the importance of *ittiṣāl* to marriage choices; Shelomo's letters are unique in suggesting how a rupture between male in-laws might directly affect the young wife whose marriage had brought them together. In this case, Shelomo's disappointment that his in-law alliance with Abū al-Faraj had not yielded an active and durable bond between them seems to have

58. T-S 10 J 18.6; PER H 85.

59. CUL Or. 1080 J 28. Similarly, in a letter to Abū al-Faraj's brother Abū al-Barakāt b. Ḥasan, Shelomo complains that he has written Abū al-Barakāt four times without receiving a reply, and has not heard from Abū al-Faraj in four months (T-S NS J 97).

60. T-S 10 J 18.6.

61. See Franklin, "More than Words on a Page," Goldberg, *Trade and Institutions*, 85–88. (Shelomo explicitly describes his correspondence with Abū al-Faraj as a form of *niʿma*, T-S 20.174.)

62. Cf. Chapter 1, around n. 78.

overshadowed his interest in the marriage itself, allowing him to mistreat Sitt Ghazāl without fear of the social consequences.

It is harder to know how Abū al-Faraj understood his role in this relationship. Only one letter of his to Shelomo has been identified. It expresses little interest in the question of their correspondence and provides no explanation for his ongoing failure to send the letters that were so important to his son-in-law. (This may reflect a more general imbalance in the correspondence between the two sets of cousins; the first letter in our group, in which Sitt Ghazāl's uncle Abū al-Barakāt tentatively approves the match, also includes his apology to Shelomo's father, Eliyyahu, for having failed to write him, here, too, using the term *inqiṭāʿ*.)[63] The letter does suggest, however, that Abū al-Faraj remained concerned about his daughter and tried to intervene on her behalf; he reprimands Shelomo and asks him to treat her well: "May God not show us ugliness (*makrūh*) in you! . . . I have only your servant Sitt Ghazāl in your care; you know that no one remains to her but you."[64]

Abū al-Faraj's letter also emphasizes a second issue at stake in this correspondence: the couple's place of residence. Even while affirming his daughter's total dependence on her husband ("no one remains to her but you"), Abū al-Faraj tried to regain a measure of control over her fate by urging Shelomo to return her to her birth family's *dār* in Alexandria, "that we may remain as we (ought), one with the other."[65] For their part, Shelomo's letters suggest both that Abū al-Faraj must have repeatedly pressed him to move to Alexandria, and that he had no intention of doing so. Although he states several times throughout this correspondence that he hopes to eventually return Sitt Ghazāl to her family's *dār*, he also takes pains to stress that the move will remain impossible for the foreseeable future.[66] Indeed, Shelomo seems to have resented Abū al-Faraj's attempts to protect Sitt Ghazāl with her relatives' physical presence in any way.

This is, at any rate, one way to understand a strange exchange over the visit that Umm Abū al-ʿIzz paid them during Sitt Ghazāl's pregnancy. In his letter from this period, Shelomo expresses outrage at the idea that Abū al-Faraj may have urged his wife to attend her daughter in childbirth.[67] Abū al-Faraj's lone extant reply, written afterward, seems to answer this charge by reassuring

63. T-S 18 J 3.15.

64. T-S 20.135.

65. Although Abū al-Faraj does not say so here, Sitt Ghazāl's move to Fustat had been at issue in the initial negotiations over her marriage. A later letter sent to Shelomo by another of her relatives after the marriage had deteriorated reminds him that her family in Alexandria had been reluctant to let her leave the city in the first place, but had finally agreed to do so in good faith, believing that he would treat her well (T-S 13 J 8.23).

66. T-S 20.174.

67. Ibid.

Shelomo that his mother-in-law had actually come for an entirely different reason ("Your aunt did not come out of love for the little one; she came to you only in hopes of [arranging] a marriage [between] your niece and her son").[68] Shelomo, it appears, wanted to remain socially connected with his in-laws, but only at a distance; he wanted their affiliation publicly recognized through their letters to him, but not reinforced by daily contact.

THINGS FALL APART

Abū al-Faraj died two or three years after his daughter married Shelomo. This event is not directly discussed in the extant corpus of documents about her, but it is revealed by two further letters, sent to Shelomo by unnamed relatives of Sitt Ghazāl's in Fustat, which describe her as an orphan.[69] These letters suggest that Abū al-Faraj's death permanently altered Sitt Ghazāl's position in her marital home, constraining her options for negotiating with her husband and his family, and eventually perhaps contributing to the demise of her marriage itself.

Both letters center on Sitt Ghazāl's ongoing conflict with both Shelomo and his mother, Sitt Rayḥān. More specifically, both letters respond to Shelomo's accusations (leveled in letters that have not been preserved) that Sitt Ghazāl continued to be disobedient and stubborn: she was lazy and failed to do her housework properly; she was impudent and did not display proper respect toward Shelomo's relatives; finally, she was personally unkempt and did not groom herself. The first letter angrily defends Sitt Ghazāl from these charges and implies that Shelomo had attempted to discipline her by beating her.[70] It opens with the fragmentary and cryptic phrase "his beating (*ḍarb*) her every Friday,"[71] and goes on to lambast Shelomo as a boor who lacks empathy for his young wife:

> You say, "She does not comb her hair!" O intelligent one! If she were well, would she fail to comb her hair?! Indeed, if she were well, her body would be perfumed, her head combed, and her eyes painted with kohl. As for your statement that she is impudent (*waqiḥa*), she is of you and yours, your (wife) and your cousin! Does one Jew call another impudent?! Do you not know that this expression is equivalent to (calling someone) an *obstinate bastard, son of impurity*?! . . . And as for what you say, that she does not do her housework—your mother cannot know this; something has been concealed from her. How can any of the

68. T-S 20.135.
69. T-S 13 J 8.23 and Bodl. MS Heb. c. 28.64, written in different hands.
70. T-S 13 J 8.23.
71. Or perhaps "week" (*jumʿa*).

> housework be accomplished if you use *her* as the servant of the *dār*—she whom you know to be alone, a stranger, an orphan, and young?

It is hard to resist reading this description of Sitt Ghazāl's lassitude as an account of deep depression. Besides depicting her misery, the letter also suggests that part of the tension between her and her in-laws stemmed from conflict over her personal autonomy from them—the same question at stake in the coresidence agreements I discussed above. Already in Abū al-Faraj's lifetime his brother had complained of her "degradation"; this more detailed account reveals a specific struggle over her subordinate status within the household and willingness to subjugate herself to her in-laws through verbal expressions of respect, domestic labor, and perhaps subjection to physical discipline.

We have no way of knowing whether this struggle intensified around the time this letter was written, or whether it describes patterns of conflict ongoing since the start of the marriage. What does clearly seem to have changed is Sitt Ghazāl's range of possible defenses. For all its outraged rhetoric, this letter does not suggest any concrete response to Sitt Ghazāl's mistreatment; in the wake of her father's death, her relatives may have been unable or unwilling to do much to help her. Most notably, they abandoned Abū al-Faraj's efforts to convince Shelomo to physically return her to Alexandria.[72] Nor did they possess the same social leverage over Shelomo as had Abū al-Faraj. Shelomo himself does not seem to have cared as much about his affiliation with his remaining male in-laws as he had about his father-in-law; at any rate, no later imploring letters of the kind he sent to Abū al-Faraj have been preserved. Nor, finally, do Sitt Ghazāl's relatives seem to have considered legal action aimed at protecting her, perhaps because their own family ties to Shelomo rendered this distasteful, or perhaps because they were impeded by the practical consideration that Shelomo's father was the chief judge of Fustat.

Within these constraints, Sitt Ghazāl's relatives directed their remaining efforts at socially shaming Shelomo into better behavior. "All of us rely on your honor, and on your valor and piety and religious knowledge and noble lineage. . . . We know that you will not mistreat her, but will comfort her with your management and fine conduct," notes one of these letters, adding more pointedly that the author's brother had "sought to enter between you," that is, to come to Fustat and defend Sitt Ghazāl, but had been deterred by concern for both sides' reputations: "He was afraid of talk and of what would be said among the people of Fustat"—perhaps a veiled threat that this visit, and the embarrassment it would cause Shelomo, might yet be in store.[73] But the author made clear in the same breath that his support for Sitt Ghazāl was limited.

72. This may have been because of financial problems; a brief letter to Shelomo notes that their "livelihood" is severely constrained: T-S 12.301.

73. T-S 13 J 8.23.

The letter ends by instructing her not to aim for domestic independence, and instead to accept a subordinate position within Shelomo's household:

> O Sitt Ghazāl! Remember the training (*tarbiyya*) of your mother and father . . . as you would perform the orders of your father or grandfather or uncle, perform those of your great master the judge, and your husband and your aunt.

The letter unfortunately breaks off here, but its final legible word, the female imperative of "kiss," reveals that Sitt Ghazāl's "orders" centered on her formally expressing respect and filial subordination to her marital relatives; kissing hands serves in Geniza letters as a standard idiom for an adult child's reverence for his parents.[74] The second letter is more blunt: "Do not disobey what your aunt tells you with respect to housework. They seek only what is best for you . . . and you know that no one remains to you but God and them, and that no one greater than the *shaykh* (i.e., her father-in-law Eliyyahu) remains in (our) extended family (*'itra*); so serve him with the best of service."[75] In other words, when Sitt Ghazāl's father died, her husband's concern for the in-law relationship between them ended—and with it, the social support that had allowed her to claim some autonomy within her marital home. Orphaned as a young bride and lacking this support, she now had no choice but to affiliate fully with her marital relatives, assuming the same dependent position toward them that she had held among her own relatives as an unmarried girl.

THE UNCERTAIN END

This bleak strategy ultimately failed. Sitt Ghazāl seems to have eventually divorced Shelomo, although we do not know precisely on what terms, nor what happened to her afterward. Three remaining texts document the likely end of the marriage: a final family letter seemingly addressed to Shelomo (although he is never named; Goitein identified it as part of Shelomo's archive based on its handwriting, which is identical to that of another letter addressed to Shelomo's mother Sitt Rayḥān), and two legal queries apparently submitted by Shelomo himself.

All three documents demonstrate that by the third year of their marriage, both Shelomo and Sitt Ghazāl were ready to divorce; but they could no more agree on how to do so than they had on anything else.

Shelomo's two legal queries present his case, one addressed to his famous contemporary Avraham Maimonides and one to a little-known official named

74. See Goitein, *Med. Soc.*, 3:240.

75. Bodl. MS Heb. c. 28.64. *'Itra*: on this term, see Chapter 1, n. 69.

Ḥisday *ha-nasi*.[76] Both texts have long been known, but have been only recently, and I believe convincingly, connected to Shelomo, by Mordechai Akiva Friedman.[77] Neither jurist's response is appended to the query, which suggests that these were drafts that Shelomo prepared as he weighed his legal options, rather than finished copies that he actually sent. Both texts describe his grounds for divorcing Sitt Ghazāl: he had been duped into marrying her against his wishes and had found life with her intolerable because of her stupidity and bad character. "I have hated her for the baseness of her character and of her deeds. . . . They deceived me from the first, until I took her *against my will*," he complains in one; the other states simply, "What prevents me from staying with her is her bad character and frivolity." Alongside this apparently sincere dislike, Shelomo hints at a more immediate irritant in his query to Ḥisday. At some point after Abū al-Faraj died, Sitt Ghazāl's widowed mother, Umm Abū al-ʿIzz, had come to live with her, either as Shelomo's dependent or perhaps in an attempt to defend her mistreated daughter. Of this turn of events, Shelomo says only, "And now her mother is here."[78] But given his previous anger about his mother-in-law's visits, it seems possible that this move also helped convince him to divorce her daughter.

Whatever his motives, Shelomo composed both queries for the same reason: in hopes that either jurist would sanction his divorcing Sitt Ghazāl without paying her deferred dower. But here her relatives drew the line, as our final anonymous letter from Alexandria demonstrates.[79] Its author seeks to hold Shelomo responsible for at least some of this money, urging him to divorce his "poor, unhappy" wife, but stressing that he must do so on terms that she and her kin can accept:

> This marriage was arranged between you . . . if you wish to leave it, the separation must be negotiated between the two of you. . . . Cease drawing distinctions between their honor and your own.

Once again, the circumstances surrounding this letter are unclear; we have no way of knowing whether the relative who wrote it did anything tangible to try to force Shelomo to honor his debts to Sitt Ghazāl. His own queries suggest, though, that he took her relatives' support of her—which this letter too frames as a matter of both sides' "honor"—seriously enough that he believed he could not easily divorce her in Fustat without at least pretending to pay her.

Demonstrating the same oddly selective attention to legal and social propriety that he had displayed throughout his marriage, Shelomo therefore

76. T-S 8 J 14.2, JNUL Heb. 4 577.5/21. On T-S 8 J 14.2 as a hybrid legal query and petition, see Zinger, "Long Distance Marriages," 32.

77. Friedman, "Marital Crisis," 73–81.

78. T-S 8 J 14.2.

79. ENA 2808.36.

suggested to both jurists that he would divorce Sitt Ghazāl immediately and without payment, but he would agree to dole out her dower in installments at some future date—which meant that he would not really have to pay them.[80] One of the queries states baldly that if she refused, he would simply run away, leaving her a chained woman unable to remarry: "I will leave her and travel far away, never to see her again, and she will be left chained in living widowhood."[81]

Husbands who abandoned their wives are a dime a dozen in the Geniza corpus, but letters openly threatening abandonment are not. (Without connecting it to Shelomo, Goitein remarked of this query, "We are revolted by this letter.")[82] This passage illustrates Shelomo's characteristic indifference to his public reputation as a husband, an indifference that is hard to explain given his exquisite social anxiety in other domains. But it also illustrates how far the death of Sitt Ghazāl's father had exposed her. Trapped in a terrible marriage to a man no longer consumed by concern for his social relationships with her relatives, she was left with few options. Whatever protection her remaining kin could offer her, it was not enough to save her from potential desertion. Her best strategy may have been to renounce her financial claim on Shelomo and request an *iftidā'* divorce—likely what he wanted her to do. Unfortunately, this is the last we hear of Sitt Ghazāl. Until the Geniza turns up evidence to the contrary, we may hope that she managed to divorce Shelomo before he acted on his threat to flee Fustat, leaving her bound in an empty marriage and unable to remarry.

Conclusions: Kinship and Female Coming-of-Age through Marriage

Both the case studies reviewed in this chapter involve women who joined patrilocal households at marriage, living with their husband's parents or siblings. These women's experiences of early marriage are most visible in the Geniza corpus not because patrilocal households were a dominant norm—they were not—but rather because this type of living arrangement was subject to the greatest degree of negotiation between the birth relatives whom a wife had left behind and the relatives by marriage among whom she now lived. This visibility in our documents mirrors the growing social visibility these same women could achieve through marriage. One of this book's central findings is that a first marriage acted as a central milestone in the early lives of Geniza women, which transformed them from subordinate dependents, constrained

80. As noted Chapter 7, n. 62; see Zinger, "Women, Gender and Law," 148–152.
81. T-S 8 J 14.2.
82. Goitein, *Med. Soc.*, 3:204.

completely by their own relatives' choices and desires, to potentially autonomous social and economic agents expected to act for themselves.

This move may have run smoothest for women like Sitt al-Nasab (whose mother-in-law and sisters-in-law promised not to take even a matchstick from her), who moved away from socially powerful relatives at marriage while retaining strong ties to them. Entering a foreign household as their own relatives' social representatives, it was these women whose fathers, brothers, and uncles were most likely to promote their domestic agency and autonomy from the nonkin among whom they lived—more so than women rich or poor who continued to live with their own kin (about whose lives and struggles we hear tellingly little), and certainly more so than women who lacked robust kinship ties entirely. As Sitt Ghazāl's story demonstrates, this success depended on many factors beyond a woman's control; not only her own relationship with both groups of kin, but also theirs with each other. Women came of age as potentially autonomous adults through first marriage. Marriage itself, a transactional and often transitory bond among Geniza people, did little to ensure a woman's economic or social stability throughout the rest of her life.

Conclusion

THIS BOOK HAS MADE TWO central claims, each resting on many smaller ones, about the medieval Jews reflected in the Cairo Geniza documents. First, women lived lives shaped by the long-term relationships they maintained with their relatives (or in some cases, with replacement relatives who had helped to raise or support them before they married). This was not because they belonged to robust extended patriarchal families of the kind often thought to have prevailed throughout the premodern Middle East: few such families appear in the Geniza. Rather, women depended on their relatives because kinship bonds were the only enduring personal ties available to women in a society ordered by such loyalties. Dyadic ties among men—rulers, state officials, merchants, scholars, scribes, jurists, judges, physicians, tradesmen, and mendicants alike—have widely been described as central to the politics and economies of medieval Islamicate states and societies. But at least among Geniza Jews, women seem rarely to have maintained such ties in any of the ways on which past scholarship has focused, either with men or with each other. Kinship is the missing link in this equation. It, too, lay mainly in individual ties rather than in corporate groups; but unlike other social loyalties, kinship ties included women. This helps to explain how women fit into the patronage-based social order that this scholarship has described.

I have argued that Geniza women took part in this social order first and foremost through their fathers, brothers, uncles, and male cousins; less visibly but still discernibly through their mothers, sisters, aunts and female cousins; and finally through the minority religious community to which they belonged, and within whose courts of law they ratified many of their transactions.

What does this finding mean for the parts of young women's lives that histories of marriage and the family more commonly address? At what age did women marry, and with what property, and how old were their husbands? What kinds of households did they live in once they married? What labor, if any, did they perform either before or after marriage, and where, and for whose profit? The Geniza suggests answers to these questions, but only tentative and partial ones. The women who appear in Geniza documents may have married relatively young, in their teens and perhaps early twenties. Their husbands may often (but not always) have been relatively older. Few women seem to have remained permanently single. Polygamy was not the norm, but was not unheard of either. Once married, many women lived in extended households with relatives besides their husbands. Still, only the last two of these findings are reasonably certain.

Likewise our evidence for women's property and labor: it is clear that Geniza women received dowries when they married, dowries that they had sometimes helped to produce; and that these dowries contained most of the property they would own throughout their lives. Efforts to prepare a dowry thus dominated most women's adolescence and helped determine when and whom they married. Here again, some details remain fuzzy. Geniza dowries worked both as women's own inheritances and as an incentive to marriage for their husbands, who legally and perhaps in reality controlled them while the marriage lasted. But it is unclear whether these motives generally overlapped, or whether they reflect distinct models of the dowry characteristic among different social strata or in different times and places, which each fueled different types of household economies once a marriage began. Similarly, families strove to use unmarried girls' labor to increase their dowries rather than for other ends. There is no way to tell, however, whether poorer women thus delayed marriage for this purpose, or whether the reverse was true: only girls financially secure enough to remain unmarried for a longer stretch of time could afford to build their own dowries by working before marriage.

Geniza marriages and households resist easy answers to these questions. This is not only because some of our data is patchy. Geniza families are also difficult to pin down precisely because kinship in this world was valued between individuals rather than within corporate groups—a focus that allowed for many different forms of families, households, and perhaps domestic economies as well. The physical spaces in which Geniza Jews lived, the specific relatives with whom they lived, and the reasons for which they did so all varied and could change rapidly. So did the individual relationships between kin that made up a given person's extended family network at any point in time. Marriage among Geniza Jews was, moreover, an unstable bond; this is one of the reasons kinship mattered for women as it did. But that instability affected households and families in turn. Husbands and wives not only divorced often (often then remarrying, and sometimes remarrying each other); some (perhaps many) married couples lived apart some or much of the time, which meant that these couples' children lived apart from one or the other of their parents too.

What remains constant in our sources is thus not the structure of the families or households to which women belonged, but the support that their relatives could offer them, the advantages that they gained from kin support, and the problems created for them by its absence. Before marriage, a girl depended on her relatives—those within her household and who maintained ties with her—in every way. These relatives seem to have controlled her in every way as well. An unmarried girl's mother or father—or grandfather, grandmother, brothers, sisters, aunts, uncles, or cousins, or their replacements—fed and clothed her (or in the case of some orphan girls, used her own property to do so); decided where and with whom she would live; chose a husband for her; gave her a dowry with which to marry him; and managed her labor to increase the value of this dowry. They also negotiated her marriage contract, which dictated how much money her husband would owe her if the marriage ended (a debt that was rarely paid in full, but whose size helped determine her bargaining power at divorce and her power to demand legal help against her husband if he abused or abandoned her). From the twelfth century onward, they might also arrange for her contract to include clauses that, at least on paper, decided what her marriage would look like—what rights she would have, for example, to move freely beyond her household, or to keep her own wages, or to prevent her husband from taking another wife or concubine, or to decide in what city she would live, or with whom, or even how much autonomy she could maintain in a household shared with her husband's relatives.

All women did not always, or necessarily, depend this much on their relatives after they married; first marriage marked the beginning of adulthood, which is to say that it could partly or fully deracinate a woman from her relatives, for better and for worse. But most of the married women who appear prosperous and socially stable in the Geniza corpus—especially in legal documents that describe women in conflict with their husbands or in-laws—had relatives, usually men, fighting for them in the background. Conversely, the poorest and most desperate women—those who wrote petitions to Jewish communal officials begging for food or for relief from an abusive husband—describe themselves as kinless, or without relatives willing to help them. This is so even though these petitions demonstrate that Geniza women did have options beyond their kin: they belonged to a minority religious group whose leaders protected its members, at least in some measure. But the same culture of personal patronage that informed Geniza kinship also explains why these leaders helped kinless women only to a limited extent. Judges, scribes, and other Jewish communal officials were better able to help women backed by relatives with social clout, relatives who had the power to retaliate against these women's husbands and in-laws. Communal leaders were also more willing to help women with such relatives, whose social loyalties they themselves valued. This left women whose kin did not help them less protected by the wider Jewish community and its institutions too.

Why did men and women (but especially men) bother to look after their daughters, sisters, and nieces? Some possible aspects of Geniza marriage—early marriage for women and later marriage for men, high rates of women marrying, and extended households formed at marriage—resemble patterns that have been described as common to societies around the historical Mediterranean (a suggestion that remains heuristically useful even if it has not always held up empirically). But the values that this and related scholarship most often associate with Mediterranean as well as Middle Eastern women's kinship only partly match those captured in the Geniza.

These values include, in the case of the Middle East, the clan-based patrilineal solidarity that I find lacking among Geniza Jews. An associated preference for cousins to marry each other to strengthen this solidarity is also mostly absent from the Geniza corpus (except when individuals paid lip service to this preference in order to create links to relatives where none had existed). Likewise, women's kinship around the Mediterranean and throughout the broader Middle East has often been understood in terms of sexual honor and shame: a range of scholarship describes men past and present in both regions as zealously guarding their female relatives' chastity to safeguard their own honor—especially the chastity of young unmarried women. This code of honor has been seen as helping to explain why Mediterranean women tended to marry young, and why in some times and places they did not work before marriage, as women routinely did in northern Europe. Yet Geniza Jews appear scarcely preoccupied with unmarried women's virginity. While both men and women strove to limit some women's physical mobility beyond the household, these efforts appear motivated either by the efforts of husbands to control their wives—not those of fathers or brothers to control their daughters and sisters—or by a view of female seclusion as an elite status indicator that could mark women at any age. No corresponding shame attached to women of less elite standing who circulated freely beyond the household, either before they married or after. In neither case do our sources reflect special anxiety focused on young unmarried women and their movements in particular, by their relatives or anyone else.

Instead men seem to have staked their honor on their female relatives in a different sense. A man who maintained his daughter or sister or niece before her marriage, and then maintained a relationship with her after it, was following a moral imperative expressed throughout the Geniza corpus. But he could also benefit through his relationship with her by marrying her to a man whose loyalty he valued: in-law ties bound men together in ways that rendered marriage a form of patronage. These bonds emerge from the Geniza as a central concern driving marriage choices, at least among the well-connected class of merchants and scholars about whose private lives we know the most. Perhaps partly for this reason, relatives who continued to support a married daughter or sister socially after marriage understood her standing vis-à-vis her husband and his family to reflect upon themselves: their own honor was affected by how he treated her, by her autonomy from her mother- and sisters-in-law, by the financial pledges that her husband had made her, and by the extent to which he honored them.

A married woman's relationship with her husband thus mattered not only to the couple, but often also to the woman's relatives. Her ties to them and theirs to her husband could likewise decide how she lived in marriage, for better and for worse, and might determine how long the marriage lasted. What happened, then, as years went by and women aged within marriage and after it? The further chapters of the story I have begun to tell in this book remain to be written. As they bore children and often divorced or were widowed and remarried, the experiences of the women described in the Geniza came to vary even more widely than those of the girls I have examined here. Some women lived comfortably within marriage, while others were abandoned by a husband, or fled him to live with their own relatives. Some managed, bought, sold, and rented real estate, while others scraped by on textile labor or depended on communal charity to survive. Some raised children alone; others did so with the help of their husbands, in-laws, and robust networks of extended relatives. Some died alone, or as dependents on their own sons and daughters, while others died surrounded by descendants and slaves who relied on them instead.

Among the questions that my findings raise about women's kinship and their social fortunes, it is worth asking how the triangular relationships among women, their relatives, and their husbands and in-laws—relationships that loomed so large in adolescent girls' lives—developed as women grew older. How did a woman's kinship bonds change over time, and as the fathers, brothers, and uncles who had championed her in her youth eventually died? How did her remaining kin—including her own sons and daughters—understand her honor, agency, and support? Could a woman who managed to maintain substantial property of her own while married eventually wield social power even without her relatives? What other forms of benefit could an older woman, long past the stage of being married off by her father or brothers, offer her relatives both young and old?

Continuing the story that this book begins also entails understanding how older women operated within the other main arena in which their lives unfolded—the Jewish community and its institutions. Here we are on firmer ground, since several excellent recent studies have examined this question from different angles.[1] These studies demonstrate the difficulties Jewish women could encounter in Jewish courts and when appealing to communal officials. But they also demonstrate how often women nonetheless continued to turn to Jewish courts and communal officials for help. What remains to be addressed is why, and what women did when and if these officials failed them entirely. This is a question about Jewish communal belonging and its limits: where within the Fatimid and Ayyubid empires, if anywhere, did marginalized

1. Especially Oded Zinger's recent dissertation, "Women, Kinship, and Law," and Mark Cohen's study of charity among Geniza Jews, *Poverty and Charity*.

Jews (especially Jewish women), who lacked the overlapping webs of patronage ties common among elites and sub-elites, fit into the social order—not only within the Jewish community but beyond it? I have argued that Geniza women's place in society depended mainly on their patronage-like relationships with relatives, and secondarily on the Jewish solidarity group to which they belonged. But was this all? Were women without practical kin thereby made entirely dependent on Jewish communal leaders, or did society at large, or the Fatimid and Ayyubid states and their officials, sometimes offer these women other options? These questions lie at the outer limits of our evidence: women angry at communal leaders for ignoring them often threatened to turn instead to a Muslim judge, but the Geniza did not preserve documents that describe what happened when and if women realized these threats. Work currently ongoing on Arabic-script petitions that Jews submitted to Fatimid state officials may offer one answer to this puzzle;[2] systematic attention to evidence for women's conversion to Islam might offer another.

Here, however, I have addressed Jewish belonging from a different angle: by considering how Jewish law structured Jews' lives. This is this book's second central claim: among Geniza Jews, women's adolescence was *not* structured by Jewish law, even though Geniza Jews carefully followed Jewish laws surrounding adolescent girls. That is, I find that they managed young women's property and marriages according to Jewish laws that they had inherited from late antiquity but that differed from their own ideas, the norms they recognized in ordinary life, about young women, their property, and their marriages.

Rabbinic (or more precisely, medieval rabbinic or Rabbanite) law casts minor girls as sexually available for marriage, allowing a girl's father (and to a more limited extent, other guardians) to marry her off in childhood. However, rabbinic law also makes a daughter independent from her father once she begins physical puberty and reaches twelve and a half years (when she becomes legally mature, or a *bogeret*). At this point she becomes responsible for her own property and legal acts and can no longer be married off by others—a stage of adolescent autonomy that ends when she marries and becomes partly subject to a husband's authority.

Geniza Jews related to this legal framework in two ways. In their legal transactions, they—at least, the rabbinic ones among them who used rabbinic courts of law—maintained rabbinic maturity law in all its details. Rabbinic courts allowed fathers who wished to do so to marry off their minor daughters. Once a daughter matured, however, the courts recognized her authority over her own marriage. They also transferred orphan girls' inheritances to them at maturity and authorized them to use this property freely, while conversely terminating the support they received from their fathers' estates—a

2. This is the subject of a book in progress by Marina Rustow.

rule predicated on the rabbinic idea that once she is independent, a mature girl must support herself.

Yet in daily life, Geniza Jews organized adolescent girls' lives differently. Men rarely married off their minor daughters even though such marriages were legal. Most Jews seem to have viewed child marriage with distaste, for reasons not expressed in classical rabbinic texts. They thus understood puberty as the point when a girl became socially marriageable, a meaning puberty does not hold in rabbinic law. At the same time, Geniza Jews did not assign puberty the meaning rabbinic law does assign it, as the start of independent adolescence. All available evidence suggests that relatives and communal officials did not really permit unmarried girls to choose their own husbands, nor to make their own economic decisions; nor did they expect them to maintain themselves. They viewed unmarried girls instead as dependents who needed others to support them, to direct their affairs, and to find a husband for them. When girls inherited property or proved capable of profitable labor, these relatives allowed them to use their own assets for one purpose only: to increase their dowries and so prepare themselves for marriage. Only once a woman married could she emerge from this dependent state and begin to act as an adult, precisely as she became less autonomous in rabbinic legal terms. Once she married, a woman was legally entitled to be supported by her husband, and he was legally entitled to control her dowry. Yet it was only at this point that a woman might socially be expected to support herself by working (or by living off her dowry) if her husband did not support her. And many married women used their dowries independently for other purposes—to conduct business on their own terms, even while acknowledging their husbands' rights to this property on paper.

Geniza Jews thus recognized a set of ordinary social norms about adolescent girls different from the religious legal norms they used to regulate these girls' transactions in rabbinic courts.

Where did these ordinary assumptions come from? It seems logical to suspect that at least some of them were not especially Jewish, but similar to assumptions held by Muslims and Christians. This suspicion is strengthened by the fact that in many places, Geniza Jews' ordinary assumptions about young women—how they should be treated, what they could and could not do, and how they differed from both prepubescent children and from married girls and women—more closely resembled those made by medieval Muslim jurists than they did rabbinic law.

Islamic legal discourse about women's coming-of-age parallels the Geniza evidence at every stage. Islamic legal texts express the same discomfort with child marriage before puberty that is reflected in the Geniza, for the same reasons, even though they also permit such marriages. Like Geniza Jews, these Islamic texts thus view girls as marriageable only once they have begun to develop physically. Likewise, although many Muslim jurists allowed adolescent girls some measure of autonomy at maturity (*bulūgh*), they nonetheless understood first marriage as the main milestone in a young woman's life, a milestone that changed her from a passive virgin (*bikr*) to an independent adult (*thayyib*). This expectation echoes Geniza Jews' expectation that adolescent girls would remain passive and sheltered until first marriage. Moreover, Jewish women who controlled their own dowries within marriage (even while acknowledging their husbands' legal authority over their contents) resembled Muslim women whose dotal property was their own.

These are the broad parallels, but smaller, more specific parallels also appear throughout the book. For example, Geniza Jews, in keeping with Islamic law but unlike Jewish law, assumed that a husband was responsible for lodging his wife. They also recognized particular norms and values mentioned in Islamic legal texts but absent from classical rabbinic ones —a wife's access to a private room of her own, or modest women's habit of leaving their households only at night. And the very legal documents produced by Geniza courts similarly embed Jewish legal norms within Islamicate cultural frameworks, recording transactions framed according to Jewish law and legitimized by Rabbanite validation formulae within mainly Judeo-Arabic documents whose forms and procedural vocabulary resemble those used in Islamic documents.

Both sides of this equation tell us something. The similarities between Geniza Jews' ordinary culture and some Islamic legal norms suggest that Geniza Jews' ordinary culture may not have been particular to Jews alone, but rather belonged to the common culture of the towns and cities in which they lived. That is, these similarities help to justify scholars' tendency to view Geniza evidence as useful for medieval Middle Eastern history and not merely the history of Middle Eastern Jews.

This is not because these similarities prove that the Jewish women I have examined here lived exactly like Muslim and Christian women. On the contrary, just as "Geniza Jews" likely differed even from each other—along diachronic, regional, and class lines that the Geniza does not always disclose—their tastes and habits may also have differed from those of Muslims and Christians in ways that the lopsided comparison I have made here (that is, between Geniza social history and Islamic prescriptive law) does not disclose. Some such differences may become more visible as the field of medieval Islamic social history continues to develop, and especially as more Islamic documents are published and studied for concrete parallels to the Geniza evidence. Other such differences may remain lost to history. Nonetheless, my findings indicate—at least with respect to women's adolescence, but probably not only with respect to women's adolescence—that these differences, whatever they may have been, were not a product of religious law. My findings thus suggest that Jews' lives were not defined entirely, and thus not set apart entirely, by the content of their religion, and that in some arenas religion's effects may have been marginal. If Geniza Jews differed in some ways from the people around them, the differences more likely reflected their class and social affiliations within their larger society, with Jews and non-Jews alike, than their Judaism. The documents these Jews left behind likewise belong to Fatimid and Ayyubid history as much as to the history of the Jews.

Nonetheless, the legal practices I have discussed throughout the book demonstrate that Geniza Jews (or again, the Rabbanite ones among them who used rabbinic courts) took Jewish law seriously. No matter how foreign the ideas embodied in rabbinic law may have seemed to them, court officials took pains to uphold this law, and the litigants who appeared before them cared that they took pains to uphold it. This matters methodologically: it means that we cannot simply gloss over Geniza documents' Jewish features, but that understanding Geniza people requires us to attend to these features closely. It also matters historically: why should Geniza Jews have worked to reproduce laws whose social assumptions they did not share? What kinds of legal practices—and understanding of the law—allowed for such discrepancy?

The book offers one answer to these questions: rabbinic law bore meaning as a *category* within the broader Islamicate social order of the Fatimid and Ayyubid empires, regardless of its content. This was thanks mainly to early medieval rabbinic jurists working first in Abbasid Baghdad and then throughout the Middle East, who had transformed the classical rabbinic heritage of late antiquity into a reproducible system of technical legal norms, grounded in written prescriptive texts and administered by legal experts. This system was one that Jews, Christians, and Muslims alike recognized; from at least the tenth century onward, members of all three religious groups viewed themselves as partly defined by their fealty to such legal systems. Moreover, this system was well suited to the political conditions in which Jewish courts operated, because the technical rules it emphasized allowed considerable social flexibility. Jewish court officials could uphold these rules in ways that often left a minimal social footprint—a model that allowed them to draw legitimacy from their legal authority, without having to demand more from litigants than Jewish courts were equipped to enforce.

On this view, Geniza Jews took pains to reproduce the technical elements of rabbinic law because its forms made sense to them, even when its legal substance—the particular rules it imposed—did not. This model helps to explain why it seems Geniza Jews did not feel especially keenly the distance between their own ideas of the world and those embodied in rabbinic law. By the same token, it helps to explain how rabbinic Judaism endured the Arabization and Islamization of the Middle East, persisting as a religious-legal system under conditions very different from the late ancient Roman and Sasanian milieux in which it had developed. Finally, it helps to explain the other main finding presented in this book: why the young women I have examined here were better off depending on their relatives than on Jewish court and communal officials. These leaders may have taken care on paper to allow women the rights that Jewish law afforded them. But the very survival of the law itself required that these rights remain contingent: that how this paper could be used, and the weight it carried, depended not only on what it said but on the people using it—the individual fathers, mothers, brothers, sisters, aunts, uncles, grandparents, and cousins on whom women relied in every arena and at every stage of life.

BIBLIOGRAPHY

Abbott, Nabia. "Arabic Marriage Contracts among Copts." *Zeitschrift der Deutschen Morgenländischen Gesellschaft* 95 (1941): 59–81.

Abd-Allah, Umar F. *Mālik and Medina: Islamic Legal Reasoning in the Formative Period.* Leiden: Brill, 2013.

Abramson, Shraga. "*Aḥat She'ela u-Shetayim Teshuvot.*" *Shenaton ha-Mishpat ha-'Ivri* 11–12 (1984–86): 1–40.

——. *Rav Nissim Ga'on, Ḥamisha Sefarim.* Jerusalem, 1965.

Ackerman-Lieberman, Phillip. "Revisiting Jewish Occupational Choice and Urbanization in Iraq under the Early Abbasids." *Jewish History* 29 (2015): 113–135.

——. *The Business of Identity: Jews, Muslims, and Economic Life in Medieval Egypt.* Stanford, CA: Stanford University Press, 2014.

——. "Legal Pluralism among the Court Records of Medieval Egypt." *Bulletin d'Études Orientales* 63 (2014): 79–112.

——. "Commercial Forms and Legal Norms in the Jewish Community of Medieval Egypt." *Law and History Review* 30 (2012): 1007–1052.

——. "Legal Writing in Medieval Cairo: 'Copy' or 'Likeness' in Jewish Documentary Formulae." In *From a Sacred Source: Genizah Studies in Honor of Professor Stefan C. Reif*, edited by Benjamin M. Outhwaite and Siam Bhayro, 1–24. Leiden: Brill, 2010.

——. "A Partnership Culture: Jewish Economic and Social Life Seen Through the Legal Documents of the Cairo Geniza." PhD diss., Princeton University, 2007.

Afsaruddin, Asma. "Early Women Exemplars and the Construction of Gendered Space: (Re-) Defining Feminine Moral Excellence." In *Harem Histories: Envisioning Places and Living Spaces*, edited by Marilyn Booth, 23–48. Durham, NC: Duke University Press, 2010.

Ali, Kecia. *Marriage and Slavery in Early Islam.* Cambridge, MA: Harvard University Press, 2010.

——. "Marriage in Classical Islamic Jurisprudence: A Survey of Doctrines." In *The Islamic Marriage Contract: Case Studies in Islamic Family Law*, edited by Asifa Quraishi and Frank E. Vogel, 11–45. Cambridge, MA: Harvard University Press, 2008.

——. "Money, Sex, and Power: The Contractual Nature of Marriage in Islamic Jurisprudence." PhD diss., Duke University, 2002.

Allony, Nehemiah. *The Jewish Library in the Middle Ages: Book Lists from the Cairo Genizah.* Hebrew, edited by Miriam Frenkel and Haggai Ben-Shammai, with the participation of Moshe Sokolow. Jerusalem: Makhon Ben Zvi, 2006.

Allouche, Adel. "The Establishment of Four Chief Judgeships in Fāṭimid Egypt." *Journal of the American Oriental Society* (1985): 317–320.

Alshech, Eli. "Out of Sight and Therefore Out of Mind: Early Sunnī Islamic Modesty Regulations and the Creation of Spheres of Privacy." *Journal of Near Eastern Studies* 66 (2007): 267–290.

'Anan b. David. *Sefer ha-Miṣvot le-'Anan*, edited by Avraham Harkavy. In *Studien und Mitteilungen*, Vol. 8. St. Petersburg, 1903.

Anderson, Siwan. "The Economics of Dowry and Brideprice." *Journal of Economic Perspectives* 21 (2007): 151–174.

Anderson, Siwan, and Chris Bidner. "Property Rights over Marital Transfers." *The Quarterly Journal of Economics* 130 (2015): 1421–1484.

Ando, Clifford. "Legal Pluralism in Practice." In *The Oxford Handbook of Roman Law and Society*, edited by Clifford Ando, Paul du Plessis, and Kaius Tuori, 283–293. Oxford University Press, 2016.

Aptowitzer, Victor. "Formularies of decrees and documents from a Gaonic court." *Jewish Quarterly Review* 4 (1913): 23–51.

Arabi, Oussama. "The Interdiction of the Spendthrift (al-Safīh): A Human Rights Debate in Classical Fiqh." *Islamic Law and Society* 7 (2000): 300–324.

Ariel, Neri. "Judges' Duties: A Reconstruction of an Anonymous Judeo-Arabic Halakhic Commentary." Hebrew. *Ginzei Qedem* 9 (2013): 51–82.

Arjava, Antti. "Paternal Power in Late Antiquity." *The Journal of Roman Studies* 88 (1998): 147–165.

———. *Women and Law in Late Antiquity*. Oxford: Oxford University Press, 1996.

Asad, Talal. "The Idea of an Anthropology of Islam." *Poznan Studies in the Philosophy of the Sciences and the Humanities* 48 (1996): 381–406.

Ashtor, Eliyahu. "Un mouvement migratoire au haut Moyen Âge: Migrations de l'Irak vers les pays méditerranéens." *Annales* 27 (1972): 185–214.

———. *History of the Jews in Egypt and Syria under the Rule of the Mamluks*. Hebrew. 3 vols. Jerusalem: Mossad ha-Rav Kook, 1970.

———. "The Number of Jews in Medieval Egypt." *Journal of Jewish Studies* 18 (1967): 9–42, 19 (1968): 1–22.

Ashur, Amir. "Protecting the Wife's Rights in Marriage as Reflected in Pre-Nuptial and Marriage Contracts from the Cairo Genizah and Parallel Arabic Sources." *Religion Compass* 6 (2012): 381–389.

———. "*Haggana ʿal Zekhuyyot ha-Isha ʿal-pi Heskemei Nisu'in min ha-Geniza ha-Qahirit u-Meqorot ʿAraviyyim Maqbilim.*" *Jamāʿa* 19 (2011): 1–30.

———. "Engagement and Betrothal Documents from the Cairo Geniza." Hebrew. PhD diss., Tel Aviv University, 2006.

———. "*Shiddukhin ʿal-pi Teʿudot min ha-Geniza ha-Qahirit.*" MA thesis, Tel Aviv University, 2000.

Assaf, Simha. "The Number of Jews in Medieval Egypt." *Journal of Jewish Studies* 19 (1968): 1–22.

———. "*Shetarot ʿAtiqim me-Ereṣ Yisra'el u-Miṣrayim.*" *Yerushalayim: Meḥqerei Ereṣ Yisra'el* 1 (1953): 104–117.

———. "*Pitom ve-Damsis.*" In *Alexander Marx: Jubilee Volume on the Occasion of his Seventieth Birthday*, 73–78. New York: Jewish Theological Seminary, 1950.

———. "*Teshuva u-Mikhtav me-et Rabbenu Barukh ben R. Yiṣḥaq me-Ḥalab.*" *Tarbiz* 19 (1948): 105–108.

———. "*Shelosha Sefarim Niftaḥim le-Rav Shemu'el ben Ḥofni.*" *Sinai* 17 (1945): 113–155.

———. *Teshuvot ha-Ge'onim*. Jerusalem, 1942.

———. "*Shetarot ʿAtiqim min ha-Geniza me-Ereṣ Yisra'el, Miṣrayim ve-Afriqa ha-Ṣefonit.*" *Tarbiz* 9 (1938): 11–34, 196–218.

———. *Mi-Sifrut ha-Ge'onim*. Jerusalem, 1933.

———. *Sefer ha-Shetarot le-Rav Hayya ben Sherira Ga'on*. Jerusalem: Azriel Press, 1930.

———. *Teshuvot ha-Ge'onim ve-Liqqutei Sefer ha-Din li-Yehuda Barṣeloni*. Jerusalem: 1927.

———. "*Bittulah shel Ketubbat Benin Dikhrin.*" *Ha-Tzofeh* 10 (1926): 18–30.

Baer, Yitzhak. "The Origins of the Organization of the Jewish Community of the Middle Ages." *Zion* 15 (1950): 1–41.

Bagnall, Roger. *Egypt in Late Antiquity*. Princeton, NJ: Princeton University Press, 1996.

Bagnall, Roger, and Bruce Frier. *The Demography of Roman Egypt*. Cambridge University Press, 2006.

Bamberger, Bernard. "Qetanah, Na'arah, Bogereth." *Hebrew Union College Annual* 32 (1961): 281–294.

Bareket, Elinoar. *Fustat on the Nile: The Jewish Elite in Medieval Egypt*. Leiden: Brill, 1999.

———. *The Jewish Leadership in Fustat in the First Half of the Eleventh Century*. Hebrew. Tel Aviv: Diaspora Research Institute, 1995.

———. *The Jews of Egypt 1007–1055*. Hebrew. Jerusalem: Ben Zvi, 1995.

Baron, Salo W. *The Jewish Community: Its History and Structure to the American Revolution*. 3 vols. Philadelphia: Jewish Publication Society of America, 1942.

Baskin, Judith. "Marriage and Mobility in Two Medieval Jewish Societies." *Jewish History* 22 (2008): 223–243.

Baugh, Carolyn. "Compulsion in Minor Marriages as Discussed in Early Islamic Legal Texts." PhD diss., University of Pennsylvania, 2011.

Baumgarten, Elisheva. *Practicing Piety in Medieval Ashkenaz: Men, Women, and Everyday Religious Observance*. Philadelphia: University of Pennsylvania Press, 2014.

Beattie, Cordelia. *Medieval Single Women: The Politics of Social Classification in Late Medieval England*. Oxford: Oxford University Press, 2007.

Bechor, Guy. *God in the Courtroom: The Transformation of Courtroom Oath and Perjury Between Islamic and Franco-Egyptian Law*. Leiden: Brill, 2011.

Becker, Adam. "The Comparative Study of 'Scholasticism' in Late Antique Mesopotamia: Rabbis and East Syrians." *AJS Review* 34 (2010): 91–113.

Becker, Gary. *A Treatise on the Family* (2nd ed.). Cambridge, MA: Harvard University Press, 1991.

Bennett Judith, and Amy Froide, eds., *Singlewomen in the European Past: 1250–1800*. Philadelphia: University of Pennsylvania Press, 1999.

Ben-Sasson, Menahem. *Emergence of the Local Jewish Community in the Muslim World: Qayrawān, 800–1057*. Hebrew. Jerusalem: Magnes Press, 1996.

———. "Varieties of Inter-communal Relations in the Geonic Period." In *The Jews of Medieval Islam: Community, Society, and Identity; Proceedings of an International Conference Held by the Institute of Jewish Studies, University College London, 1992*, edited by Daniel H. Frank. Leiden: Brill, 1995.

———. "Appeal to the Congregation in Islamic Countries in the Early Middle Ages." Hebrew. In *Knesset Ezra: Literature and Life in the Synagogue Presented to Ezra Fleischer*, edited by Shulamit Elizur, Moshe Herr, Gershon Shaked, and Avigdor Shinan (1994): 327–350.

———. *The Jews of Sicily, 825–1068*. Hebrew. Jerusalem: Ben Zvi, 1991.

———. "Maimonides in Egypt: The First Stage." *Maimonidean Studies* 2 (1991): 3–30.

———. "The Structure, Goals, and Content of the Story of Nathan ha-Babli." In *Culture and Society in Medieval Jewry: Studies Dedicated to the Memory of Haim Hillel Ben-Sasson*, edited by Menahem Ben-Sasson, Robert Bonfil, and Joseph Hacker, 137–196. Hebrew. Jerusalem: Zalman Shazar, 1989.

———. "Fragments from Saadya's *Sefer Ha-'Edut ve-ha-Shetarot*." Hebrew. *Shenaton ha-Mishpat ha-'Ivri* 11–12 (1984–86): 135–278.

Ben-Shammai, Haggai. "Is the 'Cairo Genizah' a Proper Name or a Generic Noun? On the Relationship Between the *Genizot* of the Ben Ezra and the Dār Simḥa Synagogues." In *From a Sacred Source: Genizah Studies in Honor of Professor Stefan C. Reif*, edited by Benjamin M. Outhwaite and Siam Bhayro, 43–52. Leiden: Brill, 2011.

Blau, Joshua. *A Dictionary of Medieval Judaeo-Arabic Texts*. Jerusalem: Israel Academy of Sciences and Humanities, 2006.

Borsch, Stuart J. *The Black Death in Egypt and England: A Comparative Study*. Austin: University of Texas Press, 2009.

Bos, Gerrit. "Ibn al-Jazzār on Women's Diseases and their Treatment." *Medical History* 37 (1993): 296–312.

Botticini, Maristella. "A Loveless Economy? Intergenerational Altruism and the Marriage Market in a Tuscan Town, 1415–1436." *The Journal of Economic History* 59 (1999): 104–121.

Botticini, Maristella, and Aloysius Siow. "Why Dowries?" *American Economic Review* 93 (2003): 1385–98.

Bourdieu, Pierre. *The Logic of Practice*. Stanford, CA: Stanford University Press, 1990.

———. *Homo Academicus*. Cambridge, UK: Polity Press, 1988.

———. *Outline of a Theory of Practice*. Cambridge University Press, 1977.

———. "Marriage Strategies as Strategies of Social Reproduction." In *Family and Society*, edited by Robert Forster and Orest Ranum, 117–144. Baltimore, MD: Johns Hopkins University Press, 1976.

Bray, Julia. "The Family in the Medieval Islamic World." *History Compass* 9 (2011): 731–742.

Brinner, William. *An Elegant Composition Concerning Relief After Adversity: An Eleventh-Century Book of Comfort*. Northvale, NJ: Aronson, 1996.

Brody, Robert. *Sa'adyah Gaon*. Oxford: Littman Library of Jewish Civilization, 2013.

———. "The Epistle of Sherira Gaon." In *Rabbinic Texts and the History of Late-Roman Palestine*, edited by Martin Goodman and Philip Alexander, 253–264. Oxford: The British Academy and Oxford University Press, 2010.

———. *The Geonim of Babylonia and the Shaping of Medieval Jewish Culture*. New Haven: Yale University Press, 1998.

———. *Teshuvot Rav Natronay bar Hilai Ga'on*. 2 vols. Jerusalem: Makhon Ofeq, 1994.

———. "Saadya Gaon on the Limits of Liturgical Flexibility." In *Geniza Research after Ninety Years: The Case of Judeo-Arabic*, edited by Joshua Blau and Stefan Reif, 40–46. Cambridge: Cambridge University Press, 1992.

———. "Sifrut ha-Ge'onim ve-ha-Teqst ha-Talmudi." *Meḥqerei Talmud* 1 (1990): 237–303.

———. "Were the Geonim Legislators?" Hebrew. *Shenaton ha-Mishpat ha-'Ivri* 11–12 (1984–86): 279–315.

Brody, Robert, and Menahem Ben-Sasson. *Sefer ha-Shetarot le-Rasa"g*, forthcoming.

Brown, Jonathan. *The Canonization of al-Bukhārī and Muslim: The Formation and Function of the Sunnī Ḥadīth Canon*. Brill: Leiden, 2007.

Brown, Patricia. *Private Lives in Renaissance Venice: Art, Architecture, and the Family*. New Haven: Yale University Press, 2004.

Brunschvig, Robert. "Métiers vils en Islam." *Studia Islamica* 16 (1962): 41–60.

Bulliet, Richard. *Conversion to Islam in the Medieval Period: an Essay in Quantitative History*. Cambridge, MA: Harvard University Press, 1979.

———. "A Quantitative Approach to Medieval Muslim Biographical Dictionaries." *Journal of the Economic and Social History of the Orient* 13 (1970): 195–211.

Caldwell, Lauren. "The Female Transition to Adulthood in the Early Roman Empire." PhD diss., University of Michigan, 2004.

Chan, William. "Marital Transfers and the Welfare of Women." *Oxford Economic Papers* 66 (2014): 1019–1041.

Chojnacka, Monica. *Working Women of Early Modern Venice*. Baltimore, MD: Johns Hopkins University Press, 2001.

Chojnacki, Stanley. "Getting Back the Dowry: Venice, c. 1360–1530." In *Time, Space, and Women's Lives in Early Modern Europe*, edited by Anne Jacobson Schutte, Thomas Kuehn, and Silvana Seidel Menchi, 77–96. Kirksville: Truman State University Press, 2001.

Choksy, Jamsheed. *Conflict and Cooperation: Zoroastrian Subalterns and Muslim Elites in Medieval Iranian Society*. New York: Columbia University Press, 1997.

Cilardo, Agostino. *The Early History of Ismaili Jurisprudence: Law Under the Fatimids*. New York: I.B. Tauris, 2012.

Cohen, Mark. *Maimonides and the Merchants*. Philadelphia: University of Pennsylvania Press, forthcoming.

——. "Geniza for Islamicists, Islamic Geniza, and the 'New Cairo Geniza.'" *Harvard Middle Eastern and Islamic Review* 7 (2006): 129–45.

——. *Poverty and Charity in the Jewish Community of Medieval Egypt*. Princeton, NJ: Princeton University Press, 2005.

——. *The Voice of the Poor in the Middle Ages*. Princeton, NJ: Princeton University Press, 2005.

——. "Four Judaeo-Arabic Petitions of the Poor from the Cairo Geniza." *Jerusalem Studies in Arabic and Islam* 24 (2000): 446–471.

——. "Jewish Communal Organization in Medieval Egypt: Research, Results and Prospects." In *Judaeo-Arabic Studies: Proceedings of the Founding Conference of the Society for Judaeo-Arabic Studies*, edited by Norman Golb, 73–86. Harwood Academic Publishers, 1997.

——. "Correspondence and Social Control in the Jewish Communities of the Islamic World: A Letter of the Nagid Joshua Maimonides." *Jewish History* 1 (1986): 39–48.

——. "Jews in the Mamlūk Environment: The Crisis of 1442 (A Geniza Study)." *Bulletin of the School of Oriental and African Studies* 47 (1984): 425–448.

——. "Administrative Relations Between Palestinian and Egyptian Jewry During the Fatimid Period." In *Egypt and Palestine: A Millennium of Association (868–1948)*, edited by Amnon Cohen and Gabriel Baer, 113–135. Jerusalem and New York: Ben Zvi Institute and St. Martin's Press, 1984.

——. *Jewish Self-Government in Medieval Egypt: The Origins of the Office of Head of the Jews, ca. 1065–1126*. Princeton, NJ: Princeton University Press, 1980.

Cohen, Mark, and Yedida Stillman. "Cairo Geniza and the Custom of Geniza among Oriental Jewry: An Historiographical and Ethnographic Study." Hebrew. *Pe'amim* 24 (1985): 3–35.

Cohen, Shaye. "Purity, Piety, and Polemic: Medieval Rabbinic Denunciations of 'Incorrect' Purification Practices." In *Women and Water: Menstruation in Jewish Life and Law*, edited by Rahel Wasserfall, 82–100. Waltham, MA: Brandeis University Press, 1999.

Coope, Jessica. "Marriage, Kinship, and Islamic Law in al-Andalus: Reflections on Pierre Guichard's al-Ándalus." *Al-Masaq: Islam and the Medieval Mediterranean* 20 (2008): 161–177.

Coronel, Nahman. *Teshuvot ha-Ge'onim*. Vienna, 1871.

Cortese, Delia, and Simonetta Calderini. *Women and the Fatimids in the World of Islam*. Edinburgh: Edinburgh University Press, 2006.

Cotton, Hannah. "Change and Continuity in Late Legal Papyri from Palaestina Tertia: Nomos Hellênikos and Ethos Rômaikon." In *Jews, Christians, and the Roman Empire: The Poetics of Power in Late Antiquity*, edited by Natalie B. Dohrmann and Annette Yoshiko Reed, 209–221. Philadelphia: University of Pennsylvania Press, 2013.

——. "A Cancelled Marriage Contract from the Judaean Desert." *The Journal of Roman Studies* 84 (1994): 64–86.

Coulson, Noel. *Succession in the Muslim Family*. Cambridge: Cambridge University Press, 1971.

Crone, Patricia. *God's Rule: Government and Islam*. New York: Columbia University Press, 2004.

——. "Weber, Islamic Law, and the Rise of Capitalism." In *Max Weber and Islam*, edited by Toby Huff and Wolfgang Schluchter, 247–272. New Brunswick: Transaction, 1999.

——. *Roman, Provincial and Islamic Law: the Origins of the Islamic Patronate*. Cambridge University Press, 1987.

Cuno, Kenneth. “Joint Family Households and Rural Notables in 19th-Century Egypt.” *International Journal of Middle East Studies* 27 (1999): 485–502.

Dakake, Maria Massi. *The Charismatic Community: Shi‘ite Identity in Early Islam*. State University of New York Press, 2012.

Danzig, Neil. “From Oral Talmud to Written Talmud: On the Methods of Transmission of the Babylonian Talmud and Its Study in the Middle Ages.” Hebrew. *Bar Ilan Annual* 30–31 (2006): 49–117.

David, Yeḥezqel. “*Ha-Gerushin be-Qerev ha-Yehudim ‘al-pi Te‘udot ha-Geniza u-Meqorot Aḥerim*.” Phd diss., Tel Aviv University, 1999.

Dennison, Tracy, and Sheilagh Ogilvie. “Does the European Marriage Pattern Explain Economic Growth?” *Journal of Economic History* 74 (2014): 651–693.

Denoix, Sylvie. “Notes sur une des significations du terme ‘dār’.” *Annales Islamologiques* 25 (1991): 285–288.

Dickey, Eleanor. “Literal and Extended Use of Kinship Terms in Documentary Papyri.” *Mnemosyne* 57 (2004): 131–176.

Diem, Werner, and Hans-Peter Radenberg. *A Dictionary of the Arabic Material of S. D. Goitein’s A Mediterranean Society*. Wiesbaden: Otto Harrassowitz Verlag, 1994.

Dinari, Yedidya. “*Hishtalshelut Taqqanat Mi’un*.” *Dine Israel* 10–11 (1981–83): 319–345.

Dols, Michael. *The Black Death in the Middle East*. Princeton, NJ: Princeton University Press, 1977.

Dols, Michael, and Abraham Udovitch. “The General Mortality of the Black Death in the Mamluk Empire.” In *The Islamic Middle East, 700–1900: Studies in Economic and Social History*, edited by Abraham Udovitch, 404–411. Princeton, NJ: Darwin Press, 1981.

Doumato, Eleanor Abdella. “Hearing Other Voices: Christian Women and the Coming of Islam.” *International Journal of Middle East Studies* 23 (1991): 177–199.

Drory, Rina. *Models and Contacts: Arabic Literature and its Impact on Medieval Jewish Culture*. Leiden: Brill, 2000.

Duben, Alan. “Household Formation in Late Ottoman Istanbul.” *International Journal of Middle East Studies*, 22 (1990): 419–435.

———. “Understanding Muslim Households and Families in Late Ottoman Istanbul.” *Journal of Family History* 15 (1990): 71–86.

———. “Turkish Families and Households in Historical Perspective.” *Journal of Family History* 10 (1985): 75–97.

Duben, Alan, and Cem Behar. *Istanbul Households: Marriage, Family and Fertility, 1880–1940*. Cambridge University Press, 2002.

Duby, Georges. *The Chivalrous Society*. Berkeley: University of California Press, 1980.

Duran, Shim‘on b. Ṣemaḥ. *Sefer Tashbeṣ*. Vol. 4 (*Ḥut ha-Meshullash*). Lemberg, 1891.

Edrai, Arye. “A Gift ‘From Now and After Death’ in the Mishna and Talmud.” Hebrew. *Shenaton ha-Mishpat ha-‘Ivri* 20 (1996): 1–23.

Egan, R. D., and G. Hawkes. “Imperiled and Perilous: Exploring the History of Childhood Sexuality.” *Journal of Historical Sociology* 214 (2008): 355–367.

El Cheikh, Nadia Maria. “The Harem.” In *Crisis and Continuity at the Abbasid Court: Formal and Informal Politics in the Caliphate of Al-Muqtadir (295–320/908–32)*, edited by Maaike van Berkel, Nadia Maria El Cheikh, Hugh Kennedy, and Letizia Osti, 165–186. Brill, 2013.

———. “Revisiting the Abbasid Harems.” *Journal of Middle East Women’s Studies* 1, no. 3 (2005): 1–19.

El-Leithy, Tamer. “Coptic Culture and Conversion in Medieval Cairo, 1293–1524 A.D.” PhD diss., Princeton University, 2005.

———. “Living Documents, Dying Archives: Towards a Historical Anthropology of Medieval Arabic Archives.” *Al-Qanṭara* 32 (2011): 389–434.

Elman, Yaakov. "Orality and the Redaction of the Babylonian Talmud." *Oral Tradition*, 14/1 (1999): 52–99.

Elon, Menachem. *Jewish Law: History, Sources, Principles*, Vol. 1. Jewish Publication Society, 1993.

El Shamsy, Ahmed. *The Canonization of Islamic Law: A Social and Intellectual History*. Cambridge: Cambridge University Press, 2013.

Epstein, Louis. *The Jewish Marriage Contract: A Study in the Status of the Woman in Jewish Law*. New York: Jewish Theological Seminary, 1927.

Fargues, Philippe. "Family and Household in Mid-Nineteenth-Century Cairo." In *Family History in the Middle East: Household, Property, and Gender*, edited by Beshara Doumani, 23–50. Albany: State University of New York Press, 2003.

al-Fāsī, Yiṣḥaq. *Responsa*, edited by D. Rothshtein. New York: Makhon Tzvi, 1974.

———. *Responsa*, edited by Ze'ev Biednowitz. Jerusalem, 1968. (Reprint of Bilgoraj, 1935.)

———. *Responsa*, edited by Ze'ev Leiter. Pittsburgh: 1954.

Fierro, Maribel. "Ill-Treated Women Seeking Divorce: The Qur'ānic two Arbiters and Judicial Practice among the Malikis in al-Andalus and North Africa." In *Dispensing Justice in Islam: Qadis and their Judgments*, edited by Muhammad Khalid Masud, Rudolph Peters, and David S. Powers, 323–347. Brill: Leiden, 2006.

Fishman, Talya. *Becoming the People of the Talmud: Oral Torah as Written Tradition in Medieval Jewish Cultures*. Philadelphia: University of Pennsylvania Press, 2011.

Fitzmyer, Joseph. "A Re-Study of an Elephantine Marriage Contract (AP 15)," in *Near Eastern Studies in Honor of William Foxwell Albright*, edited by Hans Goedicke, 137–168. Baltimore, MD: Johns Hopkins University Press, 1971.

Fram, Edward. *Ideals Face Reality: Jewish Law and Life in Poland, 1550–1655*. Cincinnati: Hebrew Union College Press, 1997.

Franklin, Arnold E. "More than Words on a Page: Letters as Substitutes for an Absent Writer." In *Jews, Christians and Muslims in Medieval and Early Modern Times: A Festschrift in Honor of Mark R. Cohen*, edited by Arnold Franklin, Roxani Margariti, Marina Rustow, and Uriel Simonsohn, 287–305. Leiden: Brill, 2014.

———. *This Noble House: Jewish Descendents of King David in the Medieval Middle East*. Philadelphia: University of Pennsylvania Press, 2012.

———. "Shoots of David: Members of the Exilarchal Dynasty in the Middle Ages." PhD diss., Princeton University, 2001.

Freidenreich, David. "The Use of Islamic Sources in Saadiah Gaon's 'Tafsīr' of the Torah." *Jewish Quarterly Review* 93 (2003): 353–395.

Frenkel, Miriam. "'Proclaim Liberty to Captives and Freedom to Prisoners': The Ransoming of Captives by Medieval Jewish Communities in Islamic Countries." In *Gefangenenloskauf im Mittelmeerraum: Ein Interreligiöser Vergleich*, edited by Heike Grieser and Nicole Priesching, 83–97. Hildesheim, 2015.

———. "Charity in Jewish Society of the Medieval Mediterranean World." In *Charity and Giving in Monotheistic Religions*, edited by Miriam Frenkel and Yaacov Lev, 343–364. Berlin: Walter de Gruyter, 2009.

———. *The Compassionate and Benevolent: The Leading Elite in the Jewish Community of Alexandria in the Middle Ages*. Hebrew. Jerusalem: Makhon Ben Zvi, 2006.

———. "Adolescence in Jewish Medieval Society under Islam." *Continuity and Change* 16 (2001): 263–281.

———. "*Qehillat Yehudei Ḥalab bi-Tequfat ha-Geniza.*" PhD diss., Hebrew University, 1990.

Frenkel, Miriam, Moshe Yagur, and Arnold Franklin. "Jewish Communal History in Geniza Scholarship." In "Documentary Geniza Studies in the 21st Century," special issue of *Jewish History* (forthcoming).

Frenkel, Miriam, and Nadia Zeldes. "Trade with Sicily: Jewish Merchants in the Mediterranean Trade during the Twelfth and Thirteenth Centuries." Hebrew. *Michael* 14 (1997): 89–137.

Frenkel, Yehoshua. "The *Ketubba* (Marriage Document) as a Source for the Study of the Economic History of the Fatimid Period." In *Egypt and Syria in the Fatimid, Ayyubid and Mamluk Eras III*, edited by U. Vermeulen and J. Van Steenbergen. Leuven: Peeters, 2001.

Friedl, Erika. "The Dynamics of Women's Spheres of Action in Rural Iran." In *Women in Middle Eastern History: Shifting Boundaries in Sex and Gender*, edited by Nikki R. Keddie and Beth Baron, 99–121. New Haven: Yale University Press, 1991.

Friedlander, Israel. "The Arabic Original of the Report of R. Nathan Hababli." *JQR* o.s. 17 (1905): 747–761.

Friedman, Mordechai Akiva. "Abraham Maimonides on his Leadership, Reforms and Spiritual Imperfection." *Jewish Quarterly Review* 104 (2014): 495–512.

———. "Crisis in Marriage as Reflected in Geniza Documents and a Legal Strategem in Maimonides' Responsum and their Study." Hebrew. *Pe'amim*, 128 (2011): 69–103.

———. "On Marital Age, Violence and Mutuality in the Genizah Documents." In *The Cambridge Genizah Collections: Their Contents and Significance*, edited by Stefan Reif, 160–177. Cambridge: Cambridge University Press, 2002.

———. "Two Maimonidean Letters." Hebrew. In *Me'ah She'arim: Studies in Medieval Jewish Spiritual Life in Memory of Isadore Twersky*, edited by Ezra Fleischer, 191–221. Jerusalem: Magnes Press, 2001.

———. "*Teshuvat 'ha-Rav' R. Yehuda ben Yosef ha-Kohen 'al Yetoma Qetana she-Hisi'uha ve-Na'afa.*" *Dine Israel* 20–21 (2000–2001): 329–351.

———. "On the Relationship of the Karaite and the Palestinian Rabbanite Marriage Contracts from the Geniza." Hebrew. *Te'uda* 15 (1999): 153–156.

———. "*Teshuvat r. Yeḥi'el bar Elyaqim ha-Matira et ha-Reshut.*" In *Mas'at Moshe: Studies in Jewish and Islamic Culture Presented to Moshe Gil*, edited by Ezra Fleischer, Mordechai Akiva Friedman, and Joel Kraemer, 328–367. Hebrew. Tel Aviv: The Bialik Institute, 1998.

———. "Halakhah as Evidence of Sexual Life among Jews in Muslim Countries in the Middle Ages." Hebrew. *Pe'amim* 45 (1990): 89–107.

———. "Menstrual Impurity and Sectarianism in the Writings of the Geonim and of Moses and Abraham Maimonides." Hebrew. *Maimonidean Studies* 1 (1990): 1–21.

———. "Responsa of R. Abraham Maimonides from the Cairo Geniza: A Preliminary Review." *Proceedings of the American Academy of Jewish Research* 56 (1990): 29–49.

———. "Social Realities in Egypt and Maimonides' Rulings on Family Law." In *Maimonides as Codifier of Jewish Law*, edited by Nahum Rakover, 225–236. Jerusalem, 1987.

———. *Jewish Polygyny in the Middle Ages.* Hebrew. Jerusalem: The Bialik Institute, 1986.

———. "Divorce upon the Wife's Demand as Reflected in Manuscripts from the Cairo Geniza." *Jewish Law Annual* 4 (1981): 103–126.

———. "New Fragments from the Responsa of Maimonides." Hebrew. In *Studies in Geniza and Sephardi Heritage Presented to Shelomo Dov Goitein on the Occasion of his Eightieth Birthday*, edited by Shelomo Morag and Issachar Ben-Ami, 109–121. Jerusalem: Magnes Press, 1981.

———. *Jewish Marriage in Palestine.* 2 vols. New York: Jewish Theological Seminary, 1980.

———. "Government Intervention in Qayrawān in the Divorce of a Betrothed Girl." Hebrew. *Mikhael* 5 (1978): 215–242.

———. "*Shiddukhin ve-Erusin le-fi Te'udot ha-Geniza ha-Qahirit.*" *Proceedings of the World Congress of Jewish Studies* 7 (1977): 157–173.

———. "The Minimum Mohar Payment as Reflected in the Geniza Documents." *Proceedings of the American Academy of Jewish Research* 43 (1976): 15–47.

———. "The Ransom-Divorce: Divorce Proceedings Initiated by the Wife in Medieval Jewish Practice." *Israel Oriental Studies* 6 (1976): 287–307.

———. "Pre-nuptial Agreements with Grooms of Questionable Character: A Cairo Geniza Study." *Dine Israel* 6 (1975): 105–122.

———. "The Ethics of Medieval Jewish Marriage." In *Religion in a Religious Age*, edited by S. D. Goitein, 83–101. Cambridge, MA: Association for Jewish Studies, 1974.

———. "The Monogamy Clause in Jewish Marriage Contracts." *Perspectives in Jewish Learning* 4 (1972): 20–40.

———. "Termination of the Marriage upon the Wife's Request: A Palestinian Ketubba Stipulation." *Proceedings of the American Academy of Jewish Research* 37 (1969): 29–55.

Friedman, Yvonne. "Charity Begins at Home? Ransoming Captives in Jewish, Christian and Muslim Tradition." *Studia Hebraica* 6 (2006): 55–67.

———. "Community Responsibility Towards its Members: The Case of Ransom of Captives." In *A Holy People: Jewish and Christian Perspectives in Religious Communal Identity*, edited by Marcel Poorthuis and Joshua Schwartz, 199–215. Leiden: Brill, 2006.

Froide, Amy. *Never Married: Singlewomen in Early Modern England*. Oxford: Oxford University Press, 2005.

Frymer-Kensky, Tikva. "Virginity in the Bible." In *Gender and Law in the Hebrew Bible and the Ancient Near East*, edited by Victor H. Matthews, Tikva Frymer-Kensky, and Bernard M. Levinson, 79–96. London: T&T Clark, 1998.

Fyzee, Asaf, and Ismail Poonawala. *The Pillars of Islam: Da'ā'im al-Islām of al-Qadī al-Nu'man*. Oxford: Oxford University Press, 2004.

Garcin, Jean-Claude. "Toponymie et topographie urbaines médiévales à Fustat et au Caire." *Journal of the Economic and Social History of the Orient* (1984): 113–155.

———. "Habitat médiéval et histoire urbaine à Fustat et au Caire." *Palais et maisons du Caire, époque mamelouke (XIIIe–XVe siècle)*, edited by Jean-Claude Garcin, Bernard Maury, Jacques Revault, and Mona Zakariya, 145–216. Aix en Provence: Éditions du CNRS, 1982.

Gaubert, Christian, and Jean-Michel Mouton. *Hommes et villages du Fayyoum dans la documentation papyrologique arabe (Xe–XIe siècles)*. Geneva: Droz, 2014.

Geertz, Hildred. "The Meaning of Family Ties." In *Meaning and Order in Moroccan Society*, edited by Clifford Geertz, Hildred Geertz, and Lawrence Rosen, 315–391. Cambridge: Cambridge University Press, 1979.

Gerber, Haim. "Anthropology and Family History: The Ottoman and Turkish Families." *Journal of Family History* 14 (1989): 409–421.

Gil, Moshe. *Jews in Islamic Countries in the Middle Ages*. Brill: Leiden, 2004.

———. *Yehuda ha-Levi and His Circle: 55 Geniza Documents*. Hebrew. Jerusalem: Ha-Iggud ha-Olami le-Mada'ei ha-Yahadut, 2001.

———. *In the Kingdom of Ishmael*. Hebrew. 4 vols. Tel Aviv: Tel Aviv University, 1997.

———. "The Babylonian Yeshivot and the Maghrib in the Early Middle Ages." *Proceedings of the American Academy for Jewish Research* 57 (1990–1991): 69–120.

———. *Palestine During the First Muslim Period (634–1099)*. Hebrew. 3 vols. Tel Aviv: Tel Aviv University, 1983.

———. *Documents of the Jewish Pious Foundations from the Cairo Geniza*. Leiden: Brill, 1976.

Giladi, Avner. "Liminal Craft, Exceptional Law: Preliminary Notes on Midwives in Medieval Islamic Writings." *International Journal of Middle East Studies* 42 (2010): 185–202.

———. *Infants, Parents, and Wet-Nurses: Medieval Islamic Views on Breastfeeding and Their Social Implications*. Leiden: Brill, 1999.

Gilmore, David, ed. *Honor and Shame and the Unity of the Mediterranean*. Washington, DC: American Anthropological Association, 1987.

Ginzberg, Louis. *Ginzei Schechter*. 2 vols. New York: Jewish Theological Seminary, 1928.

——. *Geonica*. 2 vols. New York: Jewish Theological Seminary, 1909.

Giovannini, Maureen. "Female Chastity Codes in the Circum-Mediterranean: Comparative Perspectives." In *Honor and Shame and the Unity of the Mediterranean*, edited by David Gilmore, 61–74. Washington, DC: American Anthropological Association, 1987.

Goitein, S. D., and M. A. Friedman. *India Book*. Hebrew. 4 vols. Jerusalem: Ben Zvi Institute, 2009–.

——. *India Traders of the Middle Ages*. Leiden: Brill, 2008.

Goitein, Shelomo Dov. *A Mediterranean Society: the Jewish Communities of the Arab World as Portrayed in the Documents of the Cairo Geniza*. 6 vols. Berkeley: University of California Press, 1967–93.

——. "Portrait of a Medieval India Trader: Three Letters from the Cairo Genizah." *Bulletin of the School of Oriental and African Studies* 50 (1987): 449–464.

——. "The Twilight of the House of Maimonides." Hebrew. *Tarbiz* 54 (1984–85): 67–104.

——. "Prayers from the Geniza for Fatimid Caliphs, the Head of the Jerusalem Yeshiva, the Jewish Community and the Local Congregation." In *Studies in Judaica, Karaitica and Islamica Presented to Leon Nemoy on his Eightieth Birthday*, edited by Sheldon R. Brunswick. Ramat Gan: Bar-Ilan, 1982.

——. "Chief Judge R. Ḥanan'el b. Samuel, In-law of R. Moses Maimonides." Hebrew. *Tarbiz* 50 (1980–81): 371–395.

——. *Palestinian Jewry in Early Islamic and Crusader Times*. Hebrew. Jerusalem: Yad Izhaq Ben Zvi, 1980.

——. "Dispositions in Contemplation of Death: A Geniza Study." *Proceedings of the American Academy for Jewish Research* 46 (1979–80): 155–178.

——. "The Jewish Communities of Saloniki and Thebes in Ancient Documents from the Cairo Geniza." Hebrew. *Ṣefunot* 11 (1970/77): 9–34.

——. "A Mansion in Fustat: A Twelfth-Century Description of a Domestic Compound in the Ancient Capital of Egypt." In *The Medieval City*, edited by Harry Miskimin, David Herlihy, and Abraham Udovitch, 163–178. New Haven: Yale University Press, 1977.

——. "Three Trousseaux of Jewish Brides from the Fatimid Period." *AJS Review* 2 (1977): 77–110.

——. "Parents and Children: A Geniza Study in the Medieval Jewish Family." *Gratz College Annual of Jewish Studies* 4 (1975): 47–68.

——. "Tyre-Tripoli-'Arqa: Geniza Documents from the Beginning of the Crusader Period." *Jewish Quarterly Review* 66 (1975): 69–88.

——. *Letters of Medieval Jewish Traders*. Princeton, NJ: Princeton University Press, 1974.

——. "New Sources on the Palestinian Gaonate." In *Salo Wittmayer Baron Jubilee Volume on the Occasion of his Eightieth Birthday*, edited by Saul Lieberman and Arthur Hyman, 503–537. Jerusalem: American Academy for Jewish Research, 1974.

——. "Formal Friendship in the Medieval Near East." *Proceedings of the American Philosophical Society* 115 (1971): 484–489.

——. "The Jewish Communities of Saloniki and Thebes in Ancient Documents from the Cairo Geniza." Hebrew. *Sefunot* 11 (1971): 9–33.

——. "Side Lights on Jewish Education from the Cairo Genizah." In *Gratz College Anniversary Volume*, edited by I. Passow and S. Lachs, 83–110. Philadelphia: 1971.

——. "A Jewish Business Woman of the Eleventh Century." *Jewish Quarterly Review* 57 (1967): 225–242.

——. "Rise of the Middle-Eastern Bourgeoisie in Early Islamic Times." In *Studies in Islamic History and Institutions*, 215–241. Leiden: Brill, 1966.

——. "Wills and Deathbed Declarations from the Cairo Geniza." Hebrew. *Sefunot* 8 (1964): 105–126.

——. "Documents on Abraham Maimonides and his Pietist Circle." Hebrew. *Tarbiz* 33 (1963–64): 181–197.

——. "The Title and Office of the Nagid: A Re-Examination." *Jewish Quarterly Review* 53, 2 (1962): 93–119.

——. "The Local Jewish Community in the Light of the Cairo Geniza Records." *Journal of Jewish Studies* 12 (1961): 133–158.

——. "Maimonides as Chief Justice: The Newly Edited Arabic Originals of Maimonides' Responsa," *Jewish Quarterly Review* 49 (1959): 191–204.

——. "A Report on Messianic Troubles in Baghdad in 1120–21." *Jewish Quarterly Review* 43 (1952): 57–76.

Golb, Norman. "The Topography of the Jews of Medieval Egypt: Inductive Studies Based Primarily upon Documents from the Cairo Genizah." *Journal of Near Eastern Studies* 24 (1965): 251–270.

Goldberg, Jessica. "Mercantile Letters." In "Documentary Geniza Studies in the 21st Century," special issue of *Jewish History* (forthcoming).

——. "Methodology." In "Documentary Geniza Studies in the 21st Century," special issue of *Jewish History* (forthcoming).

——. "Friendship and Hierarchy: Rhetorical Stances in Geniza Mercantile Letters." In *Jews, Christians and Muslims in Medieval and Early Modern Times: A Festschrift in Honor of Mark R. Cohen*, edited by Arnold Franklin, Roxani Margariti, Marina Rustow, and Uriel Simonsohn, 271–286. Leiden: Brill, 2014.

——. *Trade and Institutions in the Medieval Mediterranean: The Geniza Merchants and their Business World*. Cambridge University Press, 2012.

——. "The Use and Abuse of Commercial Letters from the Cairo Geniza." *Journal of Medieval History* 38 (2012): 127–154.

——. "The 'Maghribi Traders': Reflections on Origins, Affinities, and Identities among Geniza Merchants," unpublished conference talk, delivered at "Jews and Empire: The 7th Lavy Colloquium," Johns Hopkins University, Oct. 31, 2011.

——. "On Reading Goitein's A Mediterranean Society: A View from Economic History." *Mediterranean Historical Review* 26 (2011): 171–186.

——. "Back-Biting and Self-Promotion: The Work of Merchants of the Cairo Geniza." In *History in the Comic Mode: Medieval Communities and the Matter of Person*, edited by Rachel Fulton and Bruce Holsinger, 117–127. New York: Columbia University Press, 2007.

——. "Geographies of Trade and Traders in the Eleventh-Century Mediterranean: A Study Based on Documents from the Cairo Geniza." PhD diss., Columbia University, 2005.

Goldberg, Jessica, and Abraham Udovitch, "Lists." In "Documentary Geniza Studies in the 21st Century," special issue of *Jewish History* (forthcoming).

Goldberg, P.J.P. *Women, Work, and Life Cycle in a Medieval Economy: Women in York and Yorkshire c. 1300–1520*. Oxford: Clarendon Press, 1992.

Goldman, Brendan. "Jews in the Latin Levant: Conquest, Continuity and Adaptation in the Medieval Mediterranean." PhD thesis, Johns Hopkins University, in progress.

Goldthwaite, Richard A. *The Building of Renaissance Florence: An Economic and Social History*. Baltimore, MD: Johns Hopkins University Press, 1982.

——. "The Florentine Palace as Domestic Architecture." *The American Historical Review* (1972): 977–1012.

Goody, Jack. *The Oriental, the Ancient and the Primitive: Systems of Marriage and the Family in the Pre-industrial Societies of Eurasia*. Cambridge: Cambridge University Press, 1990.

——. *The Development of the Family and Marriage in Europe*. Cambridge: Cambridge University Press, 1983.

——. *Production and Reproduction: A Comparative Study of the Domestic Domain*. Cambridge: Cambridge University Press, 1976.

——. "Bridewealth and Dowry in Africa and Eurasia." In Jack Goody and S. J. Tambiah, *Bridewealth and Dowry*. Cambridge: Cambridge University Press, 1973.

Grayson, Jennifer. "Jews in the Political Life of Late-Abbasid Baghdad." PhD diss., Johns Hopkins University, in progress.

Greif, Avner. "The Maghribi Traders: A Reappraisal?" *Economic History Review* 65 (2012): 445–469.

Grohmann, Adolf. *Arabic Papyri in the Egyptian Library*. Cairo: Egyptian Library Press, 1934–62.

Grohmann, Adolf. "Arabische Papyri aus den Staatlichen Museen zu Berlin." *Der Islam* 11 (1934) 22: 1–68.

Gross, Andrew D. *Continuity and Innovation in the Aramaic Legal Tradition*. Leiden: Brill, 2008.

Grossman, Avraham. *Pious and Rebellious: Jewish Women in Europe in the Middle Ages*. Hebrew. Jerusalem: Merkaz Zalman Shazar, 2001.

——. "Child Marriage in Jewish Society in the Middle Ages until the Thirteenth Century." Hebrew. *Pe'amim* 45 (1990): 108–125.

Guichard, Pierre. *Al-Ándalus: Estructura Antropológica de una sociedad islámica en el Occidente*. Barcelona: Barral, 1976.

Gulak, Asher. *Legal Documents in the Talmud in Light of Greek Papyri and Greek and Roman Law*, edited by Ranon Katzoff. Jerusalem: Magnes Press, 1994.

——. "*Ṣon-Barzel be-Dinei ha-Talmud*." *Tarbiz* 3 (1931): 137–146.

Gutas, Dimitri. *Greek Thought, Arabic Culture: The Graeco-Arabic Translation Movement in Baghdad and Early 'Abbāsid Society (2nd–4th/5th–10th c.)*. Routledge, 2012.

Guzzetti, Linda. "Dowries in Fourteenth-Century Venice." *Renaissance Studies* 16 (2002): 430–473.

Ibn al-Ḥajj al-'Abdarī. *Al-Madkhal ila Tanmiyat al-A'māl bi-Taḥsīn al-Niyyāt*. 4 vols. Cairo: al-Maṭba'a al-Miṣriyya, 1929.

Hajnal, John. "Two Kinds of Preindustrial Household Formation System." *Population and Development Review* 8 (1982): 449–494.

——. "European Marriage Patterns in Perspective." In *Population in History: Essays in Historical Demography*, edited by D. V. Glass and D.E.C. Eversley, 101–143. London: E. Arnold, 1965.

Halakhot Gedolot, ed. Ezriel Hildesheimer. Jerusalem: Mekize Nirdamim, 1971.

Halivni, David Weiss. *The Formation of the Babylonian Talmud*. Oxford University Press, 2013.

Hallaq, Wael B. *Authority, Continuity and Change in Islamic Law*. Cambridge University Press, 2001.

——. "*Qāḍīs* Communicating: Legal Change and the Law of Documentary Evidence." (1999).

——. "Model Shurūṭ Works and the Dialectic of Doctrine and Practice." *Islamic Law and Society* 2 (1995): 109–134.

——. "From Fatwās to Furū': Growth and Change in Islamic Substantive Law." *Islamic Law and Society* 1 (1994): 29–65.

Hammel, Eugene, and Peter Laslett. "Comparing Household Structure Over Time and Between Cultures." *Comparative Studies in Society and History* 16 (1974): 73–109.

Hanafi, Alia. "Two Unpublished Paper Documents and a Papyrus." In *Papyrology and The History of Early Islamic Egypt*, edited by Petra Sijpesteijn and Lennart Sundelin, 45–62. Leiden: Brill, 2004.

Harkavy, Avraham. *Zikhron Kamma Ge'onim u-vi-Yeḥud Rav Sherira ve-Rav Hai Beno ve-ha-Rav R. Yiṣḥaq al-Fāsī*. Berlin, 1887.

Harrison, Matthew. "Fusṭāṭ Reconsidered: Urban Housing and Domestic Life in a Medieval Islamic City." PhD diss., University of Southampton, 2016.

Hathaway, Jane. *The Politics of Households in Ottoman Egypt: The Rise of the Qazdaglis*. Cambridge University Press, 2002.

Herlihy, David. *Medieval Households*. Cambridge, MA: Harvard University Press, 1985.

Herman, Geoffrey. *A Prince Without a Kingdom: The Exilarch in the Sasanian Era*. Mohr Siebeck, 2012.

Hjerrild, B. *Studies in Zoroastrian Family Law: A Comparative Analysis*. Copenhagen: Museum Tusculanum Press, 2003.

Hodgson, Marshall. *The Venture of Islam: Conscience and History in a World Civilization*. 3 vols. Chicago: University of Chicago Press, 1974.

——. "How Did the Early Shi'a Become Sectarian?" *Journal of the American Oriental Society* 75 (1955): 1–13.

Hofer, Nathan. "Sufism, State, and Society in Ayyubid and Early Mamluk Egypt, 1173–1309." PhD diss., Emory University, 2011.

Hoffman, Adina, and Peter Cole. *Sacred Trash: The Lost and Found World of the Cairo Geniza*. New York: Nextbook/Schocken, 2011.

Holtz, Shalom. "'To Go and Marry Any Man That You Please': A Study of the Formulaic Antecedents of the Rabbinic Writ of Divorce." *Journal of Near Eastern Studies* 60 (2001): 241–258.

Holy, Ladislav. *Kinship, Honour, and Solidarity: Cousin Marriage in the Middle East*. Manchester: Manchester University Press, 1989.

Hopkins, M. K. "The Age of Roman Girls at Marriage." *Population Studies* 18 (1965): 309–327.

Horden, Peregrine, and Nicholas Purcell. *The Corrupting Sea: A Study of Mediterranean History*. Oxford: Blackwell, 2000.

Horii, Satoe. "Reconsideration of Legal Devices (*ḥiyal*) in Islamic Jurisprudence: The Ḥanafīs and Their 'Exits' (*makhārij*)." *Islamic Law and Society* 9 (2002): 312–357.

Howell, Martha C. *The Marriage Exchange: Property, Social Place, and Gender in Cities of the Low Countries, 1300–1550*. University of Chicago Press, 1998.

——. *Women, Production, and Patriarchy in Late Medieval Cities*. University of Chicago Press, 1986.

Huebner, Sabine R. "Egypt as Part of the Mediterranean? Domestic Space and Household Structures in Roman Egypt." In *Mediterranean Families in Antiquity: Households, Extended Families, and Domestic Space*, edited by Sabine R. Huebner and Geoffrey Nathan, 154–173. Wiley-Blackwell, 2017.

——. *The Family in Roman Egypt: A Comparative Approach to Intergenerational Solidarity and Conflict*. Cambridge University Press, 2013.

Hughes, Diane Owen. "Urban Growth and Family Structure in Medieval Genoa." *Past and Present* 66 (1975): 3–28.

Humfress, Caroline. *Orthodoxy and the Courts in Late Antiquity*. Oxford University Press, 2007.

Humphreys, Stephen. "Women as Architectural Patrons of Religious Architecture in Ayyubid Damascus." *Muqarnas* 11 (1994): 35–54.

——. *From Saladin to the Mongols: The Ayyubids of Damascus, 1193–1260*. State University of New York Press, 1977.

Idris, H. R. "Le Mariage en Occident Musulman: Analyse de fatwas médiévales extraites du "Mi'yār" d'Al-Wancharīchī." *Revue de l'Occident musulman et de la Méditerranée* 1972 (12): 45–62.

Ilan, Tal. "The Jewish Community in Egypt Before and After 117 CE in Light of Old and New Papyri." In *Jewish and Christian Communal Identities in the Roman World*, ed. by Yair Furstenberg, 203–224. Leiden: Brill, 2016.

———. "Premarital Cohabitation in Ancient Judea: The Evidence of the Babatha Archive and the Mishnah (Ketubbot 1.4)." *The Harvard Theological Review* 86 (1993): 247–264.

Isaacs, Haskell. *Medical and Para-Medical Manuscripts in the Cambridge Genizah Collections*. Cambridge: Cambridge University Press, 1994.

Jackson, Sherman A. *Islamic Law and the State: The Constitutional Jurisprudence of Shihāb al-Dīn al-Qarāfī*. Leiden: Brill, 1996.

Jacoby, David. "Byzantine Trade with Egypt from the Mid-Tenth Century to the Fourth Crusade." *Thesaurismata* 30 (2000): 25–30.

Jauss, Hans Robert. "Literary History as a Challenge to Literary Theory." *New Literary History* 2 (1970): 7–37.

Jews, Christians and Muslims in Medieval and Early Modern Times: A Festschrift in Honor of Mark R. Cohen, edited by Arnold Franklin, Roxani Margariti, Marina Rustow, and Uriel Simonsohn. Leiden: Brill, 2014.

Kalmin, Richard. "The Formation and Character of the Babylonian Talmud." In *The Cambridge History of Judaism, Volume 4: The Late Roman-Rabbinic Period*, edited by Steven T. Katz, 40–76. Cambridge University Press, 2006.

Kandiyoti, Deniz. "Bargaining with Patriarchy." *Gender and Society* 2 (1988): 274–290.

Karaite Judaism: A Guide to its History and Literary Sources, edited by M. Polliack. Leiden: Brill, 2003.

Katz, Marion. New York: *Women in the Mosque: A History of Legal Thought and Social Practice*. Columbia University Press, 2014.

Katzoff, Ranon. "The Age at Marriage of Jewish Girls During the Talmudic Period." Hebrew. *Te'uda* 13 (1997): 9–18.

Kawashima, R. "Could a Woman Say 'No' in Biblical Israel? On the Genealogy of Legal Status in Biblical Law and Literature." *AJS Review* 35 (2011): 1–22.

Kelly, Benjamin. *Petitions, Litigation, and Social Control in Roman Egypt*. Oxford: Oxford University Press, 2011.

Kertzer, David. "Household History and Sociological Theory." *Annual Review of Sociology* 17 (1991): 155–179.

Khalilieh, Hassan. "Women at Sea: Modesty, Privacy, and Sexual Misconduct of Passengers and Sailors Aboard Islamic Ships." *Al-Qantara* 27 (2006): 137–153.

Khan, Geoffrey. "Remarks on the Historical Background and Development of Early Arabic Documentary Formulae." *Asiatische Studien* 62 (2008): 885–906.

———. "The Pre-Islamic Background of Muslim Legal Formularies." *Aram* 6 (1994): 193–224.

———. *Arabic Legal and Administrative Documents in the Cambridge Genizah Collections*. Cambridge: University of Cambridge Press, 1993.

Khlat, M. "Endogamy in the Arab World." In *Genetic Disorders among Arab Populations*, edited by Ahmad Teebi and T. I. Farag, 63–82. New York: Oxford University Press, 1997.

Kirshner, Julius. *Marriage, Dowry, and Citizenship in Late Medieval and Renaissance Italy*. University of Toronto Press, 2015.

Kirshner, Julius, and Anthony Molho. "The Dowry Fund and the Marriage Market in Early Quattrocento Florence." *The Journal of Modern History* (1978): 404–438.

Klapisch-Zuber, Christiane. "Women Servants in Florence during the Fourteenth and Fifteenth Centuries." In *Women and Work in Preindustrial Europe*, edited by Barbara Hanawalt, 56–80. Bloomington: Indiana University Press, 1986.

Klein, Elka. *Jews, Christian Society, and Royal Power in Medieval Barcelona*. Ann Arbor: University of Michigan Press, 2006.

Kowaleski, Maryanne. "Singlewomen in Medieval and Early Modern Europe: The Demographic Perspective." In *Singlewomen in the European Past, 1250–1800*, 38–81.

Kraemer, Joel. "Women Speak for Themselves." In *The Cambridge Genizah Collections: Their Contents and Significance*, edited by Stefan Reif, 178–216. Cambridge: Cambridge University Press, 2002.

———. "A Jewish Cult of the Saints in Fāṭimid Egypt." In *L'Égypte Fatimide: son art et son histoire*, edited by M. Barrucand, 579–601. Paris: Presses de l'université de Paris-Sorbonne, 1999.

Krakowski, Eve. "The Geniza and Family History." In "Documentary Geniza Studies in the 21st Century," special issue of *Jewish History* (forthcoming).

———. "Female Adolescence in the Cairo Geniza Documents." PhD diss., University of Chicago, 2012.

Krakowski, Eve, and Marina Rustow. "Formula as Content: Medieval Jewish Institutions, the Cairo Geniza and the New Diplomatics" *Jewish Social Studies* 20 (2014): 112–146.

Kubiak, Wladyslaw, and George T. Scanlon. *Fusṭāṭ Expedition Final Report. v. 2 Fusṭāṭ-C.* Winona Lake, IN: Eisenbrauns, 1989.

Kuper, Adam. "Changing the Subject—About Cousin Marriage, Among Other Things." *Journal of the Royal Anthropological Institute (N.S.)* 14 (2008): 717–735.

Lamdan, Ruth. "Child Marriage in Jewish Society in the Eastern Mediterranean during the Sixteenth Century." *Mediterranean Historical Review* 11 (1996): 37–59.

Lange, Christian. *Justice, Punishment and the Medieval Muslim Imagination.* Cambridge University Press, 2008.

Langer, Ruth. "The Birkat Betulim: A Study of the Jewish Celebration of Bridal Virginity." *Proceedings of the American Academy of Jewish Research* 61 (1995): 53–94.

Lanza, Janine. *From Wives to Widows in Early Modern Paris: Gender, Economy, and Law.* Aldershot: Ashgate, 2007.

Lapidus, Ira. "Muslim Cities and Islamic Societies." In *Middle Eastern Cities*, edited by Ira Lapidus, 47–79. Berkeley: University of California Press, 1969.

Lapin, Hayim. *Rabbis as Romans: the Rabbinic Movement in Palestine, 100–400 CE.* Oxford University Press, 2012.

Larson, Barbara. "Tunisian Kin Ties Reconsidered." *American Ethnologist* 10 (1983): 551–570.

Laslett, Peter. "Family and Household as Work Group and Kin Group: Areas of Traditional Europe Compared." In *Family Forms in Historic Europe*, edited by Richard Wall, 513–563. Cambridge: Cambridge University Press, 1983.

Lev, Sarra. "How the *'Aylonit* Got Her Sex." *AJS Review* 31 (2007): 297–316.

Lev, Yaacov. "Aspects of the Egyptian Society in the Fatimid Period." In *Egypt and Syria in the Fatimid, Ayyubid, and Mamluk Eras III*, edited by U. Vermeulen and J. van Steenbergen, 1–31. Leuven: Uitgeverij Peeters, 2001.

———. *Saladin in Egypt.* Leiden: Brill, 1999.

———. *State and Society in Fatimid Egypt.* Leiden: Brill, 1991.

———. "The Suppression of Crime, the Supervision of Markets, and Urban Society in the Egyptian Capital During the Tenth and Eleventh Centuries." *Mediterranean Historical Review* 3 (1988): 71–95.

Levi b. Yefet. *Sefer ha-Miṣvot*, edited by Y. Algamil. 5 vols. Ashdod: Makhon Tif'eret Yossef, 2003.

Lévi-Strauss, Claude. *The Elementary Structures of Kinship.* Boston: Beacon Press, 1969.

Levine-Melammed, Renee. "Epistolary Exchanges (with Women)." In "Documentary Geniza Studies in the 21st Century," special issue of *Jewish History* (forthcoming).

Levy-Rubin, Milka. *Non-Muslims in the Early Islamic Empire: From Surrender to Coexistence.* Cambridge University Press, 2011.

Lewicka, Paulina. *Food and Foodways of Medieval Cairenes.* Leiden: Brill, 2011.

Lewin, B. M. *Oṣar ha-Ge'onim (Thesaurus of the Gaonic Responsa and Commentaries, Following the Order of the Talmudic Tractates)*. Hebrew. Jerusalem: Central Press, 1928–1943.

———. *Ginzei Qedem*. Haifa: 1921–43.

———. "*Mi-Seridei ha-Geniza*." *Tarbiz* 2 (1931): 383–410.

———. "*Ma'asim li-Venei Ereṣ Yisra'el*." *Tarbiz* 1 (1929): 79–101.

———. *Iggeret Rav Sherira Ga'on*. Haifa, 1921.

Libson, Gideon. "Betrothal of an Adult Woman by an Agent in Geonic Responsa: Legal Construction in Accord with Islamic Law." In *Esoteric and Exoteric Aspects in Judeo-Arabic Culture*, edited by B. Hary and H. Ben-Shammai, 175–189. Leiden: Brill, 2006.

———. *Jewish and Islamic Law: A Comparative Study of Custom during the Geonic Period*. Cambridge, MA: Harvard Law School, 2003.

———. "Legal Status of the Jewish Woman in the Gaonic Period: Muslim Influence—Overt and Covert." In *Developments in Austrian and Israeli Private Law*, edited by Herbert Hausmaninger, Helmut Koziol, Alfredo M. Rabello, and Israel Gilead, 213–243. New York: Springer-Verlag, 1999.

Livingstone, Amy. *Out of Love for My Kin: Aristocratic Family Life in the Lands of the Loire, 1000–1200*. Ithaca, NY: Cornell University Press, 2015.

Lutfi, Huda. "Manners and Customs of Fourteenth-Century Cairene Women: Female Anarchy versus Male Shar'i Order in Muslim Prescriptive Treatises." In *Women in Middle Eastern History: Shifting Boundaries in Sex and Gender*, edited by N. Keddie and B. Baron, 99–121. New Haven: Yale University Press, 1991.

———. "A Study of Six Fourteenth-Century Iqrārs from al-Quds Relating to Muslim Women." *Journal of the Economic and Social History of the Orient* 26 (1983): 246–294.

Lynch, Katherine. *Individuals, Families, and Communities in Europe, 1200–1800: The Urban Foundations of Western Society*. Cambridge: Cambridge University Press, 2003.

Macuch, Maria. "Pahlavi Literature." In *The Literature of Pre-Islamic Iran*, edited by Ronald Emmerick, Maria Macuch, and Ehsan Yarshater, 116–196. I.B. Tauris, 2008.

———. "A Zoroastrian Legal Term in the Dēnkard: pahikār-rad." *Iran: Questions et Connaissances* 1 (1999): 77–90.

Madame ou Mademoiselle? Itinéraires de la Solitude Féminine, XVIIIe–XXe Siècles, edited by A. Farge and C. Klapisch-Zuber. Paris: Arthaud-Montalba, 1984.

Maher, Vanessa. *Women and Property in Morocco: Their Changing Relation to the Process of Social Stratification in the Middle Atlas*. Cambridge University Press, 1974.

Maimonides, Avraham. *Commentary on Genesis and Exodus*, edited by S. D. Sasson. Hebrew. Letchworth, 1959.

———. *Responsa*, edited by Abraham Freimann and S. D. Goitein. Hebrew. Jerusalem, 1937.

Maimonides, Moshe. *Mishne Torah*, edited by Yosef Kafaḥ. Makhon Mishnat ha-Rambam: 1983–84.

———. *Commentary on the Mishna*, edited by Yosef Kafaḥ. Hebrew. 3 vols. Jerusalem, 1963–68.

———. *Responsa*, edited by Joshua Blau. Hebrew. 4 vols. Jerusalem: Mekize Nirdamim, 1957.

Mann, Jacob. "*Inyanim Shonim le-Ḥeqer Tequfat ha-Ge'onim*." *Tarbiz* 1 (1929): 66–88.

Margariti, Roxani. "Aṣḥābunā l-tujjār—Our Associates, the Merchants: Non-Jewish Business Partners of the Cairo Geniza's India Traders." In *Jews, Christians and Muslims in Medieval and Early Modern Times: A Festschrift in Honor of Mark R. Cohen*, edited by Arnold Franklin, Roxani Margariti, Marina Rustow, and Uriel Simonsohn, 40–58. Leiden: Brill, 2014.

———. *Aden and the Indian Ocean Trade: 150 Years in the Life of a Medieval Arabian Port*. Chapel Hill, NC: University of North Carolina Press, 2007.

Marglin, Jessica. "Jews in Sharīʿa Courts: A Family Dispute from the Cairo Geniza." In *Jews, Christians and Muslims in Medieval and Early Modern Times: A Festschrift in Honor of Mark R. Cohen*, edited by Arnold Franklin, Roxani Margariti, Marina Rustow, and Uriel Simonsohn, 207–225. Leiden: Brill, 2014.

Marks, A. "*Shalosh Teshuvot le-Rav Yosef Ga'on.*" *Ginzei Qedem* 3 (1925): 57–64.

Marmer, David. "Patrilocal Residence and Jewish Court Documents in Medieval Cairo." In *Judaism and Islam: Boundaries, Communications, and Interaction; Essays in Honor of William M. Brinner*, edited by Benjamin H. Hary, Fred Astren, and John L. Hayes, 67–82. Leiden: Brill, 2000.

Marmon, Shaun. *Eunuchs and Sacred Boundaries in Islamic Society*. Oxford: Oxford University Press, 1995.

Marsman, Hennie. *Women in Ugarit and Israel: Their Social and Religious Position in the Context of the Ancient Near East*. Leiden: Brill, 2003.

Masud, Muhammad Khalid, Rudolph Peters, and David Stephan Powers, eds. *Dispensing Justice in Islam: Qadis and Their Judgements*. Leiden: Brill, 2006.

McCarthy, Justin. "Age, Family, and Migration in Nineteenth-Century Black Sea Provinces of the Ottoman Empire." *International Journal of Middle East Studies* 10 (1979): 309–323.

McIntosh, Marjorie. *Working Women in English Society, 1300–1620*. Cambridge: Cambridge University Press, 2005.

Meacham, T., and M. Frenkel. *Sefer ha-Bagrut le-Rav Shemu'el ben Ḥofni Ga'on ve-Sefer ha-Shanim le-Rav Yehuda ha-Kohen Rosh ha-Seder*. Jerusalem: Yad Ha-Rav Nissim, 1999.

Me'ir b. Barukh of Rothenburg. *Responsa*. Jerusalem, 1985. (Reprint, Crimona, 1557).

Melchert, Christopher. *The Formation of the Sunni Schools of Law: 9th–10th Centuries CE*. Leiden: Brill, 1997.

Meriwether, Margaret. *The Kin Who Count: Family and Society in Ottoman Aleppo 1770–1840*. Austin, TX: University of Texas Press, 1999.

Mernissi, Fatema. *The Veil and the Male Elite: A Feminist Interpretation of Women's Rights in Islam*. Cambridge, MA: Perseus Books, 1991.

Meron, Ya'akov. *L'obligation alimentaire entre époux en droit musulman hanéfite*. Librairie générale de droit et de jurisprudence, 1971.

Midrash Tanḥuma. Jerusalem. 1958. (Reprint, Warsaw, 1875).

Ibn Migas, Yosef. *Responsa*, edited by H. Giteler. Jerusalem, 1959. (Reprint of Warsaw, 1870.)

Mikhail, Maged S. A. *From Byzantine to Islamic Egypt: Religion, Identity and Politics After the Arab Conquest*. I.B. Tauris, 2014.

Moebius, Marc. "Narrative Judgments: The Qāḍī al-Tanūkhī and the Faraj Genre in Medieval Arabic Literature." PhD diss., Princeton University, 2008.

Molad-Vaza, Ora. "Clothing in the Mediterranean Jewish Society as Reflected in the Documents of the Cairo Geniza." Hebrew. PhD diss., Hebrew University, 2010.

Mottahedeh, Roy. *Loyalty and Leadership in an Early Islamic Society*. London: I.B. Tauris, 2001.

Motzki, Harald. "Child Marriage in Seventeenth-Century Palestine." In *Islamic Legal Interpretation: Muftis and their Fatwas*, edited by M. Masud, B. Messick, and D. Powers, 129–140. Cambridge, MA: Harvard University Press, 1996.

Motzkin, Aryeh. "A Young Couple in Thirteenth Century Cairo." Hebrew. In *Studies in the History of the Jewish People and the Land of Israel in Memory of Zvi Avneri*, 117–127. Haifa: Haifa University Press, 1970.

———. "A Thirteenth-Century Jewish Teacher in Cairo." *Journal of Jewish Studies* 21 (1970): 49–64.

——. "The Arabic Correspondence of Judge Elijah and his Family (Papers from the Cairo Genizah): A Chapter in the Social History of Thirteenth Century Egypt." PhD. diss., University of Pennsylvania, 1965.

Mouton, Jean-Michel, Dominique Sourdel, and Janine Sourdel-Thomine, eds. *Mariage et séparation à Damas au moyen âge: un corpus de 62 documents juridiques inédits entre 337/948 et 698/1299*. Paris: Académie des Inscriptions et Belles-Lettres, 2013.

Mueller, J. *Teshuvot Ge'onei Mizraḥ u-Ma'arav*. Berlin, 1888.

Muḥammad b. Idrīs al-Shāfiʿī. *Kitāb al-Umm*. Cairo: al-Maṭbaʿa al-Kubrā al-Amīriyya, 1904–08.

Müller, Christian. "Settling Litigation Without Judgment: The Importance of a Ḥukm in Qāḍī Cases from Mamlūk Jerusalem." In *Dispensing Justice in Islam: Qadis and their Judgments*, edited by Muhammad Khalid Masud, Rudolph Peters, and David S. Powers, 47–70. Brill: Leiden, 2006.

Musafia, Yaʿaqov. *Teshuvot ha-Ge'onim*. Lyck, 1863.

Musallam, Basim. *Sex and Society in Islam*. Cambridge: Cambridge University Press, 1983.

al-Nahawāndī, Binyamin. *Mas'at Binyamin*. Ramla, 1978.

Nawas, John. "A Profile of the *Mawālī ʿUlamāʾ*." In *Patronate And Patronage in Early and Classical Islam*, edited by Monique Bernards and John Nawas, 454–480. Leiden: Brill, 2005.

Neubauer, Adolf. *Mediaeval Jewish Chronicles*. 2 vols. Oxford, Clarendon Press, 1887–95.

Neusner, Jacob. *A History of the Jews in Babylonia*. Brill, 1966.

Newman, Andrew. *The Formative Period of Twelver Shi'ism: Hadith as Discourse Between Qum and Baghdad*. Routledge, 2013.

Nielsen, Jųrgen. *Secular Justice in an Islamic State: Maẓālim under the Baḥrī Mamlūks, 662/1264–789/1387*. Nederlands Historisch-Archaeologisch Instituut te Istanbul, 1985.

Okawara, Tomoki. "Size and Structure of Damascus Households in the Late Ottoman Period as Compared with Istanbul Households." In *Family History in the Middle East: Household, Property, and Gender*, edited by Beshara Doumani, 51–75. State University of New York Press, 2003.

Olmsted, Jennifer C. "Norms, Economic Conditions and Household Formation: A Case Study of the Arab World." *The History of the Family* 16 (2011): 401–415.

Olszowy-Schlanger, Judith. "Formules juridiques des documents médiévaux en caractères hébraïques et les livres de formulaires-modèle." *Annuaire de l'École pratique des hautes etudes (EPHE), Section des sciences historiques et philologiques* 143 (2012): 23–27.

——. "Early Karaite Family Law." In *Karaite Judaism: A Guide to Its History and Literary Sources*, edited by Meira Polliack, 275–290. Leiden: Brill, 2003.

——. "Karaite Legal Documents." In *Karaite Judaism: A Guide to its History and Literary Sources*, edited by Meira Polliack, 255–73. Leiden: Brill, 2003.

——. *Karaite Marriage Documents from the Cairo Geniza: Legal Tradition and Community Life in Mediaeval Egypt and Palestine*. Leiden: Brill, 1998.

——. "La lettre de divorce caraïte et sa place dans les relations entre Caraïtes et Rabbanites au Moyen Age," *Revue des etudes juives* 155 (1996): 337–362.

Oppenheimer, Aharon. *The ʿAm Ha-Aretz: A Study in the Social History of the Jewish People in the Hellenistic-Roman Period*. Leiden: Brill, 1977.

Pahlitzsch, Johannes. "Ein arabischer Kaufvertrag dem Patriarchalarchiv von 546/1169." In *Graeci und Suriani im Palästina der Kreuzfahrerzeit. Beiträge und Quellen zur Geschichte des griechich-orthodoxen Patriarchats von Jerusalem*, by Johannes Pahlitzsch, 314–324. Berlin: Duncker and Humblot, 2001.

Papaconstantinou, Arietta. "Between Umma and Dhimma: The Christians of the Middle East under the Umayyads." *Annales islamologiques* 42 (2008): 127–156.

Patai, Raphael. "Cousin-Right in Middle Eastern Marriage." *Southwestern Journal of Anthropology* 11 (1955): 371–390.

Payne, Richard. "Christianity and Iranian Society in Late Antiquity, ca. 500–700 CE." PhD diss., Princeton University, 2010.

Peirce, Leslie. *Morality Tales: Law and Gender in the Ottoman Court of Aintab*. University of California Press, 2003.

———. "'The Law Shall not Languish': Social Class and Public Conduct in Sixteenth-Century Ottoman Discourse." In *Hermeneutics and Honor: Negotiating Female "Public" Space in Islamic/ate Societies*, edited by Asma Afsarrudin, 140–158. Cambridge, MA: Harvard University Press, 1999.

Peristiany, J. G., ed. *Honor and Shame: The Values of Mediterranean Society*. Chicago: University of Chicago Press, 1966.

Perry, Craig. "The Daily Life of Slaves and the Global Reach of Slavery in Medieval Egypt, 969–1250 C.E." PhD diss., Emory University, 2014.

Peskowitz, Miriam. *Spinning Fantasies: Rabbis, Gender, and History*. Berkeley: University of California Press, 1997.

Peters, Lloyd. "Aspects of Affinity in a Lebanese Maronite Village," in *Mediterranean Family Structures*, edited by J. G. Peristiany, 27–80. Cambridge University Press, 1976.

Petry, Carl. "Conjugal Rights Versus Class Prerogatives: A Divorce Case in Mamlūk Cairo." In *Women in the Medieval Islamic World: Power, Patronage, and Piety*, edited by Gavin Hambly, 227–240. New York: St. Martin's Press, 1998.

———. "Fractionalized Estates in a Centralized Regime: The Holdings of al-Ashraf Qāytbāy and Qānṣūh al-Ghawrī According to Their Waqf Deeds." *Journal of the Economic and Social History of the Orient* 41 (1998): 96–117.

———. "Scholastic Stasis in Medieval Islam Reconsidered: Mamluk Patronage in Cairo." *Poetics Today* 14 (1993): 323–348.

Phillips, Kim. *Medieval Maidens: Young Women and Gender in England, 1270–1540*. Manchester: Manchester University Press, 2003.

Pinsker, Simcha. *Liqqutei Qadmoniyyot: le-Toledot ha-Qara'im ve-Sifrutam*. Vienna, 1860.

Piterberg, Gabriel. "Mamluk and Ottoman Political Households: An Alternative Model of 'Kinship' and 'Family'." In *Transregional and Transnational Families in Europe and Beyond*, edited by Christopher H. Johnson, David Warren Sabean, Simon Teuscher, and Francesca Trivellato, 43–53. New York and Oxford: Berghahn Books, 2011.

Pitt-Rivers, Julian. "Honour and Social Status." In *Honour and Shame: The Values of Mediterranean Society*, edited by J. G. Peristany, 19–77. Chicago: University of Chicago Press, 1966.

Poppers, H. L. "The Declassé in the Babylonian Jewish Community." *Jewish Social Studies* 20 (1958): 153–179.

Powers, David S. *Law, Society and Culture in the Maghrib, 1300–1500*. Cambridge University Press, 2002.

———. "The Maliki Family Endowment: Legal Norms and Social Practices." *International Journal of Middle Eastern Studies* 25 (1993): 379–406.

———. "The Formation of the Islamic Law of Inheritance." PhD diss., Princeton University, 1979.

Poznański, Samuel. "Karaite Miscellanies." *Jewish Quarterly Review* o.s. 8 (1896): 681–704.

Prawer, Joshua. *The History of the Jews in the Latin Kingdom of Jerusalem*. Oxford: Clarendon Press, 1988.

al-Qirqisānī, Ya'aqov. *Kitāb al-Anwār wa-l-Marāqib*, edited by L. Nemoy. 5 vols. Arabic. New York: Alexander Kohut Memorial Foundation, 1939–43.

al-Qūmisī, Dani'el. *Pitron Shnem 'Asar*, edited by Isaac Markon. Jerusalem: Meqitzei Nirdamim, 1957.

RAF: The Pahlavi Rivāyat of Ādurfarnbay, edited by Oskar Skjærvø and Yishay Kiel (in preparation).

Rapoport, Yossef. "Women and Gender in Mamluk Society." *Mamlūk Studies Review* 11 (2007): 1–45.

——. *Marriage, Money and Divorce in Medieval Islamic Society*. Cambridge: Cambridge University Press, 2005.

——. "Legal Diversity in the Age of Taqlīd: The Four Chief Qāḍīs under the Mamluks." *Islamic Law and Society* 10 (2003): 210–228.

——. "Marriage and Divorce in the Muslim Near East, 1250–1517." PhD diss., Princeton University, 2002.

——. "Matrimonial Gifts in Early Islamic Egypt." *Islamic Law and Society* 7 (2000): 1–36.

Raymond, André. *Cairo*. Cambridge, MA: Harvard University Press, 2000.

Reif, Stefan. *A Jewish Archive from Old Cairo: The History of Cambridge University's Genizah Collection*. Richmond, Surrey: Curzon, 2000.

Reher, David. "Family Ties in Western Europe: Persistent Contrasts." *Population and Development Review* (1998): 203–234.

Richards, Donald S. "Mamluk Amirs and their Families and Households." In *The Mamluks in Egyptian Politics and Society*, edited by Thomas Philipp and Ulrich Haarmann, 32–54. Cambridge University Press, 1998.

——. "Some Muslim and Christian Documents from Sinai Concerning Christian Property." In *Law, Christianity and Modernism in Islamic Society*, edited by Urbain Vermeulen and J.M.F. van Reeth, 161–170. Leuven: Peeters, 1998.

Richter, Tonio Sebastian. "Copti Papyri and Juristic Papyrology." *Journal of Juristic Papyrology* 43 (2013): 405–432.

Riskin, Shlomo. *Women and Jewish Divorce: The Rebellious Wife, the Agunah and the Right of Women to Initiate Divorce in Jewish Law; A Halakhic Solution*. Hoboken, NJ: Ktav, 1989.

Rivlin, Yosef. "The Contribution of the Geniza to the Study of the Law of Inheritance." Hebrew. *Te'uda* 15 (1999): 241–255.

——. *Inheritance and Wills in Jewish Law*. Hebrew. Ramat-Gan: Bar Ilan University Press, 1999.

——. "Women and the Law of Inheritance as Reflected in Documents from the Cairo Geniza." Hebrew. *Te'uda* 13 (1997): 135–154.

Rosen, Lawrence. *Bargaining for Reality: The Construction of Social Relations in a Muslim Community*. Chicago: University of Chicago Press, 1984.

——. "Social Identity and Points of Attachment: Approaches to Social Organization." In *Meaning and Order in Moroccan Society*, edited by Clifford Geertz, Hildred Geertz, and Lawrence Rosen, 19–122. Cambridge: Cambridge University Press, 1979.

——. "Muslim-Jewish Relations in a Moroccan City." *International Journal of Middle East Studies* 3 (1972): 435–449.

Rosen-Zvi, Ishay. "'Tractate Kinui': A Forgotten Tannaitic Debate About Marriage, Freedom of Movement and Sexual Supervision." Hebrew. *Jewish Studies Internet Journal* 5 (2006): 21–48.

Roth, Martha T. "Age at Marriage and the Household: A Study of Neo-Babylonian and Neo-Assyrian Forms." *Comparative Studies in Society and History* 29 (1987): 715–747.

Rowberry, Ryan, and John Khalil. "A Brief History of Coptic Personal Status Law." *Berkeley Journal of Middle Eastern and Islamic Law* 3 (2010): 81.

Ibn Rushd, Abū al-Walīd Muḥammad ibn Aḥmad. *Bidāyat al-Mujtahid wa-Nihayat al-Muqtaṣid*. Beirut: Dār al-Fikr, n.d.

Russ-Fishbane, Elisha. "Between Politics and Piety: Abraham Maimonides and his Times." PhD diss., Harvard University, 2009.

Rustow, Marina. "The Diplomatics of Leadership: Administrative Documents in Hebrew Script from the Geniza." *In Jews, Christians and Muslims in Medieval and Early Modern Times: A Festschrift in Honor of Mark R. Cohen*, edited by Arnold Franklin, Roxani Margariti, Marina Rustow, and Uriel Simonsohn, 306–351. Leiden: Brill, 2014.

———. "Patronage in the Context of Solidarity and Reciprocity: Two Paradigms of Social Cohesion in the Premodern Mediterranean." In *Patronage, Production, and Transmission of Texts in Medieval and Early Modern Jewish Cultures*, edited by Esperanza Alfonso and Jonathan Decter, 13–44. Turnhout: Brepols, 2014.

———. "The Legal Status of Ḍimmī-s in the Fatimid East: A View from the Palace in Cairo." In *The Legal Status of Ḍimmī-s in the Islamic West (Second/Eighth–Ninth/Fifteenth Centuries)*, edited by Maribel Fierro and John Tolan, 307–332. Turnhout: Brepols, 2013.

———. "The Genizah and Jewish Communal History." In *From a Sacred Source*, 289–318. Brill, 2010.

———. "A Petition to a Woman at the Fatimid Court (413–414 AH/1022–23 CE)." *Bulletin of the School of Oriental and African Studies* 73 (2010): 1–27.

———. "At the Limits of Communal Autonomy: Jewish Bids for Intervention from the Mamluk State." *Mamlūk Studies Review* 13 (2009): 133–159.

———. "Benefaction (Niʿma), Gratitude (Shukr), and the Politics of Giving and Receiving in Letters from the Cairo Geniza." In *Charity and Giving in Monotheistic Religions*, edited by M. Frenkel and Y. Lev, 365–390. Berlin: Walter de Gruyter, 2009.

———. "Formal and Informal Patronage among Jews in the Islamic East: Evidence from the Cairo Geniza." *Al-Qantara* 24 (2008): 341–382.

———. *Heresy and the Politics of Community: The Jews of the Fatimid Caliphate*. Cornell University Press, 2008.

Sabean, David Warren, and Simon Tuscher. "Kinship in Europe." In *Kinship in Europe: Approaches to Long-Term Development*, edited by David Warren Sabean, Simon Teuscher, and Jon Mathieu, 1–32. New York: Berghahn Books, 2007.

Sacchi, Paola, and Pier Paolo Viazzo. "Family and Household." In *A Companion to Mediterranean History*, edited by Peregrine Horden and Sharon Kinoshita, 234–249. Wiley-Blackwell, 2014.

Sasson, Ilana. "Gender Equality in Yefet Ben ʿEli's Commentary and Karaite Halakhah." *AJS Review* 37 (2013): 51–74.

———. "Methods and Approach in Yefet ben ʿElī al-Baṣrī's Translation and Commentary on the Book of Proverbs." PhD diss., Jewish Theological Seminary, 2010.

Satlow, Michael. *Jewish Marriage in Antiquity*. Princeton, NJ: Princeton University Press, 2001.

———. "Jewish Constructions of Nakedness in Late Antiquity." *Journal of Biblical Literature* 116 (1997): 429–454.

———. *Tasting the Dish: Rabbinic Rhetorics of Sexuality*. Atlanta: Scholars Press, 1995.

al-Ṣayrafī, ʿAlī b. Dāʾūd al-Jawharī. *Inbāʾ al-Haṣr bi-Abnāʾ al-ʿAṣr*, edited by H. Habashi. Cairo: al-Hayʾa al-Miṣriyya al-ʿĀmma li-l-Kitāb, 2002.

Sayyid, Fuʾād. "*Nuṣūṣ ḍāʾiʿa min Akhbār Miṣr al-Muṣabbiḥī*." *Annales Islamologiques* 17 (1981): 1–54.

Scanlon, George T. "Fustat Expedition: Preliminary Report 1965, Part I." *Journal of the American Research Center in Egypt* 5 (1966): 83–112.

Schacht, Joseph. *The Origins of Muhammadan Jurisprudence*. Oxford: Clarendon Press, 1950.

Schloen, David. *The House of the Father as Fact and Symbol: Patrimonialism in Ugarit and the Ancient Near East*. Winona Lake, IN: Eisenbrauns, 2001.

Schmid, Karl. "The Structure of the Nobility in the Earlier Middle Ages." In *The Medieval Nobility: Studies on the Ruling Classes of France and Germany from the Sixth to the Twelfth Century*, edited by Timothy Reuter, 37–59. Amsterdam: North-Holland, 1978.

———. "Zur Problematik von Familie, Sippe und Geschlecht, Haus und Dynastie beim mittelalterlichen Adel: Vorfragen zum Thema 'Adel und Herrschaft im Mittelalter.'" *Zeitschrift für die Geschichte des Oberrheins* 105 (1957): 1–62.

Schoeler, Gregor. *The Genesis of Literature in Islam: From the Aural to the Read*. Edinburgh: Edinburgh University Press, 2009.

———. "Writing and Publishing: On the Use and Function of Writing in the First Centuries of Islam." Arabica 44/3 (1997): 423–435.

Schremer, Adiel. *Male and Female He Created Them*. Hebrew. Jerusalem: Merkaz Zalman Shazar, 2003.

Schwartz, Seth. *Were the Jews a Mediterranean Society? Reciprocity and Solidarity in Ancient Judaism*. Princeton, NJ: Princeton University Press, 2010.

———. "The Political Geography of Rabbinic Texts." *The Cambridge Companion to the Talmud and Rabbinic Literature*, edited by Charlotte Fonrobert and Martin Jaffee, 75–96. Cambridge University Press, 2007.

———. "Rabbinization in the Sixth Century." *The Talmud Yerushalmi and Graeco-Roman Culture III*, edited by Peter Schaefer, 55–69. Mohr Siebeck, 2002.

———. *Imperialism and Jewish Society: 200 BCE to 640 CE*. Princeton, NJ: Princeton University Press, 2001.

Serrano, Delfina. "Legal Practice in an Andalusī-Maghribī Source from the Twelfth Century CE: The Madhāhib al-Ḥukkām fī Nawāzil al-Aḥkām." *Islamic Law and Society* 7 (2000): 187–234.

Shaham, Ron. *The Expert Witness in Islamic Courts: Medicine and Crafts in the Service of Law*. Chicago: University of Chicago Press, 2010.

Shaki, Mansour. "Dādwar." Encyclopaedia Iranica, Vol. 5.

Shatzmiller, Maya. *Her Day in Court: Women's Property Rights in Fifteenth-Century Granada*. Cambridge, MA: Harvard University Press, 2007.

———. "Women and Wage Labour in the Medieval Islamic West: Legal Issues in an Economic Context." *Journal of the Economic and Social History of the Orient* 40 (1997): 174–206.

———. "Women and Property Rights in Al-Andalus and the Maghrib: Social Patterns and Legal Discourse." *Islamic Law and Society* 2 (1995): 219–257.

———. *Labour in the Medieval Islamic World*. Leiden: Brill, 1994.

Shemu'el b. Ḥofni. *The Biblical Commentary of Rav Samuel ben Hofni Gaon*, edited by Aharon Greenbaum. Jerusalem: Mossad ha-Rav Kook, 1978–79.

Shweka, Roni, Marina Rustow, and Judith Olszowy-Schlanger. "The She'iltot, Recycling Manuscripts, and Efrayim b. Shemarya." Taylor-Schechter Geniza Research Unit Fragment of the Month, October 2011 (retrieved at http://www.lib.cam.ac.uk/Taylor-Schechter/fotm/october-2011/ on Nov. 1, 2016).

Sievert, Henning. "Family, Friend or Foe? Factions, Households and Interpersonal Relations in Mamluk Egypt and Syria." *Everything is on the Move: The Mamluk Empire as a Node in (Trans-) Regional Networks*, edited by Stephan Conermann, 83–125. Bonn University Press, 2014.

Simonsohn, Uriel. *A Common Justice: The Legal Allegiances of Christians and Jews under Early Islam*. Philadelphia: University of Pennsylvania Press, 2011.

Sirat, Colette, Patrice Cauderlier, Michèle Dukan, and M. A. Friedman. *La 'Ketouba' de Cologne. Un contrat de marriage juif à Antinoopolis*. Opladen: Westdeutscher Verlag, 1986.

Soloveitchik, Haym. "The 'Third Yeshivah of Bavel' and the Cultural Origins of Ashkenaz—A Proposal," in *Collected Essays II*, by Haym Soloveitchik, 150–201. Oxford and Portland: Littman Library of Jewish Civilization, 2014.

——. *Wine in Ashkenaz in the Middle Ages: A Study in the History of Halakhah*. Hebrew. Jerusalem: Shazar Center for Jewish History, 2008.

——. "Halakhah, Hermeneutics, and Martyrdom in Medieval Ashkenaz (Part I of II)." *Jewish Quarterly Review* 94 (2004): 77–108.

Sourdel, Dominique. *Medieval Islam*. Routledge, 1983.

Sovič, Silvia, Pat Thane, and Pier Paolo Viazzo. "The History of European Families." In *The History of Families and Households: Comparative European Dimensions*, edited by Silvia Sovič, Pat Thane, and Pier Paolo Viazzo, 1–19. Brill, 2015.

Spectorsky, Susan. *Women in Classical Islamic Law: A Survey of the Sources*. Leiden: Brill, 2010.

——. "*Sunnah* in the Responsa of Iṣḥāq b. Rāhwayh." In *Studies in Islamic Legal Theory*, edited by B. Weiss, 51–74. Leiden: Brill, 2002.

——. *Chapters on Marriage and Divorce: Responses of Ibn Ḥanbal and Ibn Rāhwayh*. Austin: University of Texas Press, 1993.

Spiegel, Shalom. "The Episode of the Pirkoi Ben Baboi Controversy." In *Harry Austryn Wolfson Jubilee Volume*, edited by Saul Lieberman, Hebrew section, 243–374. Hebrew. Jerusalem, 1965.

Stauber, Shimon. "Questions Posed to R. Abraham b. Maimonides." *Shenaton ha-Mishpat ha-'Ivri* 14–15 (1988): 245–281.

Stausberg, Michael. "The Invention of a Canon: The Case of Zoroastrianism." In *Canon and Decanonization*, edited by A. van Debeek and Karel Van Der Toorn, 257–278. Brill, 1998.

Stillman, Norman. "East-West Relations in the Islamic Mediterranean in the Early Eleventh Century: A Study in the Geniza Correspondence of the House of ibn 'Awkal." PhD diss., University of Pennsylvania, 1970.

Stillman, Yedida. "Female Attire of Medieval Egypt." PhD diss., University of Pennsylvania, 1972.

Stilt, Kristen. *Islamic Law in Action: Authority, Discretion and Everyday Experiences in Mamluk Egypt*. Oxford: Oxford University Press, 2011.

Stol, Marten. "Women in Mesopotamia." *Journal of the Economic and Social History of the Orient* 38 (1995): 123–144.

Stowasser, Barbara. *Women in the Qur'ān, Traditions, and Interpretation*. Oxford: Oxford University Press, 1994.

Strack, Hermann L., and Günter Stemberger. *Introduction to the Talmud and Midrash*. Minneapolis: Fortress Press, 1992.

Szołtysek, Mikołaj. "Spatial Construction of European Family and Household Systems: A Promising Path or a Blind Alley? An Eastern European Perspective." *Continuity and Change* 27 (2012): 11–52.

——. "Three Kinds of Preindustrial Household Formation System in Historical Eastern Europe: A Challenge to Spatial Patterns of the European Family." *The History of the Family* 13 (2008): 223–257.

Tannous, Jack Boulos Victor. "Syria between Byzantium and Islam: Making Incommensurables Speak." PhD diss., Princeton University, 2010.

Ta-Shma, Israel. "Maimonides' Responsum on the Virginity Blessing." Hebrew. *Maimonidean Studies* 2 (1991): 9–15.

Teshuvot ha-Ge'onim Sha'arei Ṣedeq. Reprint, Jerusalem, 1966.

Thompson, Elizabeth. "Public and Private in Middle Eastern Women's History." *Journal of Women's History* 15 (2003): 52–69.

Tillier, Mathieu. "Judicial Authority and Qāḍīs' Autonomy under the 'Abbāsids." *Al-Masāq* 26 (2014): 119–131.

——. "Du pagarque au cadi: ruptures et continuités dans l'administration judiciaire de la Haute-Égypte (ier–iiie/viie–ixe siècle)." *Médiévales* 1 (2013): 19–36.

——. "Les 'premiers' cadis de Fusṭāṭ et les dynamiques régionales de l'innovation judiciaire (750–833)." *Annales Islamologiques* 45 (2011): 214–242.

——. "The Qāḍīs of Fusṭāṭ—Miṣr under the Ṭūlūnids and the Ikhshīdids: The Judiciary and Egyptian Autonomy." *Journal of the American Oriental Society* 131 (2011): 207–222.

——. "L'identification en justice à l'époque abbasside." *Revue des mondes musulmans et de la Méditerranée* 127 (2010): 97–112.

——. "Qadis and the Political Use of the Mazalim Jurisdiction under the 'Abbasids." In *Public Violence in Islamic Societies: Power, Discipline, and the Construction of the Public Sphere, 7th–18th Centuries CE*, edited by Christian Lange and Maribel Fierro, 42–66. Edinburgh University Press, 2009.

——. "Women Before the *Qāḍī* Under the Abbasids." *Islamic Law and Society* 16 (2009): 280–301.

Tillion, Germaine. *The Republic of Cousins: Women's Oppression in Mediterranean Society.* Al Saqi, 1983.

Toorawa, Shawkat. *Ibn Abī Ṭāhir Ṭayfūr and Arabic Writerly Culture: A Ninth Century Bookman in Baghdad.* Routledge, 2004.

Tucker, Judith. *Women, Family, and Gender in Islamic Law*. Cambridge: Cambridge University Press, 2008.

——. "Ties that Bound: Women and Family in Eighteenth- and Nineteenth-Century Nablus." In *Women in Middle Eastern History: Shifting Boundaries in Sex and Gender*, edited by Nikki R. Keddie and Beth Baron, 233–253. New Haven, CT: Yale University Press, 1991.

——. "Marriage and Family in Nablus, 1720–1856: Toward a History of Arab Marriage." *Journal of Family History* 13 (1988): 165–179.

——. "Problems in the Historiography of Women in the Middle East: The Case of Nineteenth Century Egypt." *International Journal of Middle East Studies* 15 (1983): 321–336.

Twersky, Isadore. *Introduction to the Code of Maimonides (Mishneh Torah)*. New Haven: Yale University Press, 1980.

Tyan, Emile. *Le notariat et le régime de la preuve par écrit dans la pratique du droit musulman*. Beirut: Faculté de droit de Beyrouth, 1959.

Udovitch, Abraham L. "Merchants and Amirs: Government and Trade in Eleventh Century Egypt." *Asian and African Studies* 22 (1988): 53–72.

——. "Formalism and Informalism in the Social and Economic Institutions of the Medieval Islamic World." In *Individualism and Conformity in Classical Islam*, edited by Aman Banani, 61–81. Weisbaden: Harrassowitz, 1977.

Van der Toorn, Karel. "The Significance of the Veil in the Ancient Near East." In *Pomegranates and Golden Bells: Studies in Biblical, Jewish, and Near Eastern Ritual, Law, and Literature in Honor of Jacob Milgrom*, edited by D. Wright, D. Freedman, and A. Hurvitz, 327–340. USA: Eisenbrauns, 1995.

Viazzo, Pier Paolo. "What's so Special about the Mediterranean? Thirty Years of Research on Household and Family in Italy." *Continuity and Change* 18 (2003): 111–137.

Vidas, Moulie. *Tradition and the Formation of the Talmud*. Princeton, NJ: Princeton University Press, 2014.

Wagner, Esther-Miriam. "The Language of Women: L-G Arabic 2.129," Taylor Schechter Research Unit Fragment of the Month, January 2015 (retrieved at http://www.lib.cam.ac.uk/Taylor-Schechter/fotm/january-2015/index.html on Nov. 1, 2016).

Wakin, Jeanette. *The Function of Documents in Islamic Law: The Chapters on Sales from Ṭaḥāwī's Kitāb al-Shurūṭ al-Kabīr*. Albany: State University of New York Press, 1972.

Walker, Paul. "The Relationship between Chief Qāḍī and Chief Dāʿī under the Fatimids." In *Speaking for Islam: Religious Authorities in Muslim Societies*, edited by Gudrun Krämer and Sabine Schmidtke, 70–94. Leiden: Brill, 2006.

Wansbrough, John. *Lingua Franca in the Mediterranean*. Richmond: Surrey, 1996.

Wasserstrom, Steven. *Between Muslim and Jew: The Problem of Symbiosis under Early Islam*. Princeton, NJ: Princeton University Press, 2014.

Weber, Max. *Economy and Society: An Outline of Interpretive Sociology*. University of California Press, 1978.

Wechsler, Michael. "New Data from Saadia Bearing on the Relocation of the Palestinian Yeshiva to Jerusalem." *Jewish Studies Internet Journal* 12 (2013): 1–9.

Weiss, Gershon. "Formularies (Shetarot) Reconstructed from the Cairo Geniza." *Gratz College Annual of Jewish Studies* 3 (1974): 64–65.

———. "Legal Documents Written by the Court Clerk Halfon ben Manasse (Dated 1100–1138): A Study in the Diplomatics of the Cairo Geniza." PhD diss., University of Pennsylvania, 1970.

———. "Documents Written by Hillel ben Eli: A Study in the Diplomatics of the Cairo Geniza Documents." MA thesis, University of Pennsylvania, 1967.

Weitz, Lev. *A God-Fearing House: Law, Marriage, and Christian Community in the Medieval Islamic World*. Philadelphia: University of Pennsylvania Press, forthcoming.

———. "Shaping East Syrian Law in ʿAbbāsid Iraq: The Law Books of Patriarchs Timothy I and Išōʿ Bar Nūn." *Le Muséon* 129 (2016): 71–116.

———. "Syriac Christians in the Medieval Islamic World: Law, Family, and Society." PhD diss., Princeton University, 2013.

Woolf, Virginia. *A Room of One's Own*. Orlando, FL: Harcourt, 2005.

Yaron, Reuven. *Gifts in Contemplation of Death in Jewish and Roman Law*. Oxford: Oxford University Press, 1960.

Yiftach-Firanko, Uri. "Law in Graeco-Roman Egypt: Hellenization, Fusion, Romanization." In *The Oxford Handbook of Papyrology*, edited by Roger Bagnall, 541–60. Oxford University Press, 2011.

Yiṣḥaq b. Sheshet Parfat. *She'elot u-Teshuvot bar Sheshet*. Jerusalem, 1967 (reprint of Vilna, 1879).

Zaman, Muhammad Qasim. *Religion and Politics Under the Early ʿAbbāsids: The Emergence of the Proto-Sunnī Elite*. Leiden: Brill, 1997.

Zilfi, Madeline, ed. *Women in the Ottoman Empire: Middle Eastern Women in the Early Modern Era*. Leiden: Brill, 1997.

Zeldes, Nadia and Miriam Frenkel, "Trade with Sicily: Jewish Merchants in Mediterranean Trade in the Twelfth and Thirteenth Centuries." Hebrew. *Mikhael* 14 (1997): 89–137.

Ibn Zimra, David b. Shelomo. *She'elot u-Teshuvot ha-Radba"z*. Benei Beraq: Hekhal ha-Sefer, 1972.

Zinger, Oded. "Towards a Social History of Responsa in Medieval Egypt." Article in progress.

———. "Medieval Jewish Women in Jewish and Muslim Courts," unpublished conference talk, delivered at "The Interplay of Substantive Doctrines, Institutions and Cultural Factors in the Regulation of Jewish Marriage," Gruss workshop, University of Pennsylvania Law School, Oct. 29, 2015.

———. "Women, Gender and Law: Marital Disputes According to Documents from the Cairo Geniza." PhD diss., Princeton University, 2014.

———. "Long Distance Marriages in the Cairo Geniza." Hebrew. *Pe'amim* 121 (2009): 7–66.

———. "What Sort of Sermon is This? Leadership, Resistance and Gender in a Communal Conflict." In *Jews, Christians and Muslims in Medieval and Early Modern Times: A*

Festschrift in Honor of Mark R. Cohen, edited by Arnold Franklin, Roxani Margariti, Marina Rustow, and Uriel Simonsohn, 83–98. Leiden: Brill, 2014.

Zomeño, Amalia. "The Islamic Marriage Contract in al-Andalus (10th to 16th Centuries)." In *The Islamic Marriage Contract: Case Studies in Islamic Family Law*, edited by A. Quraishi and F. Vogel, 136–155. Cambridge, MA: Harvard University Press, 2008.

———. *Dote y Matrimonio en al-Andalus y el Norte de Africa: Estudio sobre la jurisprudencia Islámica medieval.* Madrid: Conseja Superior de Investigaciones Científicas, 2000.

Zucker, Moshe. *'Al Targum Rasa"g la-Torah: Parshanut Halakha u-Folemiqa be-Targum ha-Torah shel R' Se'adya Ga'on, Te'udot u-Meḥqarim.* New York: Feldheim, 1959.

INDEX OF GENIZA DOCUMENTS CITED

Publication data for all published documents appears in parentheses after the document shelfmark. In the case of documents that have been published or translated more than once, only the latest publication data is given, and in all cases only full editions and/or translations are included. Earlier and partial editions may be identified through the Friedberg Geniza Project (http://www.jewishmanuscripts.org). Unpublished documents for which preliminary transcriptions are available on the Princeton Geniza Project (https://etc.princeton.edu/genizaproject) are indicated by a superscript P after the document shelfmark.

Budapest: Hungarian Academy of Sciences

DAVID KAUFMAN COLLECTION

DK 238.3, 50n36, 54n52

DK 238.4, 195n50

Cambridge: Cambridge University Library

ADDITIONAL COLLECTION

Add. 3343, 37n7, 224n48, 225n53, 283n49

JACQUES MOSSERI COLLECTION

Mosseri II.133 (Gil, *Ishmael*, doc. 613), 225n56

Mosseri II.195 (Goitein, "Karaite wife"), 194n48

Mosseri IV.3 (Motzkin, "Judge Elijah," 2: 216–7), 139n89

Mosseri IV.19.1 (Ashur, *EBD*, doc. 6-ה), 56n56

Mosseri VII.6.1[P], 194n48

Mosseri VII.10.1 (Ashur, *EBD*, doc. 5-ה), 192n39, 197n57, 268n8

Mosseri VII.16.1 (Ashur, *EBD*, doc. 7-ה), 245n12, 255n40, 256n45, 268n10

Mosseri VII.27 (Bareket, *Jews of Egypt*, doc. 67), 78n28

ORIENTAL COLLECTION

Or. 1080 J 21 (Gil, *Palestine*, doc. 293), 18n41, 175n126

Or. 1080 J 28 (Motzkin, "Judge Elijah," 2:12–14), 284n52, 286n59

Or. 1080 J 58 (Goitein and Friedman, *India Book* 1, doc. 19a), 253n35

Or. 1080 J 59 (Ashur, *EBD*, doc. 5-א), 202n75

Or. 1080 J 71 (Gil, *Ishmael*, doc. 619), 227n61

Or. 1080 J 93[P], 191n36

Or. 1080 J 141 (Friedman, "Ransom-Divorce," doc. B), 166n95

Or. 1080 J 173 (Friedman, *Polygyny*, doc. 1-ט), 54n52

Or. 1080 J 263 (Goitein and Friedman, *India Book* 2, doc. 28), 221n36

Or. 1080 J 271 (Gil, *Ishmael*, doc. 470), 155n59

TAYLOR-SCHECHTER GENIZAH COLLECTION

Old series: T-S A–K

Old series: T-S number A–K

Old series: T-S Ar.

Old series: T-S Misc. (documents formerly numbered Loan 1–209 are now divided between Misc. 35 and Misc. 36)

Old series: T-S number

New Series

Additional Series

Cambridge: Westminster College

Cincinnati: Hebrew Union College

Jerusalem: Jewish National and University Library

London: British Library (formerly British Museum)

New York: The Library of the Jewish Theological Seminary of America

ELKAN NATHAN ADLER COLLECTION

Oxford: University of Oxford, Bodleian Library

Paris: Archives of the Library of the Alliance Israélite Universelle

Philadelphia: University of Pennsylvania Museum

Philadelphia: Center for Advanced Jewish Studies

St. Petersburg: National Library of Russia

FIRKOVICH COLLECTIONS

St. Petersburg: Institute for Oriental Studies

Vienna: Österreichische Nationalbibliothek, Papyrussammlung und Papyrusmuseum

PAPYRUS SAMMLUNG ERHERZOG RAINER

Washington, DC: Freer Collection

INDEX OF JEWISH AND ISLAMIC TEXTS CITED

Hebrew Bible

Genesis: *24:16*, 188; *45:9–11*, 221
Leviticus: *19:29*, 117
Numbers: *27:8–11*, 145n13; *30*, 114n2; *30:4–17*, 114n4; *36:1–13*, 213n11; *36:7–8*, 213n11; *36:7–9*, 219n29
Deuteronomy: *22:14*, 186n15; *22:16*, 131; *22:20–21*, 183; *24:1*, 193; *24:1–4*, 100n86
Ruth: *4:11–12*, 223n44
2 Chronicles: *14:6*, 223n44; *26:5*, 223n44
Esther: *6:8–10*, 228n65
Psalms: *22:7*, 285n57; *106:3*, 171n111
Proverbs: *18:22*, 224n45; *18:23*, 230n70

Mishna

Avot: *1:5*, 171n111
Bava Batra: *8:5*, 102n94, 131n65
Gittin: *1:4*, 100n86; *7:3*, 104n104; *9:3–4*, 100n86
Ketubbot: *1:5*, 188n25; *1:7–9*, 184n8; *3:8*, 114n5; *4:1*, 114n3; *4:4*, 163n84; *4:5*, 114n3; *4:6*, 165n94; *4:7–13*, 246n18; *4:8–12*, 246n15; *4:11*, 165n94; *4:12*, 246n17; *5:2*, 164n90; *5:7*, 256n47; *5:9*, 165n94, 255n39; *6:2*, 155n55; *6:5*, 173n117; *7:1–5*, 256n48; *7:4*, 195n52; *7:4–5*, 195n50; *7:4–6*, 193n43; *7:9–10*, 256n48; *9:1*, 152n46
Nedarim: *11:10*, 114n5
Nidda: *5:4*, 117n18; *5:6*, 115n6; *5:7*, 114n2, 115n7, 163n84; *5:9*, 115n6
Shevi'it: *10:9*, 131n65
Yevamot: *14:1*, 256n46

Tosefta

Avoda Zara: *3:16*, 100n86
Ketubbot: *1:4*, 188n25; *1:5*, 114n5; *4:8*, 166n94; *4:17*, 167n99; *5:1*, 118n22; *5:6–7*, 256n48; *5:7*, 256n47; *6:1*, 146n15; *6:2–3*, 146n15; *7:1–7*, 256n48
Nidda: *2:6*, 134n74
Sota: *5:9*, 193n43
Yevamot: *8:4*, 118n21

Palestinian Talmud

Bava Batra: *8:6*, 246n17
Gittin: *7:3*, 104n104
Ketubbot: *4:29a*, 145n12; *5:3*, 119n22; *5:7*, 256n47; *5:29c*, 154n54; *6:30c*, 155n55; *6:30d*, 146n15; *7:4–6*, 193n43; *9:1*, 246n17; *9:32d-33a*, 152n46; *10:33a*, 145n12; *28d*, 165n94; *29b*, 167n99
Yevamot: *1:2*, 115n6

Babylonian Talmud

Avoda Zara: *37a*, 117n18
Bava Batra: *8b*, 174nn121–22; *120a*, 214n14; *126b*, 102n94; *135b*, 104n104; *154a*, 105n107; *160b*, 104n104
Bava Metzi'a: *15a*, 105n107; *19a*, 104n104; *45b–47b*, 104n102
Berakhot: *24a*, 118n21, 198n59
Gittin: *90a–b*, 193n43
Ketubbot: *11b*, 184n7; *12a*, 188n25; *39a*, 115n6; *40b*, 115n7; *45b–46a*, 184n7; *46b*, 114n3, 163n84; *47b*, 255n39; *49b*, 165n94; *50a*, 171n111; *52b*, 145n12;

Other Rabbinic Works

Qur'ān

Gaonic Responsa

Maimonides

Other Authors

GENERAL INDEX

in-laws: abuse by, 266, 269–70; the bond between, 224, 227; disputes with, 273–80; tension with, 289–90
innovation, religious, 82n40
instability: of family, 43, 47, 56; of households, 50
intercourse: during betrothal, 188–89; with children, 134–40; and female puberty, 118n21. *See also* sexuality, female
interdiction, and female maturity, 116n11
Iraq, *yeshivot* of, 84–87, 93
Islam, definition of, 90n63
Islamization, 92
Išōʿ bar Nūn, 89
ittiṣāl, 224–30, 286

jabr, 234n83, 235
jāh, 224–27
Jews, of Geniza, 16–20, 30–31, 301–2
jurists, vs. judges, 95

Kadi-justiz, 95–96
kashf al-wajh, 175
ketubbot, 27, 38, 44, 54n50, 55n54, 96, 99–102, 108, 124, 241–57; and divorce, 269–70
Khan, Geoffrey, 25
khidma, 59
khulʿ divorce, 263
kinship, 3, 56–67, 294–95; official, 62–63; practical, 62–64, 221–22. *See also* networks, kinship; relatives
Kitāb al-Umm, 88–89
Klein, Elka, 81, 83
kohen, 185, 215–16

labor, women's, 153–54, 160–65, 177–79, 295. *See also* clauses: labor
language: legal, 103–6; and legal discourse, 89–90, 97, 103–6
Laslett, Peter, 8–10, 13
law, 4, 20–23, 69, 299–302; as an expert discipline, 90, 107; and gaonic legal writing, 83–87; and marital autonomy, 233–39; prescriptive, 83–93; religious, 24, 81–83, 301; substantive content of, 101–3; and virginity, 184–87
lawsuits, virginity, 185–87
letters. *See* correspondence
levi, and endogamy, 215–16
Lévi-Strauss, Claude, 212
Libson, Gideon, 234–35
life expectancy, 41–42
lists: dowry, 143–44, 155; memorial, 61–62. See also *taqwīm*
literary revolution, and Arabic, 92–93
litigants, as using multiple courts, 77–78
loneliness, and strict seclusion, 201
loyalties, acquired, 59–62
loyalty, social, 3, 14–16, 294–96; and endogamy, 220–23; kinship as, 58–64

madhhabs, 79n29, 88–93
mahr, 142–43, 173, 220, 241, 255–57
maiden, 114–15
Maimonides, 94
Mālik b. Anas, 88
Mamluks, divorce among, 12
mamzer, 185n10, 253
marketplace, the, women in, 191–93, 196, 200n69, 202
marriage, 3, 7–12; child, 122–28, 128–40; as economic support, 173–74; first, 42, 45, 120–28, 292, 296; instability of, 43, 47; as an orphan's support, 174–75
matchmaking, 210–11
matrilocal households, 52, 267–68
maturity, female, 116; and dowries, 157–60; and economic independence, 164–69; and marriage, 122–28; and marital autonomy, 231–39; physical, 136–37
maẓālim, 18, 28, 74, 77–80, 252; and child marriage, 134–35; and divorce mediation, 261
mediation, and divorce, 259–61
"Mediterranean" families, 8–13, 122, 297
mekhoʿar, 131–32
men: relationships among, 65–66; as women's agents, 261–62, 274–75, 280; women's dependence on, 297
merchants: and the *bet din*, 80–81; and correspondence, 27–30; and kinship, 65; and marriage alliances, 226–27
mezonot, 173–74
Middle East, family history in, 7–12
minors, female: and dowries, 156–57; labor of, 163–65; marriage of, 117–19, 122–40; seclusion of, 201–5
Mishna, and female adolescence, 114

A NOTE ON THE TYPE

THIS BOOK has been composed in Miller, a Scotch Roman typeface designed by Matthew Carter and first released by Font Bureau in 1997. It resembles Monticello, the typeface developed for The Papers of Thomas Jefferson in the 1940s by C. H. Griffith and P. J. Conkwright and reinterpreted in digital form by Carter in 2003.

Pleasant Jefferson ("P. J.") Conkwright (1905–1986) was Typographer at Princeton University Press from 1939 to 1970. He was an acclaimed book designer and AIGA Medalist.

The ornament used throughout this book was designed by Pierre Simon Fournier (1712–1768) and was a favorite of Conkwright's, used in his design of the *Princeton University Library Chronicle*.